Turning Teaching Inside Out

Community Engagement in Higher Education

Edited by Dan W. Butin

This series examines the limits and possibilities of the theory and practice of community engagement in higher education. It is grounded in the desire to critically, thoughtfully, and thoroughly examine how to support efforts in higher education such that community engagement—a wide yet interrelated set of practices and philosophies such as service-learning, civic engagement, experiential education, public scholarship, participatory action research, and community-based research—is meaningful, sustainable, and impactful to its multiple constituencies. The series is by its nature cross-disciplinary and sees its readership across the breadth of higher education, both within student and academic affairs.

Dan W. Butin is an associate professor and founding dean of the School of Education at Merrimack College and the executive director of the Center for Engaged Democracy. He is the author and editor of more than 70 academic publications, including the books *Service-Learning in Theory and Practice: The Future of Community Engagement in Higher Education* (2010), which won the 2010 Critics Choice Book Award of the American Educational Studies Association; *Service-Learning and Social Justice Education* (2008); *Teaching Social Foundations of Education* (2005); and, most recently with Scott Seider, *The Engaged Campus: Majors and Minors as the New Community Engagement* (2012). Dr Butin's research focuses on issues of educator preparation and policy, and community engagement. Prior to working in higher education, Dr Butin was a middle-school math and science teacher and the chief financial officer of Teach For America. More about Dr Butin's work can be found at http://danbutin.org/.

The Engaged Campus: Majors, Minors and Certificates as the New Community Engagement
  Edited by Dan W. Butin and Scott Seider

Engaged Learning in the Academy: Challenges and Possibilities
  By David Thornton Moore

Deepening Community Engagement in Higher Education: Forging New Pathways
  Edited by Ariane Hoy and Mathew Johnson

Turning Teaching Inside Out: A Pedagogy of Transformation for Community-Based Education
  edited by Simone Weil Davis and Barbara Sherr Roswell

Turning Teaching Inside Out

A Pedagogy of Transformation for Community-Based Education

Edited by

Simone Weil Davis and Barbara Sherr Roswell

First published in 2013 by
PALGRAVE MACMILLAN®
in the United States—a division of St. Martin's Press LLC,
175 Fifth Avenue, New York, NY 10010.

Where this book is distributed in the UK, Europe and the rest of the world,
this is by Palgrave Macmillan, a division of Macmillan Publishers Limited,
registered in England, company number 785998, of Houndmills,
Basingstoke, Hampshire RG21 6XS.

Palgrave Macmillan is the global academic imprint of the above companies
and has companies and representatives throughout the world.

Palgrave® and Macmillan® are registered trademarks in the United States,
the United Kingdom, Europe and other countries.

ISBN: 978–1–137–34302–4

Library of Congress Cataloging-in-Publication Data

Turning teaching inside out : a pedagogy of transformation / Simone
Weil Davis and Barbara Sherr Roswell [editors].
    pages cm. — (Community engagement in higher education)
Includes bibliographical references.
ISBN 978–1–137–34302–4
1. Teaching. I. Davis, Simone Weil, 1957- II. Roswell, Barbara Sherr,
1959–

LB1025.3.D38 2013
371.102—dc23   2013028874

A catalogue record of the book is available from the British Library.

Design by Newgen Knowledge Works (P) Ltd., Chennai, India.

First edition: December 2013

10 9 8 7 6 5 4 3 2 1

Contents

Part III   Productive Intersectionality: Navigating Race, Place, Gender, and Class

Part IV   Transformation? Connection as Catalyst

Part V Yardsticks and Roadmaps: Assessing Change

Part VI Leaning into the Future: Helping Change Endure

Part VII Closing Circle

The Walls We Build and Break Apart: Inside-Out as Transformational Pedagogy

Dan Butin

"Inside-Out moves through the walls—it is an exchange, an engagement—between and among people who live on both sides of the prison wall. It is through this exchange, realized through the crucible of dialogue, that the walls around us and within us begin to crumble." So writes Lori Pompa, the founder of the Inside-Out Prison Exchange Program, in the final essay to this deeply powerful book. Those words, eloquently evoking the disturbing nature of profound teaching upon our thoughts and actions, bespeak the transformational model that Inside-Out has created. It is thus an honor and privilege to write this preface for a book that stands as a testament to Lori and the Inside-Out community's work over two decades to enact an authentic means by which to transform prison education, and, in the process, the very nature of teaching and learning.

By teaching students in college ("outside") together with individuals in prison ("inside" students) in academic courses run within prison facilities, Inside-Out is one of many innovative ways to foster experiential education and community-based models of teaching and learning. Fostering respect and reciprocity among the two groups and a deep understanding of the inner workings of the criminal justice system, Inside-Out can be seen as a powerful model of connecting theory to practice and helping campus students to see the relevance of academic coursework by linking it to the lived reality outside of our textbook covers and university gates.

But Inside-Out is so much more. What Lori has pioneered and Inside-Out has systemitized is a model of education few of us dare to dream of: an educational experience so structured that it almost literally "teaches itself" at the very same time as it destabilizes our traditional notions of teaching and learning. From the crashing noises of opening gates to the destabilizing experiences of the "wagon wheel" activity where inside and outside students first dialogue as equals to the closing moments when one group of students gets to exit while another stays behind, all of the participants within an Inside-Out course enact, embody, and are enveloped by the very issues they are seemingly "only" studying. The word and the world, as Freire (Freire and Macedo, 2013) was so fond of pointing out, become conjoined in praxis.

I have long argued that antifoundational service-learning offers an opportunity to undermine our deeply held habits of mind and repertoires of actions through deliberate and distinctive learning experiences. Such culturally saturated, socially consequential, politically volatile, and existentially defining moments rupture our sense of the normal and force us to confront the constructed nature of world. It is a self-consuming pedagogy that both teaches through its content at the very same time that it exposes, through its practice, the means and modes of such teaching.

When I developed these ideas over a decade ago (Butin, 2003, 2005), I had seen but a few examples here and there of such profound teaching. For it is difficult, nay, almost impossible, to construct a framework for engaged teaching that actually performs its own principles and that does not suffer from the performative contradiction of undermining itself—by, for example, delivering a lecture about the power of experiential education.

But what I was really writing and thinking about was Inside-Out. I had read some of Lori's work (Pompa, 2002) and spent time talking to her, heard about the trainings she had been doing with faculty from around the country, and seen some of the outcomes. What I came to see was that Inside-Out was the embodiment, the most powerful model I had ever encountered, of transformative education.

The chapters in this book—written by faculty and practitioners, inside and outside students—attest to such transformation. They speak, both literally and figuratively, to how the educational experience of the Inside-Out pedagogical model makes visible how walls constrain and how they break, how cages get built and are unlocked, how closed spaces conceal as well as liberate all of us. What Inside-Out has done is begun to loosen and, yes, crumble, the preconceptions of what it means to be bound by the walls we have built to keep some people out, some people in, and all of us within our boundaries.

I do not mean to over-valorize or overpromise. And neither does Inside-Out. There are more than two million individuals in prison in the United States, constituting the highest incarceration rate in the developed world, and comprising 25 percent of the world's incarcerated population. This population is disproportionately nonwhite and poor. Almost one in three young black men are, at any given moment, either in prison or under parole (Roberts 2004). It is thus unrealistic to suggest that Inside-Out, even with the hundreds trained and thousands taught, could transform our criminal justice system.

And yet what Inside-Out offers is a transformation of thinking. Foucault (1977), in founding the Prison Information Group in 1971, argued that "The ultimate goal of [the group's] interventions was...to question the social and moral distinction between the innocent and the guilty...We wish to attack an institution at the point where it culminates and reveals itself in a simple and basic ideology, in the notions of good and evil, innocence and guilt" (227–228; see Butin, 2010, chapter 3, for an extended articulation of this argument).

What Foucault wanted, and what I believe Inside-Out accomplishes, was to make visible how an entire system, an entire culture, operated in a deeply disturbing and disturbed binary. Foucault was not attempting to whitewash evil or deny guilt. Rather, what he railed against was a system of physical and conceptual constraints to how we viewed the world, others, and thus ourselves (Butin, 2006).

Such transformations of vision and comprehension are unfortunately all too rare in a postsecondary educational system seemingly devoted to breaking down the walls of our ignorance. It is thus breathtaking that Inside-Out has created, within the very walls that bind so many of our citizens, a means to make them begin to crumble. This is engaged learning at its zenith, and an inspiration to all of us who strive for a better world.

References

Butin, Dan W. "Of What Use Is it? Multiple Conceptualizations of Service Learning within Education." *The Teachers College Record* 105, no. 9 (2003): 1674–1692.

———. "Service-Learning as Postmodern Pedagogy." In *Service-Learning in Higher Education: Critical Issues and Directions*, New York: Palgrave Macmillan, 2005, 89–104.

———. "Putting Foucault to Work in Educational Research." *Journal of Philosophy of Education* 40, no. 3 (2006): 371–380.

———. *Service-Learning in Theory and Practice: The Future of Community Engagement in Higher Education.* New York: Palgrave Macmillan, 2010.

Foucault, Michel "Revolutionary Action: 'Until Now.'" In Michel Foucault, *Language, Counter-Memory, Practice: Selected Essays and Interviews.* Dinald Bouchard, ed. Ithaca, NY: Corrnell University Press, 1977, 218–234.

Freire, Paulo and D. Macedo. *Literacy: Reading the Word and the World.* NewYork: Routledge, 2013.

Pompa, Lori. "Service-Learning as Crucible: Reflections on Immersion, Context, Power, and Transformation." *Michigan Journal of Community Service Learning* 9, no. 1 (2002): 67–76.

Roberts, Dorothy. "The Social and Moral Cost of Mass Incarceration in African American Communities." *Stanford Law Review* 56, no. 5 (April 2004): 1271–1305.

Acknowledgments

The Inside-Out Prison Exchange Program, like this volume, is by its very nature a collaborative endeavor. Countless people, in and out of prison, have been instrumental in its development. Prominent among these are the contributors to this volume, and we thank them and invite you to see first-hand the fruits of their insight and commitment. They include:

Paul Perry (chapter 4), a founding member of the Graterford Think Tank, whose suggestion in 1995 that one-time prison visits between students and incarcerated men or women should extend into semester-long experiences was the seed for the Inside-Out program,

Kay Harris, who was the chair of the Criminal Justice Department at Temple University in 1997 when Inside-Out was started and has chosen to remain involved, with deep commitment, in every aspect of the program since that time (chapter 5), and Melissa Crabbe, Inside-Out's associate director, who has been instrumental since 2003 in shaping our trainings. She adds whole dimensions to the program, both regionally and (inter)nationally through her extraordinary creativity and vision (chapter 3).

We extend special appreciation to Kay Harris and Melissa Crabbe for early shared reflection on this book project and the work it should do in the world.

Temple University, its Criminal Justice Department, and its College of Liberal Arts have afforded the staff at the Inside-Out Center, and by extension, the whole Inside-Out community, the freedom and support to flourish. Today, in 2013, Temple is joined by more than 100 academic institutions supporting faculty and students as part of the Inside-Out network, many offering college credit to all students taking courses.

The Graterford Think Tank, established in 2002, serves as the heart of the international program and over the past decade has already inspired the development of eight other think tanks across North America. The committed participants in these ongoing working groups form an ethical and intellectual backbone to the entire network. Working collectively, think tank members offer trainings, public education workshops, research projects, and other support to people in prison and beyond. In so doing, they fashion a praxis—a way of being, doing, and learning together—that undergirds the analyses in this book. Every one of the hundreds of individuals who have attended an Instructor Training has benefited from the wisdom and counsel of trainers in the Graterford Think Tank, the Theory Group in Michigan, ACE in Oregon, or the Walls to Bridges Collective in Ontario.

The talented and dedicated Inside-Out Center staff, past and present, have provided strategic leadership for Inside-Out over the past decade. These include Melissa Crabbe (chapter 3), Erin Howley (chapter 12), Francesco Campanell, Jean Lenke, Cyndi Zuidema, Simone Davis, Tricia Way, and Christiana Girvasoni. A special thank you to Tyrone Werts (chapter 17), who helped to establish Inside-Out classes at Graterford, and who, once released after more than 36 years in prison, joined the Inside-Out Team. The organization's work is also energized and deepened by the wisdom, support, and guidance of the Inside-Out Steering Committee, Research Committee, and Temple Advisory Board.

The Philadelphia Prison System took a chance on trying out this pilot educational program at its inception in 1997 and has continued to host courses ever since. Since 2002, the administrators and staff of Graterford Prison have hosted Inside-Out classes, trainings, public forums, and weekly meetings of the Inside-Out Think Tank. On behalf of each author in this collection, and the many participants throughout the network, we thank the many wardens, superintendents, Department of Corrections officials, correctional educators, case workers, and corrections officers at over 100 institutions across North America who are committed to education for all people and who have partnered with faculty and universities to bring university-based and incarcerated students together. "The devil is in the details," and their efforts to secure space, dedicate staff, and arrange schedules are key to the success of Inside-Out.

Over 460 instructors throughout the United States, Canada, and beyond have, with great trust and generosity, completed an Inside-Out training. Each of these educators, both inside the academy and beyond, brings his or her particular wisdom, creativity, and courage to the work; together, they are creating and sustaining remarkable educational collaborations in their communities.

We thank the tens of thousands of family members of the entire faculty, staff, and inside and outside students who participate in this challenging work: their lives have been impacted—and we hope, enriched—by the program, too, and they have extended untold support to their loved ones. We think particularly of Leonard Pompa who left us too early at age 99½ and his support of Inside-Out. He would have loved seeing this book in print.

We also thank the many funders over the years, especially the Soros Foundation, who share the vision of Inside-Out and have helped to keep the work vibrant and expanding.

Many thousands of inside and outside students have taken part in Inside-Out classes across the United States and Canada. We thank and honor them above all, for bringing their trust, respect, industry, wisdom, and full engagement to the Inside-Out circle, and for taking the collective insights gathered there into the rest of their lives.We are grateful to the many generous people who have lived with this book as we have and have contributed to it immeasurably. These include Dan Butin, for inviting us to craft this book and for the many ways he fosters educational opportunities that bring people together and strengthen communities; Sarah Nathan, Associate Editor at Palgrave, and Deepa John at Newgen Knowledge Works for capably stewarding this project to completion; the talented cadre of colleagues, copy editors, and thought partners whose insights and expertise have sharpened the collection, including Chandler Davis, whose incisive copy editing made this book better and also helped to make it a family affair; Inside-Out teaching assistant extraordinaire Kathryn Dehler; Goucher Peace Studies Department Chair Ailish Hopper; Goucher Prison Education Partnership Director Amy Roza; GiannaDeMedio; Michael Roswell; Naomi Roswell; committed and responsive colleagues Randell Duguid, Lora Lempert, Jane Miller-Ashton, and Shoshana Pollack; the Walls to Bridges Collective for support and insight; the staff at the Inside-Out Center; Mike Voisin at Wilfrid Laurier University; the professional Van Meter faculty secretaries, especially Cathi Price and Jamie Winter, and the Goucher Faculty Affairs Committee for a summer research grant that helped this book see light; Peter Armstrong, Lee Steel, Natalie Zemon Davis, Hannah Taïeb, and Sofia Szamosi for gifts untold; and David Roswell, Bob Roswell, and Edith Sherr for their loving championship of the project. Our warmest thanks to all the contributors to this volume for their insight and their enduring commitment both to this book and to creating change through transformative education.

Lori Pompa, Founder and Director, The Inside-Out Prison Exchange Program

Simone Weil Davis
Barbara Sherr Roswell

CHAPTER 1

Introduction—Radical Reciprocity: Civic Engagement from Inside Out

Simone Weil Davis and Barbara Sherr Roswell

A powerful classroom experience results in a radical and lasting positive change, a metamorphosis. *Transformation*. Educators seek to define that process, to account for it, and especially to incite it, to open up possibilities for the kind of engaged learning and teaching that will prove transformational. This volume offers an extended reflection on the wider implications of one uniquely powerful pedagogical model. Founded in 1997, the Inside-Out Prison Exchange Program weds community-based learning and prison education, bringing college or university students and people in prison together as classmates for a semester of shared experiential learning. Fifteen thousand incarcerated ("inside") and campus-based ("outside") students have taken at least one Inside-Out class, and in many areas, inside students are now taking multiple Inside-Out courses for credit in subjects as diverse as sociology, philosophy, performance art, social work, literature, and the law. While these academic classes are the core of our work, they have become an integral part of a larger mosaic of sustained engagement. We will see reflected in this volume the program's emphasis on alumni activities on both sides of the wall, innovative region-wide collaborations, longstanding Inside-Out think tanks in prisons that engage in public education, trainings, and research projects, and an increasing number of initiatives that take the co-learning pedagogy to sites beyond the prison entirely. This book considers the broader lessons that Inside-Out provides for community-based learning praxis and for postsecondary teaching in general, on campus, in prisons, and in other community settings.

Prisons are compelling places. Largely invisible to those who call the Academy home, they evoke our deepest resentments and most intense fears. Saturated with ideology, they operate as a hidden node connecting the network of social issues that community-based learning most often addresses—from inadequate public education to racism to poverty. They incarcerate 2.3 million Americans; ten million US children have had a parent behind bars.[1] It is no surprise, then, that prison classrooms provide an especially intense instantiation of community-based teaching and learning, where the process of crossing boundaries, engaging with difference, and entering a space imagined as other is made literal. A course that brings university and incarcerated students together provides an intensely embodied context in which to examine the walls that divide us, the institutions that support those walls, the issues and people made invisible in mainstream American culture, and—paradoxically—the power of individuals and groups to make change.

Over the past two decades, as urban communities have been increasingly impacted by the effects of mass incarceration, universities have deepened their engagements with these same communities. Service learning and civic engagement efforts have become institutionalized on almost every campus in North America. Even as programs have matured and expanded, however, the field continues to founder on several intractable contradictions and conundrums. How can an instructor create a service learning course that offers deep engagement with others as unique individuals, yet prompts undergraduates to attend to structural inequities? How does that instructor advance beyond creating a superficial "encounter" with difference to foster what the Association of American Colleges and Universities (AACU) terms "interactional diversity,"—engagements that elicit diverse perspectives as valued resources for consequential problem solving?[2] How can a university use its wealth of resources to create service projects that do not unwittingly reinscribe the deficiencies of the recipient, and the needs, rather than the assets, of a community? How, in fact, can a community-based project live up to its aspirations to be fully collaborative, engaging community members as full partners in design, inquiry, and leadership? How can universities institutionalize service learning, making programs sustainable and strategic, without sacrificing the nuanced flexibility, responsiveness to local conditions, and "tactical finesse"[3] that community-based work demands? Why, if reflection is critical to learning and growth in service learning projects, is it only required of university participants, and not participants from the community? And how are faculty to facilitate openness and risk-taking if they are not themselves challenged to step out of their familiar positions of authority?

This collection argues that, by disrupting the fundamental assumptions fueling these tensions, Inside-Out provides a critical and timely contribution to community-engaged work in the university. By enacting a particularly "thick," fully realized pedagogy of engagement, the voices of Inside-Out collected in these pages deliberately synthesize strategies from a variety of traditions to create radically reciprocal opportunities for learning. The chapters gathered here examine both the theory and the practice of Inside-Out, placing it within the larger context of community engagement in higher education, testing its claims to address some of the most vexing contradictions of most service learning initiatives, analyzing its components and their synergies, assessing its ambition to transform participants, sounding the depth of its core commitments, probing its reach, and considering the implications of a model conceived in dialogue, expanded through the collaborative efforts of all stakeholders, and now replicated in hundreds of classrooms across North America.

Inside-Out begins with the assumption that all human beings—whether they reside behind bars or on the outside—have innate worth, a story to tell, experiences to learn from, perspectives that provide insight, and leadership to contribute to the community. By bringing together campus and incarcerated students for a semester of shared course work in a prison classroom, Inside-Out creates an extended opportunity for these students to study, converse, and collaborate on academic projects as equals. Offering an alternative model of community-engaged learning unfettered by paternalistic notions of "charity" or "service," the Inside-Out model is rooted in reciprocity, dialogue, and collaboration. By examining social issues through the "prism of prison," inside and outside students come to a fresher and deeper understanding of the subject matter than might be possible in an ordinary classroom. And by collaboratively designing projects based on course readings and dialogue, students are challenged to think through change strategies and explore their personal and collective potential as change agents. The result is a constructive dialogue that inspires participants to generate new ideas and fresh solutions, catalyzing the kinds of changes that can make communities more inclusive, just, and socially sustainable.

Faculty working in fields that span the arts, humanities, social sciences, and social services have introduced Inside-Out as a novel and rewarding community-based learning opportunity to students at community colleges, research and state universities, and liberal arts colleges across North America. In the process, the program joins and advances the larger effort to return higher education programming to people in prison and jail, currently available to only six percent of those incarcerated.

As Mike Rose argues in *Back To School*, with 40 million adults in the United States possessing neither a high school diploma nor a General Educational Development (GED) Certificate and a minority of students enrolled in community colleges completing a certificate or degree,[4] "access is a necessary but not a sufficient condition for achieving a robust and democratic system of higher education. It is not enough to let people in the door; we have to create conditions for them to thrive once inside" (105). By imagining students' fullest possible development and activating not just the economic and narrowly academic, but the full range of "intellectual, social, civic, moral and aesthetic motivations" for education (133), Inside-Out offers a pathway to academic success not only for students who are incarcerated but potentially for students from other communities that have historically been underserved by higher education as well. Reimagining pathways, student and instructor practitioners of this model also interrogate and reconceive what is meant by "academic success."

Fueling this approach are seven-day intensive Instructor Training Institutes, where interested faculty learn from a team of incarcerated and outside facilitators how to build classroom communities dedicated to dialogue, critical reflection, experiential learning, and responsible collective educational inquiry. The week of professional development prepares participants to facilitate Inside-Out courses in their own disciplines, to establish and sustain functioning agreements between prisons and universities, and to pursue credit-bearing options for inside participants. The trainings bring together educators of all sorts from across the continent and beyond: faculty from across the disciplines, veteran teachers with longstanding involvement in prison or community-based education, graduate students, and community members. Inside-Out's approach to the teacher's role, developed over 15 years and evolving, has great resonance with the work of Paulo Freire, Myles Horton, restorative justice and peace-building circles, and a long history of informal educational practices in prison settings. Participating as "students" during the training in a variety of experiential activities and engaging in projects that approximate the group projects so central to most Inside-Out classes, new instructors learn by doing, share their own considerable expertise, and benefit, too, from guided meta-reflection.

Self-inquiry matters whenever we teach; when some of our students are living within the constraints of confinement, we are even more obligated to be clear on our own positions, motivations, and capacities. Why are we drawn to this work? What obstacles do we face, and where are our sources of strength and replenishment? How do group dynamics over the course of the training week reveal our own blind spots about power and privilege, and how can we interrogate and move beyond them?

Contemporary academic culture rarely brings professors face to face with their own lives as teachers, nor, specifically, are those who bring campus and community participants together often given such a thorough preparation in reflective and dialogic practice. At a time when students, community partners, and community-based learning offices are often left to navigate the partnership without the professor's involvement, Inside-Out's emphasis on teacher trainings helps to shift and integrate community engagement more fully into the academic experience. As one professor-trainee reflects:

> Learning means to travel to the battleground. Learning means to realize the true challenge before me and to strategize, to struggle, to sit in the fire so that I see what I have been avoiding, to understand what I am most afraid of, and to meet the challenge of the forces in this world that attempt to undercut humanity.. . . . Each person reflects me to myself in an entirely new and evolving way. Learning from others is to learn about myself. Learning will never be finished.[5]

Inside-Out's work has been fundamentally shaped by the perspectives of its "community partners": people in prison. In 2002, in an effort to sustain their partnership beyond the artificial limits of an academic semester, a group of inside and outside alumni of Inside-Out courses formed the Graterford Think Tank, which has met weekly at the maximum security state prison outside of Philadelphia ever since. With director-founder Lori Pompa and associate director Melissa Crabbe, the Graterford Think Tank has shaped Inside-Out's pedagogy and ethical guidelines, and it continues to play a key role in the week-long instructor trainings. Other Think Tanks have formed in Illinois, Indiana, Michigan, Ohio, Ontario, Oregon, Tennessee, and West Virginia, each with a distinct culture and mission, but each equally committed to the values and practices that animated their original Inside-Out experience.

In Inside-Out seminar classrooms and think tanks, sustained, shared inquiry lead two "populations" to build one classroom community, a negotiated "we," neither easy nor seamless, but built from shared discovery, and put into practice, allowing for continued engagement beyond the semester's conclusion.

The work of shared reflection helps to determine those engagements, because it increases participants' capacity for critical inquiry. Even as Inside-Out courses defamiliarize and challenge assumptions about "prison," they defamiliarize education and learning as well. This connection is created in one of the very first joint classes, as inside and outside students work together in small groups to consider such questions as:

> When you think of prison, what image first comes to mind? Where do these images come from? What do most people assume about people in prison? What is prison *for*? When you think of college, what image first comes to mind? Where do these images come from? What do most people assume about people in college? What is college *for*? How are college and prison different? And, how are college and prison in some ways similar?

Reflecting and collaborating together, "transcending the walls that divide us," as a program byline describes it, inside and outside students often report a powerful experience of transformed insight and motivation. Contributors to the present volume examine and attempt to theorize the relationship between a larger project of social change and the individual's classroom experience of transformed understanding of self, other, and society. *Turning Teaching Inside Out* also takes up the central challenges of this work, both practical and philosophical—partnership challenges familiar to all who lead community-based learning initiatives, put through the crucible of the penal context. What are the institutional limits on the transformation Inside-Out evokes, the sometimes vexing pressures on mission that come from collaborating with and answering to multiple stakeholders?

This volume weaves together perspectives from across Inside-Out's network, across its history, across genres and disciplines, across the continent. Peering if not leaping over watchtowers and ivory towers alike, these writers speak the story of a program in many voices.

Part I: Origin Tales: Seeding and Building a Program brings together three chapters that recount the genesis and replication of this program. They highlight two key growth moments that any community engagement educator can encounter: inception, that is, moving an idea from inspiration to manifestation; and replication, turning a strong local program into a national (and now international) model. Consideration of Inside-Out's "origin tale" and raison d'etre comes from founder and director Lori Pompa and from Paul Perry, founding member of the Graterford Think Tank and the man who first had the idea that became Inside-Out. Pompa's lead chapter provides a comprehensive introduction to Inside-Out's history, philosophy, and pedagogic strategies. Perry's "Death of a Street Gang Warrior" places Inside-Out's emergence within his own remarkable story of "cognitive metamorphosis," with an analysis and a poetry that leave formulaic tales of the rehabilitated man far behind. In an chapter with applications to a wide variety of programs that seek to scale up, associate director Melissa Crabbe, lead designer of Inside-Out's instructor trainings and coordinator of Inside-Out Oregon, walks the reader through the development of a network of highly productive partner relationships in the Eugene-Portland corridor in Oregon. Crabbe's chapter usefully offers ten takeaway lessons about program expansion, revealing some of the rich outcomes possible when informal and formal agreements and relationships are allowed to accrete and form a dense weave over time. Innovations and crosspollinations emerge and institutional players begin to recalibrate their role in the larger community in ways that catalyze systemic change.

Part II: Expanding Teaching and Learning presents a set of chapters that consider dialogic pedagogy in practice. Today we confront parallel and intersecting crises in both higher education and criminal justice, leaving campus-enrolled students with big questions about the social contract and at least 2.3 million incarcerated Americans written out of that contract. In "What the World Needs Now," M. Kay Harris, Associate Professor Emeritus of Criminal Justice at Temple University and one of the first instructors to join Pompa in teaching Inside-Out courses, explains how and why the pedagogy serves as a meaningful counter to a history of racial oppression, exploring the historical legacies and structurally embedded dehumanization that Inside-Out helps to disrupt. K. D. A. Daniel-Bey and Amelia Larson, alumni of Inside-Out courses with think tank experience, draw on their Inside-Out experiences to challenge status quo educational practices and to offer alternatives. Their chapters remind us that the move toward educational justice requires a cool look at not one but *two* of our most impactful social institutions. Charles Boyd and Mario Carines, both incarcerated coaches and think tank members who help to facilitate instructor trainings (in Pennsylvania and Michigan, respectively) consider their own roles as trainers and the impacts of this work on participating faculty. They each demonstrate that even veteran teachers are grateful for the chance to pause for a week of immersive professional development to both experience and learn more about fostering and facilitating community building and intergroup dialogue. In "Teaching Itself: A Philosophical Exploration of Inside-Out Pedagogy," Gitte Wernaa Butin explores her adaptation of Inside-Out into a three-session seminar in a halfway house as part of an introductory philosophy course. Her chapter takes readers into her classroom and offers an extended analysis of one experiential learning unit on the resonances between witnessing, experiencing, and causing harm.

Part III: Productive Intersectionality: Navigating Race, Place, Gender, and Class, at the center of this volume, examines challenges that are perhaps especially high-stakes and complex in a prison setting, but that are critical to anyone considering campus/community collaboration. The authors in this section look squarely at both the deep frustrations that can arise over endemic oppressions and some of the strategies deployed in the Inside-Out community to try to break through the stickiest and most challenging kinds of hierarchy and bias. Community-based learning initiatives require their organizers to decide how they are going to confront the manifestations of power and privilege, both when recruiting and selecting participants, and in the classroom, fostering cultural competency and ongoing opportunities for critical reflection. The section opens with a Forum on the complex ways that power and privilege can play out when race, class, gender, sexualities, criminalization, and instructor/student hierarchies all intersect. Roundtable participants, including long-time instructors, staff and think tank members, offer specific strategies that can help diverse groups engage the productive discomfort that can lead to growth and insight. "Being Human," by former program coordinator Erin Howley, and "Breaking through 'Isms,'" by artist, activist, and educator Ella Turenne, share a variety of art- and text-based workshop approaches, drawing on the work of Paulo Freire and Augusto Boal to suggest facilitation techniques that can vitalize the "growing edge" of mutual discovery. "Trusting the Process," written collaboratively by two alumnae members of Canada's first think tank, takes frank inventory of the personal impacts of their graduate level Inside-Out sociology course, showing how an explicitly feminist framework can impact classroom practices and offer lasting learning.

Part IV: Transformation? Connection as Catalyst offers a set of chapters that try—from various vantage points, in different registers, and via various methods—to ask a set of ambitious questions: What kind of "transformation" can or should the post-secondary educator or community-based learning provider hope for? Individual, institutional, systemic? Why and how does the Inside-Out process work, to the extent that it does? Will impacts endure? What is the relationship between transformative education and social change? In what becomes a sort of duet, long-time Inside-Out instructor Steven Shankman and inside Tennessee alumni Tony Vick use different discursive strategies to suggest that it is in the encounter, in the deeply reciprocal and irrefutably human gaze of our sister or brother, that we find transformation. For both authors, that transformation is linked to a new understanding of the ethical relationship that gives us our selfhood in the first place. In "Access for Whom?" Tyrone Werts, a founding member of the Graterford Think Tank and, since his 2011 release after more than three decades in prison, a key member of the senior staff on the outside, presents Inside-Out as a strikingly productive opportunity for whole-self learning as well as a significant gateway for people who otherwise might not see themselves as college-bound. In "The Reach and Limits of a Prison Education Program," Simone Weil Davis looks at the places where personal and sociopolitical transformation can be seen to intersect, and how the Inside-Out process invites exactly such an integration. The section concludes with chapters by Kristin Bumiller and Gillian Harkins that place Inside-Out within the landscapes of neoliberalism and higher education in prison. These chapters argue that Inside-Out provides an unusual opportunity for all participants—inside and outside—to see anew the sometimes homologous workings of two of our most profoundly formative social institutions. Such analysis, they each suggest, is key to advancing from educational access to educational justice.

The contributors to Part V: Yardsticks and Roadmaps: Evaluating Change ask how Inside-Out marks and measures the transformation it seeks. In "Alchemy and Inquiry," Barbara Roswell and Simone Davis reflect on a variety of explanatory models that can account for its power and on the often thorny challenges of research and evaluation that have occupied members of the Inside-Out network who are connected through an extended research community. The chapter summarizes a wide-ranging roundtable discussion among members of the program's Research Committee about the ethics, purposes, and methods appropriate to such research, about scope and scale, and about the paradigms and tools that can best analyze and assess the pedagogy's aspirations for individual and collective transformation. This section of the book explores not only which questions need asking but also what research practices can enact the program's principles by extending full partnership, in design, implementation, and analysis, to university and community participants. In answer to this question, Angela Bryant and Yasser Payne argue for the political and analytical benefits of Participatory Action Research (PAR)—and specifically for "street PAR"—as the method that can best foreground, rather than eclipse, community-participants' perspectives and agency and thus overcome the limitations of current research into community-based learning.[6] Sarah Allred, Nathan Belcher, and Todd Robinson, a faculty-alumni trio, similarly endeavor to put the commitments of the Inside-Out research community into practice. They reflect together on their own experiences as teachers and learners, identify relational learning as key to the Inside-Out experience, and share the results of their empirical study of Inside-Out's claims to foster transformation and self-efficacy.

Educators are typically given a quarter, a semester, or at most a four-year span, as the frame within which to foster engagement. For transformation to matter, it needs to persist, and two of the chapters in Part VI: Leaning into the Future: Helping Change Endure examine the means whereby students' changing roles lead to and mark their changing possibilities as agents in the world, as "alumni" opportunities allow people to stay engaged and take on new authority after their Inside-Out coursework has concluded. When Think Tank members, including those in prison, participate as leaders in the facilitation of the Instructor Training Institutes, all parties learn what "stakeholder leadership" means in practice. What is required for an incarcerated or outside student or alumnus/a to become prepared to responsibly "teach the teacher" and what gifts are shared when this work unfolds? Matt Soares speaks lyrically of this process and its myriad ripple effects. Any enduring program will prove its hardiness through the variations that spring from its original root. In a thought piece that works in dialogue with Melissa Crabbe's chapter on replication, Simone Weil Davis considers the relatively new national program that she is now coordinating in Canada, reflecting on what this crossing of national borders can tell us about the concept of "replication," program growth, shifting contexts, and adaptability. Giovanna Shay of Western New England College extends the reach of Inside-Out beyond the social sciences where it originated, and the humanities and arts where it now also thrives, to chart a first foray into law courses in the Inside-Out mode. She concludes that laws schools have a particular obligation to engage critically with issues of incarceration and suggests that Inside-Out pedagogy has an important role to play in enlivening legal education.

Perhaps the essential germ of Inside-Out is not prison; even more fundamental is the power of educational exchange and collaboration to transcend the social barriers and institutional frames that define and corral us all. On campus, adaptations of the Inside-Out approach prompt self-awareness, dialogue, and community building in such settings as first year seminars, leadership initiatives, and diversity workshops. And as the Community Inside-Out program at Drexel University in Philadelphia and incipient programs in Canada and elsewhere show us, in a host of settings, refugees, seniors, veterans, and others can join with university students to learn together in community (see Appendix 4). A praxis grounded in dialogue, collaboration, problem-solving, and sustained partnerships promises to strengthen the links between individual and systemic transformation in these noncorrectional venues as well.[7]

The book concludes with a *Closing Circle* (Part VII). Pieces by Nyki Kish and Damien Arnaout and Shawn Brown were both initially part of the proceedings of closing ceremonies for individual Inside-Out courses. The book concludes with a final, lyrical gesture from Lori Pompa, "The Essence of Inside-Out."

Notes

1. Though the United States remains a stark exception, some other Western, Asian, and "Commonwealth" countries, due in part to an exportable for-profit and risk-management approach to criminal justice, are developing policies and practices leading to a steep increase in incarceration rates, particularly for racialized communities, the poor, and women.
2. Patricia Gurin, Erik L. Day, Sylvia Hurtado, and Gerald Gurin, "Diversity and Higher Education: Theory and Impact on Educational Outcomes," *Harvard Educational Review* 72, no. 3 (Fall 2002): 330–366 and Lori J. Vogelgesang, Marcy Drummond, and Shannon K. Gilmartin, *How Higher Education is Integrating Diversity and Service Learning: Findings from Four Case Studies* (San Francisco: California Campus Compact, 2003).
3. Paula Mathieu. *Tactics of Hope: The Public Turn in English Composition* (Portsmouth, NH: Heienemann, 2006).
4. Only 30 percent of students enrolled in community colleges complete a degree or certificate or transfer within four years. Mike Rose. *Back to School* (New York: New Press, 2012).
5. See "Instructors' Voices," The Inside-Out Prison Exchange Program website, http://www.insideoutcenter.org/instructors-voices.html
6. Randy Stoecker and Elizabeth A. Tryon, *The Unheard Voices: Community Organizations and Service Learning* (Philadelphia: Temple University Press, 2009) and Devi Miron and Barbara E. Moely. "Community Agency, Voice and Benefit in Service-Learning," *Michigan Journal of Community Service Learning* 12 (Spring 2006): 27–37.
7. See Alissa Falcone, "Inside-Out Prison Exchange Course Expands Beyond Criminal Justice Courses," April 29, 2013, *Drexel Now*, http://drexel.edu/now/features/archive/2013/April/Inside-Out-update/

References

Gurin, Patricia, Erik L. Day, Sylvia Hurtado, and Gerald Gurin, "Diversity and Higher Education: Theory and Impact on Educational Outcomes." *Harvard Educational Review* 72, no. 3 (Fall 2002): 330–366.

Miron, Devi and Barbara E. Moely. "Community Agency, Voice and Benefit in Service-Learning." *Michigan Journal of Community Service Learning* 12 (Spring 2006): 27–37.

Mathieu, Paula. *Tactics of Hope: The Public Turn in Composition.* Portsmouth, NH: Heinemann, 2005.

Stoekcer, Randy and Elizabeth A. Tryon, *The Unheard Voices: Community Organizations and Service Learning.* Philadelphia: Temple University Press, 2009.

Vogelgesang, Lori J., Marcy Drummond, and Shannon K. Gilmartin, *How Higher Education Is Integrating Diversity and Service Learning: Findings from Four Case Studies.* San Francisco: California Campus Compact, 2003.

PART I

Origin Tales: Seeding and Building a Program

CHAPTER 2

Drawing Forth, Finding Voice, Making Change: Inside-Out Learning as Transformative Pedagogy

Lori Pompa

"I didn't expect to learn so much. I didn't expect to grow and change as a result of the process.... As I reflect on the power of this course, I am awe-struck and humbled."

Outside Participant

Introduction

It is a very simple concept, really: people coming together to talk about and wrestle with issues that are important to them. Yet, in this setting, it is actually quite complex and surprisingly profound. The reason is that it is all happening behind the walls of a prison. People from the outside and people from the inside study issues and work together over the course of a semester, as peers, in full collaboration. This is Inside-Out—or, by its more formal name: The Inside-Out Prison Exchange Program. And—like the student quoted above—I am, indeed, awestruck and humbled to have been able to witness the unprecedented and unpredictable developments in this program since its inception.

What follows is a short history of Inside-Out introducing the development, context, and philosophical underpinnings of the program, now active in 25 states and Canada, as well as its relationship to the concept of community-based learning. Voices of participants, interspersed throughout the chapter, illustrate the program's conceptual framework and reflect its dynamic and collaborative nature.

How It All Began: Who Knew?!?

The story begins when I first set foot in prison back in 1985. I can remember that day as if it were yesterday—the smells, sights, and sounds, a sensory cacophony of stale sweat, old sneakers, clanging bars, crumbling cement, deafening announcements over the PA system, and men...hundreds of men, who seemed to be locked in some bizarre dance, a listless fugue arrested in time. Underneath the noise and chaos, I sensed, lay silence and inertia—revealing a depth of isolation that defied imagination. This deeply disturbing feeling is as palpable today as it was then.

Something about that experience compelled me to continue going back in-several days a week—in various capacities over the next few years. I met thousands of incarcerated men and women...and the questions—and the disturbance—only grew wider and deeper. I was trying to figure out what this was all about—what this country's approaches to and levels of imprisonment meant in terms of the US social psyche. It was a mystery to me how the richest, strongest, freest country on earth could also have the most people incarcerated, in both relative and absolute terms. I came to understand, over time, that our overuse of incarceration is, at least in part, a result of the many systems of injustice that ultimately come to roost in the prison system.

Rather unexpectedly, in 1992, I was offered the opportunity to start teaching some courses in corrections for the Criminal Justice Department at Temple University in Philadelphia. So, I began to take my students—over the years, nearly 15,000 of them—to visit jails and prisons in Pennsylvania and New Jersey. Not surprisingly, I saw registered on their faces the same confusion and disturbance that I felt on my first day inside the walls.

Then, in 1995, something astonishing happened. I took some students to a state prison in Dallas, PA, three hours away from campus. We did the usual tour of the facility, followed by a fascinating, nuanced conversation with a panel of men serving life sentences there. But this conversation went places I had never experienced before—in prison, on campus, really anywhere. We talked of crime and justice, race and class, politics and economics—and how all of these strands were interrelated.

After the session was over, one of the panelists—Paul Perry—asked if I had ever considered doing this as more than just a one-time event, but rather, as a regular course. Although we could not travel the three hours each way to his institution, I promised him that I would think about his intriguing idea. And, of course, that was *all* I could think about.

Over the next few weeks, I designed a syllabus for a course: "The Inside-Out Prison Exchange Program: Exploring Issues of Crime and Justice Behind the Walls." I realized that the didactic, hierarchical methodology so often used in higher education would not be appropriate and sought to create a learning process that stood in contrast to the daily experience of life inside the prison—a liberating space juxtaposed against its repressive context. In *this* classroom, the instructor's role would be to call forth, with subtlety and grace, the voices of those in the class, through a dialogic exchange among equals.

What emerged in the development of that first course were the elements that have become the "signature" pedagogical components of Inside-Out: dialogue-focused learning, the instructor as facilitator, the group establishing its own ground rules at the beginning of the semester, the use of icebreakers and other community-building activities, specially-focused theme-based readings, experiential activities used in the class to illustrate course concepts, integrative reflection papers, group projects with real-world significance developed at the end of the semester, and a final closing ceremony, including administrators from the school and the correctional facility, to mark the achievements of the class.

The next step was to find a prison or jail that would be willing to host the course. My first choice was the State Correctional Institution at Graterford, a very large maximum-security prison about an hour outside of Philadelphia where I had been involved with programs and had good connections with the staff, but a raid on the institution resulted in its being closed to all outside people and programs.

When Graterford remained closed a year later, I approached the Philadelphia Prison System (a very large county jail complex, housing thousands of people) to pilot the program. I had no idea if it would work. As it turned out, that first Inside-Out class in the Fall of 1997 greatly exceeded my expectations: Besides learning about crime and justice, the people involved in the class came to new understandings of themselves, of others, of society, and of their relationship to society. What occurred in this course was so incredible that I just kept offering it every semester and helped a couple of other Temple faculty, including M. Kay Harris (see chapter 5) to begin their own courses.

> Most college courses are lectures and readings which, later on, we are supposed to apply to real-life situations. This class was a real-life situation itself...The students in the class gave it life—we taught each other more than can be read in a book. (Outside Participant)

In 2002, after having taught Inside-Out courses in the Philadelphia system for five years, I finally received the approval to expand the program to Graterford Prison. While arranging to teach the course, I received a somewhat shocking letter from someone incarcerated there saying, "I heard about the program that you are bringing here and we are all very excited. In fact, I am going to be helping to get the program started with some of the other men incarcerated here." And then, there was this jaw-dropping line: "You may remember me. I met you at Dallas. My name is Paul." As chapter 4 in this volume, "Death of a Street Gang Warrior," recounts, he has been, and continues to be, involved in everything that has happened since then.

The Contours of the Classroom Experience: What It Is and What It Is Not

Picture this: a group of roughly 15 campus-based college/university students and 15 men or women incarcerated in a correctional facility come together each week to read, write, study, and talk about crime, justice, and related issues. In a room deep inside a jail or prison, these 30 people gather each week in a large circle, alternately seated—inside student, outside student, inside, outside—around the circle.

In that circle, everyone is equal—with an equal voice and an equal stake in the learning process. Everyone does the same reading, writing, and grappling with complex issues together, in a shared learning process. The instructor serves as a facilitator, encouraging ongoing dialogue and collaborative work in small and large groups. Here is how one student described the experience:

> What a motley crew we made in that little program room at [the prison]. People of different colors, sexes, ages, education levels, social classes and opinions in a circle, laughing, talking, arguing and respecting each other for hours at a time. It has to make it difficult for anyone who watches to hold on to the status quo. The status quo says that doesn't happen. It says that people are different and that some things are never going to change. For two and a half hours [each week] this semester, we proved that untrue. (Outside Participant)

It is important to explain that Inside-Out is not a situation where those of us from the outside enter the prison to study the men or women on the inside; it is neither research nor voyeurism. We are also not "helping" the participants who are incarcerated; it is not charity or service of any kind. Though some instructors may choose to list their Inside-Out course under the rubric of "service learning," it is more appropriately understood as a "community-based learning" opportunity, through which *everyone* is seen as having something vital to offer in the learning process.

Additionally, while Inside-Out does not endorse any particular agenda or promote advocacy or activism *in the name of the program*, our goal is to provide more than an academic education. Inside-Out fosters analytical, productive, whole-self commitment to community and to civic engagement and helps people to actualize as contributing members of their community and society at large. By the end of the semester, both inside and outside students develop a desire to make change in the world, and we celebrate the ripple effect that has ensued.

Finally, Inside-Out is very intentional in its approach to relationships and boundaries. "Inside" and "outside" students use only first names, share no other identifying information about themselves, and have no contact beyond the classroom. The program's clear parameters and built-in limitations help to keep it safe on many levels—for participants, as well as for the program as a whole, which must operate within the security rules established by the host correctional institutions. As is discussed throughout this book (see, especially, chapters 9 and 10), after a class is over, Inside-Out often creates program-sponsored opportunities for ongoing involvement in alumni activities, including think tanks, which are comprised of inside and outside participants.

Community-Based Learning: Where Content Meets Context

This particular model of learning affords campus-based students an immersive experience that is powerful on a number of levels. Outside students are provided direct, unadulterated exposure to the exigencies of a particular context (in this case, prison). This immersion engenders deeper interaction and more intense involvement, often manifesting as a statement of solidarity with those who are struggling. It is the ultimate border-crossing experience. When students take class together as equals, borders disintegrate and barriers recede. What emerges instead is the possibility of considering the subject matter from a new context—and from the perspectives of those living within that context. The interplay of content and context creates a provocative juncture that takes the educational process to a deeper level.

> Walking out of that place every week was hard. It was hard because that was the moment that forced me to face the fact that not all of us were allowed to leave.... If prison were anything other that [what] it is, it would be a lot less traumatic to walk out that door and leave someone behind it. (Outside Participant)

It is this sort of sentiment that makes immersive learning both challenging and immensely important. Unless facilitated with great care and consciousness, however, "service" can unwittingly become an exercise in patronization, becoming the very thing that it eschews. And it can happen in subtle ways.

The crux of the problem revolves around the issue of power. If I "do for" you, "serve" you, "give to" you, that creates a dynamic in which I see myself as separate from you, and as having the resources, the abilities, and the power, with you as receiver. While benign in intent, it can be ironically disempowering and disrespectful of the "receiver," highlighting needs and deficits. Without meaning to, this process replicates the "have-have not" paradigm that underlies so many of our social problems and runs the risk of benefitting no one. The danger is that, without mutuality, service mimics charity, and "charity does not encourage the intimate connections and the personal relationships that result from service built on mutuality" (Rhoads, 128).

> Through the other, we come to experience the self. Mutuality is about how we both give and receive because we connect to the other through a concern, which, in the name of caring, bridges whatever differences we have. (139)

The notion that higher education has the responsibility to make resources available to the wider community can be dangerously one-dimensional. What we may fail to see are the many ways in which our educational institutions *need* the assets of the community—those tangible and intangible gifts that challenge, deepen, and enhance the world of higher education. For example, if we really want to understand what prisons are for or what leads to criminal activity, it seems most appropriate to at least include, if not actually foreground, the voices of people who have had experiences with the criminal justice system and have reflected deeply on these issues. Different from "studying" people as "objects," creating a space for informed community-based voices to emerge—as "subjects"—benefits everyone involved.

One of the inherent challenges of offering community-based learning opportunities with integrity is to overcome the "assets" and "liabilities" dichotomy. If community settings are defined as places where there are people with needs, that reality can become the primary filter through which the setting or group of people is viewed. It is a question of definition, perception, judgment, and labels. There is a difference, for example, between "a homeless man" and a man who is homeless, or between "a prisoner" and a person who is in prison. Labeling limits perspectives and skews the person's identity, resulting in a relationship with the *liability*, rather than with the *person*.

> The opening exercises allowed each person to get a glimpse into the other's humanity. Labels such as "inmate" and "student" fell away and were irrelevant. We were just people engaging each other on a basic human level. (Inside Participant)

Too often in community-based or service learning experiences, we can find ourselves unintentionally creating unequal relationships and then needing to contort ourselves to correct these relationships in disingenuous ways. One of the strengths of the Inside-Out approach is the dialogic interaction that takes place between and among those involved. This dialogue occurs on many levels and is multidimensional in character. It certainly includes the spoken word, through which participants share ideas, stories, perceptions, opinions—verbalizing realities and analyses with one another as coequal collaborators. More fundamentally, however, it is an experience through which people speak their lives, by the simple yet profound act of being together in an environment of mutual respect, dignity, and trust.

A Shared Liminal Space: Generating a Different Dynamic

At the beginning of any college course, everyone involved—whether consciously or not—carries assumptions about those with whom they will be sharing the semester. These judgments can be based on many factors: age, skin color, accent, dress, where one sits, how one acts—whatever is picked up through sensory cues. In the Inside-Out class, where two seemingly disparate groups come together in one space, the usual assumptions also include expectations about intelligence, dangerousness, and trustworthiness. It takes only a short time for this presumption to be dispelled, resulting in one group, whose common elements emerge more prominently than their differences.

As Robert Rhoads describes in *Community Service and Higher Learning: Explorations of the Caring Self* (1997), "overcoming our sense of alienation involves recognizing real differences, and, at the same time, understanding that we can build some common connections—that the stranger is not so different from myself and that we can engage one another in a common struggle or cause" (119).

> All I could see when I sat in class was their "blues" and I think that caused me to subconsciously form false perceptions. However, this all began to change for me when I...began to look at the [incarcerated] students as individuals, not just as blue uniforms....This was a very different perception from my first and was enlightening. I don't think I have ever felt such a strong change occur inside of me and it will be something that I hold inside for the rest of my life. (Outside Participant)

The power of this sort of realization by a student can put us directly in touch with two concomitant realities for those of us in the teaching profession: privilege and responsibility. As teachers, we are afforded the singular privilege of journeying with a group of (often young) people over several months as they grapple with concepts and try on new ideas, in the service of deepening and further preparing themselves for their lives in the world. There are few professions that provide such an incredible opportunity. And, at the same time, it is a solemn responsibility to be invited into such a hallowed place in the lives of others, as they pursue their quest for meaning and understanding in themselves and in the world. As Parker Palmer explains:

> I must take responsibility for my mediator role, for the way my mode of teaching exerts a slow but steady formulative pressure on my students' sense of self and world. I teach more than a body of knowledge or a set of skills. I teach a mode of relationship between the knower and the known, a way of being in the world. That way...will remain with my students long after the facts have faded from their minds. (1993, 30)

In *A Pedagogy for Liberation*, Paulo Freire discusses the role of the teacher in this way: that the teacher is "*not* directive of the *students*, but directive of the *process*.... As director of the process, the liberating teacher is not doing something *to* the students but *with* the students" (46). This description is reminiscent of the power of what Parker Palmer (1993) calls a "learning space." He suggests that this "space" emerges with a teacher "who not only speaks but listens, who not only gives answers but asks questions and welcomes our insights, who provides information and theories that do not close doors but open new ones, who encourages students to help each other learn" (70).

> I look forward to this class. I find it inspiring. There have been points, deep in our discussions, that I've found myself feeling at home. I know that sounds odd, but it's quite true. It must be from a combination of things. I think we all feel generally respected, affirmed, and supported in our opinions and world-views. And I feel in this dialogue of [outside] students and men on the inside an extremely critical engagement with issues of suffering and our society's account-ability to the widespread phenomenon of suffering. I've been in many settings where I feel poverty, class oppression, racism were all talked about. But somehow it still just felt like words. What is spoken in the Graterford class strikes me on a much deeper level. (Outside Participant)

In shifting the focus from the passive acquisition of knowledge to a fully integrated, dynamic process of discovery, the essential ingredient is participatory dialogue. Through both small group interaction and large group discussion, students grapple with issues in a constructive, dialogic fashion. When facilitating an Inside-Out course, the focus is on providing a framework within which the issues that we are studying can be examined in-depth. This exploration is mediated through an ongoing process in which everyone involved is afforded the space to raise questions, challenge one another, offer diverse perspectives, and wrestle with the idiosyncratic nature of our system of crime and justice. The hope is that, by the end of the semester, participants have developed more than merely the ability to take in information, but rather, the capacity to inquire, analyze, critique, challenge—or be challenged by—the information acquired.

> Even when opinions differed, it was striking to note that sometimes I thought both were right or equally reasonable. I had to redefine my concept of conflict and differences of opinion. There can be circumstances when differing opinions are equally correct, though they be mutually opposed to each other. It's not always necessary for one to be right and the other wrong. (Inside Participant)

As Palmer (1993) puts it: "tolerance of ambiguity can be taught as a way of listening to others without losing one's voice" (xviii). Additionally, understanding the relevance of context is instructive for students in a community-based learning setting because it "help(s) them understand that as human beings we do have many things in common, yet as a result of how race and class have situated us within our society, we cannot ignore important identity differences" (Rhoads, 123). This reality is profoundly evident in prison.

> It…dawned on me that having a class in a maximum security prison is…an act of resistance. By having this class, we are…questioning normative assumptions of "criminals" and "criminality" and normative reactions to those who have violated the law. Since society views offenders as immoral individuals who are not entitled to compassion or [to] have normal human relations, this class challenges those popular understandings. Every time we to go to [the prison] and have class or even have "normal" interactions with the guys there, we are in fact engaged in an act of resistance. It is a space that humanizes. (Outside Participant)

Our experience has shown that creating a space for individuals to feel comfortable and free to become engaged involves, among other things, something so simple as the arrangement of chairs in the room. This, too, is a political statement in that it reflects how power operates in a group. In a conventional seating structure, power rests in the front of the room with the teacher. In contrast, power is shared when the seats are arranged in a circle. Palmer (1993) describes it this way: "[W]hen the chairs are placed in a circle, creating an open space between us, within which we can connect,…we are all being invited to create a community of learning by engaging the ideas and one another in the open space between" (75).

> Class sessions were not "classes" by the usual standard. They were safety nets, zones by which we could come together and discuss issues commonly significant to all of us, problems and solutions that we felt were important to consider and resolve. (Outside Participant)

Attention and care are vital in fashioning a positive learning environment in which people feel safe. In prison, where trust is elusive, creating this sort of setting is a challenge. Additionally, since many of the issues explored can be difficult and sensitive, the group needs to feel that the experience is unrestricted, on the one hand, and contained, on the other. Again, Palmer (1993) sheds light on both of these issues:

"[T]he openness of a space is created by the firmness of its boundaries" (72); and "precisely because a learning space can be a painful place, it must have one other characteristic—hospitality. Hospitality means receiving each other, our struggles, our newborn ideas with openness and care" (73).

> As much as we say we are open minded, it is not until we are forced to listen to the opinions of others that we really can appreciate the perspective that each of us brings to a subject. This was clearly instructive for me personally. (Inside Participant)

One of the ways to help create a space of hospitality and openness in any community-based learning space is by offering the class the opportunity to create its own guidelines for dialogue (see chapter 14). Another critical aspect of community-based learning involves the opportunity for reflection on the part of *everyone* involved in the class. It is one thing to have an experience, even a shared experience; it is quite another to take the time and space to understand the experience and all that flows from it. Through the particular format for papers used in Inside-Out courses, inside and outside students are encouraged to focus on three areas in writing a paper based on a specific class session: *observations* of that particular week and why they were important, *integration* of the discussion in that particular class in dialogue with the readings assigned for that week, and finally, the student's personal *reaction* to the class session, its dynamics, and the topics discussed. All too rare in community-based learning initiatives, this format offers *all* participants the opportunity to use multiple dimensions of themselves in their papers, leading to a deeper understanding of both the issues and the overall experience of the course.

The Journey Continues: Depth, Breadth, and Organic Growth

The first Inside-Out class at Graterford Prison in 2002 was so on fire about the issues discussed in the course that the group decided to stay together to do a series of projects focused on reeducating the public about crime and justice. The group called itself the "Think Tank" and has been meeting weekly ever since, for more than 11 years, without interruption. Since its inception, this group has hosted hundreds of students, community participants, and civic leaders in workshops, conferences, forums, and other kinds of meetings. A major hallmark and strength of the "think tank" model is that it is comprised of and led by a combination of inside and outside participants, who are taking part in the ongoing work of the group on a purely voluntary basis. It provides a good example of where community-based learning can take those whose learning process evolves into a deeper and more long-term commitment to collaborative work on social justice issues.

One of the first decisions the Think Tank made in 2002 was to work on developing Inside-Out into a national model, which became possible through a fellowship from the Soros Foundation. After several months of preparation, we held our first National Instructor Training Institute in July of 2004—a seven-day, 60-hour intensive training—one-third of which was held inside Graterford Prison, where the

Think Tank assisted in training the instructors, offering their expertise and advice on multiple dimensions of Inside-Out's best practices (see chapters 9, 10, and 25).

These trainings have become a core function of the program. We find that, for several reasons, it is essential for instructors interested in taking on this challenge to participate in a comprehensive training. Like other community-based learning courses, Inside-Out classes are very complex, with multiple moving parts. The instructor needs to be prepared to deal with teaching within the very challenging setting of the prison, aware of the complicated dynamics of the class as a whole and the individuals in it, prepared to deal with whatever exigencies that may present themselves at the prison on a given day, able to be flexible with the flow of where the dialogue may take the group, and many other concerns. Years of faculty reflections identify Inside-Out courses as the most challenging classes they have ever taught— and, by far, the most rewarding.

The weeklong training program, crafted in collaboration with Melissa Crabbe, Inside-Out's immensely creative Associate Director, prepares faculty to facilitate these blended classes. Topics include facilitation techniques, identity and diversity issues, ethical concerns, garnering support both from one's educational institution and the local correctional institution, and understanding the context and rules of the prison. And very importantly, during the training week, instructors have multiple opportunities to reflect on this work and to consider their own "baggage" (i.e., the previously unidentified issues they may have that could impact on their efficacy as an Inside-Out instructor), while also experiencing for themselves, as "learners," many of the kinds of activities used in Inside-Out classes.

Additionally, we are very conscious of the fragility of Inside-Out and the role of each instructor and student as a kind of ambassador representing the program to multiple stakeholders. Instructors need to fully comprehend the rules and parameters of the program, and communicate them clearly. After the training, our staff remains available to instructors for further consultation as they set up and teach their classes.

To date, we have offered 31 trainings, involving over 460 instructors from the United States, Canada, and beyond. Approximately 500 Inside-Out courses have been offered in 25 states and two Canadian provinces, involving 15,000 inside and outside students. Classes are in disciplines as diverse as sociology, philosophy, theatre arts, literature, economics, and urban planning—spanning the social sciences, the humanities, and the arts. A number of law schools have begun classes, as well. Courses are conducted by every size and type of higher educational institution (major research institutions, small liberal arts colleges, community colleges) and correctional facility (minimum, medium, and maximum-security jails and prisons, including reentry facilities, for men, women, and, to a limited extent, young people in juvenile detention—located in rural, urban, and suburban areas).

Instructors have begun to utilize this methodology in noncorrectional community settings, as well, from diversity workshops on campus to courses that consider homelessness, disabilities, and immigration. The model, utilizing its core elements, is highly adaptable to many settings.

Equally important, over the years, Inside-Out has given birth to a grassroots, community-organizing structure for implementing higher education in prison on a large scale. It involves building a community of people (instructors, Inside-Out alumni, university administrators) who, in the absence of significant funding, become committed to finding innovative ways to provide college classes in prison. Our instructors are trained to do the work required to create school-prison partnerships by leveraging university resources in strategic and creative ways, providing a "win-win" situation for everyone involved: inside students, outside students, prisons, and universities. To date, instructors trained through Inside-Out have created ongoing partnerships between hundreds of schools and prisons in the United States and Canada.

As chapters 3 and 27 explain in more detail, Inside-Out has grown over the years, expanding across the country. Eight think tanks meet in the United States and Canada (in Oregon, Michigan, Tennessee, West Virginia, Illinois, Ohio, Indiana, and Ontario), each with its own mission and vision, but all providing a space for both inside and outside participants to work on projects related to social justice issues, intensifying their own civic engagement, while engendering interest in these issues among the general public through conferences, workshops, and other events (see Appendices 1, 3, and 6). Each think tank draws on the same pedagogical commitments and strategies employed in Inside-Out courses: circle processes, icebreakers, small group discussions, community-building, dialogue, reflection, and questions that open up rather than close down conversation.

Beyond the expansion of the program, we have seen intensive coordination of efforts among groups of instructors in various areas, as well as burgeoning alumni activity that has produced all sorts of creative projects, like a book club for young people incarcerated in a juvenile facility in Oregon and an Inside-Out-inspired workshop series with participants in a reentry facility in Philadelphia. From all of this—the classes, think tanks, regional development, alumni activity—the effects of this vibrant program are rippling in ever-widening circles.

The Inside-Out program is growing exponentially, both in depth and in breadth, due to its groundbreaking, cutting-edge approach to education. We understand the learning process as much more than something that happens "from the eyebrows up." Education that is worthy of the name has to involve the whole person to whatever extent possible. Given that the root of the word education means to "draw forth," this unique pedagogical approach—centered in the dialogic process—honors what education, in its deepest sense, can be—the drawing forth of the best in those gathered: the best ideas, the best critical thinking and, frankly, the best of what it means to be a human being.

> My brain never stopped processing information as each student was able to add a piece to the steadily growing mosaic. For me, this is what a college class is all about. I left class with my mind racing to place all of the pieces discussed into their proper places. (Inside Participant)

There is something both powerful and compelling about what happens within the prison classroom—for the inside students, for the outside students, and for the instructor, as well. It is an interesting, albeit ironic, twist that we are able to create a space of freedom within a context that is so often the antithesis. In this shared space, we can be who we are, say what we know, and call forth the best in each other. As human beings, we are all hungry for just these kinds of places—these sorts of opportunities—to be and express our true selves, beyond the expectations (both external and internal) that so often imprison us. This experience can have such an impact that, at the end of the semester, there is frequently a real grieving for the loss of such a liberating space.

Many inside students have even stated that, while in the class, they actually forgot that they were in prison. When instructors contact us after holding their first course, the description is remarkably similar. It is, they say, a deeply transformative experience. Assumptions are debunked...worldviews are shattered...and people begin to look at themselves, their lives, and the world in whole new ways.

> The experience has highlighted the transformative value to students of combining intellectual, emotional and experiential learning. I have expanded my capacities and deepened my knowledge as an instructor and as a human being. (Inside-Out Instructor)

Transformative Education: An Engine for Social Change

Intellectual understanding and analysis of issues combine with concern about and passion for those issues, propelling students—both inside and out—to recognize their potential as change agents, ready to take the next step in addressing a particular dilemma. Different from the idea of hands-on, engaged learning as a "feel-good" experience, which can end up both superficial and ephemeral, this approach to learning involves depth, direction, hard work, and a commitment to make change in the world.

> [W]ith enlightenment comes responsibility. We are all responsible. What is the next step after all this dialogue is done? (Inside Participant)

Community-based learning—quite distinct from charity or the "helping" modality—involves what Freire calls "conscientization" and a critique of social systems, motivating participants to analyze what they experience and then act. The pedagogy of community-based learning, when done with great care and integrity, has the power to turn things inside-out and upside-down for those engaged in it. It provokes one to think differently about the world, and consider one's relationship to the world in a new way.

> We have been fortunate. We have made the individual connections and are now faced with the challenge of what to do with our changed views. I don't begin to have the answers. But I have a great deal of hope....I don't know "how"...but I'm beginning to realize that we must also ask "who"—and I think that together, we have found some of the courage it will take to ask and answer that question. (Outside Participant)

This approach to learning captures and communicates a dynamism that inspires everyone involved to explore, inquire, analyze, and act. Thus, community-based learning provides both an impetus toward and an incubator for social change.

And it is not only university-based students who begin to see themselves as potential change agents. For many of the incarcerated students, Inside-Out provides a radical change from seeing oneself (or being seen) as the problem—to seeing oneself as part of the solution to the problem. In fact, we all come to see ourselves that way.

> [This class] has acted as the catalyst in my passion for life and human rights, and was the pivotal point where I realigned my own path. (Outside Participant)

> I will hold its ideals and values for the rest of my life—but not only to keep them with me but to act consciously with them. (Inside Participant)

And finally, from Glenn, who left us entirely too soon, these haunting words:

> Inside-Out should come with a warning label—in big black and yellow letters: *Warning: may cause severe damage if taken internally.* We have seen, first hand, the kind of damage the program can do to preconceived notions, stereotypes, and most importantly—ignorance.... Inside-Out has acted, for many of us, as a kind of eye-exam for the soul, forcing us to realize what we believe and why we believe it. And we now realize that our vision was never 20/20. We leave here with a little better vision. (Outside Participant)

References

Palmer, Parker J. *To Know as We Are Known: Education as a Spiritual Journey.* New York: HarperCollins, 1993.

Rhoads, Robert A. *Community Service and Higher Learning: Explorations of the Caring Self.* New York: SUNY Press, 1997.

Shor, Ira and Paulo Freire. *A Pedagogy for Liberation: Dialogues on Transforming Education.* Connecticut and London: Bergin and Garvey, 1987.

CHAPTER 3

Inside-Out in Oregon: Transformative Education at the Community Level*

Melissa Crabbe

Editors' note: This chapter is an excerpt of a longer case study of program replication at the state level by Inside-Out's associate director, Melissa Crabbe. The full article, chronicling the Program's development in Oregon, is archived for interested readers at The Inside-Out Prison Exchange Program website, www.insideoutcenter.org.

Introduction

Over the years I have often heard colleagues describe Inside-Out as a type of "transformative education." They are usually referring to transformation for individuals, changes in how individuals think of themselves, their potential, and their place in the world. Another way to understand "transformative education" is to consider the larger-scale transformation of social networks, communities, and institutions. This article uses Oregon as a case study to show how Inside-Out's approach can amplify and catalyze the latent potential for change already existing in colleges and universities, prisons, and other communities. These lessons may be applicable to other types of community-based education as well, in places such as K-12 schools, immigrant communities, senior centers, and more.

The key to the model I describe lies in community-building across barriers: in trainings, in the classroom, and in other programmatic activities. Just as energy is released by splitting an atom, energy is released when people come face to face with an "other" and a stereotype is shattered. This energy, concentrated through a process of dialogic learning, can fuel new alliances and initiatives, creating new pathways to leadership.

We live in a place and time when people who have been convicted of criminal offenses are generally thought of as social liabilities, as objects to be either warehoused or "fixed." We consequently fail to systematically educate and train incarcerated and formerly incarcerated people—who, more than many, have been affected by the social ills correlated with crime—for leadership in addressing those ills. As a result, we lose their contributions to creating effective social programs and policies.

When, through Inside-Out, students from our campus communities pass through the barrier of prison walls to study as peers with students who are incarcerated, they become part of a community that shares a collective lived experience and a working partnership informed by a type of academic study that we have never before seen on a large scale. We believe that members of our growing alumni community will, in coming decades, play a role in helping the United States come to terms with the human rights catastrophe of mass incarceration.

Transformative Potential

In the late 1990s I lived in an economically distressed city in California. The high school looked like a mini prison, with high walls and only a few long narrow windows. Despite the best efforts of teachers, parents, and students, our community was giving our young people the message that prison is where they belong.

A few years later, I visited a prison in Pennsylvania that had previously been the archetypal gorgeous college campus—with broad green lawns and brick buildings, the sort of thing one sees in the movies. But by that time it was a prison, with a prison's problems—crowding, uncomfortable conditions, and many varieties of misery.

So a school can literally be transformed into a prison. What an apt metaphor for the "school to prison pipeline" created by many state budgets over the past decades, with students criminalized within the schoolhouse walls and the proportion of resources for incarceration going up as the proportion of resources for higher education goes down. It seems natural to wonder whether this alchemy can happen in reverse—whether prisons can literally be transformed into schools.

The answer to that question is "yes," as philanthropists, restorative justice leaders, prison administrators, instructors working behind bars, incarcerated students, and many others have demonstrated. Most of these programs are quite small, however, dependent upon private funding, and difficult to sustain or replicate on a large scale. Knowing that higher education in prison is important for a variety of reasons, including, but most certainly not limited to, reduced rates of reincarceration,[1] the question is whether it is possible to grow higher education in prisons in an affordable way that can also influence public understandings of the complex relationships between justice and educational access *over the long term*.

What Inside-Out does well, and *differently* from most prison-based higher education programs, lies in the community building, dialogic learning, and leadership development integral to our pedagogy and program design. This is thanks, in part, to Inside-Out's unique combination of circle work, experiential classroom activities, intergroup dialogue, personal reflection, texts, and collaborative problem-solving, as well as systematic alumni leadership development. Semester after semester, the process of weaving equal numbers of "inside" and "outside" students together as peers in a learning community amplifies the transformative potential that already exists in our society both by building the capacity of students who are incarcerated and by growing the number of nonincarcerated stakeholders committed to helping bring about change.

By the time this chapter is printed, there will be more than 450 instructors trained in Inside-Out's techniques who have created more than 150 different partnerships between prisons and schools, in more than half of the states in the United States and in five Canadian provinces. This has been accomplished by strategically leveraging the modest capacities of an extremely lean organization. Inside-Out has not provided direct funding to offer courses, and its mostly part-time staff has never totaled more than four full-time equivalents. Yet if the approximately 15,000 inside and outside students who have taken courses have each spoken to just ten other people about their personal experience, that is 150,000 individuals whose opinions about higher education in prison are formed at least partly through their relationships with people who have actually taken part in it. Beyond that, Inside-Out alumni, prison-, campus-, and community-based, have started a variety of initiatives in prisons, juvenile facilities, schools, and community settings.

With more than 2.3 million people currently incarcerated in the United States only a handful of whom have access to any kind of college experience behind bars, there is a long way to go. And we are still learning what our model can and cannot accomplish. But what we have accomplished in Oregon is a start.

Now, with ten years of regional replication in the United States and Canada behind us, we have begun to think of replication in terms of stages, each with its own characteristics, lessons, and possibilities that may prove instructive for other community educators who seek to create systemic transformation. These stages of program growth are:

Stage One—The Beginnings of Community: A few key individuals come together to replicate the program in a specific region.

Stage Two—Building Institutional Support: The enthusiasm of a community of individuals is formalized as support on the part of such institutions as prisons and universities.

Stage Three—Consolidating Gains and Facing Challenges: As choices made at earlier stages have both expected and unexpected consequences, leaders troubleshoot the challenges while incorporating the strengths into the local program structure.

Stage Four—Coming Full Circle: Local alumni are systematically developed as leaders, enabling the program both to replicate and to innovate locally.

Stage Five—Optimization: The program is maximally available in all feasible local institutions, and systemic leadership development has created self-sustaining cycles of program replication and innovation (at this point, this stage is largely aspirational).

Space limitations prevent me from providing a detailed chronology here (available on the research page of Inside-Out's website at *www.insideoutcenter.org*). Instead, I share the main lessons concerning program replication we have learned from our Oregon experience, exploring their implications for others who seek to expand community-based learning or prison education program models.

Core Lessons

1. *No matter how inhospitable a particular setting, institution, or system may appear, do not assume that is the case. There may be people there who share your values and are willing to help you. It is possible that your proposed program will be embraced once partners recognize the opportunity and resources you bring.*

When I arrived in Oregon in 2003, all state-funded education including Adult Basic Education and General Educational Development (GED) courses in Oregon prisons had been cancelled, and it was actually illegal to spend state funds on post-secondary education in prisons. I was told that the education floor in Oregon State Penitentiary (OSP) was being used to store furniture. But this apparent lack of support for education was the result of insufficient resources, not insufficient will.

Today, in 2013, as far as I know, there are still no state funds directly budgeted for post-secondary education in prisons, yet instructors compete for classroom space at OSP. College courses are offered in six of Oregon's 14 adult correctional institutions through Inside-Out and two smaller local programs. Three public universities (University of Oregon, Oregon State University, and Portland State University), four community colleges (Blue Mountain, Chemeketa, Clackamas, and Portland) and one private college (Lewis and Clark) participate. Oregon now has 30 trained Inside-Out instructors. Approximately 50 Inside-Out courses have been taught since fall 2006, reaching an estimated combined total of 600 unique inside and outside students. Those outside alumni have worked to organize educational groups in local youth correctional facilities and other settings, and have also provided leadership in local and national program development. It would be a huge stretch to say that Oregon's prisons have been transformed into schools, but clearly important changes are underway.

2. *Connecting with a lower-level amenable person can be a valuable point of entry into a larger system, because that champion can introduce you to others up the chain of command. Depending upon your situation, this may be more effective than going straight to the top.*

I moved from Philadelphia to Eugene, Oregon, in August of 2003. Lori Pompa, who befriended me while I worked at the Pennsylvania Prison Society, had just begun working on Inside-Out replication. That fall, as a new Oregonian and prison volunteer facilitating restorative justice workshops, I wrote a letter to an OSP staff person describing Inside-Out. I had met him at a meeting and was impressed with his desire to promote opportunities for quality programming at OSP, and I said so in the letter.

I was not expecting a reply. But within the week he contacted me, said the program sounded exciting, and told me that he had forwarded my letter to Nichole Brown, who was overseeing reentry programs for all Oregon Department of Corrections (ODOC) facilities. Before I had a chance to contact Nichole, she contacted me. This began a two-year process of making Inside-Out presentations to various prison administrators, but rather than Inside-Out having to sell the program on its own, we essentially assisted people within corrections who said to their superiors at every level, "I want you to approve this program." (This is particularly true of Nancy Green, the DOC's Salem area education manager, without whom Inside-Out in Oregon probably would not exist.) Thus, in Oregon and elsewhere, Inside-Out did not *create* the potential for change within the system; rather, it was able to *catalyze* existing potential for change.

> 3. *Recruit through social as well as professional networks. People with whom you have multiple connections—through work, friendship, social connections, a faith community, etc.—may be more likely to become involved. At the same time, do not overlook the value of simple, low-cost outreach strategies—such as email—to find allies and partners.*

After having made contact with Nichole Brown of ODOC, the next step was to further assess local interest and begin to develop potential institutional partnerships. At first that task looked difficult, because I was a "trailing spouse" with no local professional network. Luckily, I did find a network via my faith community. My husband's job was as the associate rabbi at Eugene's largest synagogue, Temple Beth Israel. As a new "rebbitzen," I was embraced by the congregation and met many thoughtful people, including members who were University of Oregon (UO) faculty. Almost everyone I met was interested in hearing about my prison-related experiences. So, I facilitated two restorative justice workshops, and Lori spoke at the synagogue when she visited. Through this network, I met Steven Shankman, the Director of the Humanities Center at UO. He expressed an interest in prison education, so I suggested that he interview Lori on his local cable TV show. He did! Thus began an ongoing conversation between Steve and me about Inside-Out that soon brought six additional people from our overlapping circles into the program. Beyond that, with the exception of three people who came to Inside-Out via email, every person who has chosen to become a trained instructor in Oregon first interacted with Inside-Out through their work and other social networks.

> 4. *When getting started, find a way to build a community based on shared experience and values with a few key allies. That way, even if you may not know each other well, you can work together smoothly to implement your program.*

Steve Shankman, along with Portland State University's Amy Spring and Oregon State University's Michelle Inderbitzen—each of whom had heard about Inside-Out solely from a widely-dispersed email—attended early Inside-Out trainings in Philadelphia. They jumped at the chance to be part of a program that did not yet exist in the state and was still in its infancy elsewhere: another indication of the potential for change that already exists in our communities. Amy, Michelle, and Steve returned home deeply impacted by their experience of community at the training, particularly in Pennsylvania's Graterford Prison. That shared experience enabled us to work together smoothly to get the ODOC to approve Inside-Out. The participation of three public universities was particularly persuasive.

5. *Realize that a single, well-placed motivated ally, such as an undergraduate student, can be invaluable. These individuals will bring not only their skills and their passion, but their various networks as well.*

Katie Dwyer, an alumna who took an Inside-Out course as a first year student and later wrote her thesis on the program, played a pivotal role in creating an infrastructure for ongoing, self-replicating alumni leadership development at UO. She worked with me and many others to further Inside-Out programming and to promote study of prison issues (e.g., creating a prison-related freshman interest group on Inside-Out, and coediting, with an inside student, an Inside-Out literary journal that later became required reading for one cohort of honors college freshmen). Together, Katie and I conducted a focus group with outside alumni at UO, ascertaining their interest in ongoing projects. Under Katie's leadership, that focus group spun off into an ongoing alumni group, as well as an alumni-facilitated Book Club at a local juvenile facility. Katie also took the instructor training in Philadelphia in 2009. Following this, she worked as a Teaching Assistant (TA) for new instructors, reducing their anxiety about teaching Inside-Out courses for the first time and managing key logistics of bringing guests into the prison. Katie and I also cofacilitated a focus group at OSP, exploring the interest in building Inside-Out into a degree-bearing opportunity, which became the starting point for Oregon's Inside-Out think tank.

6. *Include both institutional supporters and skeptics in key events that are likely to have a powerful emotional impact, such as a closing ceremony at the end of the quarter or semester. This will make your supporters feel acknowledged and appreciated and will introduce supporters from different realms to one another; it may also lead some detractors to change their minds.*

Inside-Out instructors in Oregon and elsewhere all invited ODOC and school administrators to attend their Inside-Out courses' closing ceremonies. At these events, inside and outside students speak movingly (without being coached!) about the power of the community they have experienced in the classroom, their sense of connection to each other, and their gratitude toward the administrators who make the experience possible. These events weave together supporters within the prison and the colleges more tightly, creating a shared goal of expanding similar opportunities in the future.

7. *To establish a program within a particular system or institution, academic or correctional, bring allies together. A local steering committee can help plan and coordinate growth within an institution. If you are not part of that institution yourself, an administrative champion's knowledge of the networks within the institution can be invaluable.*

8. *Your program design should be based upon a clear set of values and principles rather than an exact blueprint of structures and policies. That way, when you hit a roadblock, you can find a way to be flexible that is consistent with the program's values, enabling you to get your program started in places that would not be as welcoming were you dogmatic about every element. In this process, you may learn*

things about potential program impacts that you had not realized. In addition, remember that a program is always evolving, so a decision made at any particular point can change if new information or new needs arise.

Just as the Oregon Inside-Out program was getting started, we faced an unexpected challenge. From its inception in Philadelphia, Inside-Out had had no GED requirement for inside students. The program saw this as a strength, because, as Tyrone Werts argues in this volume, it allows for the possibility that taking a course, and being included in a learning community, will encourage incarcerated people, who otherwise would not, to complete their GEDs. However, since two-thirds of those incarcerated in Oregon prisons already have at least a high school diploma or equivalent certification, the ODOC insisted that the GED be required for our courses. Ultimately, we agreed. Although this felt like a compromise at the time, it was also a boon. Steve Shankman invited the UO registrar, Herb Chereck, to a closing ceremony, which Herb found very moving. And thanks to the GED requirement, Herb saw that he could refute potential university concerns that the courses were not sufficiently rigorous to warrant credit. Herb repurposed a provision that allowed professionals to obtain continuing education credit for a manageable $50 per course, applying it to the inside students, who could then receive UO transcripts. This turn of events opened doors to several more opportunities for inside students—opportunities that would have been lost had we refused to work with ODOC's GED requirement.

9. *Luckily, this type of program, because it is based on the investment of time and commitment from those in your community, initially requires minimal direct funding (though as such a program grows, it will require significant in-kind support within the schools and prisons). At the same time, a budget can make it easier to build community, and can avoid some of the problems—stress, lack of communication, confusion, irritability—that arise when the members of a community are overextended. As programs scale up, capacity building funds for projects like annual reports and evaluation become increasingly important.*

10. *A successful program may look different in different places, depending upon local needs. Being willing to adapt—as long as you are consistent with your values—is a strength. At the same time, always be aware that there is a line between being flexible and losing your vision. To keep sight of that line, stay engaged with members of your wider program community.*

In closing, I would like to share a story. Inspired by his work as an Inside-Out instructor, Professor Steve Shankman organized a conference called "Prisons, Peace and Compassion" at the UO. One of the last events was a presentation by Collette Peters, Secretary of the ODOC and former head of the Oregon Youth Authority. Set in an auditorium at the law school, her session was well attended by students, instructors, and community members. The secretary was frank about the challenges the correctional system faces, and she situated those challenges within a larger social context. At one point she talked about those who are incarcerated in terms of their intelligence and skills, the loss their incarceration represents to the community at large, and also about the importance of preparing those individuals for success upon their release from prison.

During Q & A, I said something about how Inside-Out wants all of its students, inside and outside, to see each other as potential future colleagues and partners in finding ways to build safer and more inclusive communities without locking up so many for so long. As the program ended, a man I had not met before came over to me with a big smile and proudly handed me his card. "I'm one of your colleagues," he said. "I took an Inside-Out class while I was at OSP and now I am helping veterans transition back to the community."

This man might have left prison and done the same kind of work without Inside-Out. But because of Inside-Out, he knows that he is part of a larger community that welcomes him home and supports him in his efforts. This local community, its social institutions and professional networks have, we hope, begun to be transformed. It is this man, people like him, and his counterparts among all of our outside students who will help address the human rights issues related to mass incarceration.

Notes

*Many people have contributed to the growth of Inside-Out Oregon described here, including prison staff and administrators (especially Nancy Green and Frank Martin), university administrators (especially David Frank) and, of course, instructors (especially Amy Spring, Michelle Inderbitzin, and Shaul Cohen). Special thanks to the outside and inside alumni who are an inspiring, integral part of the Inside-Out Oregon community: Alex, Ben, Bob, Chuck, Eric, Francisco, Fred, Hannah, Jordan, Katie D., Kehala, Kyla, Madeline, Marc, Nestor, Paul, Phoebe, Robin, Roman, So, Socrates, Sterling, Tariq, Ted, Terence, and Trevor.

1. See, for example, Jeanne B. Contardo and Wendy Erisman, *Learning to Reduce Recidivism: A 50-State Analysis of Postsecondary Correctional Education Policy.* Washington DC: Institute for Higher Education Policy, November 2005.

CHAPTER 4

Death of a Street-Gang Warrior

Paul Perry

When applied to someone serving life in prison, there is irony in the saying "sometimes one must die in order to live." It has been more than three and a half decades since the murder trial that marked the beginning of my civic death. At 19, I caused the death of a rival gang member during an altercation. Apart from the shock of discovering that I knew the victim's mother when she took the witness stand, I had been emotionally detached throughout the entire trial. As a teenager, I had been so invested in my status as a gang leader that the risk of death or long-term incarceration seemed insignificant. I did not pause to seriously reflect on my outlaw mentality until the sentencing hearing following my trial. The hearing judge read from my file:

> The psychiatric and pre-sentence investigation indicates trouble started at the age of 15. He had seven arrests as a juvenile from the age of 15 to 17....[Charges included] aggravated assault and battery, carrying a concealed deadly weapon, disorderly conduct and vandalism. On 10–17–71, still at the age of 15, assault and battery, breach of the peace, disorderly conduct. The next month, larceny of an automobile, receiving stolen goods, conspiracy...When he becomes an adult at the age of 18, he has five arrests, three convictions and one sentence...The psychiatrist said he acts impulsively....and has given little indication that he is either able or willing to adjust favorably and acceptably to society. *Education history:* Perry did not adjust well to school. A self-confessed slow learner, he found academics difficult and was not fond of attending school. He was suspended frequently....His literacy seems marginal.

"My problem with you is," the judge said, "is there any hope for rehabilitation in your case? From reading the pre-sentence report and psychiatric report, I don't see that...They consider you a menace" (excerpts from Sentencing Hearing, September 30, 1977, 24–44).

I still remember how I swelled with rage and barked at the judge, "Dat aint me! You trynna make me out to be some kind of monster!" I realized later that my anger stemmed from the truth in the judge's words. My arrests in my youth represent only a fraction of the crime and violence I committed between ages 12 and 19. The judge shattered any delusions I had about how I was seen through the eyes of society and by victims of my crimes. Unwilling to accept the judge's conclusion that I was unredeemable, I decided right then and there to prove him wrong.

In November 1977, five months after my trial, I was at the State Correctional Institution (SCI) in Dallas, Pennsylvania. During my first week there, I took a job working in the kitchen, cleaning trays and mopping floors. I also enrolled in Adult Basic Education (ABE) classes, joined Alcoholics Anonymous, and became a member of the SCI-Dallas Lifers Association and Latin American Cultural Studies Group. By 1983, I had completed ABE classes in Math and English, 131 hours of Basic Spanish, a Basic Typing class, a six-hour workshop on the Art of Oral Communication, and an eight-week course in Personal Growth and Development, as well as an Aviation Ground School course and two years of Electrical Vocation Training. I also frequently visited the prison's law library, spending years reading court opinions and studying law books in efforts to comprehend legal jargon well enough to effectively engage in pro se litigation. My efforts to obtain freedom through the appellate court system would ultimately prove to be a major source of frustration, contributing to recurring bouts of anxiety and depression.

A deeper source of emotional strain was born of an unwavering determination to gain some insight into why and how I had so thoroughly screwed up my life. Almost from the onset of my incarceration, I began the painful process of self-examination.

I remember a five-year-old boy who once thought he had become invisible. He repeatedly pulled on his mother's dress saying, "Mommy, Mommy!" Then he tried talking to his three siblings, but they all just kept talking among themselves as if he was not even there. Without warning, fear crawled up through his stomach and coiled around his little heart. He burst out crying, immediately drawing the attention of his mother and siblings. His mother gently pulled him close and caressed him in her arms and sighed, "What's the matter, honey?" Wiping a running nose with the back of his hand, he wailed, "Nobody will listen to me." That feeling of being disconnected, of being among but not truly part of, was tattooed on his soul. Needless to say, that five-year-old boy was me. That same feeling of disconnectedness, of not being valued or truly wanted, followed me into every relationship I ever had. I remember curling up in bed in the middle of the day several times during the summer I was ten, sobbing for hours and not having a clue why. I felt out of phase with the rest of the world, missing some vital element of character. It was identical to feeling invisible at five years old, only much more painful. Well into my twenties, I began to experience similar episodes of unexplained emotional pain and finally learned that I had been suffering from clinical depression.

Growing up in a series of gang-infested neighborhoods, it was easy to get caught up in gang culture. Poverty, an unhappy home life, and underachievement made the transition into the street effortless. I got into fist fights so often that coming home with a busted lip or black eye provoked no reaction. I was shot, stabbed, and beaten up by street gangs and the police more times than I care to recall. Only in hindsight can I appreciate the seduction of the streets, how the danger and thrill provided an addictive adrenaline rush.

Being the target of violence never deterred me from participating in street-gang violence or other criminal activities. I was too attached to my self-proclaimed identity as an elite street warrior and the perceived power, recognition, and status it afforded me among peers. If anything, being the victim of violence caused me to become even more brutal when confronted.

And alcohol helped. It transformed me from a frightened, insecure little boy into a courageous, respected alpha male. Under the influence, I thought myself funny and clever, an adventure-seeking free spirit. I dropped my inhibitions and became a wild, reckless outlaw with a frozen heart impervious to remorse.

As turbulent as my teens were, there is no comparison to the visceral onslaught of pain that certain childhood memories still trigger within me. The street violence was only a continuation of the violence I experienced within my family as far back as I can remember. Though I have many pleasant childhood memories, they are mostly eclipsed by memories of my father brutally punching, kicking, and stomping my mother. Once I saw him beat her like a dog, breaking a chair and broomstick handle on her body, and leaving her stark-naked and sprawled on their bedroom floor. On another occasion, he stabbed her in the chest with a kitchen knife. When I was eight years old, I saw her leap out of their second floor bedroom window, crashing through the glass, screaming, "I can't take it anymore!"

My father's propensity for violence was by no means limited to my mother. I witnessed him beat up, stab, and shoot a number of men and physically abuse an array of women he became involved with following my mother's death. One woman had to be institutionalized after having a mental breakdown; another committed suicide by taking an overdose of pills. Not long after that, another woman he was involved with attempted suicide, but I happened to be in the house at the time and stopped her by clutching her throat to keep her from swallowing.

Living in abject poverty, our family moved from place to place, all over North Philadelphia. We stayed in many dilapidated, rat- and roach-infested houses and apartments, often spending winters without heat or electricity. After my mother's death, my siblings and I were frequently separated, sometimes sleeping on blankets laid out on the living room floor of relatives or my father's friends. I remember times when he left us alone at home for two or three days with nothing to eat while he went out to hustle money for food. Sometimes when we moved, we missed weeks of school waiting for him to take us to be registered. I frequently got into trouble in school for fighting with peers who ridiculed my ratty clothing and oversized old-man shoes.

I cannot say exactly when it started, but in my early adolescence I constructed an invisible emotional wall between my father and me that grew thicker and higher as the years passed. I never understood why he was so hard on me; he was always beating me and cursing me out, criticizing everything I did wrong, and not once praising me for anything I did right. Still, in terms of being obstinately self-willed, violence-prone, drinking, and running the streets, I was more like him than I care to admit. He and I did forge a sort of unholy bond in my mid-teens as occasional partners in crime, though, especially when he needed backup in potential physical confrontations.

Among my most painful memories is when he decided to break me out of a thumb-sucking habit during my pre-teens. After pouring hot sauce on my thumb failed to break the habit, he would sneak up on me and punch me in the mouth whenever he caught me sucking my thumb while watching television or sleeping. I finally stopped when he combined the physical attacks with psychological attacks, convincing me that the habit had caused my upper lip to poke out so much that no girl would want me.

The larger truth is that, beyond his violence and abuse of women, my father possessed a number of redeeming qualities. The most obvious was his strong sense of family. We were a chronic welfare family because my father was a third-grade dropout with crippled hands that prevented him from getting work at a regular job. Although irresponsible with money, he was an unequalled street-hustler; he fixed old junky cars, faulty plumbing, broken doors, and house wiring, as well as old radios, TVs, and things he found in the trash. He never seemed to let poverty or hard times faze him, as though it were a natural condition.

I remember how he would often take our family to visit friends and relatives. My best childhood memories of family are of the occasions he took us to the movies, a carnival that came to Philadelphia every summer, and family outings to Fairmount Park on the Fourth of July. Because we rarely had money, we usually spent the day at the carnival just walking around looking at hundreds of kids and adults enjoying cotton candy, riding the Ferris-wheel, and winning stuffed animals. On family outings to Fairmount Park, sometimes we saw live bands, groups of white folks taking off in hot-air balloons, coxswain, and scull regatta boat races in the Schuylkill River, or folks flying remote-control model airplanes. Dozens of families picnicked in the park, and we watched them barbeque ribs, chicken, hotdogs, and hamburgers.

Those family outings always left me feeling a little hollow inside. It just did not seem fair that we could not afford things that so many others took for granted. Still, those times were special because they showed me that my father genuinely loved and valued his family. Our family sank even deeper into poverty after my mother died, but no matter how many times we were separated, he always managed to bring us back together.

*   *   *

When I first came to prison, I spent a lot of sleepless nights probing my past and mourning my civic death. In a desperate effort to heal the internal maelstrom of emotional pain that process created, I ingested whatever religious materials and self-help books I could find. Questioning everything, I read books on psychology, sociology, and philosophy. In the process, something unexpected happened: I fell in love with learning.

Despite the fact that I was born during the height of the civil rights movement and had witnessed and been the victim of racial injustice on many occasions, I had no real sense of black consciousness until I came to prison. Books about slavery and the African-American experience challenged my perception of reality and changed the way I viewed myself and the world. I still feel a profound sense of shame and guilt when I think about my contributions to the pain and suffering of my own people.

While education empowered me with the ability to purge myself of a criminal mentality, I am somewhat embarrassed to admit that for the first ten years of my incarceration, I continued to associate with peers who were committed to a criminal lifestyle. One day I realized that I was a hypocrite. Not wanting to relinquish my gangsta status and associated respect, I had been trying to live in two worlds. Education and opportunities to make positive contributions to the lives of others had given me a new sense of identity and purpose, yet I continued to cling to my gangsta identity for fear that relinquishing it would make me vulnerable. Once I recognized that fear, I found the courage to surrender my outlaw identity.

In 1982, grants for higher education were still available to people in prison, and I finally got up the courage to enroll in the college program offered at SCI-Dallas. The institution had a population of about 800, approximately 60 percent African-American. I was one of seven or eight African-American students enrolled in the prison's college program, most of whom already had some college experience prior to their incarceration. They were the jailhouse intellectuals, but I was generally viewed as a street thug.

As soon as I started attending college classes, friends and associates within the prison began slinging negative comments at me. They would say things like, "*Dam*, Snake! Why you trynna git dat white man's education? Man, dat sh.. ain't gon' git you nothin'!" They acted as if I had betrayed my race and was rejecting my blackness by taking college courses. Much to my surprise, when I went on to graduate with a two-year associate's degree, I received all kinds of accolades from fellow prisoners. Moreover, not long after graduation, I noticed a dramatic increase in the number of blacks enrolled in the prison's college program, including some of the guys who had criticized me when I first started.

I had never known anyone with a background similar to mine who had graduated from college, and college was one of the more difficult challenges I had ever faced. Generally speaking, I learned very little within the classroom setting. I could not process the information the instructor shared quickly enough to comprehend what was being taught. As a consequence, the majority of classes I attended were little more than exercises in frantic note-taking, or desperate efforts to copy information scribbled on a blackboard or delivered through tortuously insipid lectures. I took notes furiously and hoped that studying them and the assigned textbook readings would provide me with enough understanding to complete writing assignments and pass tests.

One of the first things I learned in college is that the gulf between reading and studying is almost as wide as the distance between listening to music and playing an instrument. Courses I took in political science, biology, and economics during my first two or three semesters kept me in a state of frustration that nearly strangled my joy of learning. Reading assigned textbook chapters felt like driving through a deluge of alien terms and concepts with faulty windshield wipers and no headlights. I was always certain I would crash head-on into a wall of failure at test time, just as I had in elementary, junior high, and high school. Determined to not give up on myself academically this time, I studied the notes I took during classes until I memorized them. I read and reread assigned textbook chapters until the fog of incomprehension cleared and I had a firm grasp of the material.

Even though I invariably experienced anxiety during tests and was usually the last one to finish, I passed almost all the tests I took in college with an A or a B. Moreover, from my perspective, learning how to learn was my biggest achievement in college. I am not quite sure how or when, but I began to cultivate a belief in myself that empowered me to take on challenges, to pursue and achieve goals I never imagined possible.

Of all the educational experiences I have had since my incarceration, however, none has had a more profound impact on my life than the Inside-Out class I took in the summer of 2002. I read somewhere that the most important trait of great teachers is the ability to bring dormant knowledge within their students to the surface. I have been blessed to have been taught, inspired, and forever transformed by one of those phenomenal educators: Lori Pompa, founder and director of the Temple University International Inside-Out Prison Exchange Program.

I first met Lori in 1995 when she took a class of 15 Temple University Criminal Justice students on a field trip to SCI-Dallas. I had been invited to sit on a panel with a few other lifers to discuss issues of crime and justice with Lori's students. Their questions and enthusiasm blew me away. At the end of the discussion, I told Lori how much I enjoyed talking with her students and asked her what she thought about the idea of having a semester-long course with a class of college students and people in prison. I did not know at the time that she would take that idea and run with it, creating The Inside-Out Prison Exchange Program.

We would meet again seven years later, and I would be privileged to help write the proposal that made it possible for her to teach an Inside-Out course in the first state correctional facility to offer Inside-Out classes. I participated in that first course, and it turned out to be one of the most exhilarating rides of my life as we constructed knowledge organically through the dynamics of shared dialogue. Inside-Out was different from the other college classes I have taken. As Tyrone Werts also recalls in chapter 18, the class was extremely diverse. Through a variety of interactive activities, the course invited us to integrate perspectives from scholarly works, textbooks, and our own life experiences as we considered such questions and topics as:

- What Are Prisons For?
- Why Do People Commit Crime?
- An Analysis of the Criminal Justice System;
- The Myths and Realities of Prison Life;
- Punishment and Rehabilitation;
- Victims and Victimization; and
- Restorative Justice.

Every Wednesday night, most of us inside students took showers and dressed in our best uniforms in preparation to attend class. We would also get together between sessions to talk about class, sometimes sharing what we had written about in required reflection papers or bragging about grades received on essay assignments.

The Inside-Out teaching model facilitated bonding and group cohesion that provided all of us with an emotionally lived learning experience. Each class felt like a family reunion, animated with lively and sometimes heated discussions.

The first Inside-Out course had such a powerful impact on both the inside and outside students that we all decided to continue meeting after the class ended. With the approval of the prison administration, we formed the Graterford Inside-Out Think Tank, meeting once a week on a voluntary basis with the mission to reeducate the public about the criminal justice system. In 2003, we hosted Think Tank workshops with groups of students from local colleges and universities. Subsequently, armed with Lori's indomitable spirit of social activism and a shared vision of a world in which crime and victimization would be radically reduced, members of the Think Tank joined hearts and hands with Lori and several of her colleagues on a campaign to replicate the Inside-Out program nationally.

It has been ten amazing years since I began my Inside-Out journey. When we initially formed the Think Tank, no one imagined that the program would evolve into an international movement, transforming the lives of hundreds of college teachers and tens of thousands of students. Three to five times a year since 2004, between 15 and 25 college instructors from all over the United States and abroad participate in an intense, week-long Inside-Out Instructor Training, spending two or three days with the Graterford Think Tank. For the past several years, those days of training inside the institution have been held in the prison's dingy 83-year-old auditorium, a cavernous space lined with nearly a thousand ocean-blue plastic seats bolted to the floor. One or two correction officers escort the trainees into the auditorium through a set of double doors. We (Think Tank members) wait to greet them as they shuffle to an area in front of the stage where we have set up a large circle of folding chairs. With big smiles and handshakes, we introduce ourselves and welcome them to Graterford.

At each of the 25 instructor trainings I have participated in, the faces of five or more trainees would light up with excitement when I shook their hands and told them my name. Lori has made me somewhat of a celebrity among hundreds of Inside-Out instructors and thousands of students who have taken a class through her ritualized telling of my role in Inside-Out's origins, and they would say things like, "Are you *the* Paul, the one who gave Lori the idea for Inside-Out?" Embarrassed, I always respond with a smile and say, "Yeah, I'm *the* Paul."

For me, attending those trainings is like visiting a beautiful garden comprised of some of the most compassionate and wise people I have ever met. With colorful personalities and spirited hearts, they spend these days with us darting in and out of large and small group activities like hummingbirds, sustained by the sweet nectar of social discourse. Empowered with a renewed or enhanced passion for teaching, they return to their respective institutions eager to pollinate their own gardens with the seeds of Inside-Out.

Membership in the Think Tank has shifted over the years, and I am one of only three original members left. Through this evolution, I have witnessed miraculous transformations among both inside and outside members. I have never participated in any other program that imbues so many people in prison with a desire to pursue higher education while at the same time empowering them with a sense of agency that awakens a spirit of social activism. In addition to pursuing college and masters degrees, nearly every inside member has acquired outstanding facilitation, leadership, and organizational skills that they employ in programs throughout the prison community and beyond. In the same vein, most of the outside Think Tank members have taken leadership roles in diverse social justice endeavors. I have personally gained a wealth of knowledge and experience in organization building, program development, leadership dynamics, and facilitation techniques, most notably, the work I do in Ending the Culture of Street Crime under the auspices of the Graterford Lifers Public Safety Initiative (PSI).[1]

Inside-Out provided me with the skill base to expand tutoring services offered to incarcerated learners who need assistance obtaining their high school equivalency diploma (General Educational Development (GED)), and since 2006, I have been the internal director of the Graterford Prison Literacy Project (PLP) tutoring program. We have managed to increase the number of outside volunteer tutors from five to an average of 25 volunteers each semester. Moreover, since 2009, PLP has hosted five semester-long creative-writing workshops and has recently organized a book club.

On a more personal level, though I have always had a sensitive nature, my involvement in Inside-Out has both awakened and increased my capacity to care about and empathize with others. Through Inside-Out and other programs, I have been privileged to hear many heart-wrenching personal stories shared by people from all walks of life. Reflecting on how parts of so many of their stories mirror my own, I have become acutely aware of the fact that most people struggle on some level to fully connect with their own humanity and the humanity of others. While deep emotional identification can be challenging at times, M. Lydia Khuri explains that it makes learning a "lived experience informing scholarship."[2] Khuri's points about intergroup dialogue parallel the findings of a qualitative participatory evaluation project I participated in that focused on three key elements of students' learning experiences within the Inside-Out teaching model: people, setting, and curriculum.[3] Respondents included 28 of 115 incarcerated men who had taken an Inside-Out class between 2002 and 2007. Including myself, five incarcerated Inside-Out alumni assisted with the evaluation during various phases of the project.

I was taken aback by how much the language Khuri uses resembled language we use to describe the unique characteristics of the Inside-Out teaching model. I was especially intrigued by her observation that, in addition to seeking knowledge, people often engage in group dialogue to experience "feelings underlying community concern, trust, respect, appreciation, affection, and hope" (599). With a few exceptions, those are exactly the findings we garnered from our research project, highlighting Inside-Out's potential to become one of the most transformational teaching models of our time.

Data collected from six focus groups and 28 interviews highlighted several program impacts on incarcerated alumni that were attributed to Inside-Out's dialogical approach to learning. Consistent with Khuri's observations, our evaluation data suggested that emotions play a major role in making Inside-Out a positive learning experience:

It sparked a lot of emotions. It made me think about things I hadn't thought about in a long time.

In [a traditional] class, it's totally cerebral, but here you start to live in the conversation, emotions get involved....People experience pain, things you aren't going to talk about [in other classes]. To have people sit there crying, does that happen in college?

Khuri also emphasizes the importance of intergroup engagement "based on the democratic principle of shared and equal participation in civic processes" (599). For example, one respondent in our project said, "Participating in open and non-confrontational discussion on issues that have long been of great concern to me was refreshingly therapeutic." Khuri elaborates on the need to create opportunities for "authentic relationships" and "collaborative self-reflection," thus, pointing out that in intergroup dialogue, learning is facilitated through "structured, phase-specific personal sharing" (598–599). The following comments from inside alumni who were respondents in our project speak to that point:

The small and large group discussions both provided group interaction. Made it special. You got to know people on a more personal basis and share something about yourself.

This class was not like anything I had experienced before. I did learn quite a bit, but it was the interpersonal stuff that I valued most. I really felt like I connected with people on a human level.

One of the most important things I have learned from Inside-Out is that, beneath social, cultural, racial, and ethnic circumstances, people are fundamentally more alike than many of us suspect. In effect, my Inside-Out experience empowered me with an unshakable belief in the human capacity to evolve to a higher state of social consciousness. It provided me with concrete evidence that, through individual and collective effort, we can transform society into a more safe and egalitarian place to live.

There are very likely students who have taken an Inside-Out class who were fundamentally unchanged by the experience. However, I have heard and read the testimonies of too many people about the profound impact Inside-Out has had on their lives not to be convinced that it is a phenomenal education program. More than a dozen college students who have participated in one of our Think Tank workshops have told me that their experience was so inspiring that they were considering changing their major to criminal justice. The most telling evidence of Inside-Out's impact is the sprouting of a growing number of Think Tanks throughout the country and abroad. Like our Graterford Think Tank, they are comprised of inside and outside students who have taken an Inside-Out class and continued meeting on a voluntary basis. There are currently ten Think Tanks meeting in correctional facilities where Inside-Out classes are being conducted each semester.

Two or three years ago, I participated in a thought-provoking workshop with members of our Think Tank and a group of college professors. The goal of the workshop was to determine where the Inside-Out approach fits in relation to service learning and social justice education models. An unexpected outcome of that conversation was the conclusion that Inside-Out does not fit neatly into either. We decided, instead, that because of the reciprocal learning that occurs between inside and outside participants, Inside-Out is a uniquely transformative education model that might be viewed as a hybrid of both.

One participant mused: "Inside-Out is a marriage of both concepts, producing a child from that marriage that is different from both of them." I thought of a strange animal I once saw on a television program called "Animal Atlas"—a rare African mammal with the face of a giraffe and zebra-like stripes on its upper front legs and hindquarters. I thought to myself, "Damn, Inside-Out is an Okapi!"

I am still blown away by the number of inside students, outside students, instructors, and others who have boasted that their Inside-Out class, training, or workshop was a life-changing experience. Every now and then, at the end of an Inside-Out workshop or Instructor Training, Lori will catch my eye and say, "You changed my life." Flattered, but a little embarrassed, I will return her glance and say, "You changed mine, too."

Prisons are among the most inhumane and oppressive institutions in modern times. Loneliness and subjugation to incessant rituals of degradation are but two of many negative aspects of long-term incarceration. In an environment where being authentic often invites persecution, the atmosphere of contention and distrust can shrink the humanity of both the punished and the punishers. Maintaining one's sanity and sense of humanity and dignity is a constant challenge. Still, despite the dismal realities of serving life without the possibility of parole, I have been blessed to meet and work with an array of amazingly intelligent, compassionate, and conscientious people. Inspired by their example, I have taken advantage of opportunities to employ knowledge gained from life experiences and acquired education.

One of the things that keeps me motivated to do whatever I can to help facilitate the transformation of fellow prisoners is a belief in the liberating power of education. When I reflect on the violence I engaged in throughout my youth, it seems miraculous that more than 25 years have lapsed since the last time I was involved in a physical confrontation. I am not saying there are not times when I come close to giving in to anger by responding to insult or aggression with violence. Although the maturity that comes with age often quells the violent tendencies of a youth who had difficulty managing emotions, violence can be as addictive as alcohol. You have to be forever vigilant to avoid a relapse, especially in a stressful environment like prison.

If I can make so seismic a shift in my character, just about anyone, given the opportunity, proper support, and encouragement, can do the same. Like many other young men who drop out of school and become ensnared in the criminal subculture of the streets, a lot of people wrote me off as a lost cause long before I reached adulthood. Fortunately, I found the strength and will to break through a number of self-defeating psychological barriers with the support of family and the encouragement of a handful of friends. Through education and civic engagement, I managed to alter my worldview to such a degree that today I am compelled to help others afflicted with impaired social vision.

I have kept myself grounded over the past 25 years by either participating in, facilitating, or cofacilitating a variety of educational and therapeutic programs, especially programs that deal with cognitive/behavioral development. I sometimes get criticized for being involved in too many activities at once. But focusing my attention and energies outward prevents me from dwelling on matters beyond my control. More importantly, there are moments when I am gifted with psychological rewards for helping others that make it all worthwhile.

I have always been overly self-critical, questioning the value of my accomplishments and level of competence in just about everything. That has made it difficult for me to fully trust the accolades I receive from those who recognize the value of my contributions and worth as a human being. I do not know if I will ever be granted absolution, but I have received many precious gifts during my transformation that keep me on the road to redemption. I discovered the incredible psychological rewards and emotional satisfaction derived from giving instead of taking, helping to heal instead of hurting, and loving instead of hating. There was a time during the course of my incarceration when I was driven by a desperate desire for freedom. The hope of freedom had been the only thing that gave me the will to endure living in captivity. Although that hope has never diminished, at some point it became secondary to a growing desire to leave a nobler legacy than the one that brought me to prison.

Notes

1. The Lifers Public Safety Initiative Steering Committee of the State Correctional Institution at Graterford, Pennsylvania, "Ending the Culture of 'Street Crime,'" *Prison Journal* 84, no. 4 (2004): 485–685.
2. M. Lydia Khuri, "Working with Emotion in Educational Intergroup Dialogue," *International Journal of Intercultural Relations* 28 (2004): 595–612.
3. Participatory Evaluation of Inside-Out at Graterford-Temple, Report of finding submitted to The Inside-Out Prison Exchange Program on May 7, 2008.

PART II

Expanding Teaching and Learning

CHAPTER 5

Inside-Out: What the World Needs Now

M. Kay Harris

Introduction

The Inside-Out Prison Exchange Program offers a powerful tool for overcoming dehumanization, the problem that Philip Zimbardo[1] has characterized as the root of all evil. Although the precise political, economic, social, or other motivations that impel substandard treatment of any segment of a nation's population may vary, the classification of that group as undeserving of the full rights and moral consideration due to all human beings underlies such abuse. Inside-Out, by bringing college students together with a like number of incarcerated students for a semester-long course held behind prison walls, has significant potential for countering such flawed thinking. A pedagogical innovation may sound like a modest vehicle for addressing such devastating atrocities and extreme denials of human rights as genocide, ethnic cleansing, crimes against humanity, abuse of prisoners of war, acts of torture, slavery, or apartheid. Although it offers what one member of the Inside-Out Think Tank at Graterford Prison described as "the slow or scenic route" to change, rather than an immediate remedy, the world can benefit greatly from any movement in the humanizing direction that this program provides.

In making the case for how Inside-Out can contribute to overcoming some of our greatest ills, this chapter is divided into two main sections. The first section provides an historical overview of a segment of the rough road that America has followed in getting to its current status as the world's leader in incarceration. It spotlights the path from slavery to our modern-day prison nation[2] with its shocking overrepresentation of people of color. It is important to call attention to that historical trajectory in order to get at the strong cord that ties these phenomena together: the willingness to categorize a set of people as ineligible for full membership in the civic community. Yet this history remains largely unheard, or unbelieved, by much of the citizenry. This is due as much to the discourse that continues to justify the practices that got us here as it is due to deafness.

The second section of the chapter describes how Inside-Out courses can serve, for both inside and outside students, to deepen understanding and concern about both racial inequity and the overuse of incarceration, more generally. These are important accomplishments in themselves. More fundamentally, students who participate in courses that employ this educational model will be more likely to question discourse or ideology that demonizes, not just those convicted of crime, but any group of people. Inside-Out classes help bridge some of the deepest divides that separate us, a necessary process if we are to develop a more harmonious, caring, and peaceful society. Achieving that better future requires hope and belief that change is possible, as well as recognition of the individual and collective power that we have to achieve it, traits that the classes can strengthen among all participants.

In writing this chapter, I drew on my experience in teaching seven Inside-Out classes in three correctional institutions, serving as a member of the program's International Steering Committee, and being a long-time member of the Inside-Out Think Tank at the State Correctional Institution at Graterford. In addition, I used notes I took in two retreats, some parts of which were held at the prison, to identify three broad, related themes that help explain the power of what Inside-Out achieves: lifting the veil of ignorance, building connection and community, and generating hope and empowerment. I quote extensively from what I recorded in those sessions and from reflection papers written by students in Inside-Out classes I have taught.[3] Thus, material in this chapter is drawn, not only from formal, credit-bearing Inside-Out courses but also from a variety of spin-off sessions, workshops, and other activities. By weaving a rich textile of multiple voices in this way, the chapter to some extent mirrors textually the community-forming, collaborative approach of Inside-Out in the various forms it takes today.

The Contribution of Inside-Out to Building a New Social Consensus about Race and Mass Incarceration

Michelle Alexander and her book *The New Jim Crow* (2010) have drawn many people who might never before have questioned the proliferation of prisons or the policies filling them with such disproportionate numbers of people of color to examine the linkages between mass incarceration and both the historical and current status of African-Americans in the United States. She argues that a new social consensus must be achieved "about race and the role of race in defining the basic structure of our society" (15), including the interconnection between the criminal justice system and the racial caste system that she sees operating in this country.[4] She also takes the position that "this new consensus must begin with dialogue, a conversation that fosters a critical consciousness, a key prerequisite to effective social action" (15). Inside-Out courses provide an excellent ground and vehicle for undertaking these vital and interrelated tasks and achieving the knowledge and awareness required. The rest of this section highlights some of the key dimensions of what needs to be more broadly understood about the submerged texts and ideologies that support the current "prison nation" as well as the continuing existence of a racial caste system in this country. The later portions of the chapter go into more depth about how Inside-Out helps achieve both the consciousness and the will to address these fundamental problems.

Mass Incarceration and Racial Imbalance as Part of the Same Phenomenon

The popular story of the establishment and evolution of American prisons and jails traditionally told of a humanitarian march of progress, as confinement replaced widespread use of the lash, the brand, and the gallows, and as the prisoners' rights movement supplemented by progressive correctional administration led to development of cleaner, safer, and less brutal penal facilities and practices. Certainly there is truth to that narrative. Use of corporal punishment generally is prohibited in US prisons today and acceptance of capital punishment seems to be decreasing dramatically. Also, conditions within prisons and jails and their management are a far cry from what existed even 50 years ago. Yet at the same time, these carceral facilities have proven so stubbornly resistant to efforts to make them both humane and constructive as to provide rich fuel to the call for their drastic reform, if not their elimination.

Numerous human rights abuses continue to pervade punishment practices in the United States, including the issuance of life sentences for people who are minors at the time of their convictions; the widespread practice of 23-hour-a-day (or more) isolation[5] of people held in "prisons within prisons" and other forms of long-term segregation;[6] the perpetuation of penal slavery, in which people are paid pennies an hour for their work; and a host of disabling restrictions and collateral consequences imposed upon people, even after their sentences technically have been completed. In addition, many less dramatic deprivations and assaults to autonomy and dignity continue to be taken-for-granted features of what it means to be incarcerated in the United States.

There does seem to be growing awareness that a complex mix of forces and interests has played a role in creating the penal system we see today. Historian Robert Perkinson (2010) traces the rise of America's "prison empire" through a painstaking—and painful to read—history of the huge Texas prison system. Moving out from his core focus on the "uniquely calloused, racialized, and profit-driven style of punishment" (7) developed there, Perkinson argues that the dramatic shift toward mass incarceration in the rest of the country can be best understood as rooted in the same model and serving the same economic, racial, social, and political interests. After the Civil War, with the southern economy in ruins, "convict leasing" was embraced as a practical method of continuing to benefit from coerced labor while avoiding the cost of building prisons. Although not limited exclusively to black people, a great many of those turned over to private businessmen and plantation owners had been convicted under the Black Codes adopted after Emancipation, often for trivial or specious offenses. In this way, the criminal justice system was not so subtly put to the service of securing workers for hazardous and arduous jobs at low cost and at the same time achieving the resubjugation of a large segment of recently freed slaves to white domination.

In *Twice the Work of Free Labor*, Alex Lichtenstein (1996) also focuses on the Southern practice of extracting the labor of people convicted of crimes on public work crews or "chain gangs." Those who served out their sentences in "camps," like those portrayed in the movie *Cool Hand Luke*, were dispersed across Georgia and North Carolina in hundreds of shacks and wooden cages on wheels to build roads and labor on other public projects. This system, too, largely disregarded distinctions linked to matters like seriousness of offense, age, gender, or personal history, "reducing all prisoners, vicious, petty, and innocent alike, to a commodity" (xiv). With little oversight, this was a penal scheme "steeped in brutality; the rawhide whip, iron shackle, sweat box, convict cage, and bloodhound were its most potent instruments for eighty years" (xvii). Lichtenstein goes on to argue that, while the connection between economic conditions and interests and the subordination of people of color persists in today's postindustrial era, there is no longer a need for continued heavy exploitation of the labor of African-Americans, given an enormous surplus labor pool. Instead, he suggests that social control has become the sole objective for those who have been shut out of the labor market altogether. In this way, "prisons can keep young, unemployed blacks 'permanently out of the labor market,' and those lucky enough to hold minimum-wage jobs can be thankful they are not in prison" (192).

It is not uncommon today for people to think that the stories of slavery, convict leasing, chain gangs, and plantation prisons, although shocking, have little or nothing to do with modern affairs, but are simply part of a shameful history that is mainly limited to the American South. Reviewing this record is important, however, for the way in which it can help trace the origins of certain narratives and ideas that persist to this day, and which are used to support and justify—even if not explicitly—practices that would be repudiated if not supported by such myths. Oshinsky (1996), for example, describes the assertions made after the Civil War that slavery had provided a "civilizing effect" and kept the "criminal habits" and "ardent sexual appetites" (92–93) of plantation slaves in check. After Emancipation, narratives were developed positing that free Negroes were "reverting" to the "physical type" and "original morals" of their "primitive" African roots (92–93). By 1900, under the banner of science, numerous physicians, psychologists, historians, social workers, statisticians, and criminologists were "discovering" a dangerous "new" Negro, who was menacing to whites (95).

Providing a powerful counter to the idea that such views were unique to the post-Civil War South, historian Khalil Gibran Muhammad (2010) has documented some of the enduring ramifications of this disquieting narrative as it played out in cities in the North. By tracing the discourse on black criminality that linked it first to notions of black inferiority and then to black culture, Muhammad shows, as David Levering Lewis has put it, how "one of the nation's most insidious, convenient, and resilient explanatory loops: whites commit crimes but black males are criminals"[7] was created and became an enduring social construct.

> Shortly after the end of slavery, sociologists and demographers began presenting research on black failure and struggle as "indisputable" proof of black inferiority.... Census data showing that blacks were doing worse than whites in mortality, health, employment, education and crime [were seen as evidence not of] racism...but "race traits and tendencies."...At the same time, when explaining rising rates of crime, suicide and mental-health problems among whites, [blame was laid on] industrialization and the strains of modern life. (2007)

It is critical to understand that the ideology that associates blackness with criminality is on a continuum with historical notions that identified blackness with lesser levels of humanity. These pernicious ideas now go unstated, yet they remain the subtext that underlies a host of current criminal justice practices and policies. Muhammad (2012) has powerfully summarized the resultant effects:

> Racial criminalization has continued to this day, stigmatizing black people as dangerous, legitimizing or excusing white-on-black violence, conflating crime and poverty with blackness, and perpetuating punitive notions of "justice"— vigilante violence, stop-and-frisk racial profiling and mass incarceration—as the only legitimate responses.

As destructive of racial justice and equality as this discourse is, its assumptions have spread to support the more general concept that almost anyone labeled as "a criminal" stands outside the circle of full membership in the civic community. It is the default way of thinking about people convicted of crime, who are described as "monsters," "predators," and "animals" by mayors, police chiefs, prosecutors, and judges. The subjects of such animus are so demonized that worrying about their dignity or treating them with the respect to which all people are a priori entitled may come to be seen almost as an evil in itself. The pervasive ideology is that there are two kinds of people: "them"—the criminals, who are almost uniformly evil, irredeemable, and expendable—and "us"—the noncriminal, "good people" who have no need for redemption.

It will take a variety of means for a wider swath of the citizenry to understand the origins, underlying logic, and consequences of the dehumanization that characterizes so many contemporary responses to crime. It is especially critical to comprehend the full story behind, and the tragic implications that flow from, the disproportionate representation of African-Americans,[8] and then to move toward understanding why it also is true that Hispanics and Native Americans, as well as those subject to the triple threat of racism, sexism,[9] and classism, are so frequently incarcerated. This analysis, focused not on the individual but the societal level, needs to extend also to the ways imprisonment is applied almost exclusively to people on the margins more generally, including those whites who have been hit hardest by poverty and associated forms of disadvantage.

How Inside-Out Exposes Prevailing Ideology and Generates Impetus for Change

Although the need is great for a much broader grasp of the history behind America's punishment practices, remedial action and changed policies cannot wait for such an understanding to suffuse the national consciousness or conscience. Fortunately, it is possible for people to develop an understanding of these misguided and counterproductive ways of thinking. This happens best through exposure to and purposeful interaction with people whom they have been taught are one thing, but turn out to be another. It also is important for people who are incarcerated to have opportunities beyond those typically available inside prisons to participate in critical analysis and structured discussion of materials that bear importantly on their lives and experiences. The Inside-Out Prison Exchange Program is an especially valuable mechanism for exposing the flaws in the dominant discourse and inspiring the passion to create more productive and compassionate alternatives.

Lifting the Veil of Ignorance

As I write this, I am fresh from participating in a highly interactive "mini Inside-Out workshop" held by the Inside-Out Think Tank at Graterford for a set of first-time visitors from a college class. The session was cofacilitated by two regular Think Tank members, one who had been an inside student and the other a former outside student. It involved a standard icebreaker used in classes, followed by a large group-brainstorming session, work in pairs, then small groups, and a return to the full group for some discussion before the wrap up. The last agenda item was a "go-around" asking those who were participating for the first time to say, in a few words, what they would be taking with them from the evening's session. I was once again struck by how many of the students visiting for the first time commented that their preconceived notions about people in prison had been shattered and how surprised they were that the inside participants were upbeat, thoughtful, highly intelligent, skilled, and caring. These reactions were from undergraduates participating in a two-hour one-time workshop. Responses from people who complete an entire Inside-Out course are in the same vein, but magnified and intensified.

Participation in Inside-Out classes serves to raise the veil of ignorance from the eyes of those involved in several ways. One powerful dimension of this pedagogy is that the classes can shatter myths and stereotypes about other class participants, biased perspectives with which both inside and outside students may enter the classroom. Those received ideas often come bundled with expectations about the behavior and attitudes likely to be revealed by members of the other group. An outside student in one of my classes described honestly how some of her preconceptions were shattered by joining an Inside-Out class:

> I had given incarcerated men the label that my parents, school, and society tells us to give them: "bad." I remember feeling startled by how "normal" the men were; they were not people who carry the label "convicted felon" as if stamped on their foreheads. They are normal men, who have made mistakes, but can change. They have lives and families and goals just like the people on the outside of the prison walls that are so eager to distance themselves from those similarities because it's uncomfortable.

People who are incarcerated are not unfamiliar with popular stereotypes about them and this awareness may lead to a fear that the outside college students coming in will be aligned with those they perceive as being out to wreak vengeance on them. Alternatively, inside students may come to the classes believing that the outside students view them mainly as curiosities or objects of study. For their part, inside students often hold stereotyped views about their new classmates too, imagining, for example, that they all were born with silver spoons in their mouths. Both sets of students often are surprised to find that participation in the class leads to a rather different and encouraging reality. As one inside member of the Graterford Think Tank (GTT) reflected:

> Outside people care about issues. This was deeply surprising to learn. Inside-Out helps you by being engaged with people constantly; you understand that they understand. It really changes not only outside students' perceptions, but our perception of outside people caring.

Although Inside-Out classes are postsecondary courses, in which students acquire academic or "content" knowledge, that content is grasped and absorbed more thoroughly than in a conventional classroom because of the impact of experiential learning. One Think Tank member expressed this effect by saying, "We're exposing untruths in a way that's visceral, and as soon as one truth falls, it opens space to question other truths" (Inside GTT member). One of the greatest strengths of this form of participatory education is its potential to help students better understand and appreciate both differences and commonalities among the students, despite apparent distinctions. As one outside student expressed this:

> As I grew to know the inside students better, I began to see how similar I am to them. I understood that perhaps if I had grown up somewhere different, with less supportive parents, or gone to a bad school, I could have found myself in such a situation. Even if I had simply made a couple of different decisions than I did as an adolescent or young adult, I could be in their shoes. Crime doesn't happen to people who are simply "born bad"; to me, it seems to be a complex interaction of many things, many of which are beyond any one individual's control. (Outside Student)

Engaging students in examining social problems from many angles and on multiple planes leads to greater awareness of the role of context, personal values, and social forces and institutions. Another outside student captured this dawning awareness well when he wrote,

> This course has made me realize that "criminals" may not actually exist, only situations that make a person seem "criminal." Basically, we don't have to eradicate people from our societies—we have to eradicate the situations that create the illusion that people are "criminal."

Inside-Out classes do significantly more than shatter stereotypes (itself no small feat). One of the reasons that the courses are so effective is that they furnish what Kenneth Bain (2004) calls "a natural critical learning environment" (60, 99–100). The atmosphere is "natural" in the sense that the emphasis is on authentic questions and tasks that seem important to the students and "critical" in the way that participants are challenged to grapple with ideas, rethink their assumptions, and examine their mental models of reality. These are characteristics structured into Inside-Out pedagogy. An inside student in one of my criminal justice classes that delved into recent research on prisons commented in a reflection paper about how the course readings were indeed related to his life and situation:

> The assigned material was extremely informative, and surreal at the same time. The studies done, and the statistics pertaining to our criminal justice system [were] fascinating to read, but quite depressing at the same time. Reading about myself as a statistic has given me a higher level of awareness.

Dan Butin (2010) argues that the linkage of academic work with community engagement "within a framework of respect, reciprocity, relevance, and reflection" can offer a powerful means for fostering both questioning and doubt, which can lead to students' rethinking of themselves and their view of the world. He sees the greatest potential in community-engaged learning that is truly "'antifoundational' and profoundly disruptive of how students normally acquire knowledge and from whom" (vii). As Hollander notes in discussing Butin's perspective,

> Antifoundational service-learning requires students…to ask fundamental questions about justice, to hear voices rarely heard and reveal the "deep divisions" within which and through which we think about content knowledge, cultural openness, and oppression. (Hollander, as cited in Butin, 2010, vii)

An inside student in a class I taught discovered in talking with outside students over a period of several weeks that none of them was aware of having ever known or even talked to someone before who had been incarcerated. This was astonishing to him, especially because, as he put it, "Everyone I know, at least all of the men, has been in prison" (Inside Student). He said that his father and one of his brothers also were incarcerated at the time and that each of his other brothers, his uncles, and the men he "ran with" on the street all had "been to jail." "How can our life experiences be so different?" he asked. He repeatedly asked questions thereafter about the ramifications of such different experiences and exposure to the criminal justice system. An inside member of the Think Tank reflected on the ways in which participation in Inside-Out classes prompts such fundamental rethinking in saying:

> It's [exploring] shattering, foundation-shaking questions. Am I the person I think I am? It's creating the space and opportunity to shake old myths and assumptions. The veil is removed. These guys (inside students) are not who I've been taught they are. If these marginalized people aren't what I've been taught, what else isn't true? It's larger than the criminal justice system.

Inside-Out classes challenge preconceptions about members of other groups, including both college students and incarcerated people, which might never be questioned otherwise. They also enhance awareness of the significance of diverse human experiences and identities, as well as the role that larger social forces play in influencing individual behavior and in shaping the beliefs that students bring with them into the classroom. Some of the core design features of Inside-Out courses go a long way in lifting the veil of ignorance from students' eyes. As a welcoming brochure from the Graterford Inside-Out Think Tank to students coming into Inside-Out classes puts it (See Appendix 1):

> Knowledge is not only acquired from textbook material, but also generated from the learners themselves through a sharing of perspectives, beliefs and personal experiences. Crucial to the Inside-Out pedagogy is the powerful exchange that occurs between "inside" and "outside" students. It is the reciprocity and authenticity of this exchange that makes Inside-Out unique. (Welcome to The Inside-Out Prison Exchange Program, n.d.)

Building Connection and Community

Members of the Inside-Out staff and of the Think Tank at Graterford have held lengthy discussions about how best to capture the heart of Inside-Out. We often ask one another what "elevator speech" we would give about the program. In one of these sessions, Inside GTT members suggested that at its core:

> Inside-Out puts people in touch with their own humanity and others' humanity. We recognize each other as fully human. People in society are so alienated, they feel lonely. In an Inside-Out class, you develop the skill to connect to people. Inside-Out is [about] building relationships and shared humanity.

Inside-Out crosses physical walls and breaks down psychological ones. The classes typically expose participants to people who reflect a variety of differences from one another beyond those linked to their status as either incarcerated or "free world." Through interaction with colearners who may be of different age groups, races, religions, sexual orientations, socioeconomic backgrounds, family situations growing up, educational and skill levels, and reflect a variety of other distinctions, students acquire a deeper appreciation of both differences and commonalities, and of their own ability to reach across any divide.

Training of Inside-Out instructors emphasizes the importance of quickly establishing the sense that the classroom is a place where people can feel comfortable and be open to connecting with a diverse set of other people. Developing an atmosphere of trust is achieved partly through use of icebreaker and get-acquainted exercises and activities. It is further facilitated by spelling out a set of program rules and parameters within which all participants contract to stay. Beyond that, class members go on to develop guidelines for dialogue that they commit to follow as a group. Through these and other elements, a budding sense of group cohesion is established early on: "It begins: me; you. Now it's we. The tools are there to connect" (Inside GTT member).

One key to making Inside-Out classes successful is how the instructor carries herself into the space and how she sees her role, because this sets the tone for the whole experience. If the instructor is uncomfortable with herself, with being in prison, or with bringing these two groups together, that will be communicated. If, on the other hand, the instructor has developed a good sense of herself as the facilitator and as someone genuinely excited about the process in which they all are engaged, that invites everyone else to be comfortable and enthusiastic. Humor is part of creating a comfortable environment and helping members of the class overcome any initial reluctance to relate, as is body language, and most of all, holding and conveying a genuine respect and caring for each person in the room. Inside-Out classes are structured in such a way that no one is allowed to "hide," "lie back in the weeds," or avoid participation. Certainly a student can pass or not volunteer a response to a particular question, but everyone understands that their involvement is necessary to the unique chemistry of these courses. In addition, because the issues addressed are animated by learning how they play out in people's lives, even students who are ordinarily shy tend to want to be fully engaged. The result is a clear form of bonding that occurs both within and across groups of inside and outside students. One Think Tank member who took the class as a Temple undergraduate explained, "In a regular class, we never spoke all semester. In Inside-Out, it forces you to interact in ways you never would." Another member of the Think Tank who had participated in a class while incarcerated similarly noted: "That's also true inside. Before the class, we never crossed groups. Now there is genuine affection after we went through that experience together. We bonded with each other, even the guys inside."

Instilling Hope and Empowerment

Inside-Out courses inspire many students to believe that what may have seemed like intractable problems can be remedied, as well as increasing participants' confidence, skills, and commitment to playing a role in bringing about needed changes. Much of this impact is linked to the fact that students develop a deep appreciation for how the issues play out in people's lives. Once they recognize more fully how their own identities and social locations have affected them, participants come to better appreciate how people in various situations and groups are affected by social injustice. They also develop greater confidence in their abilities to develop and sustain relationships with diverse groups. This in turn allows them to feel more hopeful about the possibilities of working together across differences to achieve reform.

Participation in Inside-Out can be empowering in the direct sense that it offers educational and leadership opportunities for men and women being held in prisons, jails, and other correctional facilities that otherwise would not be available to them. For some incarcerated students, Inside-Out classes represent a first opportunity to take a college course or to reenter higher education after a lengthy hiatus. For many outside students, taking an Inside-Out class provides not only a first entrance into a correctional facility but also the initial occasion of engaging in structured conversation and collaboration with people residing in such an institution. It can help all students better find their own voices, as well as increasing their willingness to listen well and to value other people's voices.

In contrast to a conventional class in which students listen to the professor and formulate comments to earn the instructor's approval, Inside-Out courses emphasize the importance of the contributions of everyone involved. This changes students from passive to active listeners and from receivers of information to cocreators of knowledge. An inside member of the GTT emphasized that this dimension of Inside-Out classes lies at the heart of their value:

> [Inside-Out is about] (f)inding your voice where you may not have had that opportunity before—to try ideas out and explore them, practicing dialogue, perspective-taking. It allows you to empathize more. It expands perspective.

Such shifts generate greater investment and ownership, helping students feel that they are part of something larger than themselves and that they can and should help make improvements.

Students in natural critical learning environments can feel supported even while being challenged, such as when they are asked to engage in such higher-order intellectual tasks as applying, evaluating, analyzing, and synthesizing. One effective means of providing support in Inside-Out classes is achieved by making much of the work collaborative. The fostering of collaboration—literally, laboring together—means bringing more than one perspective together to work toward a new and likely richer way of seeing an issue. "It is…learning as participation—it is an active, co-construction of meaning and identity" (Cook-Sather, 2006, 25). Through collaboration, difficult tasks can be rendered less threatening and even empowering, especially when the emphasis is on solving problems and gaining understanding rather than on competition or performance for purposes of testing or grades.

For outside students, problems take on greater charge when discussed with people who may have direct experience with them. Inside students also may be provided an all-too-rare opportunity to engage in serious, structured dialogue on issues about which they have first-hand knowledge and deep interest. As one inside participant expressed it,

> Inside-Out classes help individuals think and have conversations about critical issues in an environment [within a prison] where most conversations are really goofy; they are not connected to the circumstances. They are about sports and women and cars, as if we are not sitting here inside of a maximum security institution. (Inside GTT member)

Once inside students become engaged in wrestling with more significant issues within Inside-Out classrooms, they often feel impelled to take those kinds of discussions to other people within their day-to-day circles of contact and influence.

> I see the change of guys in here. I see young guys running around on the block. Then a man is challenging three to four young guys about the political system 'cause he went through the class. [He's making clear that] it's bigger than rap and basketball. Two of those [younger] guys are now [enrolled] in the class. Inside-Out creates an opportunity for these conversations to feel safe, and to trust. (Inside GTT member)

Inside and outside students report that increased understanding about how systems operate leaves them feeling responsible, motivated, and hopeful. As one inside student reported, the class provides "an intellectual and almost spiritual lift. I feel I have been lifted from the regions of hopelessness and frustration I'd been feeling." Many outside college students similarly report that the classes motivate them to reassess their personal lives and career paths.

Both inside and outside students frequently express the desire, and even a sense of obligation, to "pay it forward" by passing along some of the new understandings they developed through the course. An outside student described this by saying:

> Thanks to the Inside-Out program, I was able to change and reform many of my ideas about who commits crime, why, and how society deals with it and see some of the greater truths that are buried beneath society's belief about our criminal justice system. In the future, I hope to have the courage to contradict and inform others who may have the same ideas I did before I participated in this program so that they can take a harder look at our ways of dealing with crime in this country.

Bain (2004) argues that the best model of education involves learners in "doing more than accumulating information; they undergo deep-seated changes, transformations that affect both the habits of the heart and mind and the capacity for continued growth" (84). From all reports, such powerful change happens regularly in Inside-Out classrooms. A brochure prepared for distribution to new groups of Inside-Out students by members of the GTT (Appendix 1) describes these benefits as follows:

> The course allows the university students to re-conceptualize what they have learned in the classroom, gaining insights that will help them to pursue the work of creating a more just and equitable society. At the same time, it challenges men and women on the inside to place their life experiences in a larger social context and rekindles their intellectual self-confidence and interest in further education. Equally important, Inside-Out encourages inside and outside students alike to recognize their capacity as agents of change—in their lives as well as in the broader community. (Graterford Inside-Out Think Tank, n.d.)

Conclusion

The world needs more of what The Inside-Out Prison Exchange Program delivers. Inside-Out classes provide a powerful model for overcoming some of the most significant problems facing us today that are associated with alienation, fear, and hostility. Mass imprisonment emerged from the profoundly dehumanizing practices and ideology characteristic of chattel slavery, convict leasing, chain gangs, and other forms of brutal criminal punishment. Beyond the devastating impact on Black Americans of the linkage in popular culture of blackness and crime, the underlying willingness to treat any group as undeserving of respect and recognition of their human dignity bleeds over into the rationalization of dehumanizing treatment of other groups disproportionately caught up in the criminal justice system, whether they are Native Americans, Hispanics, immigrants, poor whites, or any category deemed undeserving or expendable. Defining other people as inferior or evil creates social cleavages and a sense of isolation within those who are fearful, as well as between them and those they fear. It also allows treatment of others in ways that clearly would be unacceptable for members of one's own tribe.

Inside-Out is not the only means for exposing deeply-seated myths and ideologies that underlie the fissures that divide people in our society, or for generating belief in the real possibilities for creating a better future, but it is an extremely potent and accessible one. It makes a powerful contribution by lifting the veil of ignorance, building connections and community, and engendering hope and empowerment.

Notes

1. Philip Zimbardo, "The Lucifer Effect," http://www.lucifereffect.com/dehumanization. htm. Zimbardo is a social psychologist perhaps best known for his role in the Stanford Prison Experiment. In that infamous 1971 simulation that was planned as a two-week study of the psychology of prison life using undergraduate students to act as "prisoners" and "guards," those playing the "guard" role became so abusive and those playing the "prisoner" role so stressed that the experiment had to be terminated after only six days. (See http://www.prisonexp.org/ for more details.)

2. The term "prison nation" is increasingly being applied to the United States, for example, by journalist Sasha Abramsky in *Hard Time Blues: How Politics Built a Prison Nation* (New York: Thomas Dunne Books, 2002) and Beth Ritchie in *Arrested Justice: Black Women, Violence, and America's Prison Nation* (New York: New York University Press, 2012). See also the Center for the Study of Political Graphics exhibition, "Prison Nation—Posters on the prison industrial complex," at http://www.politicalgraphics. org/pdf/PRISON%20NATION.Gallery%20Guide.CSPG.pdf

3. These classes typically require students to complete five or six structured reflection papers, as well as a final paper, and to participate in a group project. Because the courses I have taught were part of the curriculum of the Criminal Justice Department at Temple University, they emphasized content in that field. However, Inside-Out courses are offered in many disciplines.

4. See generally Michelle Alexander's *The New Jim Crow: Mass Incarceration in the Age of Color Blindness* (New York: The New Press, 2010) for the argument that what exists today constitutes a racial caste system. She defines this term on pages 12–13.

5. When Charles Dickens visited Philadelphia's Eastern State Penitentiary, which opened in 1829 with a regime of strict solitude, he wrote: "I hold this slow and daily tampering with the mysteries of the brain, to be immeasurably worse than any torture of the body: and because its ghastly signs and tokens are not so palpable to the eye and sense of touch as scars upon the flesh; because its wounds are not upon the surface, and it extorts few cries that human ears can hear; therefore I the more denounce it, as a secret punishment which slumbering humanity is not roused up to stay" (chapter 7, *American Notes for General Circulation* at http://www.gutenberg.org).

6. This is a long-term condition for an estimated 25,000 people being held in federal and state "supermax" prisons—and perhaps 80,000 others in isolation sections within regular prisons.

7. This quotation from the dust jacket of Khalil Gibran Muhammad's 2010 book (*The Condemnation of Blackness: Race, Crime, and the Making of Modern Urban America* (Cambridge, MA: Harvard University Press, 2010)) is by David Levering Lewis, twice

winner of the Pulitzer Prize for *W. E. B. Du Bois: A Biography* (New York: H Holt, 1994) and *W.E.B. DuBois: The Fight for Equality and the American Century, 1919–1963* (New York: H Holt, 2001).

8. Incarceration rates for black Americans, especially black women, dropped from 2000 to 2009, while the rate of imprisonment for whites and Hispanics rose. But of the more than 100,000 women incarcerated in state or federal prisons, black women were still almost three times more likely to be in prison than white women in 2009, and black men were still incarcerated at more than six times the rate of white men. "Incarceration Rates for Blacks Have Fallen Sharply, Report Shows." *New York Times.* February 27, 2013: A12.

9. See especially N. H. Rafter, *Partial Justice: Women, Prisons and Social Control,* 2nd ed. (New Brunswick, NJ: Transaction Publishers, 1990) and Beth E. Ritchie, *Arrested Justice: Black Women, Violence, and America's Prison Nation* (New York: New York University Press, 2012).

References

Alexander, Michelle. *The New Jim Crow: Mass Incarceration in the Age of Color Blindness.* New York: The New Press, 2010.

Bain, Kenneth. *What the Best College Teachers Do.* Cambridge, MA: Harvard University Press, 2004.

Blackmon, Douglas. A. *Slavery by Another Name: The Re-Enslavement of Black Americans from the Civil War to World War II.* New York: Anchor Books, 2008.

Butin, Dan. *Service-Learning in Theory and Practice: The Future of Community Engagement in Higher Education.* New York: Palgrave MacMillan, 2010.

Cook-Sather, Alison. *Education is Translation: A Metaphor for Change in Learning and Teaching.* Philadelphia: University of Pennsylvania Press, 2006.

Hollander, Elizabeth. "Foreword." In *Service-Learning in Theory and Practice: The Future of Community Engagement in Higher Education,* Dan Butin, vii–xii. New York: Palgrave MacMillan, 2010.

Lichtenstein, Alex. *Twice the Work of Free Labor: The Political Economy of Convict Labor in the New South.* New York: Verso, 1996.

Muhammad, Khalil Gibran. "White may be Might, but it's Not Always Right." *The Washington Post* (Sunday Outlook Section), December 9, 2007: B01

———. *The Condemnation of Blackness: Race, Crime, and the Making of Modern Urban America.* Cambridge, MA: Harvard University Press, 2010.

———. "Playing the Violence Card." *New York Times.* April 6, 2012, A23.

Oshinsky, David M. *"Worse than Slavery": Parchman Farm and the Ordeal of Jim Crow Justice.* New York: Free Press, 1996.

Perkinson, Robert. *Texas Tough: The Rise of America's Prison Empire.* New York: Metropolitan Books, 2010.

Rafter, Nicole Hahn. *Partial Justice: Women, Prisons and Social Control,* 2nd ed. New Brunswick, NJ: Transaction Publishers, 1990.

Ritchie, Beth E. *Arrested Justice: Black Women, Violence, and America's Prison Nation.* New York: New York University Press, 2012.

The Graterford Inside-Out Think Tank. "Welcome to the New Inside-Out Student" (brochure). Philadelphia: The Inside-Out Prison Exchange Program, Temple University, n.d.

CHAPTER 6

Liberation from University Education: A Lesson in Humility for a Helper

Amelia Larson

> Only what you have experienced yourself can be called knowledge.
> Everything else is just information.
>
> Albert Einstein

On the first day of my Masters of Social Work degree, the faculty dean warned the students: "Don't let us school the humanity and humility out of you." Unfortunately, this is essentially what traditional education does. For most of my post-secondary education, I feigned professional conduct in an attempt to appear capable and competent, memorizing content and separating myself from the learning. Despite the alienation I felt, I was able to convince myself that I was learning and getting as much as I could out of higher education—until I participated in Inside-Out.

Ironically, the first time I allowed myself to feel vulnerable and show genuine emotion within the university context was inside a federal prison. I had the unique opportunity to study in Canada's first Inside-Out program during my initial semester of my Masters of Social Work degree. The experience informed my social work practice in every sphere and continues to do so. I have been changed. Looking at Inside-Out's lessons, this essay makes the case for including experiential learning models across university curricula.

Despite the dean's warning, I had found that traditional pedagogic practice contradicted the stated goals of the program. It emphasized expert knowledge. Large class sizes were impersonal, and the loudest, most assertive individuals dominated discussion space. Like many students, I confined myself to well-defined boundaries for fear of giving the *wrong* answer. My attempts to appear wholly professional had disconnected me from the material taught in class and the individuals I was meant to help. When I shared with my Inside-Out classmates my disappointment with my graduate studies, it became apparent that, while my inside classmates live in cages, I have been educated in one.

In the fall of 2011, 17 students embarked on an experiential learning journey, also described by Kayla Follett and Jessie Rodger in chapter 14. The course, Diversity, Marginalization and Oppression, was required for the ten outside MSW students and was taken for undergraduate university credit by the seven inside students. As a class, we examined systemic injustices, the forces that perpetuate them, and their connections with our own lives. Along the way, I constantly asked myself, "why?" observing my personal reactions (or nonreactions) toward particular topics, readings, comments, classmates, or group dynamics. Taking time to be mindful in this way helped me reflect on my own biases. Informal moments of reflexivity were bolstered by the reflection that was built into the curriculum through discussion, group activities, and writing.

The structure of the Inside-Out classroom thus supported best practices in experiential education in which the learner must be actively involved, reflecting on the experience while applying analytical, decision-making, and problem-solving skills.[1] Sitting in the circle, I could see each one of my classmates' faces at any time. We were not separated by tables nor could we avoid eye contact by furiously typing on laptops. The classroom etiquette echoed the Aboriginal Seven Grandfather Teachings (respect, love, bravery, humility, honesty, wisdom, and truth), a holistic approach in keeping with the less formalized, Socratic nature of this experiential learning process. One of the main expectations of our class was that each person would come ready to contribute and be open-minded to whatever form the process would take.[*] The underlying principle of experiential learning is holism; it allows us to recognize the humanity in ourselves and others as what connects us all.

University Education's Bad Report Card

We are taught that academic knowledge conveys power and opportunity, but how often do we escape the confines of campus to learn with and from those who are excluded from higher education? Our social work campus was recently moved "downtown," a transition intended to bring us closer to the communities with whom we would be working. While this initially seemed like a good idea, there was little communication between the school and the larger community, and we learned that community members felt unwelcome in the building. Creating and maintaining a larger, cohesive community goes far beyond physical location and superficial gestures to incorporate people who are typically excluded.

Being a university student is an isolating experience, divorced from the larger community within a world of theory and competition among peers. The university environment in fact reflects the kind of emotional poverty that modern society perpetuates. The mad drive to *achieve* and be *better* divides the whole individual into separate parts (intellectual, emotional, physical, and spiritual) and divides us from one another. Masters of Social Work programs are designed to prepare individuals for the varied forms of social work practice, which include direct practice (working with individuals, families, and groups) and indirect practice (working with communities, social planning, administration, and research). Yet in the emphasis on professionalism, the human connection is discouraged. In the Faculty of Social Work, I often hear, "Relationship heals." Can a relationship built on professionalism's strict boundaries and limited self disclosure truly heal? It is difficult to form real relationships without allowing oneself to be vulnerable. Especially in the classroom, appearing exposed violates the understanding of academic etiquette. For me, university has been a place of facts and inquiry, not emotion. How can anyone in a helping profession expect those we attempt to help to be vulnerable to heal, without being willing to do so ourselves?

The things we talk about and disclose in Inside-Out are exactly the things we try to hide in the Faculty of Social Work. We want to be seen as living on an even keel, able to deal with anything our clients throw at us; we attempt to be robots. These hidden things comprise who we are but we are socialized to be ashamed of them. By contrast, the practice of "whole-self learning" accepts emotion as part of human existence. In this class, we took individual chances that allowed for the possibility of being *wrong*, exposing emotion, and being the flawed people that we all are without fear of judgment. We were all accepted for who we are and our own individual learning paths.

The Seven Grandfather Teachings played an extremely important role in welcoming this vulnerability. I was able to admit my academic struggles to my classmates because we *respected* one another's learning and how that individually occurred; and because we recognized that *love* is needed most when people are weak, *bravery* requires us to face the foe (our own demons) with integrity, *honesty* with ourselves and others means admitting how we truly feel, *humility* is knowing that we are all equal and no one is better, *wisdom* is to be used for the good of the people, and *truth* is to know and recognize all of these things.

Ironically, the emotional, spiritual, and physical parts of ourselves that we ignore within the confines of university are the elements that most make us human and allow for connection with others as real people. Like trees, people grow in many directions; the roots grow down, the trunk up and the branches out. Experiencing and honoring all the parts of ourselves in an environment that includes self reflection and introspection allows a stronger connection to who we are as individuals and practitioners. This is the kind of reflexivity, rare in university classrooms, that should be experienced in all helping profession training programs.

One of my inside classmates stated in her Closing Ceremony address, "This world isn't an easy place for any of us." Without quantifying the difficulty of my classmates' individual experiences, we shared a collective factor that continually brought us all together: we have each been confined. Some have been and are limited in the physical sense of the word, but all of us find ourselves intellectually restricted. As university students, we have all been told that we do not know what we know from experience because it has not been tested, proven, or published by someone else with more knowledge and power. Although I value the accumulated knowledge passed down through centuries of formalized education, disciplinary knowledge does not represent the whole picture. The lifetimes of experience and knowledge that we carry with us signify multiple and much needed ways of knowing. Each student in our class was able to engage, connect, teach, and learn the topics of diversity, marginalization, and oppression because we have all lived and therefore have personal knowledge to draw upon.

Throughout elementary and secondary school years, my report cards had a section called "learning skills." In this section, the teacher rated how I was progressing in areas such as initiative, teamwork, problem solving, and cooperation with others. Once a student reaches university, there is no further commitment to developing these personal attributes. Upon graduation, however, there are few careers in which individuals work in isolation. Situations that teach individuals how to work with others, be part of a team, live in a community, and collectively enact social change should be just as valued in higher education as they were in early years. Experiential learning opportunities such as Inside-Out present methods to continue developing in these areas.

Through Inside-Out, I learned what it means to listen, and now I believe that hearing and listening are the most important skills I will bring to my social work practice. In one of my clinical classes, we studied active listening and interviewing skills and then demonstrated them through a video-taped mock clinical interview. Knowing that a large portion of my grade in the class would be determined by the interview, I was paralyzed with anxiety. I stumbled and stammered, trying to quickly recall techniques that would give my interviewee and viewer the impression I knew what on earth I was doing. Caught up in my personal presentation, I failed to really hear what my interviewee was saying. Afterwards, I felt dissatisfied with my ability to utilize essential social work techniques and suffered through the countless hours of transcribing my failure, writing off my ability to be an effective listener. Being part of the Inside-Out circle taught me otherwise: listening to actually hear is much more natural than trying to tick off a mental checklist of what one should be doing or saying. The circle carried the weight I previously felt I had to carry on my own. The constant question on my mind was, "Why doesn't everyone in the faculty get this opportunity to explore why and who they are in such a safe space?"

A necessary component of our group's success stemmed from the extensive classroom guidelines we collectively developed (see Appendix). In some other formal classes, guidelines were developed at the start of the term, but were soon forgotten. Here, the process of creating and revisiting our norms helped to reduce anxiety and create consistency. The concept of community learning is foreign to many students, so a tangible code helped set the community norms and shaped the space in this unconventional classroom. We started in small groups brainstorming answers to questions such as "How will we handle disagreement?" or "What about this class makes me feel uncomfortable?" These questions enabled us to address initial discomfort and create a space that was as safe as possible. Once crafted, the guidelines directed our interactions, from determining how contentious issues would be handled, to holding no assumptions, to knowing that within the class we are all physically safe. They acted as a unifying tool, maximizing learning while decreasing discomfort stemming from the unknown. Revisiting and referring to the guidelines often keeps them alive, ensuring fidelity or the opportunity for revision if something is inadequate or has unknowingly been omitted.

A crucial part of being in a helping profession is *unlearning* how to help in the traditional sense of the word. We are trained with tactics and techniques that are meant to facilitate others in helping themselves to improve their lives. This impulse can become so ingrained that we cannot distinguish when we are helping and when we are not; it becomes difficult to refrain from trying to help someone who wants not to be helped, but simply to be heard. There were many instances in my Inside-Out course when a classmate was talking and I wanted to ask questions or comment before my classmate had finished speaking. My urge to contribute during another's time was intended as an act of helping, to encourage further thought or insight, but the class code required that everyone had a chance to speak without interjection for as long as they needed. Every week, listening became easier and I was increasingly able to hear what my classmates were saying without a whirlwind of my own thoughts distracting me from their words. The code of entitled, uninterrupted time to speak for everyone should extend beyond the classroom circle; recognizing that individuals, friends, family, and the people we work with do not always want or need our help empowers the people in our personal and professional lives. I believe it is an important step in moving away from the client mentality and deprofessionalizing the helping fields.

Community Learning and the Whole Student

I find it astounding how much emphasis academia places on what can be accomplished alone. What might be accomplished if more emphasis was placed on collaboration and collective success, rather than individual achievement? The concept of community learning, which the Inside-Out model adopts, has helped me to reconsider the relationship between learning and teaching. In our Inside-Out circle, we were all teachers and learners. Each individual had the responsibility to be accountable for their own learning and the learning of our classmates. As such, a class norm was to come to class prepared. Being prepared in this context does not just mean having completed the weekly readings, but to have thought about those readings, deconstructed them, made connections between the material and our own lives and experience, and looked for personal relevance within the texts. We were not relying upon what our professor believed to be true, attempting to memorize what she said in order to regurgitate it in an assignment later. The majority of the class content came from the students. If all 17 of us did not come to class with something to discuss or a question to pose, we would have spent three awkward hours in pin-drop silence.

Drawing on my lifetime of experience helped me reclaim my education and shape it to best meet my own needs, a basic premise of adult education that is rarely exercised. Learning about systems that keep people marginalized and oppressed helped me to recognize how those systems operate in my own life. This recognition of systems—including the University—led me to understand the concepts of oppression and marginalization in a very real way, empowering me to push against the marginalization and oppression I witness and experience in daily life.

Embracing learning with my whole self opened my heart and mind, allowing me to challenge traditionally accepted beliefs and preconceived notions about who is a "criminal" and who is a "student." At our first class we all shared the fear of being judged by others; honest, genuine relationships and community learning squelched that fear. I have found liberation from the confines of the classroom by being heard, felt, accepted, and embraced within the Inside-Out circle.

Friendly challenge and engagement in productive, critical debate with classmates is actually *encouraged* when no one is attacked or silenced. Due to the competitive nature of the lecture format, the pressure to make oneself stand out as an intelligent individual often comes at the expense of the emotional safety of others. Before Inside-Out, I rarely admitted that I did not understand something. I was never "called out" on this, which was a great injustice to my own learning. One of the main strengths in a social work program is, I believe, the educational benefits gained from being part of a collective and developing from our shared knowledge and experiences. Experiential learning serves to unite a group rather than pitting individuals against each other. This allows students to place a higher degree of emphasis on the emotional, physical, intellectual, and spiritual learning of everyone. It helps one excel, not only academically, but also personally.

Embracing learning with my whole self has been novel and liberating. I am sorry for those who spend their entire university experience within the parameters of a campus. The most salient learning and growth I have experienced was fostered outside of the classroom, in experiential situations, from people who don't necessarily have a degree but who certainly have a great deal of humanity. Hearing multiple voices and perspectives within and beyond the context of education brings refreshing and urgently needed perspective to difficult issues. Ultimately, individuals whom we try to help are experts on their own lives. This should be recognized at the forefront of every therapeutic relationship.

Connecting the Inside-Out class content with my life experiences allowed me to learn with all aspects of my being. I tapped into multiple ways of knowing as each concept was animated through a connection I made to my life. When I used moments of my life as examples to understand concepts, I did not just learn the concept but *knew* it with my physical, emotional, intellectual, and spiritual self. At the beginning of the course, our class examined a section of Paulo Freire's *Pedagogy of the Oppressed,* discussing particularly the idea that oppressors can also be oppressed, and vice versa. The concept resonated with my own life and professional practice. I began to think back to instances where I moved between being both the oppressor and the oppressed. This reflection heightened my ability to recognize when I occupy the oppressor role, through my physical and emotional reactions to interactions. Shortly after, I was attempting to help a youth in the context of my workplace but the therapeutic relationship was becoming strained. I noted that I was experiencing reactions similar to previous instances where I identified myself as the oppressor. Being cognizant of this helped me to minimize it in further interactions, which ultimately saved the relationship we had worked to establish. The personal work of relating concepts to my own experiences resulted in an ownership and passion for the content; I did not simply study it, but lived it.

Conclusion

The conclusion of our class marked the first Inside-Out course to be completed in Canada and evolved into the first Women and Trans-people Inside-Out Collective in existence. The collective continues to meet biweekly, focusing on projects of relevance both inside and outside the institution walls.

Whenever I discussed my participation in the Inside-Out Program with others outside of the faculty of social work, I was often met with the response, "Oh, that must be so good for *them.*" This comment made my blood boil, as if offering this transformative educational opportunity was an act of charity meant solely to benefit *them.* The assumption that inside students would gain significantly more than outside students was false. I can easily say that participating in an experiential opportunity where I was not a helper but an equal has benefitted my social work practice more than I could have anticipated. Learning to help is the foundation of social work education, but unlearning to help is equally essential. Inside-Out provided a way to think about empowering others that, as Parker Palmer proposes, entails "no fixing, no saving, no advising, no setting each other straight," which came to embody what experiential learning and social work practice mean to me.[2]

Education should evoke feelings of intellectual freedom. At the beginning of class one evening, an outside classmate stated, "I am so happy to be back here; I feel free and liberated in here." We all laughed at the irony of her remark, but simultaneously recognized the truth in it. How many places of learning inspire a statement like that, especially in a locked and guarded classroom? If this is possible in an institution where people are placed in cages, imagine the potential elsewhere.

Notes

1. "Glimpse Experiential Learning." Accessed August 13, 2012, http://www.myglimpse-world.com/index.php?option=com_content&view=article&id=47&Itemid=37
2. Parker Palmer. *A Hidden Wholeness: The Journey Toward an Undivided Life* (San Francisco: Jossey-Bass, 2004), 115.

References

Freire, Paulo. *Pedagogy of the Oppressed.* New York: The Continuum International Publishing Group, 2003.

"Glimpse Experiential Learning." Accessed August 13, 2012, http://www.myglimpseworld. com/index.php?option=com_content&view=article&id=47&Itemid=37

Itin, Christian M. "Reasserting the Philosophy of Experiential Education as a Vehicle for Change in the 21st Century," *The Journal of Experiential Education* 22 (1999): 91–98.

Palmer, Parker. *A Hidden Wholeness: The Journey Towards an Undivided Life.* San Francisco: Jossey-Bass, 2004.

CHAPTER 7

The American Educational System: Abuses and Alternatives

K. D. A. Daniel-Bey

Introduction

When I was eleven, I transferred from a rural school to an urban one and experienced the culture shock that so many children go through when making such transitions. Living with an educator, my beloved grandmother, made it possible for me to examine the differences between the two school systems I had attended. Given a glimpse of the education debate years before I was consciously aware of it, I still needed many years before I was able to see the systemic problem coherently. Participating in the Inside-Out program has given me the information I need to begin a proper analysis of what needs to be done to recreate the educational system. I now see the monumental betrayal that so many of my peers and I had experienced, and I have the opportunity to do something about it.

When I moved, I realized that although the urban school was larger, the education it provided was of much lower quality. My disgust at this loss is partially to blame for my eventual incarceration. I had loved school and I still love to learn. When I came to school in the new setting, I made bad choices; my deep alienation from the education I was receiving helped me make them.

In 2008, after 15 years of prison, I took an Inside-Out sociology class. After its completion, students in my class joined what is essentially a regional steering committee, a think tank that we call the Theory Group. For me this group gave purpose to a life with little direction or significance. But Inside-Out also held up a mirror, one I had not expected, illuminating my own prejudicial, stereotypical, and stigmatic ideas. I was not always happy with what was revealed, and I have been prompted to reexamine my beliefs and broaden my perspectives.

Gathering scientific evidence and other critiques of contemporary education, I am beginning to reflect on the expertise developed through my own experiences and to hone my analysis of what was, and is, wrong with our educational system. Analysis does not automatically provide solutions. But this system-wide problem must be responded to, and proven strategies are better than none. I believe Inside-Out's methods are vital to addressing our educational shortcomings. I have watched men who were indifferent to education take an Inside-Out class and change their whole perspective toward learning. I have seen this happen time and again, and heard stories of how this happens anywhere Inside-Out has classes. There is much to be said for that.

The Problem

Many factors have brought us to the current situation. I will briefly address two of these here: historic influences on education and our collective decision-making.

In 1909, before he became the twenty-eighth President of the United States, Woodrow Wilson, then president of Princeton University, gave a speech before the New York High School Teachers Association. In that address, he argued for a two-tiered system of education that would, in practice, stratify and control the American populace. He suggested, "we want to do two things in modern society. We want a class of persons to have a liberal education and we want another class of persons, a much larger class, of necessity, to forgo the privilege of a liberal education and fit themselves to perform specific difficult manual tasks" (Wilson, 1909). Although society has radically changed since Wilson proposed this plan for a growing factory-based economy, this system continues, and its effects remain.

President Wilson further declared, ". . . what I am intent upon saying is that we should not confuse ourselves with regard to what we are trying to make of the pupils under our instruction. We are either trying to make liberally-minded persons out of them, or we are trying to make skillful servants of society along mechanical lines, or else we do not know what we are trying to do." It appears that we have chosen Door Number Three.

Perhaps the system is not broken; perhaps it works. As part of its original function, it weakens and divides us. That division leaves us conflicted with ourselves and our society. This strategy was lauded at the time as revolutionary for our university system. But Wilson's intent went beyond universities; he was speaking to a group of high school teachers. So, why haven't we investigated the persistent impact of Wilson's vision on our education system now? Probably because the answer is too ugly.

Wilson's model has two tiers. The upper tier is for those with resources to purchase a first-class education, a benefit that catapults them into leading jobs and influential positions in government and industry. They can take their place in the upper echelons of society. This good ole' boy system ensures that the affluent maintain their hold on power; only the "right" persons need apply.

The second tier trains the majority of people. These "skillful servants" (2) maintain the machinery or apparatus of society. This tier also siphons off a small number of its best minds to the upper tier, maintaining the illusion of upward mobility if you "just work hard enough." This tier gets propped up, but is never adequately funded by government or community sources. Recently in the *Detroit News,*

Governor Snyder of Michigan proposed a two percent increase in school funding. What was not explained in the proposal was that, in many places, mostly urban, that increase considered in conjunction with decreases in other government funding would actually result in "a net reduction of between two and thirty-six dollars per pupil, depending on their current state funding" (Livengood 2013). How is such a proposal beneficial?

Students graduate from high school unprepared for college; some (even some with diplomas) cannot read or perform other basic skills at grade level. Often, they have been prepared to hold jobs that are made obsolete by technology. A high school graduate cannot make a living adequate to raise a family. Unfortunately, many college graduates find themselves in the same mess, worrying that they will be or are already the invisible face of America.

One reason such severe problems persist may be that societal decision-making is plagued by dichotomous thinking. Decision-makers take narrow positions and let politics drive the conversation, and the ones who lose out in the end are the students. This problem requires creative collective thinking.

The Inside-Out Solution

How do we restructure or recreate our educational system so it provides a quality education to every student who desires it? A key piece of this puzzle involves changing our fundamental view of the purpose of education itself. Education is about life. It is learning about the world around us, who we are, the society in which we live, our responsibilities and privileges as citizens. Yet, if our education takes us so far outside of ourselves that we cannot find our way back or see its usefulness only in our everyday circumstances, then it is useless.

One of the key concerns I have with education as conventionally delivered is that it can suck the joy out of learning and thereby out of life itself. A life without joy is a life wasted. If we think back to when we were most invested in education, it was probably the first two or three years of school. Not only were we learning, but we were having fun in the process. What possible justification is there for that to change as we get older? The loss of fun, of wonder in education, also involves a loss of self—a loss fundamental to who we are. With this loss, we go from being educated to being trained. We become socialized into accepting schooling as ponderous and oppressive, told that "it must be like this" to be of value.

Schools have become breeding grounds for division, in some instances almost prisons. They fail to maximize, and rarely even address, students' gifts. Educators are not trained to help students become whole, and one size fits all methodologies and pedagogies have not worked.

Inside-Out is not a replacement for the current educational system. It is an alternative, a supplement and a complement to the tools already available. It offers another perspective from which to see the problems in the classroom and different ways of dealing with them. It is a tool that can help educators help their students, maximizing potential and satisfaction. We do this by using techniques that can adapt to different situations and that have proven effective not just in prisons, but in juvenile facilities and children's extracurricular programs, as well.

The first goal in Inside-Out is to create a safe space. It is in this space that students are able to experience the learning process differently, within an environment where all are equal partners in learning, with decreased competitiveness and a greater awareness of each other's needs. We look for what works and what does not. Together, we identify, analyze, correct, circumvent, or transcend the issues that arise. Through open and candid dialogue, refraining from accusation and recrimination, we improve our experience and thereby maintain our purpose without being counterproductive.

Our pedagogy reflects the dialogic framework expressed eloquently by Paulo Freire. Instructors are urged to use dialogue to help students unlock, explore, and gain deeper insight into what they learn. Students are shown that they have existing, indwelling knowledge which is valuable to their education. Too rarely in school are students encouraged to pose questions, reflect, or discuss their ideas with others. Freire suggests that "the program content of education is neither a gift nor an imposition—bits of information to be deposited with the students—but rather the organized, systemized, and developed 're-presentation' to individuals of the things about which they want to know more" (2009, 93). It is the authoritarian culture of our system that destroys a student's desire to know more, and often transforms that desire into a need to escape from the educator, the school, and learning itself.

Educators also have problems relating to their students on a personal, human level; most are trained to do the opposite. This, in my opinion, is the greatest block to an educator's effectiveness. Through its process, Inside-Out requires educators to demonstrate their humanity in the classroom arena. Students do not then see an enemy, but another human being with something that they need and want. Parker Palmer states simply, "Good teaching cannot be reduced to technique; good teaching comes from the identity and integrity of the teacher" (1997, 10). I can attest to this idea. When I started high school, I felt alienated from almost all of my teachers. I attended a college prep public school and the only classes where I felt human and where my thoughts mattered were elective classes like ROTC, art, and choir. In those classes, I had one-on-one time to speak with the educators, meaning that they found out who I was while I also learned who they were. In my regular classes, connecting with the teachers or even my fellow students was hard. When I transferred to my neighborhood high school due to misbehavior, happily I found that I felt that connection to my educators, again. There I ran into something fairly unique: a staff mostly comprised of alumni of the school. Even with the deficits that the school suffered under, I did not feel disconnected from my teachers. And my grades rose as a result.

From the first day, Inside-Out uses methodologies that break down the barriers that inhibit connection among classroom participants. Icebreakers are used to engage students with each other, themselves and the educator, establishing a trust dynamic that everyone in the room is part of. This safe space is a place where everyone involved becomes a trusted confederate rather than an object of suspicion. This is especially important in urban areas as a majority of students come from poorer backgrounds. Their larger culture is one of privation, distrust, and hostile authoritarian figures who automatically engender a divisive atmosphere. Is the role of a strict, unbending authoritarian necessary for effective education? People who choose this calling generally desire to help others change their lives for the better. Why use tactics that impede their efficacy? It seems counterintuitive to me. Authority is important, but authority that is accepted is more effective than authority that is imposed.

Inside-Out's pedagogy helps students by validating their understanding of what is being learned. Students themselves are not objects. This point is made clear by Palmer and Freire. Allowing students to think about the material and discuss it creates a dynamic for all to learn and teach simultaneously. In Inside-Out classes, students set expectations for themselves and for each other from the beginning. By this mutual agreement, they can strive together, helping and even correcting one another without unnecessary friction. They invest in each other.

Students typically do not feel *relevant*. This distances students from the educational process and causes lack of focus, acting out and rebellion. By engaging students, Inside-Out instructors help them feel central to the process underway, encouraging them to understand how their opinions and analyses matter. In the article, "Social Class and the Hidden Curriculum of Work" (1980), Jean Anyon notes that in two fifth grade classes she observed, enrolling children from the highest economic bracket, educators considered their students' ideas important. Teachers are quoted saying, "It doesn't matter if [what they find] is right or wrong. I bring them together and there's value in discussing their ideas," and "These children's opinions are important—it's important that they learn to reason things through." So if these principles are acknowledged for students from affluent and powerful families, why not do the same for all students? The spirit of Woodrow Wilson strikes again.

People who like a job work to do it well. If not, they avoid, rush or procrastinate. Changing how we perceive and understand a task changes the level of accountability we feel toward it. In a class with a good atmosphere, expectations rise and accountability is restored. I have watched this numerous times in my Inside-Out class. As fellow students, we corrected those we perceived as being disruptive to class harmony. Unkind remarks were addressed, either right then or later in a more private setting. Rarely did our professor have to intervene.

Furthermore, Inside-Out encourages experiential learning methods that include icebreakers, creative activities, and small discussion sessions. These strategies are developed partly to return the feeling of openness, wonder and delight that I invoked earlier in this chapter, which can make learning fun and inspiring, while at the same time maintaining a high level of educational rigor.

With properly guided students, accountability becomes a powerful tool. It provides more nuanced and sophisticated interaction between instructor and students. Negotiation, reasoning, and space for self-correction all become possible in a safe, relaxed setting. Instructors deepen their relationships with students and strengthen students' abilities to comprehend the information they are taught.

Families and communities have a responsibility and should be held accountable to the educational process as well. Here the benefits of Inside-Out are trickier to explain. Since these groups do not experience Inside-Out firsthand unless they are students themselves, they do not understand the full power of the experience. That feeling gets diluted, robbed of its power in the retelling. This is where alumni activity and the work of Think Tanks and Theory Groups become integral. Providing forums where parents and community can get a taste of that experience is crucial. Inside-Out is at its core about breaking down barriers, stereotypes, and stigmas. Familial engagement comes from properly understanding the value of a comprehensive education and can help alleviate fears for children's safety, especially if the family already knows the reality of a bad education. Think Tanks/Theory Groups work to showcase the ability we as an organization possess, as well as to encourage those invited to be involved. Showing how important their participation and input is, these groups encourage community members to "trust the process" as we do, and that trust creates opportunities for others to come into contact with it and trust it themselves.

Let me give you an example. I am a member of the Michigan Inside-Out Theory Group. Building on our shared recognition that education is a lifelong activity, it has been my privilege to have helped plan and conduct conferences, workshops, trainings, and to have aided in the formation of networks with all manner of individuals.

The Confined Minds Conference, the Theory Group's inaugural event (see Appendix for the full program), reached all the way to Washington DC, when Representative John Conyers agreed to be one of our keynote speakers. With each function hosted, we have continued to spread the idea of Inside-Out. We have hosted community leaders, corrections and law enforcement officials, media, state and federal legislators, court officers, formerly incarcerated people, and even the families of some of our group members. One outside member commented on how her family's perception of her involvement changed after attending a function focusing on restorative justice. She cried when she was able to relay how proud her family is of her work and how they look forward to hearing stories of the Theory Group now. I personally feel extraordinarily proud to have helped make such an impact upon the family of one of our members. I wish all our families could experience what hers did.

The Theory Group hopes to inspire our instructors and outside alumni to engage in even more outreach and social change. Plans for the future include ways to monitor these activities, as well as maintaining networks to provide a resource for those who want to take their work farther or need help dealing with particular problems. We look upon all of these things as part of our responsibility as a leadership group within the larger Inside-Out family.

Conclusion

Inside-Out was and is the catalyst for positive educational change in Michigan's Department of Corrections. Some of our past trainees have gone on to facilitate classes in prisons all over the state, in other states, and in other countries as well. Some focus on juvenile facilities, others on unrelated programs with educational orientations; some have become professors themselves. This movement is organic and powerful. It has had its fits and starts, has faced challenges and looks forward to more. But in the end, we are going to help solve the problems that face our educational system, and continue providing safe spaces for people to drop their barriers and allow the people they really are inside to meet the world and vice versa. We will do this because we know two things. One, we have to start where we are. Two, if no one does anything, the problems we face can never be solved. Inside-Out is facing those problems head on.

References

Anyon, Jean. "Social Class and the Hidden Curriculum of Work." *Journal of Education* 162 (1980): 67–92; http://cuip.uchicago.edu/~cac/nlu/fnd504/anyon.htm. Accessed June 13, 2013.

Freire, Paulo. *Pedagogy of the Oppressed, 30th Anniversary Edition*. Translated by Myra Bergman Ramos. 30th Anniversary. New York: Bloomsbury Academic, 2000.

Livengood, Chad. "More is Less in Snyder's School Funding Plan." *Detroit News*. February 15, 2013, sec. 1A.

Palmer, Parker J. *The Courage to Teach: Exploring the Inner Landscape of a Teacher's Life*. San Francisco: John Wiley, 1997.

Wilson, Woodrow. "The Meaning of a Liberal Education." Wikisource. http://en.wikisource.org/wiki/The_Meaning_of_a_Liberal_Education. Accessed June 11, 2013.

Related Material

"Waiting for 'Superman.'" *TakePart*. http://www.takepart.com/waiting-for-superman. Accessed June 11, 2013.

CHAPTER 8

Opened Arms, Eyes, and Minds

Charles Boyd

We shall not cease from exploration,
And the end of all our exploring
Will be to arrive where we started,
And know the place for the first time.

T. S. Eliot

One great joy of mine has been to serve as part of a supporting cast for the many professors who have come from afar to Philadelphia each year since 2004 to take an intense educational excursion into the Temple University Inside-Out Instructor Training Institute. The distinct privilege of meeting and working alongside courageous souls who are committed to a noble humanitarian effort—"teaching"—has continuously inspired me to strive toward moral excellence.

Typically, two to three days of the week-long training are conducted about an hour from Philadelphia at the State Correctional Institution at Graterford. On those days, I join with other alumni of Inside-Out courses to meet with the facilitators and professors in the prison's auditorium. With its archaic feel, paint chipping off the walls, and long, dusty red velvet curtains (to keep out the sunlight when movies are shown during holidays), this is "the spot" within the prison where each of the organizations takes turns holding their monthly meetings. The well-known Mural Arts Program also uses this space as a work site for the incarcerated artists here who are a pivotal part of their Community Outreach Project. Many other activities occur here: live band performances, lectures, Bingo (for the old heads), and Inside-Out community-based workshops. This is also "the spot" where Inside-Out convenes with participating faculty and other educators and stakeholders as part of the now international Inside-Out Instructor Training Institute.

We have shared some sweltering summer days together with only a working lunch and a few breaks in between. We have labored, taken a moment to get our bearings, laughed, and even shed a few tears. These trainings are designed to give trainees the experience of an Inside-Out classroom and prepare them to lead their own courses, and we all take turns teaching and learning, as we evolve individually and collectively.

The teachers I have met all had passion long before our paths crossed. What is distinctly different after taking the training is that some now have additional skill-sets, including empathetic listening, the confidence to step outside of comfort zones, and strategies to engage diverse learners. Others reignite and hone skills they already had.

I have come to view these educators as revolutionaries: there is no telling what the future holds for the people they encounter during each of their careers. As the participants, whether instructors, students, or alumni, become "agents of change," they impact an array of others in their worlds, creating a chain reaction as those whom they have influenced will also begin to touch the lives of others. Now, with all this movement—a constant flow of positive and creative energy—the world cannot help but shift right along with us.

During the Training Institute, educators often express concerns about their effectiveness. Even after many years as teachers, they may fear that they are losing their touch or their ability to keep participants engaged. In addition to familiarizing faculty with specific facilitation tools and experiential activities, the training creates a safe space for and supports the healthy practice of questioning ourselves every so often, to ensure that we are still fresh, engaging, and current. In the trainings, we discover firsthand—or rediscover—how essential it is to be prepared, flexible, and comfortable in one's own skin; we reconnect with what it was that inspired us to become educators.

I stumbled across an article last year in the *Christian Science Monitor* about teacher evaluation/performance that asked, "How do you evaluate the essence of a teacher who inspires a true love of learning and problem solving versus one who just gets students to master certain concepts?" (27). Although the article focused on elementary schools, the question resonated with scores of conversations I have had during trainings. One thing I know for certain, the self-examination process in which these educators were absorbed was not predicated on any form of external evaluation given by their universities. Their inquiries were based on each teacher's personal desire to be the most effective educator possible. Each was invested in their students having a life-changing educational experience.

But is that the best focus for the instructor? Not every participant in an Inside-Out circle will undergo a profound learning experience. What about the participants who are having problems at home or outside of the classroom? What about those who face peer pressure, bullying, racism, extreme poverty, or the distortions of extreme privilege: will they be able to take full advantage of the opportunities presented? What about those who simply do not want to be in school? It would be unjust for educators to evaluate their own effectiveness in terms of their capacity to reach a person whose challenges may extend well beyond their scope.

For those attending a training, perhaps the revitalization happens when the educator zeroes in on becoming more engaged him- or herself, more fully present in the classroom circle, and more able to gain from life's many lessons. I recall one professor, a middle-aged white woman who taught African American History at a historically black college. To me, she appeared almost apologetic for having been born a white female, for caring and wanting to make a difference in this world. Because of her skin, she was associated with oppression, and because she was highly valued by her administration and taught Black History, she was thought by some students to be further perpetuating white supremacy. She felt frustrated and disconnected. I well recall how her confidence soared over the week of training and, by Day Six, she was eager to get back to the classroom. She had become acutely aware of the value of an experiential approach, and of the subtle contrast between *teaching at* and *drawing from* the participants' knowledge and experience. She saw how this facilitation style could keep the climate in the classroom relational, current, live, and engaging.

"Professors who embrace the challenges of self-actualization will be better able to create pedagogical practices that engage students, providing them with ways of knowing that enhance their capacity to live fully and deeply" (hooks 22). The art of teaching echoes our life's journey. In life, we learn as we go along, often from our own and others' mistakes; life itself is a university of sorts. As we gain more clarity about who we are, we begin to view ourselves as well as others as essential parts of this bigger picture. This is part of the skill-set that the instructor training provides: together, we discover in a new way that, for those we encounter in the classrooms to be fully engaged, the educator must be fully engaged, as well. Everything starts with the tempo being set by the educator. His or her vocation is in part to provide a safe space where participants can speak from the heart, to clarify the existing boundaries and, within those boundaries, to open up themselves and share portions of their own narratives. If the instructor lets herself be open and genuine about her motivations for teaching, then once the participants become somewhat familiar with her story and feel her committed presence, conditions are created for shifts in values, perceptions, assumptions, and consciousness to emerge. Thus, although educators provide the glue that holds the class together, their role as facilitators does not preclude their own growth. It helps when they view themselves as being just as much participants in the learning process as those who are taking the classes.

"When I enter the classroom at the beginning of the semester, the weight is on me to establish that our purpose is to be, for however brief a time, a community of learners together," explains bell hooks (153). What I find is that Inside-Out removes the barriers that impede the possibility of a relational atmosphere where everyone is equal. It rejects the top-down approach that is anathema to genuine teaching-learning. Real education occurs as we begin to see ourselves as able to learn with and from every person in the room. I know I can make the same claim for myself. Above all, Inside-Out is a shared experience. As one grows, we all grow.

References

bell hooks, *Teaching to Transgress: Education as the Practice of Freedom*. New York: Routledge Publishing, 1994.

Paulson, Amanda. "The Measure of a Teacher." *The Christian Science Monitor Weekly*, August 13, 2012, 27.

CHAPTER 9

Full Circle: A Journey from Students to Trainers

Mario Carines

Walking to my very first Inside-Out class back in January 2009, I could not have imagined that a couple of years later, as part of an extended family, I would be assisting in the training of future Inside-Out instructors. For me, and for the rest of the Inside-Out alumni who form the Michigan Theory Group (TG), the student–trainer transition has been characterized by a collective willingness to make the program work. We accept and embrace our diversity; we value and benefit from the different skills each one of us has to offer; we compromise when our views conflict; and we strive to improve ourselves through ongoing dialogue, practice, and study.[1]

What is it about Inside-Out that motivates us to invest so much? If I had to use one word, it would be "love." The Theory Group follows the core structure of The Inside-Out Prison Exchange Program: a circle in which each participant has a voice. This key structure nurtures respect, appreciation, and dignity among participants. Within this space, I have found that the commonality of our imperfections strengthens our bonds and helps us to advance together. Our diverse membership includes people with a General Educational Development (GED), with some college credits, and with doctorates; one can find differences in race, gender, age, ethnicity, culture, and religious beliefs. For all of us, both inside and outside members, the TG is an intellectual and caring environment where everyone's humanity is celebrated.

This communion between supposedly polar opposites, inside and outside, is generally prohibited in prison and rare in the outside world. What is our perception of routine relations between prison staff and incarcerated men and women? When was the last time we heard of billionaires breaking bread with homeless people? Not surprisingly, the origin of the Inside-Out program in a Michigan men's prison was itself the result of selflessness and dedication from a group of incarcerated women at the Scott Correctional Facility. They had been studying college-level courses with Dr. Lora Lempert since 2002. Lempert explains:

In 2006, the American Association of University Women [granted an award] to a college program that Lora Lempert had initiated...The award came with a $5000 honorarium. The women, often incarcerated "behind a man"—that is, they killed abusive husbands, were aiders and abettors to a male partner's criminality, or were duped and used by drug dealing men who left the women holding the metaphorical "bag"—voted unanimously to use the money to "take [the program] to the men." In recognition of the generosity of the females incarcerated for life, Lempert focused recruitment for the first Inside-Out class on the male lifers. (Draus and Lempert 2013, 1)

Lempert contacted the National Lifers of America (NLA) men's chapter at the Ryan Correctional Facility in Detroit. After a year of negotiations with the Michigan Department of Corrections (MDOC), the program started in fall 2007 with 15 outside students from the University of Michigan-Dearborn and 15 incarcerated NLA members.

As is typical in Inside-Out, the class opened with a "wagon wheel" icebreaker, challenging stereotypes from the very first moment. Next, the class divided into small groups, sharing colored papers, markers, and other materials to individually represent each person's identity. During the second part of the exercise, each small group constructed a quilt out of the representations they had created. Finally, each group presented their quilt to the rest of the class.

These first-day activities and circle format set the tone for the rest of the semester. Lectures were followed by interactive exercises relevant to the day's topic. The homework assignments encouraged the students to recognize the significance of the academic subjects, the process, and their own socialization within the classroom. Both inside and outside students were graded under the University of Michigan-Dearborn standards, and the course culminated with group projects and presentations in a graduation ceremony.

A week later at a debriefing session, all outside graduates expressed a sense of loss and the wish that the semester could have continued. Luckily, after joining the National Inside-Out Steering Committee a few months following the class completion, Lempert realized that her alumni could continue to assist the program. "Thus, the congruency of Lempert's need for the institutional knowledge and the expertise of the inside students as well as the inside students' desire for 'more' continuous intellectual engagement motivated the establishment of the Theory Group" (Draus and Lempert 2013, 3).The initial plan was to meet once a month for a continuation of the theoretical discussions begun in the Inside-Out class and to respond to Steering Committee initiatives. A few outside alumni from the same Inside-Out class joined the TG; together, inside and outside members began their academic work with Erving Goffman's concept of total institutions (1961) and C. Wright Mills' *Sociological Imagination* (1959). These works generated discussions that transitioned from reflection on one's own confinement to analysis of criminal justice policy and the causes of mass incarceration. The group studied the intersections between gender and race (Crenshaw, 1995) and read Karl Marx as preparation for other subjects.

In January 2009, a few months after its inception, alumni from the second Inside-Out class, facilitated by Dr. Paul Draus, joined the Theory Group. Surprisingly, the merger gave rise to competition and friction between the two classes. Reminiscent of early kung fu movies, each side claimed that their respective teacher's style was better. At the TG meetings, they did their best to outshine each other and to dominate the conversation. Reggie, a former member, said that the conflict also arose from differences in age, with the second class enrolling mostly younger students.

The rivalry lasted several months. One inside participant, Matt, felt that the division was a sad regression to "old habits" in light of all the relevant sociological theory we had read and discussed. Steve, an outside member, was concerned about the effect of prison politics on the integrity of the program. At the same time, the nature and structure of the TG compelled all members to collaborate as a team and to listen to each other's opinions and ideas. As some members recalled, this practice in itself encouraged conflict resolution:

> Lynn and I have not always seen things the same way, and at the time I felt that we had different goals for the Theory Group. Sometimes we engaged in heated debates about which class was better. Over time, we realized that our feud wasn't helping. The Theory Group was too important for us. So, both of us toned down our emotions and worked together for the sake of the program. (Donald, inside member)

While the TG navigated these tensions, Lempert also facilitated the third Inside-Out class, into which I was accepted as a student. After graduation, Lempert explained that there were some spots available in the TG. Thus, in June 2009, about 18 months after it was created, I attended my first Theory Group meeting. Once the greetings subsided, Lempert distributed loose-leaf copies of a chapter from Ervin Goffman's *Asylums* (1961), which the group was revisiting. She instructed us to read it, write an essay on it, and be ready to discuss it at the next meeting.

Most of the concepts Goffman used to describe total institutions more than half a century ago remain relevant to our carceral environment: "storage dumps," "contradiction in goals," and "effective machines." Subsequent discussions about the relationship of society and prison culture revealed social divisions that lead us to create invisible prisons in the outside world. We also talked about the TG's potential role in bringing awareness to our communities in order to spark alternative approaches to crime and justice.

At the time I joined, the TG was in the beginning stages of planning a conference on the importance of higher education in prison. It would take place the following year in the gymnasium and adjacent classrooms. The nearly 11-month time frame we had to get ready turned out to be just right given the many aspects we had to consider, including the prison's security concerns. Our goal was to host 70–90 guests and to conduct four different workshops throughout the day, culminating in a general discussion (see the Appendix for the conference program).

By general consensus, we titled the conference "Confined Minds: Incarceration-Education-Transformation." We focused on discussing the transformative power of higher education in prison. We also wanted to bring attention to the impact that educated incarcerated people have on the communities to which they return upon release. For this purpose, we invited former incarcerated men and women to speak about their achievements and contributions to society. We also sent out invitations to judges, journalists, community leaders, and MDOC personnel. Outside TG members followed up with confirmations and contacted potential panelists identified on our guest list to arrange their participation. Lempert negotiated the security issues with the MDOC. Inside members created posters illustrating various relevant topics and prepared to facilitate group discussions, moderate panels, and serve as emcees. Other tasks included creating name tags for members and guests, participating in the various discussions, greeting guests, and overseeing food preparation and delivery.

With more than one hundred guests in attendance, the conference was a success. Once the closing ceremony was completed and the guests had left, all of us in the TG gathered in the middle of the gymnasium, standing around in a circle sharing our thoughts. In that moment, we felt like a family. One of our members reflected on the conference's significance:

> From my perspective, the conflict in the beginning was simply a lack of trust. Not knowing what each person brought to the table; not trusting that we are all on the same page. I believe we got through it under the umbrella of the Theory Group carrying out the assigned tasks. We as a whole kept our focus on what we had set to accomplish. Once the conference was over and we got the feedback from the attendees, we realized we could trust one another to perform when called to task. I learned it takes team work to progress and to make a difference. That trust is powerful. (Jemal, inside member)

We still had disagreements, of course, but we had a new collective purpose and increased trust in each other's abilities. Outside the classroom, TG members often met in the prison yard to talk about various themes related to the things we were learning. We also shared our newly gained knowledge with other incarcerated individuals with whom we came in contact. As a result, whenever a new Inside-Out class was formed, dozens of hopefuls would sign up for it.

Inspired by the conference, Michigan State Senator Michael Switalski generously offered to teach a separate sociology class on drugs, crime, and justice to the Inside-Out alumni, including TG members. In that 2010 fall semester, we read and discussed various books, wrote essays, and participated in debates. Some memorable books from this course include Upton Sinclair's classic *The Jungle* (1906), *Medical Apartheid* (Washington, 2006), and the *Autobiography of Malcolm X* (Haley, 1973).

Switalski's curriculum instilled in us a sense of the confrontations that take place in the legislative branch when discussing public policy. The assignments required us to consider legislative history, weigh competing interests for law creation, and analyze the potential dilemmas politicians face when forced to compromise their principles. At the TG, we also studied the *Handbook of Restorative Justice: A Global Perspective* (Sullivan and Tift, 2006). The benefits that restorative justice practice provides to communities around the world motivated us to plan a workshop on the subject. Building on the success of the "Confined Minds" conference, we wanted to heighten public awareness of restorative justice as an alternative to retributive justice and connect restorative justice experts with activists and other professionals who would benefit from learning about restorative justice principles and practice. Since Draus was also a member of the Detroit City Council Task Force on Prisoner Reentry, he assisted us in organizing the workshop from the outside. The guest list included former prosecutors, judges, victims of violent crime, formerly incarcerated people, social workers, activists, and academics. Meanwhile, we put together the activities program and created posters illustrating the relevant topics (Draus and Lempert, 2013, 11).

During the workshop we conducted "fishbowl" discussions, in which dialogue takes place in a small circle surrounded by listeners in an outer circle; after a designated period of time, participants switch circles. These fishbowls were facilitated by inside and outside members. We concluded with a full-circle conversation concerning the significance of the small group discussions. About a week later, Lempert brought in the gratifying responses from the guests. Another successful event!

Around this time, Lempert announced an upcoming opportunity for us to hold an Inside-Out Instructor Training. She explained that about 20 potential Inside-Out instructors, primarily university professors, would be attending the training. Since we had been designated as one of the regional training centers, the trainees would come from Michigan and neighboring states.

As Matt Soares explains in chapter 25, many of us were anxious about a trainer–trainee intellectual gap. Most of us had only a few college credits to our name, but our trainees were professors. How would they perceive us? Would we be able to connect with them? After these concerns were expressed in our meetings, we were glad to know that the preparation materials addressed these issues. Parker Palmer's *The Courage to Teach* (1998) provided the answers we needed and inspired us to take a leap of faith. Palmer explains how the prevalence of fear in our culture, including within our educational system, often prevents educators from connecting with students; this separation, in turn, prevents students from developing a relationship with the subjects they study, which can result in a lack of motivation and essential social skills. He invites us to look within ourselves and recognize those fears that paralyze our creativity and prevent us from connecting with others:

> Fear is so fundamental to the human condition that all the great spiritual traditions originate in an effort to overcome its effects on our lives. . . Though the traditions vary widely in the ways they propose to take us beyond fear, all hold out the same hope: We can escape fear's paralysis and enter a state of grace where encounters with otherness will not threaten us but will enrich our work and lives. (Palmer, 57)

During the actual training, the attending trainees would form small groups, and each group would create a 30-minute classroom activity which they would then conduct with the whole group. The purpose of this exercise would be for the instructors to familiarize themselves with the Inside-Out pedagogy and to get ideas for creating experiential learning activities for their future classes. Our jobs, Lempert said, would be to coach the instructors-in-training through the process while allowing them to come up with their own ideas for the projects. To prepare for the task, we did a practice run, forming small groups of TG members and creating 30-minute activities ourselves. The pressures associated with creating this activity—personality differences, a firm deadline, the desire for originality, and prison restrictions—gave rise to friction among some group members. In my group, for example, we had a dispute about which idea to implement and experienced discord and frustration.

For the practice presentation of these activities, Lori Pompa came all the way from Pennsylvania to help Lempert evaluate our performance. At one point, Pompa invited my group to share our frustrations with the class. This gave us an opportunity to explain the source of the disagreements, to vent our frustrations, to objectively evaluate our feelings, and to learn from that experience. It was also an occasion to apply the restorative justice concepts we had learned to a real life situation. The effects of this dialogue were instantaneous. Immediately after the session, my group members and I shook hands and shared laughs. The conflict and its eventual resolution gave us the ability to envision potential conflicts in the actual training and the tools to deal with them effectively.

A few days before the training, after becoming familiar with the Inside-Out Instructor's Manual and the Inside-Out Curriculum, we had another visit from Lori and Inside-Out Associate Director Melissa Crabbe. They helped us to brainstorm facilitation practices and addressed last minute questions. Pompa gave us additional reading materials, including an excerpt from Paulo Freire and Myles Horton's *We Make the Road by Walking: The Formative Years* (1990). This text delighted us with its enlightening simplicity. While struggling to develop an adult literacy education program in rural United States, Horton realized that the best approach was to merely "find a place, move in, and start, and let it grow." As the people began to learn from each other, Horton helped them to develop a successful curriculum based on their needs and dreams. Horton's work helped us contemplate the human values that are essential for the creation of a dialogical learning environment. This in turn eased our minds and increased our trust in the Inside-Out training process.

The week-long training took place both outside and inside the prison, and the three-day inside component included icebreakers, circle interactions, pedagogy discussions, and group activities. One of the most significant aspects of the training was the conversation between TG members and instructors about the educational system, history, sociology, philosophy, and many other subjects. We were ecstatic to have an intellectually acute audience who could understand and appreciate our educational journey.

From these interactions, the instructors also perceived the healing and transformational potential that Inside-Out and other educational programs can have, not only on incarcerated individuals but on all those who come from the outside. Many trainees reported experiencing a radical change in the way they thought about people who are incarcerated.

Our participation in the training added a new dimension to our understanding of the Inside-Out program. As students, we discovered new ways of thinking about social justice. As trainers, we understood the process that created this dialogical encounter along with the theories that make it possible.

Several TG members subsequently related to me their most memorable experiences in the training. Steve spoke about the bonds that he was able to develop in such a short period of time with the trainees, and the inspiration he drew from reading Palmer's work. Donald said the wagon-wheel ice breaker was significant because it was so much fun and made everyone feel at ease, setting the stage for all that followed. Cowboy was moved by the level of emotion expressed by the trainees. After only three days of training exercises, we felt that we were saying goodbye to family members, and the trainees felt the same way. The experience, cohesion, and confidence we gained from training strengthened our desire to continue expanding our knowledge and organizing events for the advancement of higher education in prison.

After the training, we continued our Restorative Justice studies, transitioning from Sullivan and Tifft's *Global Perspective* (2006) to Cheryl Swanson's *Restorative Justice in Prison Communities* (2009). In November 2011, we held a two-day conference entitled "Restorative Justice: Working Together for a Safer Michigan." The University of Michigan-Dearborn hosted the first day of the conference on campus. There, the guests examined the obstacles and opportunities for implementing restorative justice through real policy change. On the second day, the conference continued inside the prison with four breakout sessions where we considered restorative justice in corrections, for juveniles, the role of faith communities, and the possibilities for legislative action. Attendance exceeded 150 people. Rock, a TG inside member, reflected:

Reaching a goal is such a wonderful feeling. It gives me the motivation to do more. The sky is the limit! No matter how much I learn, with each new experience, I find myself discovering new ways of looking at things. I find that empowering.

Six months later, in May 2012, we held our second Inside-Out Instructor Training, which turned out to be very emotional due to the imminent termination of the Inside-Out program at the Ryan Correctional Facility. The prison's transition to a different custody level required the transfer of more than ninety percent of the incarcerated population, including most of the inside TG members. Fortunately, thanks to Lempert's efforts, the nearby Macomb Correctional Facility agreed to house the Inside-Out program, and after a few months, most of our membership ended up transferring there. Our first meeting at this new facility was ecstatic. After sharing our thoughts, we resumed our studies with Saul Alinsky's *Reveille for Radicals* (1989). A few weeks later, we held a workshop to debate what a society without prisons would look like. A month after that, we hosted a regional Inside-Out Think Tank Hub Meeting to exchange ideas about how to improve the Inside-Out curriculum.

At various times, we have had the privilege of interacting with accomplished writers and educators who have taken the time from their schedules to come inside the prison to meet with us. Danielle L. McGuire, author of *At the Dark End of the Street* (2010), answered our questions and signed copies of her book. Sister Helen Prejean talked about her experiences and her book *Dead Man Walking* (1994). Restorative Justice Trainer Henry McClendon Jr. gave us an informative restorative justice orientation. Hui Hui Tung offered an enlightening poetry workshop.

The contributions from our outside members have been invaluable. Aside from their significant participation in meetings and events, they always help us with needed research and have represented us at state and national Inside-Out events. Just as they inspire us to improve, we inspire them with our commitment and desire for growth. Their voice is our voice.

Similarly, for us it would be impossible to envision the Theory Group without the devotion of Professors Lora Lempert and Paul Draus. Facilitators but also fellow members, they share our commitment to be active participants in the pursuit of social change and the creation of a more humane and just world.

Our Theory Group will continue to have disagreements and occasional disappointments. However, we believe in the Inside-Out process for resolving our conflicts, finding common ground, and increasing our trust. Together, we look forward to expanding our knowledge, sharing the Inside-Out philosophy, and advancing higher education. The essence of our journey has been captured by one of our own poets in a haiku:

a sapling grows
nurtured with wisdom
to a mighty oak. (Jay, inside member)

Note

1. I want to express appreciation to fellow TG members and former members Reggie and A'don, who shared their perspectives on the early history of the TG, and to Professors Lora Lempert and Paul Draus, for their selfless commitment to the Theory Group, and whose article "Growing Pains" (*Prison Journal* 93, no. 2 (2013): 139–162) provided another important source of information.

References

Alinski, Saul D. *Reveille for Radicals.* New York: Vintage, 1989.

Crenshaw, Kimberle. "Mapping the Margins: Intersectionality, Identity Politics, and Violence Against Women of Color." In *Critical Race Theory.* Edited by Kimberle Crenshaw, Niel Gotanda, Gary Peller, and Kendall Thomas, 357–83. New York: New Press, 1995.

Freire, Paulo. *Pedagogy of the Oppressed.* New York: Continuum, 1997.

Freire, Paulo and Myles Horton. *We Make the Road by Walking: Conversations on Education and Social Change.* Philadelphia: Temple University Press, 1991.

Goffman, Erving. *Asylums: Essays on the Social Situation of Mental Patients and Other Inmates.* New York: Double Day, 1961.

Haley, Alex and Malcolm X. *The Autobiography of Malcolm X, as told to Alex Haley.* New York: Ballantine, 1973.

Lempert, Laura and Paul Draus. "Growing Pains: Developing Collective Efficacy in the Detroit Theory Group." *The Prison Journal.* Pre-published January 24, 2013. DOI: 10.1177/0032885512472691.

McGuire, Danielle L. *At the Dark End of the Street: Black Women, Rape, and Resistance—A New History of the Civil Rights Movement from Rosa Parks to the Rise of Black Power.* New York: Vintage, 2010.

Mills, C. Wright. *The Sociological Imagination.* New York: Oxford Unviersity Press, 1959.

Palmer, Parker J. *The Courage to Teach: Exploring the Inner Landscape of a Teacher's Life.* San Francisco: Jossey-Bass, 1998.

Pompa, Lori and Melissa Crabbe. *Inside-Out Instructor's Manual: Inside-Out Prison Exchange Program.* Philadelphia: Temple University Press, 2012.

Prejean, Helen. *Dead Man Walking.* New York: Vintage, 1994.

Sinclair, Upton. *The Jungle.* 1906; NY: Penguin, 2006.

Sullivan, Dennis and Larry Tifft, eds. *Handbook of Restorative Justice: A Global Perspective.* New York: Routledge, 2006.

Swanson, Cheryl G. *Restorative Justice in a Prison Community: Or Everything I Didn't Learn in Kindergarten I Learned in Prison.* Lanham, MD: Lexington Books, 2009.

Washington, Harriet A. *Medical Apartheid : The Dark History of Medical Experimentation on Black Americans from Colonial Times to the Present.* New York: Doubleday, 2006.

CHAPTER 10

Teaching Itself: A Philosophical Exploration of Inside-Out Pedagogy

Gitte Wernaa Butin

Introduction

"It's like the 'fish-bowl,'" said one of the incarcerated men to clarify a point about prison life. While I was not completely sure what the term "fish-bowl" referred to, I was certain that if I asked for clarification, the class session would no longer be a stable, controlled event. The classroom in question was a community-based learning setting which brings undergraduate (outside) students and incarcerated (inside) students on work-release together for a three-session component of an introductory level contemporary moral issues philosophy class. How many of us really knew what the "fish-bowl" was? How much did I as the teacher want control? I decided to ask for clarification.

The inside student explained how prisoners were occasionally placed in a glass box in the center of the correctional facility, in view of both correctional officers and others incarcerated there, while wearing a relatively transparent paper gown. The official rationale is to maximize efficiency when observing people who may be suicidal or violent. According to the inside students, however, the "fish-bowl" is also used in more borderline cases to address prisoner resistance. This discussion of the "fish-bowl" destabilized our presuppositions about criminal justice and the very mode of engagement in the classroom. Yet the question of the legitimacy of the device was not the only thing that changed the mood of the class. What truly transformed our discussion was the context of the dialogue, a context that negated neither the differences nor the similarities among everyone present. Suddenly, almost everybody uncrossed their arms and legs and leaned forward. The dialogue surged. Learning happened for all of us; and some sort of liberation happened as well. It was a moment of what I have come to call "teaching itself."

This chapter explores a version of The Inside-Out Prison Exchange Program approach within an undergraduate philosophy classroom. It argues that Inside-Out's nontraditional liberatory classroom practice is designed to engender such moments of "teaching itself." Critical pedagogy often assumes that the possibility of promoting "social justice" in and through the classroom is a rational and dialogical endeavor in which power relations are overcome by virtue of being made transparent. With Elizabeth Ellsworth, this article asks, instead, "What diversity is silenced in the name of 'liberatory' pedagogy?" And how can we still strive for liberation? While I generally use the term "we" to refer to the participants in the college course, when I ask how we can strive for liberation, I also use the term "we" as in "all of us"—students, educators, engaged citizens—who care about liberation in all its complex intellectual and emotional forms.

The pedagogy of Inside-Out, I argue, creates the conditions of possibility for intellectual, emotional, and academic liberation in two ways: 1) it suppresses neither the differences nor the similarities of the diverse group, using difference as a source of synergy; and 2) it displaces the content and responsibility of learning away from the instructor onto the learners, both as individuals and as a learning community. In the process, presuppositions about education are disturbed, making learning an embodied, empowering set of practices.

As such, this pedagogy and its philosophical underpinnings address the current debate in the philosophy of education concerning the role of student voice and empowerment. I first trace the general stakes of this debate, from critical theory's rejection of the "banking system of education" to poststructuralist feminist challenges to critical theory. I then link this debate to the pedagogy of "Inside-Out."

The Quandary: From "Cold-Storage Knowledge" to Transgressive Modes of Teaching

The Stakes of the Debate

Critical theorists and poststructuralist feminists agree on the failure of an education that reduces learning to a teacher depositing knowledge, in more or less sophisticated ways, into the student. This paradigm can be summed up with Dewey's phrase: "static, cold-storage knowledge," and it has been labeled by Freire (1974) "the banking system of education." Although most contemporary educators would say they reject this paradigm, we would be wise to ask ourselves on a regular basis: "Exactly how much of what I do in the classroom is grounded in a model of linear knowledge transfer? And how well do these practices work?"

As an alternative to the banking system, critical theorists such as Paulo Freire, Henry Giroux, and Peter McLaren envision liberatory pedagogy as a transformation of the social order in the interest of justice, equality, democracy, and human freedom (see, for example, Freire 1974; Giroux 1983; Hill et al. 2002; McLaren 1998). Specifically, this means developing pedagogical practices centering on analysis and rejection of structures of oppression, injustice, and inequality and empowering otherwise silenced and marginalized student voices (see Biesta 1998; hooks 1994). The presupposition is that enlightenment concerning one's situation will bring about the conditions of possibility of emancipation. In this project, knowledge and self-knowledge become dialectically linked. In short, the critical project is heavily invested in both the Marxist project of liberation from oppression and the larger Enlightenment and modernist projects, each premised on the positive valorization of reason, critical reflexivity, universality, and progress. While the flawed nature of reason is acknowledged, reason is nonetheless considered inherently positive because, regardless of the problems reason creates, the solution to the problems is employing more sophisticated reason, primarily expressed in the form of rational dialogue.

But what happens when classroom dialogue does not feel liberating? The debate within education between critical theorists and poststructuralist feminists intensified with the publication of Elizabeth Ellsworth's 1992 article, "Why Doesn't This Feel Empowering?" (see also Biesta 1998; Burbules 2000; Carlson 1998; Ellsworth 1992; Lather 1998). Ellsworth (1992) launches the following criticism against critical pedagogy:

> The pedagogical practices fundamental to the literature on critical pedagogy…are repressive myths that perpetuate relations of domination. By this I mean that when participants in our class attempted to put into practice prescriptions offered in the literature concerning empowerment, student voice, and dialogue, we produced results that were not only unhelpful, but actually exacerbated the very conditions we were trying to work against, including Euro-centrism, racism, sexism, classism, and "banking education." (91)

Ellsworth attacks critical pedagogy on a number of counts: from making itself invisible, to its inability to fulfill its own ideal of liberation, to the oppression generated, paradoxically, from this ideal. Ellsworth's counter-move can be summed up in her question: "What diversity do you silence in the name of 'liberatory' pedagogy?" To Ellsworth, critical theory's view of empowerment is ultimately an ahistorical and depoliticized abstraction, a humanism that has become too broad.

Empowerment—For What and For Whom?

The "pedagogy of empowerment" is obviously intended to liberate. However, it is based on the potentially not so liberating assumption that the agent of empowerment, in this case the teacher, is distinct from the subject of empowerment, in this case the student. In the model promoted by critical pedagogy, claims Ellsworth, the authoritarian structure of the teacher/student relation is left intact, thus promoting only the illusion of equality.

Asking for "empowerment" is a necessary but not sufficient move. What is required, demands Ellsworth, is not an ameliorative strategy of "fixing" Enlightenment reason with a dose of "better" reason. What is needed, instead, are "context specific practices" and "pedagogical modes of address that aren't founded on striving for and desiring certainty, continuity, and control" (Ellsworth 1992). The goal is to "become capable of sustained encounter with currently oppressive formations and power relations that refuse to be theorized away" (Ellsworth quoted in Burbules 2000, 10). I consider Inside-Out to be one such set of practices, which readily admits and indeed productively utilizes the acknowledgement that 1) everybody is implicated in perpetuating knowledge structures, and 2) the goal of the class is to support everybody in becoming capable of tolerating the "sustained encounter" with this cultural fact.

The contribution of poststructuralist thought to education resides, according to Ellsworth (1992), in the recognition that rational discourse is permanently partial and indeed must be interrupted by voices that resist being recuperated by the rules of reason, voices that speak from the position of the experience of personal oppression and outrage. These positions are "partial in the sense of being unfinished, imperfect, and limited, and partial in the sense that they project the interest of one side over others" (97). The partiality and partisanship must be examined, maintains Ellsworth, but "not because [these voices] broke rules of reason by grounding their knowledge in immediate emotional, social, and psychic experiences of oppression, but because they hold implications for other social movements and their struggles for self-definition" (97). Inside-Out, I suggest, can contribute to the rethinking of how such a project exceeds and interrupts the rules of reason in both theory and practice. Additionally, we must inquire into the advantages and disadvantages of this interruption. To address this dimension of the debate, I now turn to a discussion of dialogue as pedagogical strategy.

Disturbing Dialogue and "Student Voice"

The debate between poststructuralist feminism and critical theory hinges on the significance of "student voice" and the larger issue of the role of dialogue as educational tool and end. The debate's crux is whether or not dialogue ultimately possesses its own corrective by virtue of its self-reflexivity. While neither perspective rejects dialogue and "student voice," they differ in how these categories are qualified.

Critical theory emphasizes the importance, for members of marginalized identity groups in particular, of "finding a voice." The implication is that "those who previously have been silenced are empowered by reclaiming or finding a voice, one that allows them to articulate their rage at injustice, develop a social movement of empowerment, and enter into public conversations and struggles over public life" (Carlson 1998, 1).

The challenges to dialogue-as-empowerment-strategy are numerous: the fact of the empirical experience of the failure to become empowered through dialogue; the implicit and potentially unquestioned role of the mediator of the empowerment (the teacher) who in effect may be perpetuating disempowerment; and the valorization within the academic world of the analytical, reasonable voice over the personal voice (Burbules, 2000; Ellsworth, 1992). Both positions acknowledge these wedges, but their solutions to the dilemmas differ.

The critical theorists justify dialogue as inherently self-corrective: if dialogue becomes oppressive, we must resolve the oppression through more and better dialogue. If we dismiss dialogue, how can we hope to strive for open, respectful, and critical engagement (see Burbules 2000)? Don't we need the objectivity and universality implied in Enlightenment conceptions of dialogue to sustain this vision?

The poststructuralist feminists beg to differ. They question the means of arriving at such an ideal and doubt the inherently liberatory dimension of "reclaiming one's voice." "Voice," they argue, is not natural or unified but always intersectional: multiple subject positions—of gender, ethnicity, class, race—traverse our identities. Consequently, the finding and reclaiming of one's voice may take place at the expense of other equally oppressed voices.

Moreover, inviting others to find their voice may *also* be a matter of a voyeuristic desire. This has been convincingly argued by Alison Jones (2001), who analyzes her multiethnic classroom to show that notions such as "authentic voice" and "dialogue across differences" are produced by the desires of the majority group, the white students, who prefer dialogue and smaller breakout groups. The Maori and South-Pacific Island students appreciate a classroom in which they do not have to play the role of "Other." Referring to Jones' paper, Lather (1998) writes:

The colonizer's "infatuation with access to / unity with the other" is situated as the inability of majority students to see the limits of knowledge available to them and the inescapability of their collusion. Reading such desires on the part of majority students as a quest for redemption via a "Teach me! Love me" demand, Jones names this "cannibal desire to 'know the other' through being taught/ fed by her" as a voyeuristic refusal to know that the other may not want to be known. Jones concludes with a call for a "politics of disappointment," a practice of "failure, loss, confusion, unease, limitation for dominant ethnic groups" as a necessary aspect of critical pedagogy within epistemologies of uncertainty and multiplicity. (6)

How do we as teachers embrace a "practice of failure, loss, confusion, unease?" This is where we turn to Inside-Out.

The Inside-Out Prison Exchange Program

One of the purposes of Inside-Out is "to allow students and others outside of prison to go behind the walls to reconsider what they have learned about crime and justice, while those on the inside are encouraged to place their life experiences in a larger framework... the program rests on the belief that challenging individuals to stretch beyond simplistic assumptions will, over time, produce a transformation in public thought" (Pompa and Crabbe, 2004, 5–6). As Pompa argues in the opening chapter of this volume, Inside-Out is *not* an opportunity for charity, not a "doing for" but rather a "doing/being with... in which everyone serves and everyone is served" (Pompa and Crabbe, 2004, 8–9). It is ultimately presumptuous, writes Pompa, to "assume that anything that the outside students (or the instructor, for that matter) could 'do for' or 'give to' the inside students would be either desired or meaningful" (Pompa and Crabbe, 2004, 8–9). The inside students are not "people who need to be fixed" but human beings and students with contributions to make. In this framework, the instructor serves as a "site" for engaging situations involving feelings of disturbance, unease, and fear of being "othered." In short, the instructor has to embrace a pedagogy of uncertainty and disturbance as well.

Turning Stereotypes Inside-Out

I now turn to a discussion of my adaptation of the Inside-Out model. For four semesters, my Contemporary Moral Issues class met several times during the semester with people on work release at a local community organization. I also taught an upper-level philosophy course which focused entirely on imprisonment and liberation; this class met in joint fashion with the inside students throughout almost the entire semester. Generally, the undergraduate students made up two-thirds of the class, and the students from the local organization made up one-third. Additionally, the organization leader and a therapist who regularly worked with the men were present and participated on equal footing. Pompa's model was adapted to these classes because I teach in a different field (philosophy) although on occasion on a related matter (crime and punishment), and because the class met outside the correctional facility. I retained all other parameters of the Inside-Out model because of the safety they generate and I used several of its experiential learning exercises.[1]

The first session reflects on notions of time, of doing time, and time doing us; the second on the purposes and efficacy of punishment; and the third on victimization and harm. The third session's focus on victimization is a modification of an experiential classroom activity included in Pompa's curriculum. We begin by looking at a survey that students completed during the previous class reporting the number of incidents in which either oneself or a loved one has been the victim of a crime, the categories ranging from minor theft to rape and manslaughter. The numbers are always staggering: over the course of three semesters the average number of incidents each person has experienced is 1.8; the average number of incidents a loved one has experienced is 2.9. Instantaneously, it becomes obvious to all members of the class that crime affects almost everybody, both inside and outside students. Because the activity surfaces old hurts and much pain, this is a very fragile point in the class's journey together. While the experience of this sort of pain is not to be underestimated, it is my belief as well as experience that this session is extremely productive because it acknowledges something—the emotions surrounding harm—that people often think they need to hide. The communal acknowledgement brings a piece, however small that may be, to the healing process which we all can work through if we have been victimized. It is this experience of shared harm that underlies the move into the next even more unsettling part of the class.

The next phase of the activity owes much to Pompa's curriculum. It uses the language of "harm" that emerges out of restorative justice practice, rather than "crime," "victim," or "perpetrator," so as to shift participants' perspectives away from labels that come laden with stigma and accrued social meaning. Though time constraints prohibited me from doing this, the activity is intended to fall deep into the shared semester, at a point when inside and outside students have had the opportunity to build guidelines for safe dialogue and a shared sense of trust, familiarity, and respect. The instructor asks that the full exercise be carried out in silence, until a debrief at the close, which is conducted with inside and outside students together.

Forms are distributed in silence, with the assurance that one's reflections on these pages will not be turned in or shared with anyone. People are also instructed, in this memory work, to turn only to events in one's past that are not so charged that the writer will feel triggered or overly raw. The first form asks the individual to reflect on a time when she or he *witnessed* a harm being done to someone else. Questions are asked about what was seen and heard, how it felt at the time, what the student did in the moment, and what, if anything, the student lost—or gained—from this witnessing. Then the instructor asks students to quietly reflect on what they've written and to write a single summary word on a slip of paper, one that captures how they felt in the moment of witnessing. These anonymous slips are collected. In turn, two more such forms are filled out, one that focuses on a time the student *experienced* harm, and one on a time when the student *caused* harm to another person. After each, a single word capturing how each student felt is collected anonymously and placed in a bag or envelope.

The instructor then asks each student to pick one of the words from the bag and read it aloud, so that students give voice, not to their own, but to the collective experience. Ideally, the instructor writes these words on the board, so that they are collected in three distinct groupings: how it felt to witness harm, to experience it, and to cause it.

In silence, students are invited to reflect on what they see and to file up, if desired, to make circles, to draw lines or arrows—suggesting connections or significant observations about the compiled words. During the silent work and in the debrief conversation that then follows, the group often makes a startling discovery: many of the same words show up in all three categories. Whether witnessing, experiencing, or causing harm, people often feel ashamed, alone, and afraid. They lose trust, confidence, self-respect, and innocence. Thus, without lessening the accountability and pain involved, the binary distinction between a "victim" and a "victimizer" in some ways collapses. Debrief conversations can also reflect on what was lost or gained as a result of each experience, so as to consider more deeply the impacts and consequences of interpersonal harm, what needs to be restored, and often the growth that results.

In my own, modified version of this exercise, impacted by our limited shared time, a learning opportunity opened up around the experience of causing harm to another. In response to the question "How does it feel to harm somebody?," one student wrote the word "pleasure" on their slip of paper. It was extremely uncomfortable for the student who had to say the word out loud; indeed, hearing it was extremely disturbing for the entire class. Immediately I thought that the outside students would assume that only an inside student could have written the word. (So much for the instructor not stereotyping her students!) What transpired, however, was mind-blowing. Several of the inside students vehemently rejected the word as a legitimate descriptor, thereby throwing such stereotypical assumptions to the wind. In the debrief, one of the outside students continued the discussion, calling attention to the fact that when we get revenge, whether justly or not, we often experience pleasure in hurting others. This observation led the class into territory where I as teacher could never have pushed them, and rightly so, because when I as teacher surrender to "teaching itself," the students are free to lead the way, their own way, and they as much as I learn from it. Several students noted in their reflections that the incident had made them initially assume the stereotype that an inside student must have written the word, but that they then realized that they were just perpetuating a stereotype. We will never know who originally wrote the word, but I do know that, at that moment, stereotypes and assumptions were being turned inside-out in ways far beyond my imagination and beyond what straightforwardly didactic, content-focused modes of teaching could have accomplished.

The exercise is an embodied form of learning that prevents the sort of comfortable distance which makes stereotyping easy. The exercise places the personal potentially at one remove because everybody gives voice to somebody else's word, yet it is the possibility of being heard as well as the giving voice to another's "word" that make the exercise empowering.

In my view, the embodiment also manifests in the place-based specificity of being in a physical space of constraint. During class, the constraint applies to the whole group. The moment when the outside students prepare to leave the constraining space, by contrast, is at first awkward for everyone. On numerous occasions, however, the inside students took the lead in acknowledging the moment. In doing so, they changed it from what could have, using the post-structuralist feminists' vocabulary, been a voyeuristic desire to learn about the "Other" into an opportunity for shared reflection. Voyeurism from both groups was avoided due to the courage of all the students and due to the dialogue that transformed it into a learning situation.

In reflecting on the courses, I have come to believe that another factor is at play as well. When teachers embrace a pedagogical "practice of confusion and unease," we learn to stay with these moments when they occur. We may feel tempted to leap into meta-discussion that would smooth over the unease, but if we curb ourselves and "just stay" with whatever is, we model such behavior as legitimate and free students to make their own choice of attitude. To me, this is not just a cerebral activity but something we do in both body and mind. Our "staying with what is" becomes the condition of possibility for the learning and the learning is thus opened up to a spectrum that stretches from simply extracting content knowledge to engaging with complexity. Moreover, when constructive unease is the condition of possibility, the resulting learning is freed from a lot of the constraint that usually accompanies the teacher's positionality as power center. In such moments we too may encounter our "selves" as somewhat fluid and permeable, no longer needing to fully determine how knowledge is made. Inside, outside, student, teacher—they all get turned inside-out until the inevitable moment when we return to our presumably more stable selves. Nonetheless, a moment of "teaching itself" occurred.

Although the entire sequence appeared liberating for all involved, intellectual honesty makes me want to also acknowledge other possible outcomes. While the exercise centers on "giving voice" and doing so in an intersectional manner, there may still be boundaries in place. Inside students may not feel fully free to express themselves or may bear a heavier burden in the classroom; pedagogical liberation only goes so far.

Here Ellsworth's insight that all voices are partial and show partisanship is highly relevant. These aspects are not something to eradicate—as if such a thing were even possible—but as they carry implications for other partial voices, they must be addressed. The key here, in my view, is what condition of possibility is employed: is it one of striving to "fix" the "incremental liberation" or is it one of "staying with" it and its accompaniment, very real unease? If we choose the latter, I believe we have found a way to bring some of the best of critical theory together with the best of poststructuralist feminism; or perhaps, I should simply say that we have brought out some of the best in us as social beings whose selves are always to some extent reliant on other selves.

Knowing Inside-Out: Practice Responding to the Theoretical Impasses

I propose that the adapted Inside-Out class turned traditional modes of academic knowing inside-out on multiple levels. The inside-out pedagogy responds in complex and challenging ways to the stances of critical theory and poststructuralist feminism in philosophy of education. The pedagogy shares the critical theorist's call for transformation, empowerment, and the finding of one's voice; yet this teaching mode does so by taking into account the poststructuralist feminist critiques of critical theory in regards to issues of empowerment, student voice, power structures, and voyeurism.

First, the emphasis on the role of the teacher as facilitator dissolves the dilemma of empowerment as hinging on an external authority. If empowerment occurs—and there is no guarantee that it does—the subject thereof is also the agent of empowerment. That being said, the teacher cannot divest him or herself from all power. And yet, on the occasions when the teacher relinquishes the "power piece" of control and gives in to the pedagogy of confusion and unease, some self-erasure of the power takes place. Second, if students claim a voice—and again, this is by no means guaranteed—they do so in a fashion which holds everybody accountable for their own partiality. Giving voice to somebody else's word, as in the exercise on harm, is groundbreaking because it simultaneously teaches an important topic, subverts stereotypes, and removes the dialogue from the venue of "othering" people. Thus, thirdly, this exercise is emblematic of how to structure a learning environment that works against being construed voyeuristically.

Finally, power structures are subjected to critique but they are not theorized away. While the instructor is a site of power, she also embraces what the poststructuralists have named an "epistemology of uncertainty" (Lather, 1998). The teacher no longer epitomizes the sole authority of content-knowledge and certainty; in this context, life experience is knowledge, and she or he has never been incarcerated. As was the case with the "fish-bowl," it becomes permissible for her to say "I don't know" and this inspires the students to explore realms of uncertainty themselves.

Such a pedagogy of uncertainty is disturbing. Consequently, "teaching itself"— when added to any classroom—is supplementary in the sense of subverting everything else once it is "added." Unease and undoing do not signify failures in developing a coherent, universal pedagogy; rather, they acknowledge the limits of generating liberation through reason and admit that we are all still engaged in learning—perhaps even learning a sort of ease in respect to unease. The poststructuralist position acknowledges reason as inescapably fractured by various categories of struggle and it acknowledges that all knowledge production is complicit in perpetuating a normalization of knowledge. In that sense, Inside-Out pedagogy aligns with Foucault's statement that "nothing is innocent." Thus "teaching itself" is not a standard liberatory classroom practice, but a way of working within and yet resisting our complicities. Because nothing is innocent, we need to become disturbed.

Yet the story doesn't end here. We are all inside some sort of fish-bowl. Certainly, some fish-bowls are worse than others, but existing in a bowl means we have a finite perspective. Now, imagine that we are outside the bowl, that the multiverse is filled with bowls: our perspective becomes infinite. We see that finite perspectives are...just perspectives. Perhaps the intersecting of finite and infinite perspectives can open up a place where we no longer need to place each other in bowls—at least for a few moments.

Note

1. During our initial, separate meetings, both inside and outside students learned of the class format and were given the choice to opt out (at the university either by taking a different section of the course or completing an alternative assignment); over many semesters only one student ever chose the alternative assignment.

References

Biesta, Gert J. J. "Say You Want a Revolution...Suggestions for the Impossible Future of Critical Pedagogy." *Educational Theory* 48, no. 4 (1998): 499–511.

Burbules, Nicholas C. "The Limits of Dialogue as a Critical Pedagogy." In *Revolutionary Pedagogies*. Edited by Peter Trifonas, New York: Routledge, 2000: 251–273.

———. "Doubt and Educational Possibility." Forthcoming. Available at http://faculty.ed.uiuc.edu/burbules/papers/dep.html. Accessed January 29, 2006.

Carlson, Dennis. "Finding a Voice, and Losing Our Way?" *Educational Theory* 48, no. 4 (1998): 541–555.

Eby, John. Nd. "Why Service Learning is Bad." Unpublished paper available at http://www.messiah.edu/external_programs/agape/service_learning/articles/wrongsvc.pdf

Ellsworth, Elizabeth. "Why Doesn't This Feel Empowering? Working Through the Repressive Myths of Critical Pedagogy." In *Feminisms and Critical Pedagogy*. Edited by Carmen Luke and Jennifer Gore, 90–119. New York: Routledge, 1992.

Freire, Paulo. *Pedagogy of the Oppressed*. New York: Continuum, 1994.

Giroux, Henry, A. *Theory and Resistance in Education: A Pedagogy for the Opposition*. South Hadley, MA: Bergin & Garvey, 1983.

Hill, David, Peter McLaren, Michael Cole, and Glenn Rikowski, eds. *Marxism against Postmodernism in Educational Theory*. Lanham, MD: Lexington Books, 2002.

hooks, bell. *Teaching to Transgress*. New York: Routledge, 1994.

Jones, Allison. "Cross-Cultural Pedagogy and the Passion for Ignorance." *Feminism & Psychology* 11, no. 3 (2001): 279–292.

Lather, Patti. "Critical Pedagogy and Its Complicities: A Praxis of Stuck Places." *Educational Theory* 48, no. 4 (1998): 487–498.

Luke, Carmen and Jennifer Gore. *Feminisms and Critical Pedagogy*. New York: Routledge, 1992.

McLaren, Peter. "Revolutionary Pedagogy in Post-Revolutionary Times: Rethinking the Political Economy of Critical Education." *Educational Theory* 48, no. 4 (1998): 431–463.

Pompa, Lori. "Service-Learning as Crucible: Reflections on Immersion, Context, Power, and Transformation." *Michigan Journal of Community Service Learning* 9, no. 1 (2002): 67–76.

Pompa, Lori and Melissa Crabbe, *The Inside-Out Prison Exchange Program: Instructor's Manual*. Philadelphia, PA: Temple University, 2004.

PART III

Productive Intersectionality: Navigating Race, Place, Gender, and Class

CHAPTER 11

From Safe Space to Brave Space: Strategies for the Anti-Oppression Classroom

Shahad Atiya, Simone Weil Davis, Keisha Green, Erin Howley, Shoshana Pollack, Barbara Sherr Roswell, Ella Turenne, Tyrone Werts, and Lucas Wilson

This chapter recounts a Round Table Discussion on power, privilege, and classroom dynamics convened in September, 2012 among nine members of the Inside-Out community, including instructors, Steering Committee members, staff, Think Tank members, and alumni.

Simone: Welcome everyone. Perhaps we can begin by naming some questions for today's discussion. I am particularly interested in hearing about those times in the Inside-Out classroom when insidious or challenging dynamics around racial or other inequities arise, or when some lived dynamic felt oppressive, when you realized that something was occurring that was not fulfilling your best goals for what Inside-Out could be. How we can become more conscious of and responsive to those moments?

Barbara: I'm also interested in exploring the ways we may experience or exclude dimensions of identity in our classes. For example, when I participated in the Training Institute, several of us who are white also identified as Jewish. I've been very grateful to Ella and Keisha for introducing me to the "Circles of My Multicultural Self" exercise, which enables people to unpack and think beyond the most obvious categories. I'll always remember the conversation that this activity provoked in a workshop at Graterford, when an inside Think Tank member reflected on his identity not as "incarcerated," or as Latino, but as a son.

Shahad: I also struggle with how to identify myself. I'm a Middle Eastern female. If I identify myself as white, other students say, "You're not white." And they are right, but I'm also not Pacific Asian; the census sheet has no category that fits me.

Keisha: Shahad, your comment suggests that we might spend more time in our trainings or workshops examining what Kimberle Crenshaw terms *intersectionality*. In my own context, teaching an Inside-Out course in the South, for example, I found it complicated to be at an institution where most of the staff and incarcerated women were African-American, but because admission to the course was based on prior conduct or course participation, the women selected to take the course were disproportionately white. The white women in the course were reluctant to talk publicly about race, in part because of fear that anything shared in class might be repeated in general population, where they were the minority and might have to deal with undersirable fallout. The outside students and I could leave the prison. The white inside students still had to live, bathe, eat, and work with the black women who were in the class.

Ella: I would also like to think about how gender plays out in our conversations and interactions. In the same way that you experienced resistance to talking about race, I've experienced contexts where gender becomes highly contested or the elephant in the room, particularly if the inside students are young men and the outside students are mostly women. Each of those groups brings in all their baggage around gender, making the classroom a potentially volatile space. It's not that the men *want* to bring in that baggage, they just bring in all of the stereotypes and behaviors that they have been used to navigating the world with. . . . And there are the young women who, perhaps since being in college, have taken a very critical stance about gender. This creates a clash, and our job as facilitators is to get each side to think through their own and each other's comments.

Tyrone: Maybe we're not really being as inclusive as we think when we talk about diversity. Many of us—facilitators and faculty and administrators and even students—automatically default to race and we don't consider gender, sexual orientation, spiritual affiliation or maybe even political affiliation.

Ella: This issue is not limited to Inside-Out. This is a national dilemma, that when we think about "diversity" or race, we automatically default to black and white. The challenge is, even when the physicality of who is in the room is narrow, to be able to open up the conversation and challenge ourselves to think about other dimensions of diversity. Because, back to the original question about oppression, these other modalities of difference are not necessarily visible. And so when they become invisible and we reinforce that invisibility by failing to acknowledge or value them, that's when we start creating the oppressive environment that we're intentionally trying to deconstruct.

Simone: Right. So there are times where, in the moment, a facilitator might be able to see ways to intervene productively. And prior to that, as facilitator, you would want to have developed an increased sensitivity so that those moments would sort of flash neon for you, and you would have a conscious sense: this is a moment when things could either go in a more oppressive or a less oppressive direction. What do we need to respond to this need for in-the-moment interventions? And are there things that can happen early on which allow for group discussion of the dynamics, so that everyone in the room can shoulder a collective responsibility? How can a classroom community build some kind of shared comfort so that bringing such dynamics into the open wouldn't feel accusatory, but more like a collective commitment to best practices?

Erin: Oppressive situations happen all the time. If the person who's feeling the oppressive situation is feeling fear, there's this activation barrier, like you have to get your guts together so that you can say something. It's a risk, and you have to determine if it is worth it, or how truthful you want to be, and how safe the environment is. It may feel way more comfortable to stay quiet. The question becomes, is this a space where it's okay? Can I reveal myself in this space? Sometimes as facilitators, we have no idea what is triggering students, and around what issues, because they remain silent and keep up the mask. It's their job to speak up, but it's our job to help create a setting where they can do that. I had that feeling when I first took the training as an undergraduate in a roomful of professors, feeling very young, and insecure. Toward the end of the training, we did an excellent exercise where we were asked to pair up with one other person and talk about our experiences in the training, a sort of meta-narrative, and I was able to voice all of my feelings in a way that wasn't so intimidating. The curriculum provided a way for me to be honest, appropriate to the setting and circumstances. People are constantly searching for how to place themselves, how to belong, how to contribute. It's a matter of creating a space where people can speak those inner narratives out loud.

Plus, there's a tension between covering a certain ground academically and allowing the space for people to breathe and grow personally. Breaking open and challenging oppressive moments, and the important learning that results, sometimes involves conflict. This conflict can arise because people may project power onto an authority figure who is seen as holding the key to what is allowable and what is not. Especially in institutional settings like the prison or traditional academia, the professor often plays out this role of the regulator. How as facilitators can we create a space where students and trainees can also be the ones to choose what enters into the conversation? Part of the work of changing patterns of oppression is being able to have nonviolent conflict in the lived moment, in a way that is not merely theoretical.

Shahad: The facilitator has to know when to stay in the background, when to step in, when to use humor.

Ella: I think that Erin has a really good point about conflict. It's easy to fear conflict, but conflict is a place where you can grow. The concept of "safe" spaces is tricky because safety implies that you're always going to be comfortable. But when you're exercising, you're going to feel a stretch, you're going to feel some pain, and that's how you know your muscles are working. And so you don't want a space where everybody always feels good. That is not the marker of progress. But you still want it to be a respectful space where everyone is held and feels like they're in community working through these issues together. That's why establishing and taking ownership of the ground rules is key. Then, even when there is conflict, the group respects and trusts each other enough to stumble through the conflict together.

Erin: Right. There's a distinction between violent conflict and nonviolent conflict. Violent conflict actively continues the cycle of oppression. That is not safe. But to develop people's ability to be in conflict and do it nonviolently is essential to create change.

Shoshana: During my Inside-Out training, conflict emerged because there was silence on issues of gender and sexuality, so people started going underground and talking in subgroups at breaks, and working themselves up into a sense of anger and resentment and then some conflict emerged. But difference and silence don't have to imply conflict. I think that "discomfort" is a better way to frame this.

Simone: I've found it striking that many outside students come to Inside-Out with a sense of entitlement to safety in the classroom. Their vision of safety, hard won, emerged in part out of the second wave feminist movement—the idea that we have a right not to feel like we're in danger. That *is* productive, but it's impossible for certain kinds of productive work to happen without discomfort, sometimes even acute discomfort. So you can have a class with some outside students who believe they have an automatic entitlement to what they experience as safety and a majority of inside students who have become accustomed to being treated, themselves, as sources of danger. To build a productive classroom dynamic, we need to be mindful of how all of these assumptions can be institutionally shaped.

Shoshana: We encountered this in my classroom when we were setting guidelines for dialogue. One inside student said she wanted the outside students to know that they were safe. Although some students interpreted that as emotional safety, she was responding to stereotypes and wanted to reassure more literally that the inside women were not going to hurt the outside students. And so that kind of put the whole thing on the table around what safety means.

Shahad: Something that challenged me in my class was that, as a female, I always thought men wouldn't feel the way I would feel in a dark parking lot. And then we did that exercise where you put pieces of paper on the ground, the facilitator offers a statement, and you stand on one side of the room or the other, depending on whether you agree or disagree with the statement. And one inside student shared a story during that exercise. He's African-American and he said, "If I was in an unfamiliar neighborhood and three Black guys were coming my way, I would move to the other side of the road." I was surprised that, even though he was incarcerated and convicted of a crime, he knew what it feels like to be vulnerable, as well.

Barbara: So we're thinking about what we collectively do to create a space that is neither a comfort zone nor a panic zone, but is somewhere in that middle learning zone, like Zygotsky's "zone of proximal development." What else do you do to create that space where people can enter discomfort and still feel safe enough to stay there?

Keisha: After we create the guidelines together, we also use an activity I learned from *Teaching for Diversity and Social Justice* to identify psychological signs indicating that we have been triggered. So sometimes my class decides that we'll have a box available for people to be able to get up and drop in a note about when they might have been triggered or when they notice someone else was triggered. The note can be anonymous. We make a pact to address that moment, either pausing right then or coming back to it in another class. It doesn't always work—we're not always attuned to how other people are responding—but it does at least help people start to observe body language, nonverbal things that we may overlook. In my youth development workshop experience with an organization called Project South, we call this strategy a "Whoa!" moment and we literally say "whoa—we need to stop." Bascially, the goal is to figure out ways to identify that there's a tension present and to try to navigate it or negotiate it together.

Ella: I like the idea of the *whoa* moment, Keisha. Another strategy is to have a trigger word—"purple," for instance. When something happens in the space, or someone is triggered, they can use the word and the group knows that something needs to be addressed. A facilitator can also offer some prompts that can be used in difficult discussions. One of them is to preface a comment by saying "First draft." That signals that you have something to say, but it's not completely formed and so you're asking for permission to speak without being judged. Another helpful phrase is "Do over." This gives you the opportunity to restate what you intended. These strategies help keep the space open and productive.

Shahad: Something that helped create productive classroom dynamics for us was Allan Johnson's *Privilege, Power, and Difference,* that argues that, for anything to change in society, the people with privilege have to say, "I'm going to give up some of my privilege so we can talk about something here." Before reading the book, I assumed that the "privileged" were white men. But since I got to drive my car out of the prison and go home, the dynamic of who was privileged was shifted and I became the privileged one. Until you see an inside student's vulnerability, you don't know how to address it. You don't know how to think from an inside student's perspective until you walk in their shoes, until they kind of meet you halfway. So, I'd add that students need to be comfortable with each other on a personal level, and it would help if the professors allowed more "water cooler" conversation, maybe a five minute break between activities when students can interact one on one and share more personal stories. Everyone is thirsty to share some part of themselves related to the readings or to connect with each other to respond to class activities. The students will feel more empowered and that would take some pressure off the professors to control the space. I don't know if you read the *New Yorker* article about LeBron James and how he's been choking at free shots: it's mostly because he's thinking too much about the process rather than just shooting the ball. And I think a lot of Inside-Out professors do that because they know so much and they want to do so much. I'd say, hey, relax, let the process take its course.

Simone: But there's another side to this. Have any of you had to struggle with the experience some outside students can have, where they become paralyzed by recognition of their own privilege and for a time simply don't know what to do with that new awareness?

Keisha: Yes. I felt like the experience for students at Emory participating in the Inside-Out class was sometimes overwhelming to a point of silence. Reflection papers and arts activities were very helpful; students reported feeling greater comfort expressing themselves and their ideas without necessarily having to talk.

Lucas: My experience entails some interesting role reversals. I am often the only male in the group, and even though it has been easy to talk about sexuality, gender, race, and ethnic difference, I have felt troubled in my own authority around issues of sexual violence. We once did an exercise that I learned from another Inside-Out instructor in which the group considers five scenarios that escalate in terms of their intensity and complexity. One of the later scenarios describes a date rape. An outside student, on hearing it, felt safe enough to tell the class that scenario had happened to her. She had not previously talked to anyone about it and had not processed it; she said that she had put that experience in a box, sealed the box and tucked it away. It was quite raw in the classroom. I've learned the hard way to be really careful about materials and texts that even figuratively deploy sexual violence in careless ways. Years ago I used a film in an African-American studies class, a film called *Ricochet* with Denzel Washington and John Lithgow. I was totally unaware of how prominent bodily penetration by phallic objects was in the film until a couple of students suggested that, if someone in the room had experienced sexual violence, our discussion of the film could likely feel like a reenactment. That was a very important lesson for me. It changed how I evaluated and framed discussion of texts. So, in this Inside-Out class, I had an outside facilitator who had some sexual counseling training talk with the student. But after the break, the inside students were very sophisticated about talking to the student and the class as a whole about what my outside student had shared. It was a very real opportunity for us to merge discourses. Until that point, the educational and intellectual work the inside students had been asked to do tended to be in the form of personal responsibility and "I" stories, and explaining why they are incarcerated in terms of the choices they made. Outside students tended to think about "structured privilege" stories—advantage and disadvantage in the world—as a consequence not simply of personal decisions but of structural forces. In this moment, we all saw this dichotomy dissolve, as structures shaped agency, and as agency permitted an identification of and analysis of structural influences. So, being uncomfortable allowed us to be creative.

Simone: Lucas brings us back to those moments when, as a class, you discover that there is a bridge between the microexperience of group dynamics in the room and macroquestions, so that the artificial divide between structural and interpersonal power dynamics gets addressed and traversed. This reminds us that the Inside-Out facilitator has the opportunity and the obligation—the constant, sometimes humbling and always educational opportunity—to think hard about his or her own positionality in the room. Also striking in what you said is the role of *collective* education: often the facilitator can and should step back, as you did here, and watch people engage in generous acts of mutual illumination.

Ella: One way that I've discovered to help students move beyond paralysis is to focus on the structures in which power and privilege play out. Because in my own experience, I found that when students get hung up on analysis of privilege, it's because they're personalizing these issues and thinking of themselves as racist or homophobic. Trying to get them to take a step back and look at structures that perpetuate inequalities gives them perspective, helps them understand how they may be a part of this system, but the weight of this is not wholly on their shoulders. It also gives them a context to think about what to *do* about these inequalities. Inside-Out courses can be very charged, and after having had deep conversations and building relationships, students want to do something. The question is how to channel that energy in a productive way. What I've tried to tell my students is that there's a time to overhaul and completely change or abolish everything. But that's not necessarily this space. And so we have to try to stay true to the space that we're in and then also think about all of these other external things and other spaces we inhabit where we have the tools and opportunity to facilitate change.

Erin: Once a person moves through that paralysis and starts understanding the larger situation, there's a certain sense that "I'm an active body, I'm here and I can do things." And it becomes a personal quest. Inside-Out has struggled to develop alumni opportunities and to ask, "What does Inside-Out do to usher people forward?" But I think one of the most effective things about Inside-Out is that it creates a space for people to see themselves as agents. It prompts students to ask, "What is my skill, what are my abilities, what are my talents, what is my calling?" Inside-Out creates an activation zone, transforming paralysis into motion.

Simone: So what is standing out for me is that, not only is it important for the instructor to stay reflective during class time, but we also need to confront things about our needs, our blocks, our resources and our motivations, and to stay current with this "personal growth" work.

Keisha: Right. And I've encountered people wanting to be in carceral spaces for all kinds of reasons. I want people interested in such work to know that prison education is not a cool, exotic thing to do, but rather, that it's life work. Choosing to be a part of educational programming inside prison facilities is an ongoing commitment, a philosophy, a way of thinking and being in the world.

Tyrone: Some really tough issues have come out in this conversation. I keep thinking about that very first Inside-Out class at Graterford. It was really diverse: graduate students, undergrads, three or four African-American students from outside, four white students from inside. More and more, I'm thinking that, in addition to the wagon wheel, that first class should also find ways to name these issues from the very beginning, to address diversity and power and privilege.

Shoshana: One of the things that's sticking with me are Lucas's comments about the individualistic and therapeutic narrative that inside women are given to regurgitate, to show that they are "reformed or remorseful or now a reduced risk." One of the fascinating things that teaching Inside-Out does inside women's prisons is it opens up a space for another kind of narrative in which the personal engages with the structural. So maybe, as a group, we can think about how Inside-Out classes play out differently in women's prisons.

Lucas: Let me just add to what Shoshana just said. What complicates my involvement with inside students is this: with the possible exception of *one* student, every inside student I've ever taught has had, prior to the event or events that led to her incarceration, a chemical or substance abuse issue. Now, obviously there are individual factors. But what students confront is a set of structural conditions, "environmental hazards," that "I" stories cannot account for. Address the substance abuse differently and incarceration may be unnecessary. That's a matter of broader opportunities—policy structures—in a given society. The ideology of the "I" story ignores structure's role, treats it as immaterial to the "facts" of the case. This ideology contributes to the public's tendency to view incarcerated persons as irresponsible. What else to do but to immerse them in languages and practices of deep personal responsibility as the sign of rehabilitation? As a result, inside students struggle, often dissembling to move through imprisonment toward parole, with being "too responsible" in their lives. But this erroneous conclusion belief that the only thing that matters is what "I" can "control" ignores structural or social conditions. The second issue I'd like to raise is the perspective of employees at the jail. They are often forced to work two and three jobs to support their families and resent that inside students get the educational opportunity provided by Inside-Out. As an instructor, I want to figure out ways for everyone at a prison to have the option to enroll in a class and be transformed by it.

Shahad: I think the most interesting thing that I'm going to walk away with is this whole discussion about definitions and communication. As I mentioned, I identify myself as a Middle Eastern feminist, but when I would say that, some students think "feminist" means "lesbian." It might help in classes to stipulate some working definitions. I remember a class on "revolutions" in which a professor said, "before talking about anything, I'm going to put a definition of revolution on the board that we will use for the discussion." I use that strategy all the time in trainings for new instructors. It enables us to say, for the purposes of this discussion, here's what we'll mean when we say "race," or "white," or "African-American."

Simone: Building rather than assuming a common pool of definitions.

Erin: The main thing that this whole conversation has opened up for me is that word "empowerment." It's so many things; maybe we don't have to have a single definition. But we do have assumptions about what it should look like, especially what we think it means for *other* people. I see empowerment unfolding in all kinds of subtle ways through spaces we open up in order to struggle, create new definitions, and develop individual and collective agency.

CHAPTER 12

Being Human

Erin Howley

A human being is a part of the whole, called by us "Universe," a part limited in time and space. He experiences himself, his thoughts and feelings as something separated from the rest—a kind of optical delusion of his consciousness. The striving to free oneself from this delusion is the one issue of true religion. Not to nourish it but to try to overcome it is the way to reach the attainable measure of peace of mind.

Albert Einstein[1]

I am a human being. Nothing human can be alien to me!
Maya Angelou (quoting Publius Terentius Afer (185—159 BC))[2]

"What does it mean to be fully human?" This question emerged from a conversation with my inside colleague Kempis "Ghani" Songster in the Graterford Think Tank. Erudite and always profound and graceful in his speech, Ghani posed the initial question, and I have returned to it again and again. Reflecting on what it means to be human is like trying to define the ever-changing sky. It is an inquiry that feels fleeting and cumbersome because "being human" is relevant in the widest of settings and disciplines, yet at the same time, too commonplace to note. My life story gives testimony to my own growth and development as a human, but there must be as many ways to talk about "being human" as there are people on this planet.

Ghani's question is deeply relevant to the work of the Think Tank, since we consider education to be a process of evolution and progression toward our own individual and collective potentials, regardless of what side of the wall we return to when the meeting is over. As a group, we are committed to the process and practice of education, and to honing our work at the crossroads of education and social change. Hosting dozens of public education workshops and instructor trainings to further the reach and impact of education across prison walls, time and again we have experienced interactions and dialogue that are deeply transformational and life-affirming. Our focus is implicitly on growing and becoming, and on increasing the capacity of our peers to do the same. Understanding and achieving our potential as human beings, as best possible, are central and ongoing motivations for our work together at Graterford Prison.

Spurred by the energy and focus of our conversations, Ghani and I set out to facilitate a workshop to explore what it means to be human, with an emphasis on the personal life experiences of members of the Think Tank. We convened, as we usually do every Wednesday evening, in a circle of about 15 inside members and ten outside members, in one of the classrooms of the "School." A corridor of rooms, a library, and regularly spaced motivational posters reminiscent of junior high, the School is close to the end of the quarter-mile walk from one end of the prison to the other. After our familiar routine of chattered greetings, Ghani and I began our workshop with gusto; we had prepared the session with the aim of inviting a grounded, contemplative, and generative conversation (the full Workshop Outline appears in appendix 5).

The session started with Ghani's steadfast and stalwart voice quoting Albert Einstein and Terence (by way of Maya Angelou) followed by a simple query to the group: "What do these quotes mean to you? What do they reflect or say about what it is to be human?" The quotes were an entrance, a passageway, into the topic. Once the responses started flowing, and the energy surged in response, we asked the group to go deeper by taking ten minutes to write about "what is involved in the quest to be fully human, from your position, circumstance, environment, or status." I watched the silent group as they wrote. Some faces showed meditative searching, some consternation, and some serenity. Once hands rested and heads turned up, Ghani and I invited everyone to share their insights.

As people took turns revealing what emerged, I was struck by my own presumptions about what it means to talk about diversity in the context of "being human." I had assumed that the group would talk about the particularities of individual experiences, as well as about how we have group affiliations that create multiple other layers of similarity and difference: "*female or male, Black or White, poor or wealthy, gay or straight*" . . . and so on along a familiar chain of social position and status. The conversation, however, revealed a different spectrum altogether.

The group talked about our limited ability as humans to perceive reality in its totality. We sense things temporally and spatially, but to be whole, we must also investigate the connection of inner reality to outer reality, of self to the environment, world, and universe. We must seek to understand more fully how we are part of something larger and more significant than our individual selves. One participant, Tuesday, reflected:

The body we live in is a filter for the world around us, and we cannot see all of the layers. I am recognizing that every part of existence is me, so I must treat each part with respect as I would treat myself—a flower, an old man, a curtain. To damage them is to damage myself. All this is me.

The exchange had a circular, repeating theme, endowed with concern for the well-being of all things, and the dissolution of the barriers between self and other.

Another recurring theme was that we could reach our full human capacity (and the twin notion that we have likely not yet reached that capacity) through our chosen actions and emotional and spiritual acuity. As relayed by various members of the group, our potential as humans involves acceptance, respect, empathy, and self-love. If we practice these things, we can develop and witness our essential and authentic selves.

> To reach the full potential of our humanity, we must be able to elevate our ability to empathize with others. If I can increase my potential to empathize, I believe that increases my humanity. I can respond in a productive way if I am not reactive. (Paul)

We also considered the conditions that prevent us from realizing our full potentials: poverty, disadvantaged beginnings, and inadequate education, for example. Oppressions and social ills can induce fear and self-hatred, and to let our true selves come forth, we need to make good choices as we contend with these limitations. Yet the challenge of growing against all odds cannot be understated, and the process of becoming more human also necessarily demands a change in societal conditions. Becoming fully human incorporates self-realization and self-actualization in a cyclical process that is akin to metamorphosis, a building and emergence oriented toward personal growth that is neither selfish nor isolated, but bound with a concurrent concern for others, as well as recognition of and focus on changing what holds us back.

Along with the sense that we can realize our capacity as humans through our own will to act and think in productive, self-fulfilling ways, came distinction around the concept of *humanity*, which is something more expansive than the matter-of-fact nature of our physicality and individuality.

> We have to accept ourselves and each other to promote individuality in the context of a larger world community. First we belong to the planet. We fall within that. Individuality without a greater context of belonging promotes dehumanization. When we perceive ourselves only as individuals, we see less of the humanity of others, to the point where someone doesn't matter at all, and that is how prisons arise. The shift is difficult, because we live in a culture that promotes individuality. How many people would actually sacrifice themselves for the country and for the world? (Tuesday)

Humanity, as it was discussed in our group, is a concept that connects individuals to larger social and environmental contexts and communities. Tuesday's comment conveys a sense that our well-being depends on respect and even *sacrifice* to a collective ethos; we detract from humanity by disrespecting, seeking revenge, and acting out of hate. Humanity can be viewed through the scope of social responsibility and interdependence, a capability to intervene in and stop cycles of violence and harm to self and others.

Critical to this deliberation was the obvious and striking fact that our conversation took place inside of a maximum security prison. Some of the members of our group are free to enter and leave, and others are confined. The context of prison was immediately relevant, and brought forth a conversation on the meaning and significance of freedom in relation to being human and dehumanization.

> I wrote about my freedom, and the cost of my freedom. Being dehumanized is not to be able to come and go on your own. It is what gives us the feel of being like an animal. (Saadiq)
>
> I agree that it is about freedom. Freedom, the less freedom you have, the less human you are, the more it holds you down. A dehumanizing experience is the physical and mental restrictions being put on us. But at the same time, there is no right or wrong with being human. Is there a choice to be human or not? (Harry)

Saadiq and Harry brought forth what seems like an impossible contradiction between the inalienable fact that they are human beings, and the simultaneous dehumanization they experience as incarcerated people. Freedom of body and mind are inherent to the process of humanization, and the alienation and restriction of freedom they experience on a daily basis is a deeply felt reality.

While some members spoke about the daily impacts of prison and confinement, prison was also discussed in a metaphorical sense. Freedom was associated with our ability to live up to our full potentials, while prison was linked to control and denial of that potential from internal, emotional, and psychological restrictions, such as self-denial and lack of self-love.

> I want to talk about our internal prison. We all carry within ourselves ways that we are not free. I trip myself up. I spent much of my life being insecure and not liking myself. Being fully human has something to do with being internally free. (Lori)

To be free means not having externally enforced restrictions that prohibit expression and range of movement *or* internally imposed mental and emotional impediments. In both the literal and metaphorical senses, the discussion about prison revealed how freedom is related to humanizing experiences and the quest to become fully human. There is an implicit sense of the need for choice and self-will in determining one's life—a freedom to choose how to act, think, and feel. A humanizing process of education should be liberatory; even if it is not possible to immediately change physical restrictions, it encourages critical awareness and incentive to act upon limitations in all their forms.

In our conversation, freedom and humanity were aligned with self-betterment, a faith in the ability to contribute, to explore the relationship between self and others, and an underlying sense that, along with the quest to become fully human and to contribute to humanity, comes validation of what is good, right, and endowed with respect. But there was also a resistance to this notion that emerged at various turns as the evening went on. Simply put, in Terrell's words, "Isn't being human also *not* being able to empathize? Being judgmental, evil, bad? That stuff is human too." Moving against the current of the ideal human self was a challenging notion that we were idealizing the topic. We were choosing to put forth images that supplemented our self-concepts, but in reality, there are a whole other range of orientations, actions, and approaches to life that are not so ideal, but are yet just as human. To leave out or deny these perhaps undesired parts of our existence is dangerous, because it means that we are defining what is and is not worthy of the title "human" and what is banished from the circumscribed definition of "humanity."

> If my environment or society says being human means I have to be this way or that way, and it restricts me from being who I am, then it takes from my humanity. Am I allowed to be me and what I think it means to be human? If I can't embrace what society says, does that make me less human? Can outside influences dictate my humanity? Influences say how I should be and behave, and that isn't how I see myself. Then it takes away from my humanity because I have to live up to that idea. That is freedom of choice. (Silk)

What if claiming freedom of choice also means risking and, in fact, being excluded? If we are in agreement regarding expectations and social norms, then consensus on what it means to be fully human in relation to others does not seem so far out of reach. But experiences, desires, and motives are not standardized, and our society is riddled with oppressive forces and pressures that dampen the spirit rather than contribute to common well-being. Perhaps more often than not, there are great contradictions between individual interests and an all-inclusive notion of humanity.

> I'm trying to understand the phrase, "fully human." What does being fully human actually mean? At least part entails a full-on embrace of all things human. What are the challenges of that? Does it mean I would have to embrace even a person who poses a threat to humanity? If that is the case, I'm not sure I can be fully human. I'm more wired to fight against that individual. How do I be fully human, if it means embracing them? (Kareem)

To be required to accept the threatening, criminal, unhallowed parts of ourselves and others can be difficult because it means grappling with harms and abuses and the deep challenges of recognition and acceptance. The contradiction of which Kareem speaks is a very relevant concern within the Inside-Out classroom. Education as a humanizing and freeing process may seem easier in the ideal, since the practice of dialogue and facilitation is faced with the challenge of incorporating many different histories, priorities, choices, and motives into circles of inclusion.

This angle of the conversation, which appeared again and again as if it was coming up through a fissure, introduced those aspects of our nature for which we do not receive approval and acceptance, the characteristics that are ostracized, that do not contribute to the overall progression of "humanity." It also revealed the struggle of differences of perspective, in that there is no single approach to what it means to be a full human. Contending with this is perhaps a difficult truth; we did not reach consensus about what is allowed entrance and what is relegated to a realm outside human status.

The struggle to find common ground appeared to me personally through my entry point into this conversation as a white woman. My interest in co-facilitating this workshop was prompted in part by the ongoing conversations I have with cherished friends and colleagues about race and identity. I have pondered the meaning of my race, the ways in which it has morphed and changed in various settings and situations according to how I see myself and how others see me, as well as by social and historical realities. How can I *ever* become fully human in a society where my race is defined in juxtaposition with other racial distinctions of black and brown, creating divisions of privilege, freedom, status, and treatment that limit the full potential of everyone's development, including my own?

I had no simple answer—and I still do not. But in the conversation that unfolded, the Think Tank challenged my assumptions about the *meaning* of difference, my surefootedness about the ground to be covered, and the salience of race, sex, gender, class, and ability—the familiar frames of reference in academic and activist communities. Our conversation brought forth a deeply important joint question of how to define, talk about, and act in recognition of our differences. Yet rather than seeing difference as a permanent or static "othering," or an academic or politicized categorization of how we stand in relation to one another, we can shift our perspective. Instead of asking, "How can we co-exist together despite our differences?," we are able to consider the alternative question, "Given our differences, how do we become more fully human together?" The Think Tank is a setting that allowed us to consider this question (and its challenges) in connection with authentic and genuine understandings of self. The group allowed for exploration, because through our interdependence as colleagues and peers, we recognize that our differences coexist in relationships full of commitment and integrity.

The Think Tank is an environment where we as participants are all responsible for expressing our own understandings, for offering up our honest perspectives, and in the process, learning about others and ourselves. The group process returns us to our own expertise and experience in ways that can be newly productive, removing the predetermined answers outside of ourselves, the sieve of expectations. In querying what it means to be human, we were fully present to seek and create. This way of learning let me embody this exploration of humanness as I facilitated the group along a winding path of dialogue. It broke open my preconceptions, and turned over new ground for my thinking and for my work in groups.

Our dialogue also showed the value of an educational model that allows for what is authentic to emerge, that relies not on a prearranged set of materials, but that offers up an entryway into lines of questioning that can break us out of our assumptions, our well-tread routes of thinking, our expectations about who we are and why we are in a classroom together. The setting of the Think Tank, modeled after the Inside-Out classroom, allows for a reordering and reorientation of perspectives because learning happens as a function of relational growth. Facing the possibilities and challenges in grappling with diversity requires us to truly listen and respond to each other as unique people, a skill that in turn allows us to function with greater capacity and perspective as educators, facilitators, and peers.

Since its inception, a motivating interest within the Think Tank has been to explore how we can increase our capacity as individuals and as a group to create social change and positive impacts within our communities. What I gained from our conversation on "being human" is that we have potential, not just in the ability to resist, but also to create, to generate an investigation in which self and other are intrinsically linked. Education merges with social change via a honing of inner perception. To the degree that we can increase self-awareness, as well as awareness of others, we can have greater influence and impact within our relationships, environments, and communities. When we have a sense of how our own unique development as humans is connected to a larger humanity, and a deeper understanding of the meaning of freedom in the context of our own lives, we can steer our motivations and actions with a deft and keen perception.

Because of how we are situated in our own unique lives, we are all being challenged in different ways to discover what is at the heart of the question of what it means to be fully human. Our real differences show us that we cannot determine this meaning for any other person, yet we have a deep interdependence with each other for discovering our own answers. The classroom can be a place where we explore our potentials as well as our limitations, take responsibility for our collective well-being, and help each other to grow. Perhaps with this understanding, we can actively and collectively work to create and generate further settings where we can be fulfilled in this quest.

Notes

1. Albert Einstein, *The New Quotable Einstein*, ed. Alice Calaprice (Princeton: Princeton University Press, 2005), 206.
2. Maya Angelou, "A Poem for Haiti," in *The Zombie Curse: A Doctor's 25-Year Journey Into the Heart of the AIDS Epidemic in Haiti*, Arthur M. Fournier (Washington, DC: The National Academies Press, 2006), 297–298.

CHAPTER 13

Breaking Through "Isms"

Ella Turenne

> I am more and more convinced that true revolutionaries must perceive the revolution, because of its creative and liberating nature, as an act of love. For me, the revolution, which is not possible without a theory of revolution—and therefore science—is not irreconcilable with love. [T]he revolution is made by people to achieve their humanization. What, indeed, is the deeper motive which moves individuals to become revolutionaries, but the dehumanization of people?
>
> Paulo Freire[1]

In a preliminary meeting in juvenile hall with a group of incarcerated young men, my coinstructor and I shared our vision for the class we would soon begin with them and a group of college students. We offered the workshop as a space where we would talk about topics they wanted to explore, would create art together, and could be open and honest with each other. After we finished our pitch, I asked for questions. One young man raised his hand.

"You said you want us to be honest. Will you be honest with us, too?"

"Of course," I said. But the question caught me off guard. It reminded me that we were still interlopers who had not yet gained trust from these young men. I asked him to clarify. He went on to say that many people in the facility, in their lives, in the *system*, rarely told them the truth, even if it was a painful truth. Would we be honest and courageous enough to confront the good, the bad, and the ugly and share with them when they were out of line? No coddling. Just being real. I assured him that we would be. I can say we kept that promise and so did they.

Something about the Inside-Out model offers people who would not normally be in the same room with each other the resolve to be their best—and perhaps their truest—human selves. So much militates against this elusive aim. Peer pressure, societal norms and constructs, personal insecurities: these factors all perpetuate the routine habits and behaviors that prevent us from truly listening and responding to fellow human beings with compassion, understanding, and dignity. As Thich Nhat Hanh explains, our day-to-day perceptions and assumptions are often detached from reality:

> Because of forgetfulness and prejudices, we generally cloak reality with a veil of false views and opinions. If one clings merely to a system of concepts, one only becomes stuck. The meditation…is to help one penetrate reality in order to be one with it, not to become caught up in philosophical opinion or meditation methods. The raft is used to cross the river. It isn't to be carried around on your shoulders.[2]

The Inside-Out Prison Exchange Program provides a kind of meditation, a raft in the praxis of liberation work. It is effective in its ability both to bring together groups of people from often disparate backgrounds and to facilitate an educational process. It creates spaces for people to be students and humans, for opinions to be valued, and for counternarratives to be cultivated and explored. Spaces such as these, where we give ourselves permission to be the most human, are all too rare.

We live in a society that is plagued by "isms," where the word "post-racial" is an idea avidly discussed by some and fiercely dismissed by others. Potentially explosive issues related to race, class, gender, and a host of other socially constructed categories—the election of the first African-American president, the rash of recent suicides by LGBTQ youth, yoyo-ing legislation around abortion—occupy independent and mass media, academic conferences, and dinner-table conversations, yet little understanding emerges.

We are hard pressed to find ways to come to grips with how these issues affect us as individuals, communities, and society. Especially in college and university settings, faculty and administrators struggle to respond to these charged current events as "teachable moments" that can motivate genuine dialogue. Such a task is daunting; as discussed in chapter 12, students are unaccustomed to being stretched beyond their comfort zones or to experiencing the tension that can lead to growth. Although there is no magic formula for how to do this work, the Inside-Out model, I suggest, offers a productive pedagogical approach with which to tackle these charged issues.

What Do We Mean by "Breaking Through Isms?"

Brazilian artist and activist Augusto Boal, who developed Theatre of the Oppressed (TO), calls his use of theater as a tool for social change a "rehearsal for revolution."[3] TO, as described by Marie-Claire Picher, "is a participatory theater that fosters democratic and cooperative forms of interaction among participants. Theater is emphasized not as a spectacle, but rather as a language designed to: 1) analyze and discuss problems of oppression and power; and 2) explore group solutions to these problems."[4] Boal argues that part of the problem with oppression is that it is difficult to imagine circumstances outside of what one is accustomed to. By actually "acting" out a solution to a problem, one can even begin to manifest its reality. In the classroom, this idea of rehearsing revolution through dialogical interactions has roots in Paulo Freire's theories about education and critical transformation. Freire believed that "Within the word we find two dimensions, reflection and action, in such radical interaction that if one is sacrificed—even in part—the other immediately suffers. There is no true word that is not at the same time a praxis. Thus, to speak a true word is to transform the world."[5]

Considering these two quotations in tandem, a model emerges of learning geared toward the transformation of thought into action. This model places students at the forefront of learning and expects that they will actively wrestle with creating shared spaces where such transformation will unfold. The practice of engaging students experientially rather than in purely traditional analytical and theoretical ways stretches their ability to think critically and investigate how reality intersects theory. As a result, the revolution is the act of disrupting and then dismantling the outside hegemonologue dominating the thoughts and behaviors of each student inside the classroom. Collectively, they are engaged in the practice of social dramaturgy, a process they *rehearse inside* the classroom and *act outside* of the classroom.

Boal also writes, "To surmount the situation of oppression, people must first critically recognize its causes, so that through transforming action they can create a new situation, one which makes possible the pursuit of a fuller humanity. But the struggle to be more fully human has already begun in the authentic struggle to transform the situation."[6] One of the greatest attributes of the Inside-Out model is the ability it fosters to see participants as fully human. Especially in a space such as a prison, where people are routinely subjugated, told when to wake up, what to eat and with whom to speak, to be seen and respected as a human being is critical. There are real injustices at play within as well as outside of prison walls. The "isms" exist on a global level. However, students bring this global baggage into the classroom with them, which is then sometimes enacted through micro aggressions and other forms of unchecked manifestations of privilege. On two levels, structural and pedagogical, Inside-Out models how we can get to the heart of addressing these issues and possibly bring about transformation.

On a structural level, Inside-Out has long been involved in tackling issues of inequity within the program, such as improving the training around diversity, privilege, and power issues as well as developing initiatives like Degrees of Freedom, which works to address the question of sustained access to higher education.[7] In addition, the presence and participation of the Think Tank, a body of incarcerated men at Graterford (who are mostly lifers), with whom the Inside-Out staff, the International Steering Committee, and trainees meet on a regular basis, also represents Inside-Out's continuous efforts to foster equity and share leadership among all stakeholders within the organization. These structural considerations are important to note when we reflect on the dynamic of who occupies Inside-Out spaces. An organization in which the structure mirrors—or strives to mirror—its work and values sends a strong statement and further legitimizes the work.

Depending on geographic location and the demographic of the participating college and correctional facility, it is common for most of the inside students in an Inside-Out class to be middle-aged men of color and for most of the outside students to be younger white women. In addition, to date, most Inside-Out instructors are white women. As inside and outside students learn together, multiple "isms" are constantly in play in a dialectical way: assumptions about race, gender, class, age, and a host of other categories. This dynamic is not exclusive to the Inside-Out program, but rather a national, historical trend that permeates programmatic work in prisons, education and social justice, and social service work in general. For instance, according to the National Center for Education Statistics, in 2007–2008, close to 76 percent of public school teachers were female and 83 percent were white.[8] To ignore the historical inequities that have contributed to these dynamics would be antithetical to the principles of anti-racist organizing and pedagogy.

The goal of Inside-Out is not to sweep these dynamics under the rug, but to work through these issues collectively as authentically as possible. We are asked to be intentional about our awareness of these "isms" in structural ways and to work to subvert them while staying true and honoring each person's identity. This work requires a great level of trust and openness and necessitates that each person bring his or her authentic self to the conversation, regardless of how difficult that conversation is. Respectful dialogue almost always results in a deeper appreciation for another's perspective, even if one still ends up not agreeing. In her groundbreaking book, *Teaching to Transgress*, bell hooks writes that "To engage in dialogue is one of the simplest ways we can begin as teachers, scholars, and critical thinkers to cross boundaries."[9] This brings us to the pedagogical question of how to help students learn how to have productive, respectful dialogue and to approach what the People's Institute for Survival and Beyond calls the "growing edge."[10] Freire writes, "Mobilizing and organizing have in their nature education as something indispensable—that is, education as development of sensibility, of the notion of risk, of confronting some tensions that you have to have in the process."[11] It is in the doing—both by being in the classroom as a group and working on classroom projects—that Inside-Out has been successful. In a similar way, TO challenges people to shed the identity of passive spectator and become "*spect-actors*," or agents of transformation. You cannot rehearse the revolution if you are not actively engaged in it. TO allows for people to be an integral part of the process of critiquing issues and coming up with solutions to bring about change. In similar ways, the Inside-Out model demands that all students be active participants. Even the faculty member, like the joker in the Theatre of the Oppressed, is considered a facilitator, not a teacher employing the "banking" method of education.[12]

Small group activities and projects facilitate this pedagogical idea within the Inside-Out model. Small group work, which encompasses the bulk of project-based work, assists in fostering community and respectful dialogue. In creative ways, it allows students to work together toward a common goal, which often means having to exhibit a great deal of compromise, patience, and empathy. It is in those moments where people have to listen to each other that some important work happens. As we have seen Boal and Freire urge, the process of dialogue begins to transform into action.

As is discussed elsewhere in this volume, the practices of collaboratively creating guidelines for dialogue, small group activities, and group projects all contribute to the creation of a space where students can agree *and* disagree without harboring ill feelings toward each other. The skills for participation in respectful dialogue that students develop promise to have a ripple effect, potentially altering not just the classroom but our larger society's perception of and response to a variety of inequitable situations and ideologies.

I began doing this kind of liberatory work in prisons in 2001 with an organization called the Blackout Arts Collective,[13] a group of artists, activists, and educators of color based in New York City who sought to empower communities of color through arts, education, and activism. One of our main programs was Lyrics on Lockdown (LOL),[14] a tour that used the arts to educate the public about the prison industrial complex, created spaces for incarcerated people to think and act critically about their oppression, and built coalitions with existing grassroots organizations and movements doing anti-prison and prison abolition work. We travelled across the country, performing at venues such as the Nuyorican Poets Café, Rikers Island,[15] and the World Stage.

Out of this tour grew the idea to develop a college course that would take students inside the prison walls for a collaborative and transformative experience with incarcerated young people. Like Inside-Out, the LOL methodology employed critical pedagogy and popular education to engage young people in examining social justice issues using language and the cultural rhetoric of their time. While the two programs differ somewhat in detail and logistics, both models use small group and project-based work to foster dialogue and build community. My experiences with these programs in tandem offer powerful models for incorporating elements of the TO, music, writing, and popular culture to explore personal narratives and various perspectives on the criminal *in*justice system and to imagine change.

Art is an essential tool in this pedagogy. There are numerous documented practical reasons why art is such a potent tool, such as those found in a study conducted by the California Endowment:

> Arts programs for incarcerated youth have been shown to reduce violations, result in...fewer injuries for offenders and staff, allowing more time for constructive activities. When compared with control populations, arts programs for incarcerated youth and youth on probation have resulted in lower recidivism rates and fewer court referrals. Youth...who have participated in art programs display important pro-social and mental health characteristics, including greater self-efficacy, the ability to express themselves, improved attitudes toward school, and appropriate behavior and communication with adults and peers.[16]

We know that the arts have other powerful effects. Engaging in the arts allows people to develop their voice and their own sense of agency. As many of the incarcerated participants I have encountered have told me, it offers a space of "freedom," whether for the short time that class is in session, or when they are working on a poem or collaborating with outside students on a project. Art allows critical messages to be explored, often in ways that might be considered radical in other forms. Finally, art is also a medium for the expression of profound social ideas; sometimes it functions as the miner's canary. From the beginning of time, artists have used creative expression to spark awareness and dialogue about critical societal issues.

Class projects are one of the hallmarks of an Inside-Out class. The project-based nature of the Inside-Out model ensures that students: 1) engage in dialogue; 2) are continuously in a position where they challenge their assumptions; 3) collaborate; 4) have a chance to use their strengths and discover their own agency; and 5) deepen their understanding of the challenges and complexity of inequity. In her critique of critical pedagogy, Elizabeth Ellsworth writes about the dangers of oversimplifying privilege and oppression. She writes, "To assert multiple perspectives in this way is not to draw attention away from the distinctive realities and effects of the oppression of any particular group. It is not to excuse or relativize oppression by simply claiming 'we are all oppressed.' Rather, it is to clarify oppression by preventing 'oppressive oversimplifications' and insisting that it be understood and struggled against contextually."[17]

Here is where the intersectionality between "isms" exists. You cannot think about race without considering gender or class. You cannot discuss ability without taking into account how size-ism might be a factor. Intersectionality makes conversations about the oppressed and the oppressor both richer and more complex. In an Inside-Out classroom, the building of community requires that each individual understand the multiple layers of "isms" present in the room and how they play out based on any number of dynamics. Then it requires that everyone create a collaborative environment while together balancing the weight of these "isms."

Bobbie Harro's model of a "cycle of liberation"[18] mirrors these steps and helps to explain how Inside-Out supports the process of moving toward critical transformation. The first stage is "waking up"—encountering something that causes someone to rethink or change their core beliefs and/or values. For many students in an Inside-Out course, simply entering a prison, or encountering an individual who is incarcerated or in college, is enough to begin that process. Harro describes the second stage as "getting ready." In this stage, she writes, "once we know something, we can't *not* know it anymore."[19] In this stage students take their waking-up moment and think about its implications on a systemic level. They are reading and gathering information to contextualize the questions that are now swirling in their minds. It is also the stage where they begin to dismantle the discriminatory and privileged views that they have been socialized within and to begin building a new understanding and vocabulary that is anti-oppressive. The next stage is "reaching out." In this stage, students move beyond their interior understanding to explore the expertise of others. The reaching out stage allows students to get feedback about their developing views.

In an Inside-Out classroom, these three phases are taking place concurrently, as students dialogue and work on small group activities. The significance here is that assumptions and norms brought in from years of socialization are suddenly cracked wide open while, at the same time, new ideas are being developed, debated, and tested. While this is taking place, the next phase, "building community," also blossoms. The Inside-Out classroom becomes a microcosmic community, one that includes people of different genders, races, ages, and socioeconomic backgrounds. In the final stages, "coalescing" and "creating change," the final project creates the exigency to synthesize and shape the learning from the early stages into one concrete, tangible action. The groups, having taken what they have learned, now put into action their theories, all the while still embodying these new ideas and values through their own interactions. The final project that arises from a semester of dialogue among the inside and outside students brings about the critical transformation that makes the model so successful.

Several projects illustrate this process in action, prompting the kind of dialogue that requires deeper introspection. In one project designed and facilitated by college students for a shared workshop, participants chose an issue and created a performance representing that issue without using words. In another, students were asked to pick a topic and develop a public service announcement (PSA) about the issue. We began with intense discussion about PSAs—What are they? Whom do they target? Do they always achieve their goals? The class watched examples of PSAs and also came up with others they had seen and analyzed them with a partner. Then, the students broke into groups and created their own PSAs about a topic of interest to them. What emerged from this project was an interesting array of messages, from warnings about violence to information about drug use. Appendix 3 includes the full student-developed plan for the workshop.[20]

During this workshop, typical of Lyrics on Lockdown and the Inside-Out classroom, the students worked collectively, had equal voice in the conversation, and felt as if their opinions were valued even if others disagreed. Heated debates over issues of class and race were discussed and shared in the groups; however, there was no hostility in the room, only impassioned voices asking questions, looking for answers and, most importantly, listening. The students challenged each other at every turn. This, however, only seemed to validate that everyone was experiencing the discussion in the moment. In other words, the recognition of "isms" was useful for dialogue and understanding, but did not create an atmosphere of intimidation or mistrust. People felt they could ask each other honest questions about race, gender, and class dynamics and get equally honest answers without fear of resentment or suspicion or anger. Everyone understood that the challenging and the questioning are educational processes meant to contribute to personal and collective growth, not personal attacks. Students are able to remain objective both because of their understanding of how *systems* contribute to the "isms" (developed through discussion of assigned readings as well as lived experience) and because of their initial establishment of guidelines for interaction with each other.

Other projects developed more long-term initiatives. For example, in an Inside-Out class taught in Portland, Oregon, the group decided to work on a proposal to create a recycling program at the facility. The conversation began with the idea that white, middle-class communities mostly activated the environmental movement while low-income communities of color were affected (sometimes negatively) by the policies stemming from that movement. The students put together the proposal to launch a recycling program in the facility, which was eventually approved by the administration. The benefits of this were that the students got to wrangle with complex issues of race and class and then had the opportunity to do something about it together, in a way that was equitable and meaningful.

One final key element is the use of icebreakers and other fun, small group exercises. In the same way the projects foster an atmosphere of collective understanding, icebreakers allow for the gradual building of the trust such a group dynamic requires. In trying to foster conversation about "isms" and break down socialized barriers, these activities can serve as very useful tools to reveal complex issues in nonthreatening ways. For instance, my class once did an icebreaker in which students listened to a variety of songs containing the same word—for instance, "mother"—identified similarities and differences among the songs, and discussed what it meant that the songs were created by people of different genders, races, or classes. One of the songs, a pop song, was by a white female artist named P!nk. As it was played, an inside student, a young black man, jumped up and began singing the song. He knew every word and, I might add, had a great time dancing to it. Both inside and outside students looked at him quizzically, partly from the shock of his sudden exhibition, but more because his classmates never expected him to even know that song. After a few moments, he looked around and yelled out, "What? I love this song!" That moment was a turning point for all in the class because it shattered every stereotype we collectively held.

During another class, the group exercise invited students to analyze lyrics of an explicit rap song. The students entered into a heated discussion about identity and masculinity. The female students (all of whom were outside students) challenged the male students (mostly inside students) about stereotypes of women and how they were portrayed. The male students challenged those notions and discussed society's hand in shaping notions of masculinity. Each student in that room had to think seriously about what they knew, why and how they knew it, and how they were going to be thinking about it moving forward.

These examples illustrate a finding in a recent report from Campus Compact on access to education and civic engagement:

> The practice of moving theoretical academic content from the lectern to engaged applications has grown significantly at higher education institutions over the past 20 years. This practice has been shown to help campuses fulfill several key goals of higher education, including producing critically, civically, and globally minded graduates who possess problem-solving and leadership abilities.[21]

The Inside-Out model reaches a step further by pushing students—both inside and outside—to see the humanity in others, in turn challenging them to be critical about societal norms and stereotypes. In this way, it moves beyond the Campus Compact criteria for successful civic engagement initiatives. To be sure, as administrators and faculty, we are always intent on achieving reciprocity. It is recognized as a critical element to the success of our partnerships. However, the academic institution usually focuses on the benefits of the experience not for community participants, but for its campus students. The Inside-Out model challenges institutions to expand, to see all students in that classroom as their students: all capable of critical transformation; all capable of beginning the process of deconstructing oppression; all capable of being agents of change.

> At the risk of seeming ridiculous, let me say that the true revolutionary is guided by great feelings of love. It is impossible to think of a genuine revolutionary lacking this quality. (Che Guevara)[22]

As we try to build understanding in our communities about complex issues and "isms"—and as we educate the next generation of inside and outside students who will be lawyers, judges, law enforcement officers, social workers, community organizers, artists, citizens, and voters—the Inside-Out model provides critical strategies and tools with which those struggles can be transformed into positive learning experiences for all students.

Each time I teach Inside-Out or LOL, I poll the students at the end of the semester and ask each group what their impression of the group was at the beginning and end of class. The inside students usually say that, initially, they thought the outside students would be stuck up and judgmental. The outside students usually say they thought the inside students would be intimidating and also judgmental. By the end of the course, both groups agree that they found the other group accepting and open-minded, and were surprised that they had more in common than they anticipated. This realization could not have come from just reading about college students or incarcerated students in a book.

Thich Nhat Hanh writes, "We have to strip away all the barriers in order to live as part of the universal life. A person isn't some private entity traveling unaffected through time and space as if sealed off from the rest of the world by a thick shell."[23] Inside-Out aspires to this vision in its structure and its pedagogy. We enter the prison to strip down its raison-d'être, keeping certain people in and shutting certain people out. We interact with each other to ignite and challenge the ideas located within the pages of our books. We do this because, as Paulo Freire writes,

> If it is in speaking their word that people, by naming the world, transform it, dialogue imposes itself as the way by which they achieve significance as human beings. Dialogue is thus an existential necessity. It is an act of creation; it must not serve as a crafty instrument for the domination of one person by another. The naming of the world, which is an act of creation and re-creation, is not possible if it is not infused with love. Love is at the same time the foundation of dialogue and dialogue itself.[24]

This idea of love, echoed by Guevara, is at the center of opening up our authentic selves to such an experience. A love for humanity dictates that we must be empathetic. To be empathetic is to understand suffering, and once we understand suffering, there is no reason to fear the unknown. There is only the desire to move toward action, to relieve or abolish the oppression. Inside-Out gives us tools that facilitate the revelation of humanity in people and situations. It allows us to see, through praxis, what we only otherwise assume, based on factors such as how we were raised, the environment in which we live, and what we see in the media. It offers us firsthand knowledge of a human's insight, not a collective stereotype of a group's behavior. Herein lies the power of the collaborative model coupled with the arts: that we bring our authentic selves to these confined spaces where freedom of thought, creativity, and movement are greatly suppressed and oppressed. We do this work in order to break through walls but also to move toward respect, compassion, and—ultimately—freedom.

Notes

1. Paulo Freire, *Pedagogy of the Oppressed* (New York: Continuum, 2005).
2. Thich Naht Hahn, *The Miracle of Mindfulness* (1975; Boston: Beacon Press, 1976).

3. Augusto Boal, *Theatre of the Oppressed* (New York: Theatre Communications Groups, 1985).
4. Marie-Claire Picher, *What is Theater of the Oppressed?* (New York: TOPLAB, 2002; revised 2011).
5. Freire, *Pedagogy of the Oppressed*.
6. Boal, *Theatre of the Oppressed*.
7. Degrees of Freedom is a program of The Inside-Out Prison Exchange Program (in development) that extends the classroom experience by supporting incarcerated men and women to to continue their higher education endeavors post release.
8. National Center for Education Statistics, Schools and Staffing Survey, Teacher Data Files, 2007–2008.
9. bell hooks, *Teaching to Transgress: Education as the Practice of Freedom* (New York: Routledge, 1994).
10. From my notes from the People's Institute for Survival and Beyond training, Undoing Racism, January 2006.
11. Freire, *Pedagogy of the Oppressed*.
12. The banking method of education was described by Freire as the traditional way in which it is assumed that teachers bring all knowledge to students. Students are like a bank, empty until knowledge is "deposited" in them.
13. The Blackout Arts Collective was founded in 1999 and now loosely exists as a network of artists and activists. http://socialjustice.ccnmtl.columbia.edu/index.php/BlackOut_Arts_Collective
14. The Lyrics on Lockdown tours took place from 2001 to 2009. An artist's review of LOL: http://www.litrave.com/archives/archives27.htm
15. Rikers Island is America's second largest jail system. http://www.forbes.com/2009/07/10/jails-houston-recession-business-beltway-jails.html
16. Susan Anderson, Nancy Walch, and Kate Becker. *The Power of Art: The Arts As an Effective Intervention Strategy for At-Risk Youth* (Los Angeles, CA: California Endowment for the Arts, 2004).
17. Elizabeth Ellsworth, "Why Doesn't this Feel Empowering?" *Harvard Educational Review* 59 (1989): 297.
18. Bobbie Harro, "The Cycle of Liberation," in *Readings for Diversity and Social Justice, 2 edition*, edited by Maurianne Adams, Warren J. Blumenfeld, Carmelita Castañeda, Heather W. Hackman, Madeline L. Peters, and Ximena Zúñiga. (New York: Routledge, 2010), 52–58.
19. Harro, "The Cycle of Liberation."
20. Lauren Bille and Danielle Laura, *One Mic* (New York: Andre Maurice Press, 2006), http://www.corporatebboyism.com/one-mic/
21. Christine M. Cress, Cathy Burack, Dwight Giles, Julie Elkins, and Margaret Carnes Stevens. *A Promising Connection: Increasing College Access and Success Through Civic Engagement* (Boston, MA: Campus Compact, 2010).
22. Che Guevara. "From Algiers, for *Marcha:* The Cuban Revolution Today," in *The Che Reader* (New York: Ocean Press, 2005), 393.
23. Nhat Hanh, *The Miracle of Mindfulness*.
24. Freire, *Pedagogy of the Oppressed*.

CHAPTER 14

Trusting the Process: Growing and Liberating Self-Reflective Capacities Behind the Prison Walls

Kayla Follett and Jessie Rodger

Pre-conceived notions. We are all guilty of harboring them. Notions of what we think things are supposed to be. Things like prison, and education. Of what and who the student is, and what and who the convict is... Today those lines are blurred. Today there is no distinction between student and convict and education and prison... because today, right here, we are all students. Learning. Evolving. Erasing. Celebrating.

Inside-Out Alumna, currently incarcerated

When we first heard that there was "an alternative educational opportunity" being offered in our Masters of Social Work (MSW) program at Wilfrid Laurier University in Kitchener, Ontario, we were intrigued. Our most memorable lessons have been those where we have a chance to interact with, support, and walk alongside others. So, as first year MSW students, we enrolled in Shoshana Pollack's required course, "Diversity, Marginalization, Oppression." In this chapter, we join together to reflect on the ways our experiences in this Inside-Out course have changed our professional and personal lives.

Introduction

"Diversity, Marginalization, Oppression" (DMO) explores the ways that intersectional oppression affects populations, communities, and individuals, making it well suited to the Inside-Out approach. The course is designed to reveal the preconceived notions and biases used to label and stereotype people, how these labels can affect how you relate to yourself and the world around you, and the implications of privilege for social work practice.

We remember thinking that the course would feel risky or touchy, and we worried that it would not be possible to talk openly about diversity and oppression with people who were themselves "oppressed." Little did we know that challenging assumptions just like this one was all part of what Shoshana called "trusting the process"—listening to our inner selves and feeling confident that what we were experiencing was all part of learning and growing.

The course pushed us to the limits of our understanding of ourselves as individuals, as members of the larger group, and as budding social workers. We have gained a nuanced appreciation for the vital importance of openness. Being open to feeling some discomfort, analyzing it with others, and transforming it for personal and professional growth reminds us of the words of Paulo Freire: "Washing one's hands of the conflict between the powerful and the powerless means to side with the powerful, not to be neutral" (122). We feel empowered to talk about the bad shit.

On Feminism

After all this time, now I know: women do need women. It takes a woman to teach a woman how to be a woman. A man will tell a woman what he thinks she wants to hear, but a woman will tell a woman what she needs to hear. The life lessons I learned by creating relationships with women helped me to become the phenomenal woman I was born to be. I can never repay these women for the love they gave to me. I can give the love to another sister. There are so many diamonds in the rough that just need to be polished. Who said women can't get along?

Elizabeth Leslie

Our feminism strives to foster connection and empowerment through nonjudgmental openness with others and self. We value individual experience and choice. We question the patriarchal society around us, how it tries to lead us to believe that women cannot get along. We are critical thinkers who always try to apply an anti-oppression and social justice lens.

Jessie's Feminist Perspective Vignette

My feminism had been honed over many years working with women and children, and it provided me with a keen sense of self and purpose. Feminism was not always welcome in the MSW program on campus, however, and I spent a lot of time establishing my feminism in the room, learning when to speak up, learning when to share my feminist perspective, and also negotiating when to keep quiet.

Complicating this process was the illusion of safe space in my faculty classrooms. Within the walls of the university, we were encouraged to speak up and often, but rarely spoke to one another, usually directing our comments to our professor, the authority in the room.

Our Inside-Out classroom, by contrast, was facilitated, rather than taught. We were encouraged to respond, not just to course material, but also to each other. In addition, our Inside-Out classroom facilitator not only guided us to create a list of guidelines for our time together, but revisited them with us, helping us slow down at times and check in with one another. If there was a moment in the dialogue that was challenging, we would sit and reflect, talk and dissect what was happening and how we were feeling about the content, and engage one another in thoughtful and frank dialogue. The conversations and dialogues that resulted continue to resonate with me today.

Early on in our class it was made clear that our space was a safe space, and this commitment was reinforced week after week. It was not the absence of being challenged that enabled me to mature as a feminist. I knew that there were varying levels of feminist perspective in the room, and we did not ignore the differences. We were encouraged to share perspectives, listen to one another, and reflect on how the content made us feel. This was refreshing, and my feminist perspective was deepened in an environment where I did not have to temper my opinions or deal with the commonly held belief that feminism was pure anger.

Kayla's Feminist Perspective Vignette

When I first started Inside-Out, I had just recently stopped volunteering with a grassroots feminist organization, where I had peer-counseled survivors of sexual assault. This organization is tight-knit and, being the extrovert that I am, I was happily right in the middle of the chaos. I developed comfortable relationships and a "feminist rapport" almost instantly with several women, and within a short period, we were friends for life. We accepted differences of opinions and perspectives but stuck together for the common good—our fight against sexual violence and the damaging impacts of inequality.

When I went into the Inside-Out classroom, I brought this deep feeling of solidarity, this feeling of "we're all in this together." I thought: here we are, in the middle of a federal prison, stomping down those walls together. In my mind there couldn't possibly be anything more empowering. But to my surprise, I wasn't getting the same feelings of solidarity back in return. Each week, I would walk into the classroom thinking, "Okay, today is the day we will begin to collectively build our feminist rapport like the strong women we are!" And class after class, I didn't feel it. We would spend three hours together one week, and by the end of it, we would be laughing and enjoying one another's company; a week would pass and coming into the classroom felt awkward and unusual all over again.

It wasn't until the course was over that I realized the difference between *my assumptions of how unity should feel* and the unity that existed in the group. The unity in our group was based on showing up to every class prepared, being present in the circle, providing space for all voices to be heard, embracing difference, and working together to build the ideal circumstances for authentic experience. I didn't fully appreciate this unique and wonderful unity at the time because I was too busy imposing my own assumptions about feminist rapport development, or *my* felt-sense of feminist unity. I spent the whole time feeling "something was missing," which prevented me from *just being*. Moreover, my sense of feminist rapport was defined largely by my experiences with a previous group, where we had all come from similar (if not identical) social locations: white, cis-gender, heterosexual, able-bodied, middle-class university students or professionals. Being deeply embedded in the privilege that I assume, I had a shallow understanding of what building a feminist rapport was really all about. And the fact of the matter is, I come from a social tribe that is more different from than similar to many of the women in our Inside-Out circle. How could I ever think that we were "in this together"? In what together? Life? The prison? Not a chance. Not even close. The DMO Inside-Out curriculum gave me the opportunity to challenge my feminism, and to grapple with how that applies to the social work I intend to do in the future. I have gained a deeper perspective on the power of assumptions (no matter how well-intended), the process of relationship building, and the intersectional complexities of life, experience, and feminism.

On Transfeminism

As you will read from our vignettes, embracing transfeminism was a personal challenge. We are not trans-identified. Through Inside-Out, we can both now proudly say that our feminism will not be held back by fear, judgment, or societal boundaries that separate trans-identified and non-trans-identified individuals.

Kayla's Transfeminism Vignette

Our group's final project was to design a format for our ongoing work together. Several of us had written a paragraph together and were reviewing it out loud with the full group. One part of it, which I happened to love, said "with women, by women." So simple, so powerful.

With a slight hesitation, a group member spoke up and asked, "What about trans people?" I am not sure what my facial expression revealed in that moment, but my heart skipped a beat and my mind started to whirl. Instantly I realized that I knew *nothing* about the issues that trans people face. For incarcerated people who identify beyond the gender binary... I knew even less. More than that, however, I felt scared. Not scared of trans people, but afraid that if we were not "with women, by women" then something was going to be taken away from the group. After all, women still have a long way to go in this world. Do "we" really have the capacity to broaden our horizon like that? I knew in my mind that this was not the right reaction—I knew I had no right to *build* a wall when I touted breaking them down—but my heart wasn't there.

I clearly needed to learn more about the issues that trans-identified people face and turned to Scott-Dixon's *Trans/forming Feminisms*. Scott-Dixon makes the point that if feminism is to avoid repeating historical mistakes, then broadening one's vision is essential, not just to "feminism" as a value, but more importantly for trans people. In time, I have come to realize what that "something" was that I felt would be taken away from the group if we chose not to embrace the "with women, by women" adage. That something was my own internalized oppression, my own feelings of inferiority, wrapped neatly in a package of anxiety and fear. It fooled me into believing that social boundaries and inequality would keep me safe.

Jessie's Transfeminism Vignette

My own response to the challenge of transfeminism mirrors Kayla's very closely. There had been fleeting moments prior to our Think Tank discussion about the issues surrounding the trans community. Every time the subject came up, I knew that it was important, but I did not feel well-read enough in the subject to contribute thoughts. I now recognize this was a barrier that I was using to avoid the question. It was a way to stop myself from having an uncomfortable confrontation within myself. When it came to the question of including "trans people" in the mission of the Think Tank, there was a silence in our group. Like Kayla, part of me knew that it was important that we include trans people in our work moving forward. This was especially true when we were advocating for those who are most vulnerable and marginalized in our criminalized society. But when it came time to include "them" in our conversation, to my chagrin, I remained quiet. I, too, was concerned about the possibility of "watering down" an idea of having a woman-focused think tank. Feeling conflicted, I realized that I needed to educate myself further.

I liked to think that before this exercise I was well-read on the subject, taking a deliberate and pointed step in the direction of understanding gender as social construct and biology as only being a small aspect of identity. What I learned through this moment was that I was very quick to identify myself as "trans inclusive" in my ideology, but when push came to shove, I needed that big push to realize my own insecurities and opportunities for growth.

I would not go so far as to say that our Inside-Out classroom facilitated great dialogue about trans rights in prison. Most of us were not prepared to have that conversation during our semester together, knowing little about trans rights, much less the trans experience in prison. But this moment prompted me to explore not only the topic of people who identify as trans but also my own initial resistance. I am still not where I want to be in terms of my understanding about how the trans identity is experienced, but I'm on my way and feeling eager to adapt and to be a more thoughtful and just social worker.

On Social Locations

On the surface, social location is simply a person's place in society, including but not limited to, race, gender, sexuality, culture, and ethnicity. From a critical social work perspective, social location has much to do with the unequal distribution of power and privilege and the dominant-subordinate relations that ultimately protect the powerful to the detriment of the marginalized. Being white, middle-class, English-speaking, Canadian-born, non-Aboriginal, able-bodied, non-trans, MSW students, our social locations are of privilege.

Kayla's Social Location Vignette

In the first week of the MSW program, I had a conversation with a woman from the Caribbean about privilege. She told me that she does not want to be called an "immigrant," a "woman of color," a "black woman," a "brown woman"...she just wanted to be *her*. She said to me, "Look at you, with your curly hair and your white skin." With hurt feelings and a tinge of anger, I reacted, "That's not fair, you don't know what I've been through in my life and you're totally judging me by how I look." She told me I didn't get it. I didn't understand what she was talking about. She explained that when I walk into a clothing store or a restaurant, or I apply for a job, I receive preferential treatment solely because of the color of my skin and my pretty hair. She said that it didn't matter what I had been through in my life or what she had been through, because society doesn't care. This was the *first time* in my life I stopped for a moment and really, truly *felt* the unfairness of privilege from someone else's perspective. She, as a Caribbean woman, had been living within this reality her entire life.

When I walked into the prison for the first time, unlike my family, I wasn't worried about my safety or intimidated by the officers. What I *was* worried about was the way I was going to be perceived by the women inside. Because of a conversation with my MSW colleague, I was painfully aware of my identity and my privilege, and I worried they were going to see me as privileged, prissy, or entitled. In our Inside-Out classes, especially when we learned about the hardships women face inside, this awareness felt particularly raw and painful. I often drove home in tears. Other weeks, when I was given the opportunity to just interact one-on-one or in small groups, this awareness within me was met with kindness from the women living inside; sharing laughter during an ice-breaker felt like fond acceptance and I believe that as I worked through challenging my own assumptions, so too did some of the women inside. Indeed, the acceptance that I have received from the women living inside has helped me to acknowledge that I cannot change who I am. What I *can* do is be authentic, work toward being open to events that make me stop and check myself, and trust the process.

Jessie's Social Location Vignette

Examining my social location in our Inside-Out program was an interesting exercise by virtue of the context. In the classroom at the Faculty of Social Work, I was able to sit back and be very self-satisfied in my examination of my own power. I was able to relax, converse with my professors and fellow students, and present myself as a self-aware, self-reflective social-worker-to-be. I felt comfortable and pleased with myself and mostly got positive feedback. On campus, it was easy, even routine, to acknowledge my privilege. Why? The risk to me was minimal. I knew I was surrounded by people who had had life circumstances similar to my own. While some of us were taking on debt to do this work and some were not, we all shared the privileged vantage point of those able to access advanced higher education.

When faced, literally, with women who are incarcerated and whose life experiences had been so radically different from my own, the level of comfort I had had in the on-campus classroom disappeared. I was more easily seen through by my Inside-Out colleagues, and that was frightening. This confrontation with my privilege was different from anything that I had experienced. In the past, we had always framed our social location with the understanding that we were not racist, biased, or prejudiced. Conversations would invariably end up with people saying how hurt they were that marginalized groups would assume that they would be prejudiced. We would play the "hurt card" and then all of a sudden we would become the victim. Looking back, it is incredible to think about how we were able to turn a conversation about supporting marginalized and oppressed population into a conversation where we validated our own insecurities.

The first few weeks of the MSW program were littered with conversations about social locations. It was the cool thing to do: locate yourself, find yourself, and proudly (but humbly) declare who you were to everyone. I could do it in my sleep. But for some reason, when you gave me a dedicated amount of time to reflect, the same old script no longer came out as readily as it had before.

This experience made me question everything. I stopped and thought critically about who I am and who I acknowledge myself to be in the context of social work. Being in the Inside-Out classroom did not afford me the luxury of invisibility: I had to participate and be present.

I felt an additional struggle when reading and reacting to the course materials. I did not want to become a student—or eventually, a social worker—who espoused the virtues of criminalized people in order to prove how supportive and understanding I was of marginalized people. So I was challenged to ensure that my participation was not opportunistic or performative, but genuine and thoughtful.

In the months that followed my Inside-Out experience, I continued to question and reflect. The experience was so intense that, six months after the class wrapped up, I found myself revisiting conversations and questioning my identity. Months after, I experienced a profound movement in my self-perception. I found myself working through some challenging and difficult realities of who I am and becoming comfortable with myself. It came as no surprise to me, after these months of self-reflection, that I came out as a gay woman in the wake of my Inside-Out experience. I am more convinced than ever that this coming out process for me was in some way facilitated by the space that was created in our Inside-Out course. I would not have felt comfortable acknowledging or saying this out loud if I had not been challenged and given the chance to process my true self.

Conclusions

Kayla

What my social location further exemplified for me in a way that I had never experienced was how pervasive my privilege is in my life. Time after time I have had a chance in this Inside-Out experience to understand and see how I benefit from my privilege, as well as how my privilege has impacted others negatively. If I benefited from the color of my skin, it meant that another person was challenged because of the color of theirs. If I was able to succeed because of my parents' socioeconomic status, another person was set up to fail because of the circumstances of their family.

I live in a world where my experience of privilege is the norm. I work with those who have gone on to postsecondary education, I socialize with people who have never had to utilize social services themselves because of their positions (or if they have, they certainly do not discuss it because of the stigma attached), and I go to a school where conversations about how "poor" we are is a regular staple. Part of my realizing the impact of my social location is the very clear understanding that I now have—that my experiences are not the norm.

Jessie

The Inside-Out model forced me to confront this reality face to face in a very literal way. We were challenging ideas not only academically. We were dialoguing with people who had first-hand knowledge, in a way that I have never had before, about the treatment they had received through a criminal justice system slanted against ethnic, racial, and religious minorities.

At the end of this experience I came to a very startling understanding. Had I been born in different circumstances, I could have very well been an inside student rather than an outside student. The assumption that those who commit crime "deserve their punishment" or have a "choice between right and wrong" dissolved. The reality of our criminal justice system setting people up for failure felt heavy and frightening.

*　*　*

These experiences, and the competing thoughts that followed, showed us that we are not as centered and self-aware as we thought we were at the beginning of our semester. Self-awareness is a lifelong process—an ever-changing, painful, and challenging process that is full of opportunity for growth, empowerment, and capacity building. As social workers, we strive to own the fact that our perspectives are shaped by our privilege. As we work with people and communities, it is paramount that we constantly remind ourselves that people will know their situations and their lives far better than we ever could. We will listen and value individual lived experience. We will learn from the instances when we judge someone. These experiences, just like in our Inside-Out classroom, provide opportunities to deconstruct self, become more critical, and build authentic connections.

In social work education, the acknowledgment of power, privilege, and dominant-subordinate relations is presented as the first step toward becoming an empathic social worker. We challenge that "first step" model: acknowledging the impacts of power and privilege should be a lifelong, ever-emerging, and changing process. It takes genuine and committed dialogue across difference, going beyond your comfort zone, and learning how to *just be* with people. If we do not have these dialogic experiences, social work students may be at risk of gaining a false confidence in their capacity to acknowledge their "self" and the privilege that goes along with it.

So we find ourselves wondering, "What's next?" How can these efforts translate into something that will better meet the needs of the individuals and people we will work with and serve? One of the hallmarks of the Inside-Out program is the group project. Each Inside-Out class creates something together, and students are evaluated on the process, rather than the outcome. Our class knew what we wanted to do together. We created the first Canadian Inside-Out think tank, joining our colleagues in Pennsylvania, Oregon, Michigan, Ohio, Indiana, Tennessee, and West Virginia as the first international Inside-Out think tank, and the first to advocate for women and trans people. Our charter appears in appendix 6.

The process of creating the Walls 2 Bridges Collective was not easy. It took hard work, collaboration, and lots of time. Today, a group of Inside-Out alumni meets at Grand Valley Women's Institution every two weeks to work on public education projects, learn together, consider the issues that divide us, and talk about what connects us. Not talking to our inside colleagues between meetings slows down our process and can be frustrating. This frustration, however, is a very tangible reminder of the walls that divide us. And when progress is slow, we are reminded to connect. We believe in showing up, being present, and finding solutions together. Allowing experiences that disrupt our sense of self to change us, we strive to be more open, more empathic, less judgmental, and always willing to learn.

References

Freire, Paulo. *The Politics of Education: Culture Power and Liberation*. Westport, CT: Bergin & Garvey, 1984.

Leslie, Elizabeth. "Who Said Women Can't Get Along?" in *Interrupted Life: Experiences of Incarcerated Women in the United States*. Edited by R. Solinger, P. C. Johnson, M. L. Raimon, T. Reynolds, and R. C. Tapia. Berkeley, CA: University of California Press, 2010.

Scott-Dixon, Krista. *Trans/forming Feminisms: Trans/feminist Voices Speak Out*. Toronto: Sumach, 2006.

PART IV

Transformation? Connection as Catalyst

CHAPTER 15

Turned Inside-Out: Reading the Russian Novel in Prison after Levinas

Steven Shankman

"The ego [*le moi*] is...a being divesting itself, emptying itself of its being, turning itself inside out [*à l'envers*]."[1]

"A feeble-minded person can be inspired.... This is a type that exists in Russia. It is *The Idiot* of Dostoevsky. The human pierces the crust of being. Only an idiot can believe in this goodness."[2]

Emmanuel Levinas

Turned Inside-Out

When I participated in the Inside-Out Training Institute in the summer of 2006, most of the classes taught in the program were in criminal justice. And that made good sense. If the subject you are studying is criminal justice, it seems perfectly fitting for a professor to bring his or her college students inside to give them a firsthand experience of the prison environment. But the teaching of literary texts? This question haunted me the first time I taught an Inside-Out class. Why do it here, in this particular environment? But I wanted to teach literature and ethics inside, particularly the novels of Dostoevsky, and I was struck by Dostoyevsky's alleged claim that "the degree of civilization in a society can be judged by entering its prisons."[3] So reading Dostoevsky in a literature class taught in a prison seemed a good fit, although it was only after I became an Inside-Out instructor that I discovered just how deeply relevant to the Inside-Out experience Dostoevsky's great texts would prove to be.

I taught my first class in spring 2007 on *House of the Dead*, Dostoevsky's semi-autobiographical prison memoir, and *Crime and Punishment*, which was the first novel Dostoevsky wrote after he was released from his four-year prison sentence followed by another six years in exile in Siberia. As a novice Inside-Out instructor in the Oregon State Penitentiary (a maximum-security facility in Salem), I wasn't sure that the inside students would possess the necessary academic skills for more advanced, upper-division work. So I taught a lower-division class, officially the third quarter of a year-long survey class taught in the Clark Honors College at the University of Oregon. Similarly, concerned that the prose would be forbidding to those not schooled in the history of philosophy, and especially in phenomenology, with its sometimes specialized vocabulary, I felt it wasn't appropriate to focus the class in the way I would have preferred, that is, on ethics as understood by the great philosopher of ethics, Emmanuel Levinas, whose work was, and still is, having a deep impact on my own thought and experience.

My outside students were wonderful. They were open and very capable but, because they were mainly first-year students, they were very young. The inside students, it turned out, were much better readers and writers than I had imagined. After debriefing with them at the end of this first course, I decided to teach my next Inside-Out course as a senior-level colloquium, where it would be possible to achieve the sharpness of focus the more mature incarcerated students were capable of and looking for, and to place Levinas and his notion of ethics front and center.

My spring 2008 class was, for several reasons, a breakthrough experience for my teaching of Inside-Out. First, there was the consistent interplay between Dostoevsky's great novel, *The Brothers Karamazov*, and Levinas's thought, as seen in a series of interviews with Levinas included in the book *Ethics and Infinity*, which was deeply influenced by Dostoevsky, and particularly by *The Brothers Karamazov*. Second, Levinas's thought—and Dostoevsky's novel—began to reveal, for me, much of what makes the Inside-Out experience so powerfully transformative. We not only read about the ethical encounter in both Levinas and Dostoevsky, but the class itself powerfully enacted this encounter in its interpersonal dynamics. Third, both my inside and outside students took joy in slowly and patiently unpacking Levinas's densely evocative prose, sentence by sentence. What seemed impossible to grasp on a first reading began slowly to make sense, and to inspire the students with a vision of a remarkable human generosity and kindness that was affirmed on a regular basis in the interactions they experienced with their fellow students in the classroom.

I have continued to teach "Literature and Ethics," using a variety of texts to explore a certain way of reading the Russian novel, and particularly Dostoevsky, in the twenty-first century, specifically in the wake of the moving and influential writings of Emmanuel Levinas, who died in 1995. In the third year, we read Cervantes' *Don Quixote* and Dostoevsky's novel *The Idiot*, whose protagonist, Prince Myshkin, is modeled on Cervantes' hero. We also read a selection of transcriptions of the last set of lectures, on "God and Onto-theo-logy," that Levinas delivered at the Sorbonne in 1975–1976. In the fourth year, we read Vasily Grossman's great novel *Life and Fate*, a Soviet version of *War and Peace*, alongside a series of interviews with Levinas entitled *Is it Righteous to Be?* These experiences opened up these great novels and Levinas's thought to me, and to my students, in amazingly deep ways.

Levinas was born and raised in the shadow of a prison, in the town of Kaunas, Lithuania, where his father owned a bookstore that sold mainly Russian books. Before he read philosophy, the young Levinas encountered a preoccupation with ethics, as he would come to understand ethics, in Russian literature and especially in Dostoevsky's novels, which he read in the original. To read Dostoevsky after Levinas is, for me, to read Dostoevsky for the inspiration that Levinas, the great philosopher of ethics, found in Dostoevsky's novels. Levinas was fond of quoting Father Zosima's brother Markel, in *The Brothers Karamazov*, whose idea is reiterated by a variety of characters in the course of the novel: "Each of us is guilty [or 'responsible,' *vinovat*] of all and for all men before all, and I more than the others."[4] Levinas redefines subjectivity in terms of the responsible "I." No one can take "my" place. "I" am inescapably responsible for the Other, who is absolutely other, separate from me, and who is likewise unique and irreplaceable. Ethics goes from the unique to the unique.

Levinas, whose work participates in the phenomenological tradition of philosophical analysis, was a student of Husserl and Heidegger and was the revered teacher of such thinkers as Jacques Derrida, Jean-François Lyotard, and Luce Irigaray. Levinas sought to rethink the relationship between philosophy and ethics, alarmed by philosophy's apparent complicity with ethical turpitude and indifference, as evidenced by the great philosopher Heidegger's association with Nazism. Levinas argued that ethics must precede ontology (the science of "being"), which is always in danger of betraying ethics. By ethics Levinas means the face-to-face, concrete encounter with a unique human being for whom I am uniquely and inescapably responsible.

Face-to-face! Those of us who teach Inside-Out classes will immediately think of the Wagon Wheel, the signature Inside-Out ice-breaking exercise we use with our students. The Wagon Wheel consists of two concentric circles of facing chairs. The inside students sit in the outside circle, the outside students in the inside circle. The facilitator asks a "fill-in-the-blank" question. Inside and outside students share their responses for a minute or two. Then, with a signal from the facilitator, those in the outside concentric circle, consisting of inside students, rise up from their seats and move to their right, sitting in a chair facing a different outside student, a procedure that is repeated until each and every inside student sits, face-to-face, opposite each and every outside student. It is crucial that it be the outside students who sit in the stationary, inside circle. Were it the inside students sitting stationary, it could create the impression that the inside students are being made objects of the gaze of a group of tourists from the outside.

The face-to-face encounter is central to the way in which Levinas explains the ethical relation. Although Levinas is not interested in proving the existence of God, he holds that "in the access to the face there is certainly also an access to the idea of God."[5] In *Totality and Infinity*, Levinas writes:

> The facing position, opposition par excellence, can be only as a moral summons. This movement proceeds from the other. The idea of infinity, of the infinitely more contained in the less, is concretely produced in the form of a relation with the face. And the idea of infinity alone maintains the exteriority of the other.[6]

The Other is absolutely other. He or she cannot be contained by me, by my perceptions, by my attempts to know him or her, by my consciousness. As we learn in the Inside-Out Instructor's Manual, there is much wisdom contained in our rule that inside and outside students know each other only by their first names. This rule teaches, the manual suggests, that the need to know *about* the other may well inhibit our ability to live *in relation to* the other.

My encounter with the other breaks the trance of presence, of being, of knowing. The other is infinite, cannot be contained by my consciousness. He or she is infinite in this sense, and in the sense, as well, that I am never finished with the other, that my responsibility is never completely fulfilled. I am always, infinitely—without end—obligated to the other. "The best way of encountering the Other," Levinas says, "is not even to notice the color of his eyes! When one observes the color of his eyes one is not in social relationship with the Other. The relation with the face can surely be dominated by perception, but what is specifically the face is what cannot be reduced to that." Levinas continues:

> There is first the very uprightness of the face, its upright exposure, without defense. The skin of the face is that which stays most naked, most destitute. It is the most naked, though with a decent nudity. It is the most destitute also: there is an essential poverty in the face; the proof of this is that one tries to mask this poverty by putting on poses, by taking on a countenance. The face is exposed, menaced, as if inviting us to an act of violence. At the same time, the face is what forbids us to kill.[7]

Likewise, in the Wagon Wheel, one feels both vulnerable and responsible at the same time.

Inside-Out. The name of the program refers to the fact that each class taught in the program consists of incarcerated students—students on the inside—and those from outside the prison walls. But to me, the phrase "inside-out" suggests something that happens, emotionally, to those participating in the class. You are turned inside-out, emptied of your ego as you transcend labels and categories—"student," "teacher," "murderer," "prisoner," "criminal"—and respond to the other as fully human. The class becomes a community of learning based on the dignity of every individual. It is a transformative experience for those involved. We not only read about and discuss ethics in my classes, but the students enact the ethical encounter in which the ego (the "*moi*"), as Levinas describes this encounter, is experienced as "a being divesting itself, emptying itself of its being, turning itself inside out [*à l'envers*]."

Levinas, Dostoevsky, Transcendence, Incarceration

Both Dostoevsky's and Levinas's lives were deeply influenced by exposure to incarceration. In addition to being raised near a prison, for five years during the Second World War, Levinas, by then a French citizen, was captured by the Germans and incarcerated in several prison camps before being sent, from 1942–1945, to a facility for French military officers in Germany near the town of Hanover and Bergen-Belsen. His French military uniform saved him, as a Jew, from being sent to a concentration camp. When he was released at the war's end, he discovered that many of his closest relatives—including his parents, his two brothers, and his brother- and sister-in-law—had been murdered by the Nazis. Readers of French now have access, through the recently released first volume of a projected edition of the collected works of Levinas, to Levinas's prison notebooks.[8]

Dostoevsky, like Levinas, was deeply transformed by his incarceration. Dostoevsky was arrested in 1849 for having joined a circle of political activists with Utopian ideas. He entered the prison as a young radical from a privileged class with advanced, European ideas about social equality who thought he knew what was best for Russia but who was, at first, unable to connect emotionally with the largely peasant population of convicts whom he had initially found so repellent. Like Raskolnikov, the protagonist of the first of his four great novels, Dostoyevsky emerged four years later as a humbled Christian whose first impressions of his fellow convicts had been dramatically reversed by his prison experience, and who had, in the process, gained a life-long sense of fraternal intimacy with Russia's peasant class and with many of those less fortunate than himself.

What transformed Dostoevsky was an experience he describes in *A Writer's Diary*. Wandering on his father's estate, the nine-year-old Fyodor, terrified by a wolf, is comforted by his family's serf, the illiterate peasant Marey, whose selfless kindness, unnoticed by others, went unrewarded. When, in prison, Dostoevsky suddenly recalls this moment,

> through some sort of miracle, the former hatred and anger in my heart had vanished. I went off, peering intently into the faces of those I met. This disgraced peasant, with shaven head and brands on his cheek, drunk and roaring out his hoarse, drunken song—why he might also be that very same Marey; I cannot peer into his heart after all.[9]

Dostoevsky now encounters each of the men imprisoned with him as a "face" in Levinas's sense of the term—infinite, unknowable—that evokes his inescapable responsibility for the other.

Reading, Responsibility, Transcendence

Dostoevsky draws on his prison experience in a remarkable passage in *The Brothers Karamazov*. The novel's moral beacon, Father Zosima, remarks that it is not truly possible to be "a judge of anyone." Zosima continues:

> For no one can judge a criminal, until he recognizes that he is just such a criminal as the man standing before him, and that he is perhaps more than all men to blame for that crime. When he understands that, he will be able to be a judge. Though that sounds absurd, it is true. If I had been righteous myself, perhaps there would have been no criminal standing before me.[10]

How can "I" possibly be responsible—as Dostoevsky's revered Father Zosima insists that I am—for someone else's crime? I asked my students to think about this extraordinary passage from *The Brothers Karamazov*. An inside student named Terry remarked that he had been thinking deeply about this passage ever since he first encountered it the week before. He resolutely refused to allow anyone else to take responsibility for his crime. "If I did not commit my crime," Terry insisted,

> people would not have had their precious lives cut short by my selfish act. Putting it any other way feels like an avoidance of the truth and a violation of the memory of the lives of my victims.[11]

Danny, an outside student, broke the hushed silence that followed Terry's disarmingly honest words. Danny said that his best friend from high school, at the age of 19, was killed in a fight in a parking lot after a major league baseball game. Since his friend's death, Danny said, he "swiftly passed judgment on his murderer, and there was not a doubt in my mind," he observed in his final paper, "that he [i.e., the murderer himself] was solely responsible for his actions." After reading Father Zosima's words, especially within the context of the feelings of deep friendship that developed between the inside and outside students in our class, Danny said that he had reflected upon the ways in which he may have contributed to the murder. "My actions in high school condoned violence. Fighting others was a rite of passage. It exemplified masculinity and dominance, and was even glorified. I have accepted the possibility that my involvement in these actions helped create an atmosphere that shaped the outcome" of his friend's death.

This, for me, was one of the most extraordinary moments of my teaching literature and ethics in the Inside-Out program, for several reasons:

First, there is the absolute honesty of this exchange, an honesty that is rare in a conventional academic setting, and that encourages students to be vulnerable and to take risks. A large part of what makes Inside-Out classes so special is the fact that inside and outside students come to class, like Prince Myshkin in Dostoevsky's novel *The Idiot*, without an agenda. In the class I taught in spring 2009 on *Don Quixote* and the *Idiot*, the students and I had the opportunity to connect Myshkin's disarming—even disruptive—openness towards others to the atmosphere of the class itself. We noted how often the notion of emptiness came up in the course of the novel, and I discussed the doctrine of *kenosis*, of Christ's emptying and humbling himself, that was so central to Dostoevsky's understanding of the Eastern as opposed to the Western church. Roman Catholicism, for Dostoevsky, equated spiritual with temporal power, and hence with a triumphalist notion of Christianity epitomized by the crusades. Even Don Quixote, despite or rather because of his idealism, continually exerts his will upon others, not restraining himself from physical violence in pursuit of his ideals, although his weapons are generally hapless and ineffective. Don Quixote has an agenda. In the complex, materialistic, competitive, and upwardly mobile social world depicted in *The Idiot*, everyone has an agenda, exemplified in Ganya Ivolgin's quest for marriage with Nastasya Filippovna, whom Ganya tries to purchase as if she were a thing rather than a human being. What is remarkable about Prince Myshkin, the students maintained, was that, in his relations with others, he has no agenda.

Inside and outside students, in their respective worlds, also typically encounter those who have an agenda. On campus, Honors College students, like Dostoevsky's characters in fashionable St. Petersburg society, sometimes find themselves trying to impress those who are capable of advancing their careers. They have an agenda. Inside students come to distrust many of the people around them in the prison environment. Even gestures of apparent kindness can be viewed, with suspicion, as insincere forms of manipulation. When they cross the threshold of the Inside-Out class, though, inside and outside students come to study together without an agenda. Students know each other only by their first names. Once the class is over, no further contact is permitted. This helps to insure that neither inside nor outside students misuse their friendships.[12]

Second, this moment confirms for me the reason why I was drawn to teaching literature–great literature–inside. Inside-Out classes bring two very different worlds together.[13] Reading a shared, great literary text creates community. A great text has the potential of eliciting powerful individual responses. Indeed, it *requires* such responses. While outside students often have better training as academic analysts of literary texts, the inside students teach the outside students how to read great texts on a profoundly experiential level.

Third, the exchange between Terry and Danny illustrates key aspects of the ethical encounter upon which Levinas insists. For Levinas, the "I" is absolutely responsible for the other. No one can take my place: "Each of us is responsible for all before all, and I more than all the others." I more than all the others! This is what Terry was insisting, as was Nat, another inside student, in his written response to this passage, in which Nat remarked that "I can ask mercy for all others, and refuse it for myself." At the same time, indeed precisely because of this untransferable responsibility of the I, it is only "I" who can save the world. For Levinas, what the other does is his or her affair. If there is injustice in the world, *I* need to step up. I am responsible for the other, for the world. I can do more. If only I had been more righteous, perhaps there would not be a criminal standing before me now, perhaps, as Danny observed, if I had worked to create a more peaceful, more loving environment in my high school, I might have thereby prevented the death of my best friend. What is my role in the phenomenon of crime? Of mass incarceration? What have I done to address the deep social ills that have created the current crisis? I am responsible!

Charity, Justice, and Other Others

All of these lessons found fruition in a closing ceremony of an Inside-Out class I taught in spring of 2012, in which we had read the great Soviet-era novel *Life and Fate* by Vasily Grossman alongside a series of interviews with Levinas collected in a volume entitled *Is It Righteous to Be?* In part because of the "no contact rule," the final closing circle in an Inside-Out class is truly final, and always a difficult rite of passage. I try to share with the students my own reflections on something positive we find in those painful, fleeting, closing moments and what we can learn from being so fully present for the three hours a week that we come together, present in ways that we are not always so present in our day-to-day lives. I tell the students that this is the result, in part, of our awareness, from the very first moment of the class, of how limited, how finite is our time together. If we brought this kind of awareness to our lives outside of the Inside-Out classroom, imagine how much more present we could be, how much more available to those around us!

When I asked the students to share something that they will take away from the class, Sam, an inside student, said that

a huge reason why this class has had such a powerful effect on me was the atmosphere in every class [meeting]. I came from a world full of stereotypes, prejudice, and "violence against the other." And walked into a sanctuary. I wasn't judged for my circumstances or my past. I was welcomed into a community where we respected, even admired, each other's differences. We encouraged participation and respected the right to just listen. After crossing the threshold into class I felt free in every sense of the word.[14]

When it was time for an outside student to share, Bianca spoke of her high regard for all of the inside students, and said that she could not understand why they were being "punished" by serving a prison term or what good that punishment could possibly accomplish.

I, too, had a very high regard for the inside students in the class, but Bianca's comments made me uncomfortable, especially because a prison officer was there with us, at this charged moment, and I was concerned about how the officer would take Bianca's comment. Inside-Out classes would hardly be welcomed by prison officials if these officials thought that the explicit point of these classes was to dismantle the prison system or excuse criminal behavior. I decided that we should discuss Bianca's comments during the outside students' debriefing session. So I drew their attention to the subject of our class, literature and ethics, reminding students about what Levinas means by "other others," which came up a number of times during our class discussions. Why, I asked the outside students, might someone feel uncomfortable with Bianca's saying that she could not understand why our classmates on the inside were being "punished"? Again, no response from the outside students. Was this non-response, I wondered, the effect of my outside students having been so completely turned inside-out by the faces of their classmates on the inside, so hollowed out by the face of the other, so transformed, that they had somehow become oblivious of the other others, of the victims of the crimes perpetrated by their classmates?

In our readings from *Is it Righteous to Be?*, we confronted, on a number of occasions, what Levinas calls "the third party." When I encounter the other, for Levinas, we are not "alone in the world." We are

> at least three. Two plus a third. If I heed the second person to the end, if I accede absolutely to his request, I risk, by this very fact, doing a disservice to the third one, who is also my other. But if I listen to the third, I run the risk of wronging the second one. This is where the State steps in. The State begins as soon as three are present. It is inevitable. Because no one should be neglected, yet it is impossible to establish with the multiplicity of humanity a relation of unique to unique, of face to face. One steps out of the register of charity between individuals to enter the political. Charity pursues its fulfillment in a demand for justice. It takes a referee, laws, institutions, an authority: hence the State, with its tyrannical authority.[15]

In the face-to-face relation, I am obligated to be charitable toward the other, to respond to him or her: to exercise my respons-ability (the word "responsibility" is significantly spelled, in French, *responsabilité*), to exercise my *ability* to respond to, even to answer for, the other. But I am also responsible to the third who comes along, and to all the other others. The other, in the face-to-face relation, is infinite, cannot be limited, reduced, categorized. But now, with the appearance of other others, I must compare incomparables. Here is where "justice" enters, and the State. Levinas even goes so far as to say that "justice constantly has a bad conscience" because "the demand of charity which precedes it remains and beckons it."[16] Justice can always be better. Our charity for the other, the bad conscience that accompanies judgment, demands that we work for more and more perfect justice in the world.

In *Life and Fate*, Vasily Grossman describes how, in even the most horrendous and oppressive of situations—in a concentration camp, in a gas chamber, in a gulag, in the midst of bloody military conflicts—individual human beings have performed extraordinary, unexpected, seemingly random acts of kindness. In their anthology, my students chose to cite, as one of their favorite quotations from Grossman's novel, the following passage from *Life and Fate*, spoken by a character named Ikonnikov, a preacher of the creed of senseless kindness:

> Human history is not the battle of good struggling to overcome evil. It is a battle fought by a great evil struggling to overcome a small kernel of human kindness. But if what is human in human beings has not been destroyed even now, then evil will never conquer.[17]

Bianca, in her affection for her classmates from the inside, had clearly tapped into that remarkable energy of irrepressible kindness generated by, and born witness to in, Grossman's remarkable text. She had perhaps forgotten, for the moment, about the other others who had been harmed by her classmates on the inside.

At the end of this class, I held separate debriefing sessions with the inside and outside students. I met first with my outside students. In the debriefing session with the inside students, Shawn asked what his classmates from the outside had to say in their debriefing session. I mentioned our discussion about Bianca's comment during the closing ceremony. One inside student applauded Bianca for saying what she believed. Two others, however, had misgivings. Sam said that, at first, he was glad to hear what Bianca said, but then he felt more cautious and, finally, almost embarrassed by Bianca's attempt to exonerate him. "It's not as if I'm not in prison for a reason," he said, almost surprised by his refusal to accept a free pass for failing to live up to his responsibility for the other. Sam, as did Terry and Nat in our class on *The Brothers Karamazov*, is here affirming Dostoevsky's insight—first articulated by Father Zosima's brother Markel and then adopted by Father Zosima himself—about the nature of the "I," about true subjectivity: "Each of us is responsible for everyone and everything, and I more than all the others."

Is it likely that Bianca would have made the same concluding remark that she did if she had taken an Inside-Out class that was focused exclusively on the criminal justice system or on *The Brothers Karamazov* rather than on a novel about the brutal crushing of freedom by the Nazi and Stalinist totalitarian regimes during the Second World War? When Inside-Out classes are offered in the field of criminal justice, students have the opportunity to learn just how complex a phenomenon crime is. Criminal acts are committed within a broad cultural context rife with injustice at every level. This, I take it, is the force of Father Zosima's insistence that "If I had been [more] righteous myself, perhaps there would have been no criminal standing before me."[18]

If I were more righteous, perhaps there would be no prisons at all. But since there are prisons, it is my responsibility to do what I can, as an Inside-Out instructor, to offer my students the opportunity to be turned inside-out by the other, to transcend labels and prejudices, and to help transform the prison environment into a more compassionate and just one. Each of us who has been turned inside-out can then do everything in our power to create an increasingly just society for the benefit of each other, and for all the other others, inside and outside the prison walls, until, one day, there are no prison walls and no prisons at all.

Notes

1. Emmanuel Levinas, *Autrement qu'être ou au-delà de l'essence* (Paris: Brodard & Taupin/Livre de poche, 2001), 185 (originally published by M. Nijhoff in Dordrecht, Netherlands, 1974); *Otherwise than Being or Beyond Essence* trans. Alphonso Lingis (Pittsburgh: Duquesne University Press, 1981; rpt. 1998), 117.

2. Emmanuel Levinas, interview with Myriam Anissimov (1985), trans. Jill Robbins and Thomas Loebel; published in *Is it Righteous to Be? Interviews with Emmanuel Levinas*, ed. Jill Robins (Stanford, CA: Stanford University Press, 2001), 89–90. Levinas makes these remarks about Dostoevsky's *The Idiot* in the context of his admiration for Vasily Grossman's great Soviet-era novel, *Life and Fate.*

3. This quotation is attributed to Dostoevsky, though it cannot be found in his published works.

4. Fyodor Dostoevsky, *The Brothers Karamazov*, trans. Constance Garnett as revised by Ralph E. Matlaw and Susan McReynolds Oddo (New York and London: W. W. Norton & Company, 2011), 250. I have modified the translation. Cited by Levinas, *Ethics and Infinity: Conversations with Philippe Nemo*, trans. Richard A. Cohen (Pittsburgh: Duquesne University Press, 1995), 98.

5. Emmanuel Levinas, *Ethics and Infinity: Conversations with Phiippe Nemo*, trans. Richard A. Cohen (Pittsburgh: Duquesne University Press, 1995), 92.

6. *Totality and Infinity: An Essay on Exteriority*, trans. Alphonso Lingis (Pittsburgh: Duquesne University Press, 1969), 196.

7. *Ethics and Infinity*, 86.

8. Emmanuel Levinas, "*Carnets de captivité*," suivi de "*Écrits sur la captivité*" et "*Notes philosophiques diverses*," in *Ouevres Compl*ètes, Tome I, eds. Rudolph Calin and Catherine Chalier, with a preface by Jean-Luc Marion (Paris: Grasset et Fasquelle, 2009).

9. From *A Writer's Diary*, February 1876, chapter 1.3; trans. Kenneth Lantz, *A Writers Diary*, Vol. I, 1873–1876 (Evanston, IL: Northwestern University Press, 1994), 135.

10. Dostoevsky, *The Brothers Karamazov*, 276–277.

11. *Dostoevsky and Levinas Face to Face* (Eugene, OR, 2011), ed. Aisha, Jordan, Eryn, Carmela, Kevin G., Nick, and Jeffrey (students in my spring 2011 Inside-Out class, "Ethics and Literature," taught at the Oregon State Correctional Institution), 44. This is the anthology composed by my students at the end of the class.

12. For the anthologies the students assemble at the end of each class. I ask each inside student to write a brief, anonymous appreciation of an outside student and each outside student to appreciate an inside student, also anonymously. Anonymity is key. It empties the appreciation of ego. I present these appreciations during the graduation ceremony when I hand the certificates to the students in recognition of their completion of the class. As each student steps forward, I read the anonymous appreciation composed for that particular student.

13. Paul Perry (see chapter 4) made this comment to me during an Inside-Out Steering Committee meeting in Graterford after I taught my first Inside-Out class in 2007. Since

my class focused on literature, hearing these words from Paul meant a great deal to me. When Paul articulated his broad conception of an Inside-Out class, it was as if a prophet had spoken!

14. *Zhizn' i Sud'ba* [*Life and Fate*], an anthology of student writings from my spring 2012 Inside-Out class on "Literature and Ethics: Levinas and Vasily Grossman's *Life and Fate*," ed. Pepe, Abs, Seth, Talon, Steve, Carolina, Robyn, and Anna (Salem, OR: Oregon Corrections Enterprises, Oregon State Correctional Institution, 2012), 7.

15. Emmanuel Levinas. *Is it Righteous to Be?: Interviews with Emmanuel Levinas*, ed. Jill Robbins (Stanford, CA: Stanford University Press, 2001), 193–194. This chapter is entitled "In the Name of the Other." The original interview was conducted by Luc Ferry, Raphaël Hadas-Lebel, and Sylvaine Pasquier and was published, in French, in *L'Express* (July 9, 1990). The translator is Maureen V. Gedney.

16. *Is it Righteous?* 194.

17. *Life and Fate*, trans. Robert Chandler (New York: New York Review of Books, 1985; rpt. 2006), 410.

18. Dostoevsky, *The Brothers Karamazov*, 277.

CHAPTER 16

Look at Me!

Tony Vick

Are you a recycler? Do you spend any time separating your refuse into different bins in order to spare the world from expending unnecessary resources? The fact is that if we only consume, and never find additional uses for materials, the supply will one day become exhausted. Yet we can't imagine living without paper products, or drinking water, or bottles and cans to hold our beverages. It seems that society is beginning to understand the importance of being more "green."

We have learned that society's choice of whether and how much to recycle depends basically on economic factors. Recycling becomes economically attractive when the cost of reprocessing waste or recycled material is less than the cost of processing new raw materials.

I suggest that we also need to begin recycling human life—the greatest material and resource that we've got. Perhaps we don't consider this to be a valid recycling project since new humans are being born every minute of every day. Maybe we feel like it's not worth the energy and trouble it would take to pick through the human refuse to see if any vitality and good is left.

Right now, Tennessee has over 21,000 humans in large refuse centers: prisons. These people are hoping and praying that they will be recycled. Will someone see the value that they still have for society? Will someone take time to separate them from the unusable waste that surrounds them? To do that you must *look at them*, not as statistics like the one I just mentioned, but as *people*—people who have a pulse, life, worth, and sustainability.

So, look at me! Look into my eyes so you can see that I am flesh and bones—not a statistic, not a product of the justice system—but a human being. After you see me and I see you, we can no longer pretend that the other does not exist. Once we realize that, we can move forward in ways that benefit us both. Programs that bring outside people to our inside world behind these fences are a great avenue for connecting humans to humans, eyes to eyes.

We are visual creatures. When we can visualize something, we can make it a reality. So when people look into each other's eyes they become real beings that take up this world's space. We only have so much space in our world for garbage, so we must begin to recycle even human beings. While Tennessee has these 21,000 pieces of recyclable products—what is being done to refine the material? How are citizen's tax dollars being spent to make these rough materials into productive, useful and viable members of the world?

In 2011, Tennessee claimed that they recycled over 14,000 people housed in their storage centers and released them back into the community to serve the world once again. However, Tennessee also contends that almost half of these 14,000 return to prison, their transformation somewhat defective. With that logic, what if you sent 14,000 cans to the recycling center and half of them returned with holes in them? Would that be an acceptable return on your investment?

Perhaps we have to look at the source of the problem, as Peter Rollins does in his book *Insurrection*.[1] He suggests, "Donating money to the poor without asking why the poor exist in the first place, for instance, allows us to alleviate our guilt without fundamentally challenging the system that perpetuates poverty. As the Brazilian archbishop Dom Helder Camara once said, 'When I give food to the poor, they call me a saint. When I ask why the poor have no food, they call me a Communist.'"

This concept can be further explored by looking at eighteenth-century theologian Jonathan Edwards, a slave owner who strongly advocated for the fair treatment of slaves. While he condemned the policy of taking people from Africa, he never directly attacked the system that sustained slavery. This move was left to people like his son, who questioned the very conditions that supported slavery. The point was not to be kind to one's slaves but to create a world where slavery did not exist.

Therefore I suggest to you that until we look at the system and how we are giving up on our most precious materials—human lives—people will continue to be taken to faulty recycling centers across the nation, left there to sit, without being converted into new and precious beings.

So look at me, face to face, and then tell me that I am not worth your thoughts, your time, and your prayers. Until then, you are only using your tax dollars to cover up your own guilt, your own shame, or your own disregard for human life, building recycling plants that fail all of us.

Note

1. Peter Rollins, *Insurrection: To Believe Is Human, To Doubt Divine* (London: Hodder and Stoughton, 2011).

CHAPTER 17

Access for Whom? Inside-Out's Opening Door

Tyrone Werts

In 1975, I was convicted as an accomplice to a second-degree murder and sentenced to life in prison without parole. Pennsylvania is one of six states (with Illinois, Iowa, Louisiana, Maine, and South Dakota) where a life sentence comes without the possibility of parole—essentially a death sentence (Nellis, 2010). I served my time at the State Correctional Institution at Graterford, in Pennsylvania, a maximum-security prison housing approximately 3,500 men 30 miles outside of Philadelphia.

Graterford Prison is a foreboding place. Built in 1929 to house 2,000 men, it has five cellblocks, two football fields long. Each block has 400 cells with a top and bottom tier, constructed in the shape of a huge coffin. When you drive up to Graterford, you are confronted with a massive, 30-foot concrete wall. As I passed through the gates, the noise hit me: the clanging gates, the jingling keys, and the barking of orders from the guards. Reflecting back now, I am reminded of Dante's *Inferno* . . . I had entered Hell without even knowing it.

What I remember most about my first day was the last question asked before I was led away to the six foot by 12 foot cell where I was to spend the rest of my life. The intake person looked me in the eye and asked, "Where do you want your body sent?" I was sure I hadn't heard the question correctly. I responded, "What did you say?" Looking deeper into my eyes, he repeated, "Where do you want your body sent?" I do not know now how I replied. I do remember that walking in a daze to my cell, carrying my few belongings, I knew I had to do everything in my power to get out of this place.

I spent the next 25 years appealing my case in the courts. After each denial, I would file again and again, trying to convince any court that would listen that I didn't deserve to die in prison. As the years ticked by, it became obvious to me that no one was listening. After my last appeal failed, I accepted my fate. I was going to spend the rest of my life in Graterford Prison.

When I first arrived, I was angry, bitter, and resentful toward a legal system that had sentenced me to die in prison for something of which, at the time, I thought I was innocent. I lacked formal education and had no desire to change that: education held no value for me.

I think back to one teacher I had in elementary school. She had clearly made a commitment to a career in teaching and she must have cared about the work—but she really lacked the personality to inspire young, impressionable children. I witnessed her routinely belittling and embarrassing other children over the school year.

My own most memorable run-in with her happened when the class was given an assignment to write a brief paragraph explaining what we wanted to be when we grew up. In my neighborhood, there was an older guy who had a telescope on his back roof. I used to go up there to sit with him and he would tell me about the universe. He would let me look through the telescope as he pointed out the stars and the planets. He would talk to me about the speed of light, how the planets revolved around the sun, and the vastness of the cosmos. I was fascinated by the universe as a result of the knowledge he passed on to me.

When Monday arrived, each student was called to the front of the class to read their paper: *I want to be a teacher, I want to a fireman, a doctor, a policeman,* and on and on it went. After each person finished, at the urging of the teacher, the other students would clap. I could hardly contain myself as I anxiously awaited my turn. When my name was called, I headed to the front of the room, paper in hand. I read what I had written: *I want to be an astronomer when I grow up.*

Ms. Gomez looked at me sternly and asked, "Where did you get that from? You might as well get that idea out of your head. You're not smart enough to be an astronomer, boy."

My final humiliation came when the rest of the students began to laugh at me. I walked back to my desk wanting to cry but held back the tears. I sat there, sunk in my own thoughts as the class assignment continued and each student got round after round of applause. I wanted to run out of the room and never return.

As I look back, I realize that it was this incident that first caused me to internalize the belief that I wasn't smart and couldn't learn. I lost any desire to continue going to school and did so only to hang out with friends, until I finally dropped out in the tenth grade.

When I arrived at Graterford at age 23, I was given a battery of psychological, educational, personality, and IQ tests. Mr. Ernie Bello, not only a counselor at the prison but also an Adult Basic Education (ABE) teacher at night in the education department, administered the assessments and reviewed the results with me. It was then that I learned that my reading, math, and comprehension skills were at second and third grade levels. I was not surprised and, frankly, I didn't care. The scores confirmed what I already knew: I wasn't smart and I didn't have the confidence to compete academically. Mr. Bello, however, convinced me that my interpretation of the scores was misguided. Not only was I smart enough to manage college, but I was capable of truly succeeding academically. At his urging, I registered for his evening Adult Basic Education (ABE) class and passed the General Educational Development (GED) test a year later. That was one of my proudest moments, and it gave me the confidence that I could do college level work.

Feeling more confident about my ability to learn, I registered at Villanova University's Graterford campus and Montgomery County Community College and began taking college courses, eventually earning an Associate of Science degree from Montgomery County and a Bachelor of Arts degree from Villanova.[1]

Education was an eye-opening experience. It made me realize how much time I had wasted. I had prematurely given up on my own life because I hadn't understood what I was capable of academically. With my newfound awareness, I participated in a lot of activities and programs around Graterford, and rose to become president of the largest organization in the state prison system in Pennsylvania, Lifers Incorporated.

During my 36 years inside, I met and worked with a number of incredibly committed and dedicated people, prison volunteers and other professional people working to bring hope and inspiration to those of us housed at Graterford. One of those incredible people was Lori Pompa. I met Lori in the early 1990s in my capacity as president of the lifers' organization when we served together on the board of directors of Reconstruction, Inc., a holistic reentry program assisting men in successfully returning to the community. Lori and I collaborated on a whole host of other projects, too, during her years working for the Pennsylvania Prison Society, a prisoner rights advocacy organization established more than 200 years ago.

Eventually, Lori joined the Criminal Justice faculty at Temple University and would regularly bring her students into Graterford and other prisons in the area to give them a real-world perspective on the criminal justice system. I would often serve on a panel, answering students' questions about incarceration, the prison system, and possible reforms.

One day in 2002, Lori told me about The Inside-Out Prison Exchange Program, which she had developed and had begun to offer in the county jails. It seemed like just another prison college program: it would offer an opportunity to those few individuals inside who were operating at a successful level, who already had their lives together. For me—by then deeply involved in finding ways to empower people whom others discarded as unreachable—this did not immediately strike a chord. That is, until I learned that the requirements to participate in the class were vastly different from other prison college and university programs.

A number of colleges and universities have initiated programs that allow people in prison to take college courses and work toward degrees.[2] This is valuable work. Research clearly indicates that those in prison who graduate from college have a lower recidivism rate than noncollege graduates.[3] And many incarcerated people are quite capable of doing college level work. When given the opportunity, they usually do well and even excel.

I remember back in the early days when I was just starting out, I would watch the men going to college in prison with envy. Proud, confident, well-spoken, and eloquent, they were the elites in the prison, the "cream of the crop," who had changed their lives and worked to change the lives of others in the prison and out in the community. I wanted to be like them. I wanted to demonstrate that same confidence and knowledge. And I came to realize that if I had never had the educational experience provided to me by Mr. Bello, I would never have imagined the possibilities for myself.

Therefore, while many college degree-bearing programs are giving incarcerated people great opportunities and this work should be supported, I would like to point out that those who cannot meet the requirements or who do not have the confidence to obtain a college education are left behind. They are what I think of as the "throw-away people"—men and women who recidivate because no one showed them compassion or kindness or demonstrated a belief that they could survive the rigors of a higher education. I was one of those people.

So, what piqued my interest in the Inside-Out program was finding out that, to take this college course, you didn't necessarily need a high school diploma or GED; you didn't need college experience and might not even recognize that you have the intellectual abilities to compete in an academic setting.[4] This resonated with me powerfully. I knew first-hand that there were literally hundreds of thousands of men and women incarcerated, not just in Graterford, but across the country, who were essentially like me when I first came to prison: people who were smart, but didn't know it; who suffered from low self-esteem; who lacked confidence in their abilities; who saw no value in education; who needed a chance and the opportunity to find out about their capabilities. I realized that this program would provide them with that opportunity, the same opportunity that was given to me.

All that the applicants needed was the willingness to do the work and fully participate in the sessions. Many of these men and women are the very people who would probably fall short of regular college requirements, or believe they would. Yet, those who take Inside-Out classes without these tools build confidence in their abilities. Once they go through this engaging experience, participants develop a new perspective, a new understanding about themselves and their ability to learn, as well as a desire to seek other educational opportunities. In many ways, Inside-Out serves as a gateway to higher education for these participants, which translates into lower recidivism, lower crime rates, and reduced prison populations.

I initially balked at the very idea of taking this course when it was first offered at Graterford, because my life was already on an upward trajectory. As someone who already had a college degree, I figured I had already learned the value of education. And, though I had absorbed an enormous amount of information through Villanova's Graterford college program, the experience just hadn't been as earth-shaking as I thought it should have been. Instead, it was isolating. I would go to class and listen to the lectures, take my notes, read my books, and write my papers. I passed my classes and eventually graduated. I left college happy—happy with the degree, and happy never to have to list to another dry lecture or write another paper.

So, when I was asked to take this Inside-Out course, I resisted. The syllabus required that I read six books—some research and statistics heavy—and write eight papers. This did not appeal to me. Additionally, as a Villanova graduate, I dismissed the Inside-Out course as a class for beginners, only worthwhile for people just starting out. I was proud of my academic achievements and I flaunted my degree as a badge of honor.

Once I had been convinced to take this course, however, I discovered that it was radically different from anything I had experienced in college, or even in a prison program, before. It wasn't lecture-based; it was centered in dialogue. This was not about being talked at; we were being urged and inspired to talk among ourselves. It was not instructor-focused, it was peer-focused. When we spoke, we didn't address a single individual, we engaged the whole group.

Each week, there was a different topic and, instead of facing the front of the room listening to monologues from the instructor, we sat in a circle and talked to each other. Because of this focused exchange, I gained a deeper understanding of the topic under study, and the class discussions made it much easier to digest what I was reading and to write my papers.

On a deeper, more personal level, I expanded as a human being. In doing so, I learned what my college degree truly meant for my future. I found a larger vision for myself and began to understand how I could impact the world in a more meaningful way. My leadership abilities expanded, and I learned how I was connected to my community and the rest of the world. As aware as I thought I was, this class experience opened me up further, ripping away prejudices and biases of which I had been totally unaware.

But more than that, what I witnessed among my fellow "inside" classmates was astounding. Some I knew, others I did not. The energy generated in the class carried over into the prison, where men were studying together, competing cheerfully for the best grade against one other, and having positive impacts on their peers. Before this opportunity, some men hadn't shown any interest in activities that were beneficial to their growth and development. Yet, here they were, changed men, eager to find ways to further their growth and build healthy lives.

Like the man in Plato's Allegory of the Cave, who breaks free from his chains and escapes the false reality of the shadows on the walls, I watched with extreme pride as each of my classmates left the shadow-streaked caves of their present experience and stepped into the bright sunlight of a new reality. The cosmos became ours to explore after all. But even more important than that, most of these students have gone on to work to free others among their peers still caught up in their own self-created caves, still fascinated by the shadows on the walls.

To my great surprise, although I had convinced myself I was going to die behind that 30 foot wall, my life-without-parole sentence was commuted to 36 years to life by former governor Ed Rendell on December 30, 2010, and I walked out of Graterford Prison on March 14, 2011.

For me, Inside-Out is what has been missing in our prisons, jails, communities, colleges, and universities. While its focus is education, one central outcome is a reclamation of "throwaway" people—thousands of changed lives that will, in the end, change our world.

Notes

1. Villanova's Graterford program offers both Bachelors and Associates degrees and has been in place since 1972. For a one-page description see *A Volume of Community Engagement, Community Service and Service Learning.* Office of Planning and Institutional Research: Villanova University. April 2009. 38. www1.villanova.edu/content/villanova/mission/campusministry/service/_jcr_content/pagecontent/download/file.res/CommunityEngagement.pdf.

2. In 1994, people in US prisons lost eligibility for Pell grants, closing most higher education programs inside. In recent years, an increasing number of programs have begun to fill that gap, including the Education Justice Project at the University of Illinois Campaign-Urbana; Goucher Prison Education Partnership; the Bard Prison Initiative; The Prison University Project in San Quentin; Hudson Link for Higher Education in New York State; University Beyond Bars in Washington State; and the Saint Louis University Prison Program.

3. See, for instance, M. E. Batiuk, K. F. Lahm, M. Mckeever, N. Wilcox, and P. Wilcox, "Disentangling the Effects of Correctional Education." *Criminal Justice* 5, no. 1 (2005): 55; *Changing Minds: The Impact of College in a Maximum Security Prison.* Collaborative Research by The CUNY Graduate Center & Women in Prison at the Bedford Hills Correctional Facility, 2001. Site visit April 16, 2010. http://web.gc.cuny.edu/che/changingminds.html; Jeanne B. Contardo and Wendy Erisman, *Learning to Reduce Recidivism: A 50-State Analysis of Postsecondary Correctional Education Policy.* Inst. for Higher Education Policy. November 2005. Site visit April 16, 2010. www.ihep.org/Publications/publications-detail.cfm?id=47.

4. As this volume makes clear, many Inside-Out programs now do offer credit for inside students, and these credit-bearing courses generally do require the GED or high school diploma for eligibility.

References

A Volume of Community Engagement, Community Service and Service Learning. Office of Planning and Institutional Research: Villanova University. April 2009. 38. www1.villanova.edu/content/villanova/mission/campusministry/service/_jcr_content/pagecontent/download/file.res/CommunityEngagement.pdf

Batiuk, M. E., K. F. Lahm, M. Mckeever, N. Wilcox, and P. Wilcox . "Disentangling the Effects of Correctional Education." *Criminal Justice* 5, no. 1 (2005): 55.

Changing Minds: The Impact of College in a Maximum Security Prison. Collaborative Research by The CUNY Graduate Center & Women in Prison at the Bedford Hills Correctional Facility.2001. Site visit April 16, 2010. http://web.gc.cuny.edu/che/changingminds.html

Contardo, Jeanne B. and Wendy Erisman. *Learning to Reduce Recidivism: A 50-State Analysis of Postsecondary Correctional Education Policy.* Inst. for Higher Education Policy. November 2005. Site visit April 16, 2010. www.ihep.org/Publications/publications-detail.cfm?id=47

Nellis, Ashley. "Throwing Away the Key: The Expansion of Life Without Parole Sentences in the United States." *Federal Sentencing Reporter* 23, no. 1 (October 2010): 27–32.

CHAPTER 18

Inside-Out: The Reach and Limits of a Prison Education Program*

Simone Weil Davis

Prison bars are meant to keep people in; they are also meant to keep people out. In tandem with the other powerful social forces that keep us divided, especially those that cluster around race, class and gender, the tall walls and razor wire fences of North American prisons and jails ensure that our internalized maps of what we consider home are skewed, pitted with lacunae. These blanks, blind spots, and alienations do not just impoverish us; they make it possible for things as they are to continue—including the United States' unprecedentedly high rate of incarceration. With our sense of connection, community, place, and identity distorted, our ability to militate for change—or even to envision it—is severely limited. Inside-Out seeks to loosen the foundations beneath the *conceptual* walls that our carceral system throws up.

* * *

The Inside-Out classes that I have facilitated to date were all in Western Massachusetts: creative writing and literature classes that brought students from the small, all-female liberal arts college where I then taught together with women incarcerated in that county. My co-facilitator, Lysette Navarro, herself formerly incarcerated, is a creative-writing teacher, then working with a nonprofit in the region that offers creative-writing workshops to incarcerated and formerly incarcerated women.[1] My work as an Inside-Out instructor has deepened my questions not only about the way we define and enact crime and punishment in North America, but also about the way we conceive and practice another of our central institutional projects, education. Whether critiqued as "cultural capital" or lauded as "money in the bank," education is often described as something that one acquires and then possesses *as an individual,* a currency that can buy you benefits, the key to individual social mobility. As a result of my engagement with this program, I join Paulo Friere, Myles Horton, and others to endorse not only far greater access to education but also its radical reconceptualization: a redefinition that emphasizes community creation and collective purpose rather than individual self-"betterment" and "upward" mobility, one that turns literacy from a noun to a verb, from a possession one acquires and owns into a practice between people.[2]

Here, I also challenge the assumption that when women reveal themselves through writing, their story must necessarily follow the conventions of either the confession or recovery narrative. Even with therapeutic writing designed to confront trauma, these tales of the individual are not all that's told, when women sit in a circle and write. In my own Inside-Out courses, our work did indeed lead to reflections on gratitude, guilt, and personal healing; importantly, it led just as inexorably to analysis of social inequity and calls for political change. In the present chapter, I use accounts and documents from the Inside-Out classroom to propose that it is only via heavy-handed shaping and funneling of the therapeutic discourse that questions about systemic institutional and political violations *can* be bracketed off and disregarded, in favor of the "merely" personal. How can an unorthodox seminar or an impassioned poem or story change anything? That is my focus here.

* * *

Maybe my own Inside-Out education began in earnest on the day the first paper was due, during my first time running the course in Spring 2006. It was February 17th, and I planned on collecting the papers at the end of class. On the agenda for class time was a discussion of the assigned reading, and I was struck by how slowly comments seemed to be coming, in stark contrast to our last class session. "What's the problem?" I wondered, grumpily. Finally, one inside student, Joanie, raised her hand and said, "I don't know about anyone else, but I wrote my paper all night last night, and I worked hard on it. I wanted to read it out loud and get feedback."[3] So we changed tack and devoted much of the rest of class time that day to student volunteers reading their entire papers aloud, and sharing our responses. This marked a shift, as women in the circle claimed ownership over the process we were inventing together. The assignment had been to write about "jailface" (like pokerface squared, this is author Patricia McConnel's term) and to respond to this related passage about "corázon" from Jimmy Santiago Baca's memoir, *A Place to Stand.*[4] In Arizona's notorious Florence State Prison, Jimmy's friend Macaron tells him:

All you got here is heart *corázon.* Only *corázon.* And if you don't have it, every day will be a hell you've never imagined. When the mind says, I am human, the heart growls, I am an animal. When you wish to scream, the heart says, Be silent. When you feel hurt, you numb yourself. When you're lonely, you push it aside. Strip yourself of every trace of the streets, because it will hurt you here. Here you have no feelings, no soul; only your heart will help you survive. Forget everything except survival. Don't ask why—there are no reasons. You didn't exist before coming here; your life before here never happened. The only thought that drives you on is to be alive at the end of the day, and to be a man, or die fighting proving you are a man. That's the code of the warrior. (131)

Joanie responded, in part:

"The jail face," as terminology puts it, is having to say nothing, do nothing, but you act as if anyone who dares to cross your imaginary line becomes the bait. You are like a magnet; others run to you for a "sense of belonging." They take orders like soldiers readying for battle; nothing is too hard for them to accomplish. Like you, they probably came in "jail-faced," but found out quickly that it takes more than a look, you need heart. Perseverance, the relentless effort to get back up no matter what, ability to carry on even after the soul breaks, the eyes blind, the spirit dies.

How strong are you, really? [...] Relying only on our own strength, it is impossible to reach beyond a break. I had never seen the good in me. For as long as I could remember, everything I'd loved had left me. I had done too much to go back and too much to go forward. I couldn't change, but my heart that lives inside me wanted desperately to see what all the suffering was for, why I had to resort to imprisonment, and why I was running.

With nuance and probity, Joanie's insights in the above passage detail the depth of experience that looms behind the silent mask, a threatening veneer of invulnerable cool. So, her essay read aloud to inside and outside students breaches not only education's "ivory" strongholds, but the protective scaffolding of "jailface," as well. A sheltered outside student, in other circumstances and without a class like this one, would likely "read" the text of that mask's surface and skitter off, uncomprehending.

One could understand and appreciate Inside-Out solely as an innovative way to help get educational programming to an underserved population, but in instances like this, its participants make it rather more. What we mean by education is itself mutated when Joanie insists on turning her paper from evaluative fodder into a communicative beam. From that day on, students voluntarily read course papers aloud to one another and then provided feedback. The point of writing for class changed: not hoop-jumping for a grade, but the creation of community through expression and careful listening. Just as the specific use value of an object can flatten out and fade away behind the glare of its exchange value once it has become a commodity, so too does the content of a student paper become almost moot, once it has been dubbed with a letter grade. In this classroom, by contrast, it seemed on the face of it perverse for writing to be generated and then not shared.

A noticeable portion of the writing we did, whether in dialogue with assigned reading or in reaction to a creative-writing prompt, was personal, often grippingly so. To share such work in the circle, then, is already itself a charged entrusting of the group that had its own memorable impact. This "confessional" mode isn't by any means central to all Inside-Out courses, but it was consistently part of my own, which leads me to the following reflections about the very gendered practice of writing that is dubbed "therapeutic." Questions about the scope and potential of this kind of writing in my own course converge with my broader investigation here of the reach and the limit of Inside-Out's transformative possibilities more generally.

Confession: This narrative project drove Saint Augustine, of course, and, more than a thousand years later, Jean-Jacques Rousseau.[5] The need to come clean about one's sins—or to justify them—and to shape a plot around crisis and conversion, is one central motor driving the genre of autobiography and even the emergence of the novel form.[6] Of great currency today and often conflated with confession is *therapeutic* writing, whereby written expression is seen as one path to liberation from the effects of endured trauma. When we suffer a traumatic experience, perhaps its worst affront is the sense that jurisdiction over our lives and experience has been forcibly ripped away; when a survivor of trauma writes about the experience, he or she gets to grab the narrative reins back and reshape the story over which someone or something else had wrested control. If he or she shares the work, both writer and audience benefit. The breaking of silence, combined with the fact of mutual gain in a safe space, makes overwhelming ghosts dwindle, somehow, to a manageable size. This converging of literature, medicine, pedagogy, self-help, and feminist praxis has resulted in some very powerful writing, along with a regular cottage industry of publications about writing's use in healing.[7]

To call a piece of writing "confessional,"—in spite of all this or, perversely, because of it—is to level a feminizing slight. Michael Skube describes women's memoirs that treat incest as "awfully tiresome," "nonliterary and faddish." He shudders, "people are spilling their guts out, confessing the unimaginable and sometimes the purely imaginary."[8] When people think about women writing, especially about avowedly "personal" topics, ideas about the healing powers of writing on trauma get strangely interwoven with profound literary disdain for gut-spilling; gendered disdain for "womanish whining"; encrusted ideas about sinfulness and redemption; pop-Freudian notions about repression and confessional discharge; and voyeuristic yearning for the tell-all. How do women negotiate with this, when they pick up their pens? Canadian scholar Irene Gammel insists on

> the experimental and creative energy with which women have negotiated their positions within the larger realms of confessional politics. Many "real-life" stories encode an awareness of [...] possible appropriation and recolonization of their life stories [...], signaling that theirs is not the unmediated cry from the female heart, [working to create a] safe space in which to articulate their personal and sexual lives, while defying confessional entrapments.[9]

Perhaps the theme of "entrapment" is over-determined in an Inside-Out classroom. To write as a convicted and incarcerated woman is to write into the implicit assumption of predetermined guilt and an oft-reiterated obligation to rehabilitate on paper. The work of emerging from crisis becomes dangerously blurred with the mea culpa, and both are stage managed, as much as can be possible, by the correctional context.

Fending off more punitively minded colleagues, well-meaning rehabilitators working within corrections consider it a key piece of their mission to offer gender-responsive treatment. They note that the great majority of women behind bars are there for nonviolent drug-related offenses, that a very significant majority of women who wind up incarcerated struggle with addiction and depression and have been the victims of sexual and domestic violence.[10] So they seek treatment and programming solutions that will address these social and psychological ills.

This emphasis on a complex of personal dysfunctions and psychological vulnerabilities, however, can overshadow *another* set of demographic facts about the women who go to jail and prison: overwhelmingly, the imprisoned are women of color, poor, under- or unemployed, lacking adequate access to education and health care, and increasingly, facing homelessness.[11] (As a reminder, people *break* drug laws at a remarkably equivalent rate, regardless of race or class—the staggering demographic discrepancies emerge only when we look at who is arrested, and especially who goes to prison, for these infractions.)[12] Across the board, for women who wind up in prison, social services may have proved inadequate, absent, or even an active aggravation of their difficulties. The violence they have survived may well be not domestic, or not solely domestic, but state-sponsored.

Perhaps the United States is criminalizing poverty, giving corporate criminals carte blanche while tracking poor people of color toward a prison-industrial complex that has ballooned into a juggernaut, unmatched around the world. Perhaps the prison industry lobbies to construct more and more carceral spaces, which then gabble to be filled until they burst. Perhaps as a society, we are normalizing tyranny, what Fyodor Dostoevsky called the "habit" that will "coarsen and stupefy the very best of men to the level of brutes," and growing inured to it when we tune into shows like *Prison Break* and *Inside San Quentin*.[13] Perhaps white celebrity convicts (e.g., Martha Stewart, Robert Downey, Jr., Lindsay Lohan) function as the entertaining exceptions that mask the entrenched inequalities of the carceral system. (In recent years, celebrity mug shots have become an almost iconic new index of notoriety.)[14] If all these processes are underway, what ends are they serving? And how can they be interrupted?

These questions do persist. They are not necessarily welcomed by rehabilitators, who seek empowerment for "their clients," but who face an unspoken imperative that the elicited agency must be limited to "personal" healing and recovery. Reflection on structural, institutional injustice—reflection that might challenge the very system in which rehabilitators work—is dubbed whining, a shirking from the accountability that makes personal transformation possible.

This stance is unsurprising and emerges from a long, gendered history of rehabilitative corrections. From their inception in the nineteenth century, gender-specific rehabilitation and reform philosophies have urged that for women harsh punishment be replaced by *a training in norms*. Thereby, the successfully retooled woman would embrace self-regulation, a submissive femininity and a vigorous gratitude, ready to sign on unquestioningly to an American Dream that may well have no place for her beyond permanent subjugation.[15]

The common contemporary therapeutic emphasis in criminal justice theory on low self-esteem, addiction, and the coercive boyfriend seems to keep its focus squarely upon the female "offender" (and a dangerous partner), and thereby to lift scrutiny away from state practices and social conditions that may have had a sweeping impact on a woman's choices.[16] Perhaps all the psychologizing is simply a stand-in for political analysis, a distraction, a way to discredit and dissipate a well-earned rage that should not be "healed," but turned toward activism. What's needed, surely, is not purging, but protest, not rehabilitation, but radical change.

One could argue that, as practiced, "therapeutic" writing of the sort often generated in my Inside-Out courses is at heart about releasing steam and recreating acceptable confession narratives that presume guilt and emphasize only gratitude. One might hearken back to a warning issued 30 years ago by Michel Foucault to those who rushed to celebrate all "voice" as liberation.[17] Looking around today, we can see what is valid in his warning: from the judge to the priest to the oral examiner to the therapist to the talk show host, the person who shapes the discourse often has more social power than she who gushes forth, on cue, with a volley of responsive words. Yes, not every talker gains from her outpouring—think of the ridiculed guests on daytime talk shows or the rejected contenders on reality TV, their lowbrow expressivity instigating guffaws. And by contrast, think of the power held by the wizard of Oz, omnipotent only so long as he is tucked silently away in his curtained box, unmarked as he pulls the levers and orchestrates the showy hegemony out front. He is potent precisely because he keeps his own voice unheard.

As an object lesson in this regard, we might reflect on Eve Ensler's wonderfully titled video, "*What I Want My Words to Do to You.*"[18] (The title quotes a creative-writing prompt that inspires several great poems featured in the film.) Ensler's 2003 documentary introduces her long-standing creative-writing workshop for women incarcerated in upstate New York at Bedford Hills. This valuable project is marred somewhat, I would argue, by its structural commitment to eliciting the penitence tale and by Ensler's unquestioning claim of the right to act as confessor. In classroom sequences, she pushes workshop participants to come to terms with their crimes as if that were the only story they, by rights, had to tell; she appears consistently to funnel the writers' speech into the confessional mode. Again and again the participants gently, insistently deepen the conversation, and carve out more room for nuance than her initial stance allowed.

Must these women's writing process be above all about acknowledging their own guilt? What is lost when that storyline is made to predominate above all others? As former Weather Underground member and workshop participant Judith Clark recites in Ensler's documentary, "I want my words to leave you thirsty for complexity and the deep discomfort of ambiguity… I want to make you wonder about your own prisons. I want you to ask why." *What I Want My Words to Do To You* shows both the (partly voyeuristic) impulse to demand confession from incarcerated women and the "complexity" that is possible when the familiar narrative arc of transgression and repentance is superseded.

It looks to me, from within another workshop circle, that reading and writing in barrier-bending communities can lead precisely to the fruits and the "deep discomfort[s] of ambiguity" that Judith Clark called for in Ensler's documentary[s]. Such charged encounter between people who are in and out of prison—conversation that is productive, surprising, sometimes even uncomfortable—ushers in the possibility of change. And in this process, the personal cannot be disentangled from the political, except via a carefully manipulated tunneling of the conceptual field. If second wave feminism has left us with one lesson supposedly learned, it would be that.[19] In our classes it seemed always obvious that "low self-esteem," domestic violence, sexual abuse, and all the tragic corollaries that spring from them do not occur in a vacuum. They occur across the full span of society, in every regional, cultural, and economic niche. In fact, one telling and very gendered bond between us, in the Inside-Out circle, was how many of us, as women, knew first-hand about this kind of harm.

None of the authors we read limited themselves to either the personal or the political; all talked about both domestic and institutional violations and the crucial interplay between them. Jarvis Jay Masters, a Buddhist on death row at San Quentin, writes about the scars from childhood beatings marking his own body and those of his friends on the yard; he also reports the groans and astute commentary on his floor the day Thurgood Marshall resigned from the Supreme Court.[20] In her nineteenth-century abolitionist memoir, *Incidents in the Life of a Slave Girl,* Harriet Jacobs details the sexual harassment she endured from her owner, and with equally visceral disgust she lambastes the 1850 Fugitive Slave Law that turned Northerners into willing bounty hunters.[21] When we discussed Dorothy Allison's *Bastard Out of Carolina,* our conversation turned to the fact that all abuse unfolds in a larger context and is shaped by that context.[22] Violent men are themselves shaped by power and privilege differentials. Bone's stepfather in *Bastard* is an exploited employee and humiliated son. When he compounds the struggles of his family members through intimate violence, he works in concert with the very systemic forces he himself resents. And the impacts of at-home violence are either treated or aggravated by conditions beyond the private sphere. Access to health care, housing, employment, even transportation and education opportunities, all contingent upon economic means, are relevant here. Students pointed out that many of the women in Allison's novel are forced by poverty to persist in violent marriages; these energetic women are not hogtied victims by any means, but because of class inequities, they negotiate between an array of bad choices. (During one term, this led to one of the most multifaceted and charged debates about sex work that I have ever witnessed in a classroom setting.)

Thanks in part to the careful circumscriptions provided by Lori Pompa's pedagogic model, our reading and writing circle was a well-bounded safe space; in this class, our intellectual and creative work often did emphasize healing, in a way utterly foreign to standard procedure in a college classroom. Consistently, the scope of our conversation widened from personal healing to broader, social, and political issues about class disparities, racial tension, and the often-triggering dehumanizations of the criminal justice system itself. Maxine, an inside student in our class, argued that complaining about society or the government can be a way for an individual—especially an individual who is addicted—to evade the hard work of thinking about his or her own accountability. But must it be? All told, our conversations suggested that someone ready to embrace responsibility for her own actions is *also* ready to function as an active agent in the civic sphere, and that includes the demand for justice. A person cannot be an effective agent of change, or of much else, if the wounds from violation go unaddressed. Transformative justice principles, which play a role in the Inside-Out classroom, teach us that once we have begun to think in deep ways about the times we have caused, witnessed or survived harm, we will soon turn to the systems and contexts that depend upon and produce injustice. Shoshana Pollack, fruitfully critiquing the typical deployments of "self-esteem discourse" among criminologists, remarks that "*political agency,* the opportunity for effecting change in women's lives, provides the context in which *subjective agency* evolves."[23] I would argue that some version of the reverse is also true: subjective agency, once arrived at, will—if given free reign and not corralled by the discursive pressure to self-pathologize—lead inexorably toward political agency, or the hunger to seize it.

And that might be how a poem could be said to change anything. George Oppen, a poet and political activist who felt that poetry and activism should not be conflated, insisted that we recognize poetry's limits: "We must cease to believe in secret names and unexpected phrases which will burst upon the world" and through their sheer lucidity wreak political change.[24] To address this lingering challenge, I turn to the preface of a chapbook of writing by women at Riker's Island (cited in Judith A. Scheffler's anthology of women's prison literature, *Wall Tappings*): The chapbook preface declares:

> [T]his anthology is a crime. A crime of conspiracy, an informed, fully-consenting adult decision to commit poetry, an invention of the imagination that will never tear down the bars or break the system's back, but has ripped off some room for people to "breathe together" (another definition of "conspiracy") and pulled off a heist of institutional supermind, liberated the space as a continuum. This anthology is about possibilities.[25]

The chapbook itself is provocatively titled *Songs from a Free Space,* and that is what creative collaboration can do: it may not "break the system's back" all at once, but it can claim a liberated space, between women or maybe just between the ears. One inside student writes: "So here I must stay in / those rooms in my head. Take my rights, take my pride, / But this soul it is mine." And that leads to "possibilities."

In profound ways, those possibilities are expanded upon, when the working circle brings together incarcerated and nonincarcerated students, as with Inside-Out. If power exists and asserts and replicates itself via a web of relations, concretized in institutional spaces and naturalized through repetition, then a shift in "empowerment" can itself only truly manifest via changing relations. Inside-Out's careful commitment to a de-hierarchized pedagogy, to education as nexus rather than capital, and to the work of collaborative inquiry can set the stage for and even set in motion what Iris Marion Young calls "participatory democracy, critical self-reflection and collective action."[26]

Our responses to Jarvis Jay Masters' work (the Buddhist living on San Quentin's death row) were sent directly to the author and each time we received from him a vivid, lengthy reply, taking the dialogic principle well beyond our own circle. Reading a text like Masters', though, means something different for readers who have never themselves been thrown into solitary confinement or heard violence break out in the middle of the night, never been strip searched or had their visiting privileges revoked on a whim.

One approach to this experiential gap came through the writing that inside students generated and shared with classmates. Nan's poem "Confinement" proved a lesson to the outside women in her class, while sounding the music that the inside women in the group all knew too well and felt moved to hear articulated:

> It is not being put in a physical space and made to stay that is the prison.
> It is the sound of the sally-port as it "CLANGS" into place behind you, the "CLICK CLICK" of the cell door latch locking in.
> The air pressure's "HISSSSS" of the cell door settling permanently into place.
> The sound of the loud speaker, "Lock in, lock in for count."
> The sound of the correctional officer's well-shined shoes, "clack, clack, clack, clack,"
> Pause "Clack, clack, clack, clack," as he tallies his prisoners.
> The sound of seventy plus women in a cement and metal room all talking of the lives they had, a roar of laughter, regrets and threats of doing it again.
> The sounds of voices building relationships through a ventilation shaft, "Hello, who's that? Your baby's daddy?" Or a rap song drifting up from the hole. [. . .]
> It's the sound of someone waiting in anguish, shedding soft silent tears, that secures the soul and confines the mind.
> To survive the sound of confinement one must remember the sweet sounds of freedom, your daughter's voice, the purr of your cat, the wind in the treetops . . .

Nan's careful building of a soundscape here lets her readers hear how carceral power can ring along the senses; crucially, its clangs and hisses cannot drown out the contained but vibrant agency of the confined women Nan conjures in her poem. In a prose piece about the onset of confinement structured around descriptions of her own changing face, inside student Becky addresses her readers directly, with a challenge: "I am then led [from the courtroom] to a waiting area with holding cells. My face takes on another appearance at this point. 'O.K.—this is really happening.' *Imagine that look.*"[27] So, in instances of expressivity like Joanie's paper, Nan's poem or Becky's prose, we see "empowerment" linked not to the power of positive thinking, but to the work of communication. The writer's expressivity must be *matched in kind* by the reader's understanding ("imagine that look"), with the purpose of changing social relations by fostering a new comprehension across the deep divisions of stigmatization, class, and race.

That leads to a final point: the force of generosity in the class. Class time was studded with moments of kindness between students, when individuals took an assignment or in-class exercise as an unbidden opportunity to help another classmate. This generosity flowed in all directions, and never bore the one-way strain of philanthropy. Students gave voice to each other's concerns, stepped in with words of encouragement when another student's spirits flagged, never dismissed one another for a failure to understand, and looked beyond and beneath classed and raced stereotypes about "college girls" and "convicts" to address the intellect and personality beyond. Examples included inside students supporting outside students who had loved ones facing prison time . . . and who had never mentioned that fact in a school setting before. Then there was Maxine.

Unlike some inside students who parlayed their in-class inspiration into a return to school upon release, Maxine apparently didn't do well after class ended; she was absent when we held an admissions event for inside participants at end of term. She had concluded her sentence a couple of days earlier, and according to a staff person, just 15 minutes after she'd landed at the voluntary rehab program and halfway house for which she'd signed up, "she was seen on the streets, walking rapidly away, smoking a cigarette." The difficulties that loomed in her life so soon after our graduation in no way undermine the contributions she made as a student; they certainly do put the brakes on a too-utopian sunniness about Inside-Out's project of social transformation. As a criminalized woman facing stigma, poverty, a history of abuse, violence, and addiction, and a dearth of meaningful resources, Maxine returned to the streets in the face of a complex web of social, political, economic, institutional, and individual forces.

Staring directly at the limits of Inside-Out and other "change agents" in the face of such magnetic, cumulative, tragic force, one hopes that these agents are nonetheless working—the way a powerful undertow works in the ocean (to use an image of Pompa's) to elicit a profound upheaval, a paradigmatic shift, even against the force of such tides. As the program's work has continued, many stories have emerged that counter Maxine's trajectory, stories that could far more readily be pointed to, to suggest "program success." I want to recognize here that Maxine's academic work in the course and her generous contributions to the classroom community *were* successes; perhaps "impacts" assessments that cannot detect these need to be retooled.

The first year I taught the class, one student's final paper took up the topic of generosity. Anna begins with a catalogue of the many restrictions placed on any Inside-Out class, including, "No smoking allowed, and gift exchanges are unacceptable under any circumstances. Respect confidentiality; no full names. No point of contact after the class." She soon points out that, contraband regulations notwithstanding,

> gift exchanges became the focal point of our classroom. In fact, we all exchanged massive gifts that we may not have known we had . . . How did we get by the metal detectors and uniformed officers without being caught in the act? How could they not have noticed? While we were being monitored for our clothing and the items we brought into the classroom, our large gifts were invisible to anyone who was not a part of our precious circle. Our secret presents flooded our classroom, expanding across the room, bringing each person closer together. . . . While we weren't allowed to tell one another our last names, I learned more about the women in my class than I know about my close friends. . . . Through this class, I've learned that words make the best presents. The best words are spoken honestly and trustingly.

So, perhaps we can benefit from thinking of education as part of a gift economy, rather than as cultural capital; we can go further and think of it as *contraband,* remembering the Riker's Island chapbook previously cited: "this anthology is a crime of conspiracy [. . .] to 'breathe together' (another definition of conspiracy)." My co-facilitator Lysette Navarro remarks,

Inside-Out shows you that your mind and soul still belong to you. And then when that happens, there's a revolution in the room. You contribute something and speak out yourself, and then all of a sudden, everyone wants to give something, throw something in, you can feel the room shift, the automatic clicking as connections are made ...[28]

People typically talk about education as opening doors, and I will, too. Those doors open, however, not just to provide a point of entry to hopeful individuals eager to buy into society's predetermined avenues for upward mobility. No, these doors allow not just entry, but *egress*. And they leave us with a new map of where we live, new means to traverse social distance, and a new capacity to act collectively.

Notes

*Excerpted reprint: "Inside-Out: The Reaches and Limits of a Prison Program," in *Razor Wire Women: Prisoners, Scholars, Activists and Artists*, ed. Ashley Lucas and Jodie Lawston (Albany: SUNY Press, 2011), 203–223. Thanks to Lois Brown, Melissa Crabbe, Lori Harriman, Holland Hendrix, Jacqueline Johnson, Kim Keough, Ashley Lucas, Lysette Navarro, Don O'Shea, Lori Pompa, Yedalis Ruiz, Don Weber, and Lindsey Whitmore.

1. *Voices from Inside* offers creative writing workshops to incarcerated and formerly incarcerated women, trains interested participants to lead workshops, and provides avenues for public dissemination. http://www.voicesfrominside.org.
2. Myles Horton and Paulo Freire, *We Make the Road by Walking: Conversations on Education and Social Change* (Philadelphia: Temple University Press, 1991).
3. All student names listed here are pseudonyms.
4. Patricia McConnel, *Sing Soft, Sing Loud* (Flagstaff, AZ: Logoria, 1995), 61 and Jimmy Santiago Baca, *A Place to Stand: The Making of a Poet* (New York: Grove Press, 2001).
5. Augustine of Hippo, *The Confessions of St. Augustine*, trans. Rex Warner (New York: Signet, 2001); Jean-Jacques Rousseau, *The Confessions, and Correspondence, including the Letters to Malesherbes*, ed. Christopher Kelly, Roger D. Masters, and Peter D. Stillman, trans. Christopher Kelly (Hanover, NH: University Press New England for Dartmouth, 1995).
6. Patrick Riley, *Character and Conversion in Autobiography: Augustine, Montaigne, Descartes, Rousseau and Sartre* (Charlottesville: University of Virginia Press, 2004).
7. Charles M. Anderson and Marian M. MacCurdy, "Introduction," in *Writing and Healing: Toward an Informed Practice* (Urbana, IL: National Council of Teachers of English, 2000), 7; Charles M. Anderson and Marian M. MacCurdy, *Writing and Healing: Toward an Informed Practice*, (Urbana, IL: National Council of Teachers of English, 2000); Special issue, *Literature and Medicine* 19.1 (Spring); Isha McKenzie-Mavinga, "Creative Writing as Healing in Black Women's Groups," in Working Inter-Culturally in Counselling Settings, ed., Aisha Dupont Joshua (New York: Routledge, 2004), 10–27.. *Working Interculturally in Counselling Settings*, ed. Aisha Du-Pont-Joshua (New York: Routledge), 14–38; Ann Hudson Jones, "Writing and Healing," *The Lancet* 368 (December 23, 2006), S3–S4.
8. Michael Skube, writing in the *Atlanta Journal-Constitution*, in Sue William Silverman, "Confessional & (Finally) Proud of It: For Women Only." Site last visited May 29, 2008. <http://www.suewilliamsilverman.com/work4.htm>.

9. Irene Gammel, "Introduction," in *Confessional Politics: Women's Sexual Self-Representations in Life Writing and Popular Media*, ed. Irene Gammel (Carbondale: Southern Illinois University Press, 1999), 2.

10. In 2005, 73.1 percent of women in state prison were identified as mentally ill (compared to 55% of men held in state prison). In 1999 that almost 60 percent of women in state prisons had experienced physical or sexual abuse prior to their incarceration, the figure for women in jails was 48 percent. More than 33 percent of women in US prisons and jails the same year reported childhood sexual or physical abuse, while the prevalence for same among women in the general population is estimated at between 12 and 17 percent. See "Women in the Criminal Justice System: Briefing Sheets," *The Sentencing Project* (Washington DC, May 2007), www.sentencingproject.org and Lawrence A. Greenfeld and Tracy L. Snell, "Women Offenders." Bureau of Justice Statistics Special Report, United States Department of Justice. December 1999/ revised 2000, Table 20, 8. <www.ojp.usdoj.gov/bjs/pub/pdf/wo.pdf> Caroline Wolf Harlow, "Prior Abuse Reported by Inmates and Probationers." US Department of Justice, Bureau of Statistics. <www.ojp.usdoj.gov/bjs/pub/press/parip.pr> All sites mentioned here last visited January 2, 2008. From corrections sources, see Margaret Shaw, "Conceptualizing Violence by Women," in *Gender and Crime*, ed. E. Dobash, R. P. Dobash, and L. Noaks (Cardiff: University of Wales, 1995). Kate DeCou and Sally Van Wright, "A Gender-Specific Intervention Model for Incarcerated Women: Women's V.O.I.C.E.S. (Validation Opportunity Inspiration Communication Empowerment Safety)," 2002. Gerald Landsberg, Marjorie Rock, Lawrence K.W. Berg, Amy Smiley., eds. *Serving Mentally Ill Offenders: Challenges and Opportunities for Mental Health Professionals* (New York: Springer), 172–189.

11. http://www.wpaonline.org/pdf/Focus_December2003.pdf "WPA Focus on Women and Justice: A Portrait of Women in Prison," Women's Prison Association (December 2003).

12. "Whites and African Americans report illicit drug use and illicit drug sales at similar rates. However, at the local level, African Americans are admitted to prison for drug offenses at much higher rates than whites. In 2002, African Americans were admitted to prison for drug offenses at 10 times the rate of whites in the 198 largest population counties in the country." And "as of 2003, twice as many African Americans as whites were incarcerated for drug offenses in state prisons." Phillip Beatty, Amanda Petteruti and Jason Ziedenberg, *The Vortex: The Concentrated Racial Impact of Drug Imprisonment and the Characteristics of Punitive Counties*. A Justice Policy Institute Report, December 2007, 2–3. http://www.justicepolicy.org/. Site last visited December 28, 2007. See Michelle Alexander, *The New Jim Crow: Mass Incarceration in the Age of Colorblindness* (New York: New Press, 2010).

13. Fyodor Dostoevsky, *The House of the Dead*, trans. David MacDuff (New York: Penguin, 1985), 242. Dostoevsky wrote *House of the Dead* in 1861, after having spent four years in a Siberian prison camp.

14. For two examples, see www.mugshots.com or www.thesmokinggun.com/mugshots/celebrities. Sites last visited April 18, 2013.

15. See Estelle B. Freedman, *Their Sisters' Keepers: Women's Prison Reform in America, 1830–1930*. (Ann Arbor: University of Michigan Press, 1984); Dana Britton, *At Work in the Iron Cage: The Prison as Gendered Organization* (New York: New York University Press, 2003); Paula Johnson, "Introduction," *Inner Lives: Voices from African American Women in Prison* (New York: New York University Press, 2004); Meda Chesney-Lind and Lisa Pasko, *The Female Offender: Girls, Women, and Crime*, 2nd ed. (Thousand Oaks, CA: Sage, 2004).

16. See Beth E. Richie, *Compelled to Crime: The Gender Entrapment of Battered Black Women* (New York: Routledge, 1996). Despite the book's significant contributions, Richie's emphasis on domestic victimization has the effect of downplaying both the reality of women's agency and the role of larger social conditions.

17. See, for instance, Michel Foucault, *The History of Sexuality: An Introduction, Vol. I* (1976; New York: Vintage Reissue, 1990).

18. *What I Want My Words to Do to You.* Prod. Eve Ensler, Carol Jenkins, and Judith Katz (PBS, 2003). The high profile cases and the high percentage of women in for murder in Ensler'sworkshop mean that *representativeness* is not one of the movie's virtues. In the county system where I taught, 85 percent of the women are there for nonviolent offenses.

19. See Donna M. Bickford's Women's Studies listserv discussion on the origins of the phrase, "the personal is political." http://userpages.umbc.edu/~korenman/wmst/pisp.html. Site last visited February 3, 2008.

20. Jarvis Jay Masters, *Finding Freedom: Writings from Death Row* (Junction City, CA: Padma Publishing, 1997); "Scars," 67–72; "Justice Marshall Resigns," 89–90.

21. Harriet A. Jacobs, *Incidents in the Life of a Slave Girl, Written By Herself* (New York: Penguin Classics, 2000).

22. Dorothy Allison, *Bastard Out of Carolina* (New York: Plume, 2005). A highlight of our course came when Dorothy Allison visited one class session in May 2007. We discussed her work and she joined our writing circle.

23. Shoshana Pollack, "Reconceptualizing Women's Agency and Empowerment: Challenges to Self-Esteem Discourse and Women's Lawbreaking," *Women and Criminal Justice* 12, no. 1 (2000): 75–89.

24. George Oppen, *Selected Prose, Daybooks and Papers*, ed. Stephen Cope (Berkeley: University of California Press, 2007). Cited in James Longenbach's review, "A Test of Poetry," *The Nation* 286, no. 5 (February 11, 2008): 30.

25. Carol Muske and Gail Rosenblum, eds. *Songs from a Free Space: Writings by Women in Prison* (New York: New York City Correctional Institution for Women/Free Space Writing Program), n.d. Cited in Judith Scheffler, ed. *Wall Tappings: An International Anthology of Women's Prison Writing, 200 to the Present* (New York: Feminist Press at CUNY, 2002), 223.

26. Iris Marion Young, "Punishment, Treatment, Empowerment: Three Approaches to Policy for Pregnant Addicts," *Feminist Studies* 20, no. 1 (1994): 50. Cited in Pollack, "Reconceptualizing Women's Agency and Empowerment," 86.

27. Emphasis mine.

28. In conversation with author, March 2007.

CHAPTER 19

Transformative Learning in Prisons and Universities: Reflections on Homologies of Institutional Power

Kristin Bumiller

Proponents of community-based education claim that this teaching offers positive results for the university and the community, enriching student learning beyond traditional classrooms and providing benefits to organizations in the community. Far-reaching transformations are also imagined, such as revitalizing civic engagement and fundamentally changing the mission of higher education to broaden its global impact. These aspirations follow from an ideal of transformative education that has a deep history and diverse ideological foundations, ranging from missionary teaching to progressive left activism. Community-based learning both draws upon these diverse foundations for transformative education and offers new challenges and opportunities for collaboration between the university and the community.

Long before community-based learning became an established component of higher education, my scholarly life was in the community, as an ethnographer of the sociology of law and everyday life.[1] Consequently, my scholarship has been dominated by intellectual problems at the heart of the connection between the researcher and the community. In particular, like most ethnographers, I have devoted serious reflection to the ethical challenges of turning community members into research "subjects." These reflections have often turned to the question of what constitutes transformative sociology and the role of interpretation of personal accounts in the production of sociological critique.[2] In approaching community-based education from this intellectual tradition, the confident pronouncement of its transformative potential is both longed for and received cautiously. Despite this skepticism, I have been deeply committed to teaching inside prisons for the past seven years as an Inside-Out instructor. This experience provides a perspective from which to examine the ideal of transformation as the model of Inside-Out teaching imagines it and to reflect upon the implications for the community-based learning movement.

Transformation in the Inside-Out Model

The Inside-Out educational model (as described on its website) promises "transformation" for participants, the prison, and for the larger community. In the context of a "dynamic partnership between institutions of higher learning and correctional systems," Inside-Out courses are presented as unique opportunities for dialogue and leadership development among diverse students. These opportunities bring about a "paradigm shift" in thinking about crime and social justice that potentially fuels "an engine for social change."[3]

In these pronouncements, the potential for transformative learning is linked to the ways the innovative course format allows participants to traverse boundaries between the university and the prison, boundaries that have been created and reinforced by a culture of law and order. Crossing boundaries is theorized as the engine of transformation—the act of going behind walls, both figuratively and literally, creates openings for and deepens dialogue. Creating space for dialogue, in turn, is linked to both the potential for personal redemption and furthering a social change agenda. These conversations "behind the walls" are instrumental to the breaking down of participants' demonizing stereotypes of the criminal, and this transformation of consciousness is essential to resisting the underlying psychological dynamics that fuel mass incarceration.

This description of the transformative effects of the Inside-Out experience is experientially familiar. Inside-Out instructors (myself included) report remarkable conversations in the classroom that are made possible by the diversity of background and experiences of the students and by the prison setting. Testimonials from both inside and outside students often report "life-changing" effects of participating in a course, such as finding a direction in the pursuit of social justice or renewing their commitment to higher education. These accounts provide evidence of impactful experiences in the classroom that stimulate broad reflection about personal and societal issues. Evaluating whether these impactful experiences are indeed transformative, however, requires a more complex analysis of how the learning is situated in systems of power and domination.

There is another reason to reflect more seriously about the meaning of these accounts. While they attest to the significance and the often-inspirational quality of the course experience, they tell us little about the dynamic processes in a classroom that produce a paradigm shift in students' thinking about crime and social justice. Specifically, does the crossing of boundaries between the prison and the university produce this transformation? This is the most salient assumption at the core of the transformative ideal of the Inside-Out program: the notion that the conversion of thought and action is linked to the bringing together of the prisoner and "typical" college student, as well as how these courses produce an all-too-rare engagement between two institutions that appear to be fundamentally at cross purposes.

This commentary explores the transformative effects of crossing boundaries and demystifies the distinctions that are often made between academic settings and carceral institutions. The metaphor of crossing boundaries brings with it powerful assumptions about how universities and prisons are configured in relation to each other within democratic society. This metaphorical distinction is reinforced within each setting; each is laden with symbolic ritual and form that puts the distinction between the university, as the home of freedom and opportunity, and the prison, as a total institution, in stark relief. However, learning happens in both places, and it may arise unexpectedly and unintentionally, and in ways that are truly transformational. The ideal of transformational learning might be better understood by clarifying how the university and the prison represent bounded institutions, while at the same time exhibiting many of the same aspects of institutionalized power and restraints on citizen action. In fact, transformational learning might arise not so much from the unconventional format of an Inside-Out course, but from the opportunity it provides to scrutinize how even revelatory educational practices are deeply entrenched within the power arrangements they seek to change.

The Homology of Universities and Prisons

Inside-Out instructors work within and between two highly bureaucratized organizations, the university and the prison. This means that instructors get a "double-dose" of bureaucratic entanglements (often in their most virulent forms as each resists the implementation of a new program). It also offers an opportunity for insight through a "mirroring effect": providing a vantage point from which to view the congruity and the discrepancy between them. This vantage point facilitates the participants' capacity to critique: it allows for recognition of how both institutions, while maintaining distinctive symbolic meaning and function, engage in similar managerial tactics.

While critics have brought attention to the growing tendencies of universities to bend to the will of corporate interests and consumer demands, these critiques often rely upon a comparison with (or lament the growing distance from) the golden age of academe, characterized by faculty governance and autonomy. Such critiques fail to take into account how legalized accountability is fully incorporated into university life.[4] Under these conditions, the university is a highly regulated environment similar to private workplaces and public institutions. The belief that the university is a unique environment preserved by academic freedom is in contradiction with the fact that faculty are increasingly forced to respond to institutional directives that are wholly inconsistent with the pursuit of knowledge or the achievement of excellence.

Likewise, prisons in the United States are increasingly scrutinized for their exercise of brutalizing power and excessive violence. Yet, over the past 20 years, the correctional system has undergone "modernization" similar to private organizations. This has led to the institution of efficiency measures, flatter management practices, accountability measures, demands for "cultural competence," and employment of gender-specific management styles. These changes often focus on the performance of correctional officers and their expanding role as "case managers." The image in the mirror is strikingly similar—as both the university and the prison have their relative autonomy eroded vis-à-vis the state and economy. This is clearly illustrated by how strict compliance to professional norms is achieved by the same devices in seemingly incongruent settings. Both prisons and universities create pressures on employees (both fit into the category that sociologist Lewis Coser classically described as greedy institutions[5]) that discourage innovation and maintain conformity. Under conditions of advanced capitalism, greedy institutions insist on employees' loyalty and time (despite the pretense of "family friendly" policies). The overwhelming force of greedy institutions is acutely reflected through their capacity to put in place widely accepted and irresistible new standards, and tie together professional competence with adherence to these standards. As a result, workers in prisons and universities follow similar professional directives. One of the most pervasive and defining directives is risk management, where the "risk" being conceived and contained is both monetary and physical, which tightly grips both types of organizations despite the differential factors contributing to potential hazards.

The homology of institutional structures is most evident and striking in the context of day-to-day interactions that confuse or disorient perceptions about "who is making the rules." The Inside-Out program, upon the initiation of each course, blurs these boundaries when it requires all participants to agree to a "contract" that includes the standard set of rules for visitors in correctional institutions (dress code, restrictions on contraband, communication guidelines, etc.) and reinforces them with the potential threat of academic failure. This sets the scene for heightened awareness throughout the course of both formal and informal compliance schemes. Ultimately, the complicity of the Inside-Out program in the forms of institutional power against which it imagines itself to be in opposition sets the stage for critical thinking.

Symbolic Oppositions

Despite the trend toward institutional homology, universities and prisons are steeped in symbolic forms that remind those within and outside of their distinctive character. These powerful symbolic structures serve many functions, including creating the public face of the institution, establishing its political purpose and necessity, reinforcing the idea of its "relative autonomy" (or institutional independence), and defining the institution's role in the delegation of state violence. Universities and prisons exist symbolically in manifest opposition to each other. Consider, for example, how these symbolic divisions are often posed as incontrovertible, while restingupon debatable presuppositions.

- Criminals need reform; students need education.
- Prisons will be unsafe without the opportunity to employ force; universities will fail without academic freedom.
- Prisons require a military chain of command; universities rely upon self-governance.
- Prisons contain surplus populations; universities preserve the domain of the elite.
- Prisons impose rules arbitrarily; universities base decisions on enlightened reason.
- Prisons follow the law's command; universities reinforce standards.

- Prisons reduce risk; universities produce knowledge.
- Prisoners experience total domination; students learn in freedom.
- Violence is endemic to prison life; violence shocks universities.

In an age of mass incarceration, presumptions about crime, criminals, and the prison system are buttressed by the sway of these emblematic boundaries on public opinion. In political discourse, condensation symbols (emotive images that mobilize both fear and the punitive desires of the mass public) further reinforce the image of tightly bounded institutional forms.[6] Hence these symbols are most potent as abstract cultural ideas.

In post-Fordist capitalist society, this representational apparatus plays another crucial function: masking the expansion of managerial practices of neoliberalism. As Luc Boltanski and Eve Chaipello argue in *The New Spirit of Capitalism*, over the past 30 years capitalist enterprise has evolved to incorporate a network-based form of organization.[7] This furthers a style of management that relies upon meritocratic criteria to hide and legitimate domination. Under the new spirit of capitalism, the firm both neutralizes opposition and increases profitability by incorporating more "lean" forms of management. Most of these reforms occur at the level of middle management, and include such "innovations" as flexible labor, teamwork, multi-skilling, and less hierarchical management practices.

Community-based learning courses, like Inside-Out, may be preparing students for new capitalism rather than providing a radical alternative to it. Ironically, innovative courses often offer skills that are well suited to performing effectively as workers in middle-level management. While traditional college courses often lack such skill-building opportunities, students in community-based learning classes are encouraged to collaborate and develop leadership skills through completing group projects. These forms of interactive and flexible learning (central to the Inside-Out model), therefore, are derived from the new spirit of capitalism rather than essential elements of its critique. Likewise, "community based learning" opportunities are touted as promoting connections with "communities" that are more diverse, politically responsive, and representative of democratic interests. This is an especially dubious assumption for the Inside-Out program, which functions alongside the carceral apparatus and its industrial complex. The community is neither a more democratic nor responsive community, but is a thicket of forces that promote state violence and private profit.

Luc Boltanski has recently argued that despite the emergence of new capitalism, workers (and, in this context, students) experience moments of acute awareness of their situation. He describes these as "metapragmatic moments" that "*increase in the level of reflexivity*" and "during which the attention of participants shifts from the tasks to be performed to the question of how it is appropriate to *characterize* what is happening."[8] At these moments, people question the self-evidence of the process, causing them to look to "rules" and questioning their applicability and fairness. These moments reveal more clearly to workers their position vis-à-vis the firm, but they also expose how the organizations justify their "existence and mask the violence they contain."[9]

In the discussion that follows, I suggest that Inside-Out classrooms are well situated for metapragmatic moments: students within these forums are effectively positioned to observe the conditions that sustain institutionalized violence within both the university and the prison. Such observations may define the transformative experiences of instructors and students. Transformative learning happens when the symbolic framework breaks down and managerial practices within each institutional setting are consequently made more visible and can thus be called into question.

The Emancipatory Classroom

The metaphor of crossing boundaries, while accurately describing many aspects of the educational experience, seems like a poor fit to describe the potential insights gained from participating in the Inside-Out program. Instead, the enduring impact of Inside-Out courses may arise from the opportunities they provide to observe how the conditions of institutionalized power in universities and prisons are in many ways more similar to each other than forces in dramatic opposition. In this sense, the participants see each institution in "reflection" to the other (as opposed to "crossing into" unknown, rigidly bounded, and totally unfamiliar space). Both inside and outside students, through observation and dialogue, are well positioned to observe the *boundlessness* of many of the forms of social control that pervade modern institutional life. In this sense, students are not the subjects of a transformation, but rather observers of it. Their vantage point allows for an acute recognition of how all citizens, whether or not in the custody of the state, are vulnerable to managerial forms of power. The practice of transformative learning, accordingly, is akin to gaining the skills of an ethnographer. Students learn the art of sociological critique—the capacity to question how institutionalized power is instrumental in the production of knowledge.

What are the aspects of Inside-Out teaching that might heighten students' awareness about institutional power? In many ways, mindfulness is fostered for the outside students by the expectation of viewing the administration of actual force inside a prison; these expectations, whether realized or not, draw attention to the "real" violence of state authority. This expectation also encourages "reality checks"— instances in which participants are able to compare their assumptions (about the symbolic authority of both prisons and universities) with empirical observations. The classroom scene has the effect of making the following questions ever present in the participants' consciousness:

- Boundaries—How permeable are they? How is action governed by the state of lockdown?
- Fairness—How is it contingent upon the prerogatives of those exercising institutional control?
- Recognizability—How is the identity of who is an insider and who is an outsider being maintained (despite the efforts to create a learning environment that deconstructs this distinction)? How are all participants (whether from the inside or outside) marked by intelligible signs of class and status?

The primacy of these questions is reinforced both by incidents (clashes with prison authorities that are bound to happen every semester) and by the substantive material discussed. Even more provocative are the connections between the incidents and the academic material.

My Inside-Out course, "Regulating Citizenship," provides an exploration into the foundations of liberal democratic citizenship as well as examples of situations in which persons gain or lose their rights of citizenship, in the broadest sense of exercising their capacity to a full and meaningful life. We begin the course by reading John Locke, a text that allows them to think about tacit agreement not only with the state but also within the prison.[10] This awakens students' common-sense notions about power and legitimacy, in particular, the uncertain foundations of taken-for-granted rules and institutional norms. Discussing Locke enables students to more acutely recognize that the legitimation of the state mostly relies upon "freely given" consent and submission to the anticipation of force. Traditional political science courses produce the same kind of familiar insights. Regulating Citizenship, however, provides the context for students, as prisoners or as citizens who delegate their prerogative to punish to the state, to question the unfounded, but commonplace, assumption that confinement negates thecitizenship rights of those behind bars. Inside students, in particular, often enter the course believing they exist as noncitizens, essentially in exile, rather than knowing that the power of the state to confine is carefully delineated (by the proportionality of appropriate punishment and the requirement that the state act in the interest of the "common good"). This immediately forces students to confront their shared power, as citizens invested in the common good, as well as their shared powerlessness (imposed not by wrongdoing against the state but by the bargain that induced consent to democratic governance). In this way, their equality, as citizens and students, is established not only by the practices of the Inside-Out teaching model, but also by the foundations of democratic theory.

At the same time, students also encounter the notion of political responsibility, as it is defined not only by obligations to obey state authority, but also by the vigilance required to assure that a democratic government fulfills its promise to promote the common good. This inquiry forces a redefinition of how most students have been taught to think about what it means to be a "responsible citizen." Prior teachings about responsibility often have immediate potency, especially for inside students who, simultaneous to taking an Inside-Out course, are compelled to complete programming that urges them to take individual "responsibility" for their addictions, obligations to work (rather than steal), and for harm caused to others.[11] Many of the outside students, who enjoy the benefits of a liberal arts education, simply assume that acting responsibly as citizens is inherent in their "goodness," manifested by the rewards of status and privilege they enjoy. Both groups of students come to realize that neither strategy promotes responsible citizenship, in the sense of exercising their duties to question the legitimacy of state power.

Moreover, classroom discussion reveals how the liberal foundation of politics are deeply depoliticizing: while Locke invested the right to revolution to remain with the people, living in a democratic society provides rather limited opportunities for the political experience of ruling and active participation in shaping public affairs. To live responsibly in a democracy, therefore, citizens must retain their "political sensibilities" (for equality, democracy, and participation) after agreeing to the social contract. This broader notion of political responsibility is all the more important to acknowledge under the conditions of new capitalism. A managerial society is intrinsically depoliticizing—as market forces squeeze out the consideration of social values that lack relevancy to the promotion of economic efficiency. This process of discovery in the context of an Inside-Out course is often not abstract; it is experienced as students risk disciplinary consequences for publically speaking about unjust practices inside the prison and ideas for group projects are quelled by rules (often paradoxically designed to protect the prisoners' rights under conditions of confinement). Through these experiences, students learn that, under the conditions of new capitalism, creativity and rebellion are only allowed within delineated parameters.

In the Inside-Out classroom, students are often able to create moments of democratic participation, as they reinvent themselves as a collectivity of diverse citizens. The idea of responsibility reemerges, in being accountable to each other, as the community establishes trust and adopts an ethos of local citizenship. The students engage in a collective experiment in which they practice conducting themselves as responsible citizens in the broadest sense. In this community, like all political communities, trouble arises from inevitable conditions that create unfairness and inequality. When trouble occurs, it provides occasions to reflect upon their responsibilities as individuals, even under conditions of coercive institutional control. For example, the outside students at times are confronted by situations or conversations in which they realize their role in keeping the inside students confined (e.g., specifically by following the prison rules that are ostensibly designed to prevent escape or, more abstractly, by implicitly consenting to the excessive penalty that has led to the growth of the prison population). Sometimes this realization is dramatic. Halfway through the semester, one of my inside students is reassigned from the full security section of the facility to "minimum." My outside students are not aware of this particular student's change of status, and as we leave the class the inside student, fairly nonchalantly, walks beyond the usual corridor to which he has been confined and joins us in the "trap". In their silence (and expression of puzzlement on their faces), I see my students ponder: Who is watching? Should I "tell" on my classmate? Am I entrusted with the "security" role as an outsider? Does the prison care, or need to care, if this individual walks out? If the whole purpose of this maximum-security facility is to keep "them" inside, why is it so seemingly easy to get out? Possibly, the inside student muses—why does walking into the trap create shock in the eyes of fellow students who just convincingly treated me as a peer?

Institutional power is also made more transparent when security measures seem excessive, redundant, and intrusive. The class period is always interrupted by two "counts" (periodic lockdowns in which the correctional officers officially record the presence of every inmate) within 40 minutes of each other. Counts are serious business—if all inmates are not accounted for the facility will remain in lockdown. The correctional officer enters the classroom during counts and attempts to do his job, hindered by the quite striking capacity of an Inside-Out course to create an isolated environment of freedom in the midst of a correctional institution. During counts, the students observe remarkable aspects of the relationship between correctional officers and the people who are imprisoned there.They take note that every officer exercises a different style of control, ranging from respect and friendliness to officiousness and rudeness. My unwillingness to stop the class is tolerated by all of the officers despite the fact it causes them problems. Many of the officers don't know the inside students' names despite living under conditions of forced intimacy;

as a consequence, they sometimes mistake an outside student as a prisoner. This display causes the students to question the purpose of the counts, especially when identification of who belongs inside becomes awkward. Ultimately, counts provide educational moments in which the authority of the classroom community runs up against the power of an institution defined by its security mandate. The seeming casualness of the exercise of power is a demonstration of assuredness of the security function of the prison. When students watch the performance of counts by correctional officers, they gain awareness about how coercive violence is exercised in a managerial organization. Throughout the course, students are given abundant opportunities to consider whether "what feels like freedom" under these conditions is actually closely guarded thought and behavior.

The Transformative as Ordinary Education

What I have described as transformative education in my course Regulating Citizenship is played out in Inside-Out courses that explore quite different subject matter and pose other interesting theoretical questions. What is crucial to creating opportunities for transformative insight is students' direct confrontation with the dynamic tension between the symbolic framework of the prison and the everyday exercise of managerial power within the classroom. What makes Inside-Out a project of transformative education is inherent to any setting that allows for this kind of questioning of institutional arrangements. Inside-Out courses are positioned to present these opportunities in abundance; this is primarily due to the fact that instructors and students are deliberately engaged in establishing a community (amidst a backdrop of a symbolically opposing idea of community) in which questions of boundaries, fairness, and recognizability can be actively addressed.

Moreover, the idea of transformative education offered here reinforces the notions that learning bears close resemblance to scholarship. Students, like critical scholars, struggle to understand not only how power operates under the conditions of late capitalism, but also how emancipatory impulses can be realized in a depoliticized and market-driven society. The methodology of transformative teaching is essentially ethnographic; it depends on observing contradictions and uncertainties as they manifest themselves in everyday life.

Although this analysis has emphasized the homology between universities and prisons, it is important to qualify how Inside-Out courses present different opportunities for transformative learning depending on which institution is your home. Despite their similarities, the prison and the university both function independently, and in opposition to each other, to powerfully determine the life chances of two separate groups of young adults in American society. Incarceration results in lost educational opportunity, poor employment prospects, and the reinforcement of racial and ethnic discrimination. Conversely, admittance to university usually enables students to maintain or improve class status and prospects for a career. Prison education programs hope to close this gap, but only a fundamental transformation in the function of both prisons and universities would break down the existing forces that are at work. The presence of a single "college class" inside a maximum security prison may have some demonstrable effect on the quality of life on the inside, yet it would be absurd to suggest that it significantly changes the institutional mandates of prisons. Prisoners who benefit greatly from higher education face a litany of institutional barriers once released. Likewise, even the most transformative curriculum taught inside prisons pushes against, rather than fundamentally challenges, the academic conventions that define knowledge and learning within accredited institutions of higher education. The enormity of these problems, and their rootedness in an unequal opportunity structure, provide a backdrop that allays far-reaching claims for the transformative potential of community-based education.

Yet with the scarcity of vitally necessary college programs in prisons, Inside-Out courses provide extraordinary opportunities for learning. The classroom experiences allow both groups of participants to think reflectively about their institutional lives and to experiment with new forms of democratic participation. In a neoliberal society, educational opportunities that stimulate metapragmatic reflection are both rare and significant to furthering the larger political objective of building spaces for freedom.

Notes

1. See, for example, Kristin Bumiller, *The Civil Rights Society* (Baltimore: Johns Hopkins University Press, 1988) and *In an Abusive State* (Durham: Duke University Press, 2008).
2. For a discussion of these issues confronting sociology, see, for example, Pierre Bourdieu and Loic J. D. Wacquant, eds, *An Invitation to Reflexive Sociology* (Chicago: University of Chicago Press, 1992).
3. http://www.insideoutcenter.org.
4. For further elaboration on the effects of legalized accountability, see Charles R. Epp, *Making Rights Real* (Chicago: University of Chicago Press, 2010).
5. Lewis A. Coser, *Greedy Institutions* (New York: Free Press, 1974).
6. Murray Edelman, *The Symbolic Uses of Politics* (Urbana: University of Illinois Press, 1964).
7. Luc Boltanski and Eve Chaipello, *The New Spirit of Capitalism* (New York: Verso, 2007).
8. Luc Boltanski, *On Critique* (Cambridge: Polity, 2011), 67.
9. Boltanski, *On Critique*, 156.
10. The students read sections of John Locke, *Two Treatises of Government* and the appropriately critical companion piece by Sheldon Wolin, "Fugitive Democracy" in *Democracy and Difference: Contesting the Boundaries of the Political*, ed. Seyla Benhabib (Princeton: Princeton University Press, 1996), 31–45.
11. For a critique of this programming see my recent chapter, "Incarceration, Welfare State, and Labor Market Nexus: The Increasing Significance of Gender in the Prison System," in *Women Exiting Prison: Critical Essays on Gender, Post-Release Support and Survival*, ed. Bree Carlton and Marie Segrave (New York: Routledge, 2013), 13–33.

CHAPTER 20

Access or Justice? Inside-Out and Transformative Education

Gillian Harkins

By working to serve individual students, do we suggest the correctness and justness of the institutions and systems that they find themselves in and that we support with our own work? Conversely, by working to address the manifest injustices in such a system, do we neglect the individual lives presently caught within it? I would argue that, at least in spirit, these are questions almost any teacher in any institution could ask about the work they do.

Kirk Branch, Eyes on the Ought to Be[1]

In scholarly research, answers are only as good as the further questions they provoke, while for activists, answers are as good as the tactics they make possible.

Ruth Wilson Gilmore, Golden Gulag[2]

In keeping with the spirit of the epigraphs offered here, this essay raises more questions than it answers. How do we imagine and institute the aims of higher education in systems that have historically separated "scholarly research" and "activism"? And how do we shift our tactics to address recent changes in these systems brought about by neoliberal reforms, which combine a philosophy of free-market enterprise with policies limiting state support for education and increasing state support for incarceration? Given this context, how can we strategize to link efforts to increase access to higher education inside prisons with the broader goals of education justice? Efforts to answer these questions are already underway among activists and scholars working within the constraints of existing institutions. This essay adds to the conversation by exploring how higher education in prison programs can create institutional mechanisms or systems that contribute to broader education justice movements. Focusing specifically on the historical context of neoliberalism, I ask how providing increased access to higher education—specifically access that crosses prison walls—can become a strategy in broader educational justice efforts rather than another component of neoliberalism's restructured access to higher education.[3] My goal is to situate the Inside-Out Prison Exchange Program in relation to the broader impact of neoliberal incorporations of education justice efforts and higher education programs in prison more generally.

We are at a peculiar crossroads entering the second decade of the twenty-first century. The economic, political, and social reforms known as neoliberalism have enacted wide-scale reform of the very meaning of public education in the United States. Early formulations of neoliberal theory developed by Friedrich von Hayek and Milton Friedman in the 1940s were slowly adopted in the United States during the late 1970s and 1980s, working to wed liberal ideals of freedom to neoclassical economics through a shift away from social collectivity and Keynesian government to radical individualism and macroeconomic strategies. Often referred to as privatization and deregulation, neoliberalism more accurately describes the shift from state-regulated redistribution "downward" (via taxation, social welfare, and entitlement programs) to semi-regulated market redistribution "upward" (via protections for capital and corporations).[4] David Harvey lists four features of neoliberalization: (1) privatization and commodification; (2) financialization; (3) management and manipulation of crises; and (4) state redistributions that "strip away the protective coverings that embedded liberalism allowed and occasionally nurtured."[5] These features created "uneven geographic development" (Harvey 87) and new surpluses in population and political power, effects that led to the dismantling of public entitlements (such as education and welfare) and the construction of alternate versions of the social safety net: prisons. Economic and political commitments to prisons were on the rise while those targeting education waned. From the 1980s onward, public education—including traditional institutions of higher education—became increasingly subject to economic reforms and evaluation on the grounds of efficiency rather than other measures of effectiveness, while incarceration seemed to promise neoliberalism a strangely efficient investment strategy for capitalizing on crises in populations and politics.

So what is the role of college programming in prison in this new century, while public higher education itself is under concerted attack? In the later twentieth century, following the 1971 Attica uprising and demands from people inside and outside to provide greater access to education, education programs in prison flourished. In 1994 the Violent Crime Control and Law Enforcement Act restricted access to Pell Grants for incarcerated people (which had been available since 1965), severely impacting the ability to offer accredited college programs on the inside.[6] As a result, roughly 350 college programs in prison closed. But college programs in prison continue to offer postsecondary education to people behind bars around the country, with more programs being developed through new partnerships between colleges, nonprofits, and Departments of Correction.[7] Current education programs in prison have diverse aims and institutional structures, from state-supported Graduate Equivalency Diplomas (GED), English as a Second Language (ESL) curricula, and vocational training to volunteer offerings in creative writing and reading groups or degree-granting programs affiliated with accredited higher education institutions on the outside (including community colleges and four-year universities).[8]

This chapter situates Inside-Out within the impact of such uneven incorporations on higher education programs in prison. Working from frameworks and questions raised by the 2007 Incite! collection *The Revolution Will Not Be Funded*, I ask how transformations of public and private funding, often linked to the NGOization or privatization of political activism and social movements, impacts efforts to offer college programs behind bars.[9] We face a historical juncture where the discourse of "access" to higher education supports increased investment in online learning over and against campus-based pedagogies, a potentially democratizing opening of the campus that does not however address core issues of educational equity. College programs in prison provide one site where the relation between access and equity can be raised, specifically drawing attention to how the digital divide only reinforces the caste system already created for the currently and formerly incarcerated (estimated to make up 8.6% of the national population).[10] College programs in prison are well positioned to partner with broader community- and university-based activists and scholars to fight for transformation of higher education by placing currently and formerly incarcerated students at the center of movements for education justice.

Education Justice

So how did we get here? While systems of incarceration have been intertwined with systems of education from the inception of the United States, many critics link the late twentieth-century boom in carceral systems (including the construction of new prisons as well as the development of massive infrastructures of policing, detention, and administration) to a broader shift from the Welfare–Warfare to the Workfare–Warfare state. According to Ruth Wilson Gilmore, the "welfare" function of the Welfare–Warfare state was replaced in the neoliberal era by a "post-Keynesian state-building project" (53) that turns welfare into workfare. People de- and re-territorialized throughout the twentieth century to meet the national needs of capital suffered new forms of domestic abandonment as capital is liberated (via trade "deregulation") and labor is opened globally to uneven geographic exploitation-without-development.[11] Within the United States, this transformation has been linked to the turn to mass incarceration (and dismantling of systems of mass access to education, healthcare, social services, and jobs). The building of prisons for mass incarceration seemingly resolved problems associated with surplus populations (warehousing some portions of the surplus population in regions that create jobs and political capital for others), surplus capital (providing sites of investment as well as extraction), and surplus state power. Neoliberal governance derived political power from claiming to shrink the state, specifically its welfare functions, while actually building the state apparatus through anti-immigrant legislation, three strikes laws, and drug-related mandatory sentencing.[12]

The rise of post 1970s mass incarceration is not therefore merely about prisons per se, but more broadly about a transformation in the systems (including education) that define and distribute human value, including what precisely humans deserve, and who is accountable to provide this for them. In the 1960s and 1970s, radical movements for racial, sexual, and gendered liberation crystallized long-standing struggles over state power, including its function in the redistribution of wealth, its regulation of labor and financial markets, and its commitment to infra-structural support for all. These movements included educational access as part of infrastructural redistribution; affirmative action and (limited) open admissions are among the more famous limited outcomes of these demands for full educational equality. The 1980s and 1990s might be equally characterized as periods of radical struggles over economic justice, but this time the welfare state itself was the target. Here neoliberal activists (both politically liberal and conservative) sought to shrink the state's role in redistribution, regulation, and infrastructural guarantees, includ-ing a specific attack on public access to higher education. This entailed a rhetorical and legal move away from explicitly race-based and racist restrictions on political, economic, and social access to an allegedly race-neutral focus on "crime" as the logic of disentitlement.[13] This shift actually expanded categories of criminalized activities and police powers while exacerbating racial disparities in education and incarcera-tion, moving a huge swath of the human population from state-supported education into state-supported incarceration. This is what Erica Meiners calls the "school to prison 'nexus,'" a deepening interpenetration of systems of education and incarcera-tion that transforms who counts as a deserving "human" and who must be counted among the undeserving mass of society's debris.[14]

This new redistribution of humanity, and the economic and social redistribution it entails, naturalizes the current transformation of systems of mass education into systems of mass incarceration, with civil subjectivity the horizon of political pos-sibility for the elite and entitled few. Theorizing more broadly, Dylan Rodriguez suggests that "the prison is less a 'destination' point for 'the duly convicted' than a post of *massive human departure*—from civil society, the free world, and the mesh of affective social bonds and relations that produce varieties of 'human' family and community."[15] Such a "massive human departure" is paradoxically facilitated in the late twentieth- and early twenty-first century by the promise of a "selective human return": philanthropic efforts help to lift up the most worthy among the disentitled masses. As public entitlements shrink and market-based responses rise, nonprofit organizations frequently step in to provide distributive and service functions. What were once grassroots struggles against the welfare state have become through neo-liberal pressure part of what Ruth Wilson Gilmore calls "the shadow of the shadow state," which "take[s] responsibility for persons who are in the throes of abandon-ment rather than responsibility for persons progressing toward full incorporation into the body politic."[16] These organizations play a specific role in "buffering" lim-ited access for the poor or working classes, seeking a combination of public and private funding to offer minimal versions of a social safety net.[17]

In relation to education, neoliberal activism targets systems of public entitle-ment to higher education, offering private solutions to raise worthy individuals from their mass problems. Increasingly philanthropic and private efforts are called upon to provide even minimal access to what was once "public" education. This seems particularly true as I draft this essay, while state universities across the country are under attack for everything from unionization and teacher salaries to offering ethnic studies and humanities curriculum. According to Bill Gates in his 2011 Speech to the National Governors Association:

> Now in the past, it felt fine to just say, ok, we're overall going to be generous to this sector. But in this era, to break down and really say what are the categories that help fill jobs and drive the state economy in the future, you'll find that it's not across the board in terms of everything that the state subsidizes in higher education.[18]

Here we see a shift in the meaning of "public" education away from community-based demands for state redistributive mechanisms and into market-based delivery systems in the service of capital.[19] In an era when high-interest-bearing private student loans allow debt-based access to higher education, especially for the dwindling middle classes, we are seeing the financialization of education for the benefit of the very philanthropists who will later refinance it. The restructuring of higher education, including its turn to greater on-line access to credits and degrees, speaks the language of economic empowerment and democratization while often creating increased inequities in accumulation and debt.

The financialization of education sharpens our responsibility to make alliances between those seeking education equity and justice and those working for prison abolition. This feels particularly true for programs seeking to provide access to higher education within prisons. Critics of prison-based programs working to provide access to existing institutions of higher education have argued that these programs risk complicity with broader neoliberal reforms. Simply providing access to higher education in prison does not necessarily challenge the project of mass incarceration and the dismantling of mass education in which it is situated and may in fact institute new partnerships between state institutions (such as the Department of Corrections and public colleges and universities) and seemingly nonstate actors (volunteers and nonprofits). Within these complex systems, state authority itself may be diffused through new formations of "hybrid" governmental processes incorporating administrators, teachers, students, and activists.[20] Thus the selective return to humanity promised by education programs in prison could actually legitimate new relations between neoliberal subjects of governance as well as new systems and institutions of "humanization" and selective politicization. Yet these same dangers are faced by those teaching exclusively on two- and four-year college campuses on the outside; the problem may in fact be exacerbated by ignorance about how these academic institutions actually intersect with carceral institutions. Rather than acknowledging how these institutions are economically and politically interdependent, many external colleges and universities promote the illusion that sponsoring programs in prison is itself a kind of educational philanthropy (spreading cultural capital where it has been denied). It seems important not to isolate and critique teaching that takes place inside prisons, but instead take accountability for how various institutional settings intersect. This means that we must face the overarching problem of providing access to a system—shifting one's given position within it—rather than demanding justice from it, which requires a transformation of its institutions, values, and practices.

College in Prison Programs

We might usefully approach higher education programs in prison as one key terrain of critical and tactical struggle among various academics and activists (including those on the inside) over "access to higher education" as an education justice issue. In effect, our current moment exposes the long-standing site of higher education as a struggle between state-, market-, and community-based activists, a struggle over and at times against the will of academics who sometimes see themselves as institutionally apart and protected from such struggles.[21] This is where we find college programs in prison engaged in a broader "praxis" of education justice—struggling in the interstices of state, private, and nonprofit institutions to foster intellectual expansion and educational justice amidst distributive arguments over higher education more generally.

Higher education programs in prison, or post-GED programming, have one primary goal: to create curricular offerings and pedagogical approaches that offer the best access to the broadest range of courses that meet the goals, needs, and interests of students. This goal requires the recruitment, training, and (preferably collaborative) supervision of qualified and appropriate educators (paid or volunteer). But to achieve this primary goal, programs face three unique challenges posed by the interinstitutional relationships described above. They must (1) develop institutional relationships that enable high-quality education to be delivered inside prisons, which requires by definition the permission of the Department of Corrections and, if college credit is sought, a matriculation agreement with an accredited college or university; (2) create organizational structures that match the expectations of one or all of the following: private funders, state funders, accreditation partners, and/or 501(c)(3) by-laws and Boards of Directors; and (3) create program goals that define recognizable and measurable outcomes that demonstrate the "effectiveness" and "efficiency" of the program delivery model so that it can be sustained over time (i.e., meeting the expectations of financial and institutional partners). The first overarching goal is often dependent on achieving the next three, as the delivery of relevant and high-quality curriculum is often evaluated according to the institutional protocols outlined in the three subordinate goals. This creates obstacles to the interinstitutional transformation needed to shift education access into education justice.

This is the problem confronted by efforts to create access to college education in particular: neoliberal college education is not free. In the context of formal credit-bearing institutions, value assigned to learning is assigned a specific monetary value. This means that college programs inside prisons reflect and refract the structural problems posed to educational values on the outside. Learning outcomes are overall subsidiary to program outcomes (here tied to broader institutional outcomes), measured by students enrolled and dollars delivered. College credit can be purchased *without* any demonstrable learning taking place, as has been the complaint about some private on-line universities. But, except in the rare case of honorary degrees, it cannot be earned without a monetary transaction or through learning alone. Course credit by examination, the lowest cost formula, still requires a fee for "testing out" of a course based on learning beyond the classroom. Prison-based programs could forego college credit and focus instead on the value of learning at the college level. But most students feel strongly that college credit is a key value—it appears to promise improved confidence and greater job access post-release as well as a credential whose value transfers across the walls. While college credit does not guarantee improved postrelease outcomes, and as Dylan Rodriguez points out beliefs in the magical powers of formal higher education are often overstated, there is no doubt that receiving college credit for their learning is important to students on the inside.

We cannot transform the conditions of education on the inside if we do not transform those on the outside, and we cannot transform conditions of education on the outside if we do not transform those on the inside. The educational experiences and leadership of people who have been caught up in this system must be foregrounded in overall equity efforts focused on higher education. It cannot merely be a question of access. It must be aimed at justice. This requires the transformation of the relation between institutions of education and institutions of incarceration. Higher education programs in prison cannot be asked to carry out this work in isolation: they operate in an interstitial realm between institutions and people with very different aims, and they serve students who deserve the highest quality education possible. This is not work to be undertaken in individual classrooms but rather the structural and institutional work of building relationships across institutional walls. This requires partnerships among leaders resisting the neoliberal restructuring of the university system and public education more generally. Unless we connect our work to broader strategic agendas for education justice, access to higher education inside prisons runs the risk of being pressed into the most restricted forms of educational delivery, rather than institutional transformation. This can create a zero-sum game of choosing between providing transferable value without value transformation, or value transformation without transferable value.

Despite these pressures, higher education programs in prison are doing important work facilitating new modes of education and working through (and against) existing parameters of higher education in neoliberal times. The Inside-Out model is particularly interesting in this regard, developing alternative spaces where students from campus and prison can come together to create new educational paradigms. The model trains instructors in activity-based pedagogy that can bring together diverse learning styles and allow for shared learning and dialogue. Students are given the chance to learn together and to question how different institutional spaces shape the meaning of education and equity, as well as how their understanding of education changes when they shift institutional spaces and relationships. At its best the Inside-Out model creates longer term learning communities among inside and outside students in the Think Tanks and Theory Groups that continue to meet on the inside after the class has stopped. At their best, such programs can create genuine alliances in critical thought that challenge our current system's demobilization of intellectual and political exchange and educate people in resistance to its new caste system.

But like all models, it will only be as successful as its implementation. The implementation of this model by individual teachers and institutions raises many of the same questions facing other programs today. By creating an alternative pedagogical experience that takes place only inside prison walls, it runs the risk of creating an "experimental" education that does not in fact transform educational values more broadly. This can exceptionalize prison space as outside the values of higher education while leaving those values intact on main campuses. At its worst, poorly instituted Inside-Out programs can run the risk of creating "contact zones" between inside and outside students that do not transform the meaning of education or incarceration. The biggest problem faced by Inside-Out and other programs is how to create transformative systems across the diffuse institutions and practices of higher education. Transformative education is therefore both an ideal and a goal. It provides a lens for self-critique within our programs and allows us to build alliances across institutional spaces. Pursued thoughtfully, it can help us achieve strategies for education justice that place at the center the leadership of currently and formerly incarcerated students.

Recent collaborations among programs and institutions have developed some shared practices to help build exactly this type of transformative education. In conclusion, I will simply summarize four of these practices: (1) national coalition-building; (2) shared assessment protocols; (3) constituency-based accountability; (4) interinstitutional collaboration. First, college programs in prison can work together to share best educational and program practices; this includes supporting the initiative to return Pell Grant eligibility for incarcerated people. Second, such a coalition can develop assessment protocols that introduce our own measures for success. This is crucial if we want to implement practices that ensure transformative education on terms that work for program participants (rather than funders or outside institutions). Three, each program can develop its own constituency-based accountabilities, including supporting the leadership of currently and formerly incarcerated students and building relationship with communities impacted by educational inequity and mass incarceration. Finally, each program can seek collaboration, rather than sponsorship, from its accreditation partner. This is required work if we are to create and sustain meaningful access to higher education; it is required work if we are to define education justice as the end of the prison industrial complex and start of meaningful education for all.

Notes

1. Kirk Branch, *Eyes on the Ought to Be: What We Teach When We Teach about Literacy* (Stanford: Stanford University Press, 2007), 7.
2. Ruth Wilson Gilmore, *Golden Gulag: Prisons, Surplus, Crisis, and Opposition in Globalizing* (Berkeley: University of California Press, 2007), 27.
3. Shana Agid, Michael Bennett, Kate Drabinski, eds, Special Issue: "Teaching against the Prison Industrial Complex," *Radical Teacher* 88 (Summer 2010); Kate Drabinski, Gillian Harkins, and Shana Agid, "Teaching Inside Carceral Institutions," Special Issue of *Radical Teacher* 95 (Winter 2012). 3–9.
4. Lisa Duggan, *The Twilight of Equality? Neo-Liberalism, Cultural Politics, and the Attack on Democracy* (Boston: Beacon Press, 2003); Clarence Lo, *Small Property Versus Big Government: Social Origins of the Property Tax Revolt* (Berkeley: University of California Press, 1995).
5. David Harvey, *A Brief History of Neoliberalism* (New York: Oxford University Press, 2005), 168. Harvey argues that China, Chile, the United States, and the United Kingdom developed neoliberal policies and practices somewhat at odds with the early theoretical formulations.

6. While only 1 percent of Pell Grant funding was distributed to people behind bars, public rhetoric emphasized the condition of "less eligibility" to argue that the Pell Grant created unfair access for imprisoned people. Efforts to restore Pell Grant eligibility are lead by the Education from the Inside-Out Coalition: http://www.eiocoalition.org/.

7. Jeanne B. Contardo and Wendy Erisman. *Learning to Reduce Recidivism: A 50-State Analysis of Postsecondary Correctional Education Policy.* Inst. for Higher Education Policy. November 2005. Site visit 21 September, 2013. www.ihep.org/Publications/publications-detail.cfm?id=47.; Minatiya Dawkins and Erin McAuliff, "Higher Education Behind Bars: Postsecondary Prison Education Programs Make a Difference," *Centerpoint*, American Council on Education (October 14, 2008): CenterPointEditor@ace.nche.edu.

8. The most detailed survey of programs can be found here: http://prisonstudiesproject.org/directory/.

9. Incite! Women of Color against Violence, eds, *The Revolution Will Not Be Funded: Beyond the Non-Profit Industrial Complex* (Cambridge: South End Press, 2007).

10. Statistics estimate 7.2 million currently on probation, parole, or in jail or prison. Statistics including formerly incarcerated people or those convicted of a felony who did not serve time estimate 19.8 million persons. Sarah Shannon, Christopher Uggen, Melissa Thompson, Jason Schnittker, and Michael Massoglia, "Growth in the U.S. Ex-Felon and Ex-Prisoner Population, 1948–2010": http://paa2011.princeton.edu/papers/111687.

11. What Harvey calls "accumulation by dispossession" has been practiced throughout colonial history and is a key feature of indigenous exploitation and migrant labor exploitation (including earlier legalization such as the Bracero Program). This recent phase dismantles white civil entitlements to national protection of labor through tariffs and unions.

12. Michelle Alexander, *The New Jim Crow: Mass Incarceration in the Age of Colorblindness* (New York: The New Press, 2010); Joy James, ed. *States of Confinement: Policing, Detention, and Prisons* (New York: St. Martin's Press, 2000).

13. Discussions of the Thirteenth Amendment focus on whether or not a "badge of servitude" was justly imposed by race or crime. Longer histories of impressment, enslavement, and incarceration include: Scott Christianson, *With Liberty for Some: 500 Years of Imprisonment in America* (Boston: Northeastern University Press, 1998); Peter Lindebaugh and Marcus Rediker, *The Many Headed Hydra: Sailors, Slaves, Commoners and the Hidden History of the Revolutionary Atlantic* (Boston: Beacon Press, 2000); and Luana Ross, *Inventing the Savage: The Social Construction of Native American Criminality* (Austin: University of Texas Press, 1998).

14. Erica R. Meiners, *The Right to be Hostile: Schools, Prisons, and the Making of Public Enemies* (New York: Routledge, 2007).

15. Dylan Rodriguez, *Forced Passages: Imprisoned Radical Intellectuals and the U.S. Prison* (Minneapolis: University of Minnesota Press, 2006), 227.

16. Ruth Wilson Gilmore, "In the Shadow of the Shadow State," *The Revolution Will Not Be Funded: Beyond the Nonprofit Industrial Complex*, ed., INCITE! Women of Color Against Violence (New York: South End Press, 2009), 41–52.

17. *The Revolution Will Not Be Funded* historicizes philanthropy as the result of massive disinvestment in governmental and state processes of redistribution and the rise of the "Non-Profit Industrial Complex" (NPIC) from the early 1900s to the present. See in particular Christine E. Ahn, "Democratizing American Philanthropy," *The Revolution Will Not Be Funded: Beyond the Nonprofit Industrial Complex*, ed., INCITE! Women of Color Against Violence (New York: South End Press, 2009), 63–76.

18. Bill Gates, "Do's and Don'ts for Higher Education Improvement," *Bill & Melinda Gates Foundation*, Uploaded by Gates Foundation (March 1, 2011): http://www.youtube.com/watch?v=BSn4ShnDEk0&feature=autoplay&list=SP59A85238C8B52C62&index=3&playnext=4.

19. As in the case of labor and capital, education is globally de-territorialized as elite out-of-state and international students paying increasingly high fees to attend US public universities (while in state residents face diminished access) and US universities create distance-learning and international campuses largely unknown to their domestic faculty.

20. Lynn A. Haney, *Offending Women: Power, Punishment, and the Regulation of Desire* (Berkeley: University of California Press, 2010), 8, 15.

21. Christopher Newfield, *Unmaking the Public University: The Forty Year Assault on the Middle Class* (Cambridge: Harvard University Press, 2008); Roderick A. Ferguson, *The Reorder of Things: The University and Its Pedagogies of Minority Difference* (Minneapolis: University of Minnesota Press, 2012).

PART V

Yardsticks and Roadmaps: Assessing Change

CHAPTER 21

Alchemy and Inquiry: Reflections on an Inside-Out Research Roundtable

Sarah Allred, Angela Bryant, Simone Weil Davis, Kurt Fowler, Phil Goodman, Jim Nolan, Lori Pompa, Barbara Sherr Roswell, and Dan Stageman

In 2008, The Inside-Out Prison Exchange Program convened a Research Committee to (1) facilitate a collective, critical, and professional consciousness about social justice, crime, and incarceration through the exploration of the Inside-Out program pedagogy, impact, and effectiveness; (2) develop and encourage proposals for various types of research that focus on The Inside-Out Prison Exchange Program; and (3) establish ethical guidelines for inquiry that would meet and exceed the federal human subjects guidelines in research practices. In fall 2012, Research Committee members Sarah Allred, Angela Bryant, Phil Goodman, Kurt Fowler, Jim Nolan, Lori Pompa, and Dan Stageman joined with Simone Davis and Barbara Roswell for a roundtable discussion of the central claim that Inside-Out is "transformative." This chapter frames and summarizes that conversation.[1]

The pressure to research and evaluate successful programs is certainly not news to faculty and professionals responsible for community-based learning, prison education, or—in the case of Inside-Out—the nexus between the two. Diverse stakeholders are interested in better understanding program impacts, from funders and administrators who want to know about the effects of their financial and institutional investments, to staff who may use program evaluation to improve training or curriculum, to faculty and campus professionals who want to understand and improve community-engagement practices and pedagogies. Others see campus-community partnerships as fertile ground to advance knowledge in a range of disciplines (and perhaps to add to their own publication records as well), and view community-engaged work not as the focus of but as a site or context for research.

Just as the prison context offers a particularly intense instantiation of community-based learning, it also heightens concerns about research in community settings. Research without consent has a long and deeply troubling history in the prison context, and people who are incarcerated have realistic concerns about being treated as objects for research that may be exploitative, harmful, or invalid. Phil Goodman points out that this issue has deep roots "in the rise of 'criminology' as a 'scientific' discipline and a particular modernist/contemporary power-knowledge project to know the 'offender'. . . . While we can say that research on Inside-Out can and should be less horrific than past research, left unanswered are questions about the ways in which *all* research in this area is necessarily implicated in the larger project of punishment."

These concerns resonate with those of community-engagement scholars, who, similarly concerned about exploitation and reinforcing power differentials, ask, "Where's the *community* in community-based teaching and research?" As a result, the Inside-Out research community has been occupied with a series of fundamental questions: Who conducts the research? What or whom is being studied? What questions should be asked? What qualifies as success? What tools and methods should be used? How can we assess claims of transformation? What kinds of inquiry does Inside-Out make uniquely possible?

A felt sense of transformation—a deep knowing that community-engaged work makes a difference—will be familiar to readers who teach in prisons or bring campus and community together. It is what we know when we read a grateful email from an alumna expressing thanks for the experience that gave her purpose and shaped her career, when an incarcerated student recounts an animated phone conversation with his son about the essays they are each writing, when a group of previously disengaged students join together with their neighbors to campaign for social justice in their community. Equally familiar, likely, is the hankering to explain and prove—and the wish to look beyond the class, beyond the semester, and to engage with scope and reach. For this we need longitudinal studies, and yet these require both care and innovation: both ethical and methodological challenges arise when people are leaving prison. As Phil Goodman and Sarah Allred concluded during our roundtable, the traditional scientific model with a contained, tightly defined, and operationalized unit of analysis may not be the most useful here.

Plus, as Angela Bryant notes, the question of "who sets the agenda" cannot be divorced from the paradigms and larger social analyses that a research agenda upholds. Researchers only seek answers to the questions they know to ask. Content analysis of reflection papers, for example, can help focus attention on themes and questions salient for campus and community participants. Even more critically, Participant Action Research (PAR, see chapter 23) is key to inviting the participants themselves to be involved not only in naming the questions but also, as Turnbull et al. show, in conducting inquiry and developing participant leadership. Inside-Out joins a wider effort to challenge the assumptions of the research and practitioner community, to empower community participants *as* researchers, and to "push the envelope of what is considered mainstream research." This challenge can itself be an impetus for social change.

This is especially true today, when evaluation of both educational and criminal justice outcomes typically focuses on individual—rather than group or institutional—transformation, thereby obscuring broad-scale challenges to social systems and institutions. In the case of penal research (and assessment of a program like Inside-Out), this almost always involves a demand for recidivism rates. Just as "retention" or "graduation rates" are at best "partial indicators of student success" that "work around the edges of students' actual learning"—necessary but scarcely sufficient, as Carol Schneider writes, recidivism is a similarly distorting and reductive measure of "success" or impact, not only unable to account for the impact of education on those still incarcerated, but also unable to address impact on family, self-esteem, employment, future education, or a whole range of other reasons for education, from the development of critical thinking to civic participation.[2] Recidivism is additionally problematic as a purported measure of individual success or failure because of the ways it disregards the systemic flaws that can return people to prison over very minor parole violations.

The motivations for inquiry—and the shapes that inquiry may take—run much deeper, of course, than the documentation of narrowly defined outcomes for external audiences. This volume, in fact, is filled with a kind of wonder. Multiple authors included in these pages use the phrase, *"There is something about Inside-Out that..."* as they seek to define that *something* that encouraged risk, deepened engagement with complex texts, disrupted the stereotypical thinking, or enticed people disaffected with school to embrace learning. Each chapter, in its own way, seeks to explain Inside-Out's transformative power, to describe the "crucible" for learning, or the "alchemy" of the Inside-Out model.

While these metaphors of alchemy at first seem to romanticize and mystify the "magic" of Inside-Out, they are actually very telling in the ways that each calls attention not to one method or strategy, but to the program's unique, intense, and carefully sequenced and calibrated mixture and juxtaposition of strategies that makes the whole larger than the sum of its parts. Ella Turenne, for example, invokes Harro's "cycle of transformation," Paul Perry employs Khuri's analysis of the role of emotion in intercultural dialogue, M. Kay Harris draws on Bain's construct of a natural critical learning environment. One approach to Inside-Out research, then, is to ask, "What theoretical frameworks can account for this interpenetration of high impact practices as the source of the transformational power of Inside Out?" Given the explanatory power of these models, how might researchers test a hypothesis about how Inside-Out creates transformative learning? How, in turn, might research into Inside-Out as praxis inform and contribute to our theoretical understanding of civic engagement in higher education?

Perhaps most impressive, of the ten well-documented "high impact" practices identified by George Kuh for the Liberal Education and America's Promise (LEAP) initiative—with the modest goal that every student participate in two of these during his or college career—each single Inside-Out course integrates the key features of *seven*:

- First-Year Seminars
- Learning Communities
- Writing-Intensive Courses
- Collaborative Assignments and Projects

- Diversity/Global Learning
- Community-Based Learning
- Capstone Projects.[3]

In his extensive study of the conditions that enable adults returning to school to thrive, Mike Rose similarly identifies an interlocking set of best practices that align with Inside-Out's combination of key elements: a welcoming space, a meaningful context for learning, a small community of learners engaged in a shared enterprise, opportunities to develop "soft skills" and higher order thinking, and, perhaps most significant, metacognitive language and attention to learning itself, with multiple and scaffolded opportunities for students to reflect on their own journey and the process, not just the products, of learning.

Where LEAP identifies large curricular and institutional structures, in his study of "What the Best College Teachers Do," Ken Bain seeks out the ingredients of individual teachers' practice that lead to transformative, or deep learning, what he terms "sustained, substantial, positive influence on how students think, act and feel" (5). He highlights teachers' understanding of teaching as creating conditions for learning, the connection between personal and intellectual development, collaborative work with other students that requires higher order thinking about significant questions, and asking students to make a commitment to the class and the learning. Perhaps most critical to these qualities is the key skill emphasized in Inside-Out's Training Institute, the instructor's ability to "do intellectually, physically or emotionally what they expect from the students" (112).

Even more obvious as an extensively studied explanatory model is Jack Mezirow's ten-stage description of transformative learning. On the basis of a meta-analysis of the empirical literature, Edward Taylor suggests that fostering transformative learning involves the integration of a set of interdependent core elements that, like the Inside-Out approach, include activation of individual experience, critical reflection, dialogue, creation of shared norms, a holistic orientation toward teaching (including affective and relational ways of knowing), awareness of context, and authentic relationships, all made possible through learner-centered teaching.

Beyond the educational literature, one can find explanations of Inside-Out's unique contribution in its emphasis on helping students simultaneously to build what Robert Putnam identifies in *Bowling Alone* as "bonding capital" (often deep connections among homogeneous groups) and "bridging capital" (the ability to work with diverse others). As Amy Gutmann concludes, "The more economically, ethnically and religiously heterogeneous the membership of an association is, the greater its capacity to cultivate the kind of public discourse and deliberation that is conducive to democratic citizenship" (25). The Inside-Out classroom creates the conditions where students develop the types of close bonds of trust and affiliation typical of "bonding capital"— *while* bridging divides and working with diverse others. Gurin and her colleagues' distinctions among "structural" (demographic), "classroom" (reading, discussion, theory) and "interactional" (peer and informal relationship) forms of diversity offer a related and also well-researched framework; Inside-Out can be understood to maximize the educational value of diversity by activating and connecting these three dimensions of diversity that in most educational settings are distinct or absent.

Over the years, research into Inside-Out, like other forms of community-based learning, has used frameworks like these to test the claim that the program contributes to change in individuals' attitudes, beliefs, self-perception, etc. Using Likert scale items (Strongly Agree, Agree, Disagree, Strongly Disagree), the Research Committee has considered such pre- and posttest questions as:

- One individual can make a difference in changing society
- I can only learn from an expert or authority
- The criminal justice system treats people of all races equally
- Punishment is the best way to deter crime
- I believe that I have the ability to successfully complete a college degree.

As chapters 22 and 23 elaborate, an approach like this will be of most value only if it is embedded in other forms of inquiry and if it is enriched through the contributions of a networked research community: students, alumni, and think tanks participate in projects and conduct inquiry; crossinstitutional multisite content analysis projects yield themes to be investigated further; and instructors who are interested in different questions, models, and approaches share with and inform each other, creating a collaborative research community.

It was members of that research community who participated in this roundtable discussion. So we put the query to them:

What Sorts of Questions Do You Want to Ask?

Dan Stageman (DS): I would ask someone who had completed a class, "How has this transformation manifested in your interactions with a community, with your desire to stay involved, with how you act?" If this has long-term effects, people need to be acting on the transformation in other contexts and over the long term.

Lori Pompa (LP): In the original Inside-Out curriculum, the first part of our final reflection paper asks about process—it elicits observations about group process, dynamics. We could add, "Where will you take this from here? What will you *do* with this?"

Angela Bryant (AB): But at that stage (the end of a semester), they may not know what they will do.

LP: Over the years, I've often gotten letters from alumni, who say things like, "I'm a lawyer and what I'm doing was influenced by Inside-Out..."

Simone Davis (SD): So would that require a longitudinal study, and what are the ramifications there

Sarah Allred (SA): We definitely need a way to broaden the net.

Jim Nolan (JN): I think that we all shy away from focusing on individuals in prison as objects as study, in part because it is worrisome whether they can truly give consent. So focusing on context is a good way of proceeding. I ask, to what extent does the classroom change? I want to know whether someone is waiting for the teacher's direction or is involved in and sharing responsibility for a group project—in my classes, typically, a class-created "white paper" that goes to the commissioner in the state office. I want to know: Do students take changes in perception back into their respective communities?

AB: How has this work changed our own communities, our learning, and our knowledge production? Roswell and Bryant went on to voice an interest in the program's impacts on participating instructors. How has participation in Inside-Out changed instructors' teaching, research, self-concept, or civic engagement? For example, what do instructors learn as a result of working in correctional settings and confronting institutional barriers? Interviews, syllabi, statements of teaching philosophy would all serve as data sources for this inquiry.

In class, students often shake instructors free from preconceived ideas about the pedagogy's purported benefits. Thereby, students point the way toward different evaluative yardsticks. Here are three examples from our conversation.

1) *SA*: The transformation that I have observed and been able to share in does not seem to be a unilateral experience. It does not necessarily center on the group project. As we've discussed, moments of unanticipated conflict or disruption may be transformational. And it's hard to plan for this in advance. I once took a class on a tour, and had a horrible experience with the staff member who led it. So the learning does not unfold uniformly. We need a way to respond to something when it happens, to learn how it is labeled.

2) *JN*: When I started doing Inside-Out, what I observed was that the inside students internalized their role as "criminals." During Inside-Out training we were given warnings against labeling language, but during class, it became a kind of joke, because the inside students used the word "convicts" to describe themselves. The prison is full of language about "choice" and "making the right choices" and inside students use this terminology a lot. The outside students in the class were enrolled in a sociology program, and they put much more emphasis on context, on places—college and prison—where habits and dispositions are re-formed. In this difference, we found a jumping-off point for learning.

3) *AB*: We talk about group projects as something that brings people together. What we learned from talking with students was that this blurring of lines was not what they say they found most monumental in their thinking. They weren't completely transformed—they went back and forth and revisited old roles and identities and divisions. As an instructor and researcher, I was trying to quash these divisions, but when given an opportunity to contribute, participants corrected me.

We talked about scope. What's our frame—a single class or a community that persists? Inside-Out exists both in its form as a single semester experience and as an opportunity for ongoing programmatic involvement. And we talked about the consequences of the various tools deployed in this research.

LP: Inside-Out classes are delimited by nature, less than 15 weeks long. What impact does that have, compared to, say, a Think Tank that is ongoing?

SD: What does its boundedness make possible or curtail?

LP: At closing ceremonies, so moving and significant, there is quite a bit of mourning that happens, but it is mourning for more than just the relationships; it's for the loss of the liberating space itself. What is made possible by the knowledge that this has an end? How might this "boundedness" heighten transformation or the perception of transformation?

JN: It hurries it along and makes it more intense.

AB: I'd like to know, for how many people does the experience really end? In Ohio [and across the network], more and more alumni are staying involved in one-credit reading groups, Think Tanks, and independent studies. So when we are measuring the impact of the classroom, we need to do longitudinal work. How do we ask, "What happens when the work *doesn't* end?"

SD: Certain kinds of transformation require as a foundation the trust that can only be built through sustained relationships. We see this in the ongoing work of think tanks, et cetera, as Angela suggests.

JN: I'm wondering if conceptualizing the entire structure of Inside-Out as a grassroots community would be a more productive avenue of research [which suggests a very different set of frameworks and tools (see Grant and Holley)].

DS: If I were to look at one researcher and one model, it would be Michelle Fine who eschews more restrictive ideas of units of analysis and looks at circuits, like the "Changing Minds" work with Bedford Hills or her more recent work.

SD: This leads back to questions about method, voice, story.

Kurt Fowler (KF): This makes me wish for something like "Story Corps"—idiosyncratic, contextualized. We need a repository of stories and a way to explore what this means in terms of method and moving forward.

SD: People working in the Inside-Out community have expressed the wish for an anthology, an archive of narrative and qualitative research. For me, what's relevant about process in this regard is that stories aren't just the content of the stories themselves. When research projects are collaboratively designed and implemented in a participatory way, shared stories can become active engagements, connective tissue, and crucial context, performances in the Austinian sense.[4] Telling and listening to a story can be a way of healing and building community. Jim asks, "What is happening in the room, what do you want to have happen?" This is an invitation for the participant to think about agency. It's an invitation to create a story about your own role in community.

Notes

1. The full text of the roundtable is available at www.insideoutcenter.org.
2. Just as Carol Schneider, the President of the Association of American Colleges and Universities, calls on higher education to better align metrics with what we know about deep integrative learning and what makes it possible, Vernor Munoz Special Rapporteur to the United Nations suggests that human dignity should be a fundamental concern of models and measures of education in detention, not simply "a utilitarian add-on should resources allow it."

3. George D. Kuh, *High-Impact Educational Practices: What They Are, Who Has Access to Them, and Why They Matter* (Washington, DC: Association of American Colleges and Universities, 2008). Internships, student research, and study abroad are also identified as high-impact practices.

4. J. L. Austin described some speech acts as far more than descriptive or analytic: they are a kind of doing or making. When we say "Happy Birthday!" our words are themselves a (verbal) action. See J. L. Austin, *How to Do Things with Words* (Oxford: Clarendon Press, 1962).

References

Austin, J. L. *How to Do Things with Words.* Oxford: Clarendon Press, 1962.

Bain, Ken. *What the Best College Teachers Do.* Cambridge, MA: Harvard University Press, 2004.

Fine, Michelle and Jessica Ruglis. "Circuits and Consequences of Dispossession: The Racialized Realignment of the Public Sphere for U.S. Youth," *Transforming Anthropology* 17, no. 1 (2009): 120–133.

Grant, Heather. *Transformer: How to Build a Network to Change a System: A Case Study of the RE_AMP Energy Network.* Monitor Institute, 2010. www.monitorinstitute.com/reamp/.

Gurin, Patricia, Eric L. Dey, Sylvia Hurtado, and Gerald Gurin. "Diversity and Higher Education: Theory and impact on educational outcomes," *Harvard Educational Review* 72, no. 3 (2002): 330–366.

Gurin, Patricia, Gerald Gurin, Eric L. Dey, and Sylvia Hurtado. "The Educational Value of Diversity." In *Defending Diversity: Affirmative Action at the University of Michigan*, edited by Patricia Gurin, Jeffrey S. Lehman, and Earl Lewis. Ann Arbor: University of Michigan Press, 2004, 97–188.

Gutmann, Amy. "An Introductory Essay," *Freedom of Association.* Princeton, NJ: Princeton University Press. 1–27.

Harro, Bobbi "The Cycle of Liberation." In *Readings for Diversity and Social Justice*, edited by Maurianne Adams, Warren Blumenfeld, Carmelita Casteneda, 50–60. New York: Routledge, 2000.

Holley, June. *Network Weavers Handbook: A Guide to Transformational Networks.* Athens, OH: Network Weaver Publishing, 2012.

Khuri, Lydia "Working with Emotion in Educational Intergroup Dialogue." *Journal of Intercultural Relations* 28 (2004): 595–612.

Kuh, George L. *High-Impact Educational Practices: What They Are, Who Has Access to Them, and Why They Matter.* Washington, DC: Association of American Colleges and Universities, 2008.

Mezirow, Jack. *Transformative Dimensions of Adult Learning.* San Francisco: Jossey-Bass, 1991.

———. "Transformative Learning: Theory to Practice," *New Directions for Adult and Continuing Education* 74 (Summer 1997): 5–12.

Muñoz, Vernor. "The Right To To Education of Persons In Detention." Report of the Special Rapporteur on the Right to Education, United Nations Human Rights Council, 2009.

Rose, Mike. *Back to School: Why Everyone Deserves a Second Chance at Education.* New York: New Press, 2012.

Schneider, Carol Geary. "Losing Our Way: On the Meanings of Student Success," *Liberal Education* 99, no. 2 (Spring 2013), http://www.aacu.org/liberaleducation/le-sp13/schneider.cfm.

Taylor, Edward. "Fostering Transformative Learning." In *Transformative Learning in Practice: Insights from Community, Workplace, and Higher Education*, edited by Jack Mezirow and Edward Taylor, 3–17. San Francisco: Jossey Bass.

Turnbull, Ann P., Jean Ann Summers, Betsey Santelli, Ursula Markey. "Truths Converging: Empirical Support for Intuitive Understanding," *NHSA Dialog* 5, no. 2 and 3 (2002): 386–389. http://www.beachcenter.org/research/FullArticles/PDF/PAR8_TruthsConverging.pdf.

CHAPTER 22

Relational Learning and the Inside-Out Experience: A Pathway to Building Capacities, Transformative Perspectives, and a Deeper Understanding of Self, Community, and Others

Sarah L. Allred, Nathan Belche, and Todd Robinson

Introduction

Our chapter is a collaboration of three members of the Inside-Out community who, among us, have taken the roles of teacher, student, researcher, study participant, and civic project contributor. We focus here on transitions in the learning processes experienced by students in an Inside-Out course in which we all participated. Specifically, we describe shifts in students' assessments of their closeness to other students as learners, academic self-efficacy, and perceptions of the course as a transformational experience.

The differences between our stories, our present social positions, and our pathways toward this collaboration are important to the work itself, and we believe that its value would been diminished had the project been conceived, implemented, and analyzed by a specialist or "expert" taking a single vantage point. At the time we write, Allred is a tenured faculty member, a trained Inside-Out instructor, and a member of the Inside-Out Research Committee. Robinson and Todd are incarcerated alumni of an Inside-Out course. These significant differences in experience, perspective, and immediate structural constraints were partly bridged by three primary experiences that we share: learning and teaching within an Inside-Out course, developing a peer health education program, and writing a manuscript. To the extent possible, our relationship has progressed with open discussion about the power dynamics that too often remain unexamined within collaborations between community constituents. We have come to think of each other as "neighbors" in this process, sharing in civic fellowship and viewing each other with respect and admiration.

In the fall of 2012, we met to discuss our mutual interest in writing an essay that would frame, summarize, and discuss the findings presented here. Although simple in design, as far as we know, this study is the first of its type: a pilot project designed to test basic hypotheses about the Inside-Out pedagogy. Our methodology, "in keeping with accepted practices of hermeneutic and ethnographic qualitative research" (Sandy and Holland, 2006), involved a place-based focus with regard to the college and community constituents (inside and outside students learning together in a prison setting) and our work. Our collaboration was informed by an "ethic of reciprocity."[1] Because Belche and Robinson were incarcerated, our only means for direct communication were face-to-face meetings, augmented by crucial practical support of a staff liaison. During lengthy meetings in prison, we shared notes, discussed thematic interpretations of qualitative data, proposed hypotheses for quantitative testing, and outlined the contours of the story told here, about what took place in our class and why.

Author Frames and Experiences

Trainee, Instructor, Researcher, Community Partner

Despite feeling skeptical about the value of a "a 7-day, 60-hour intensive training,"[2] in the summer of 2007, Allred attended the Inside-Out Training Institute. She entered into the week with powerful reservations about an approach that did not "feel" or "look" academic and did not seem able to accommodate the substantive topics she regularly teaches—until she began the work at Graterford Prison, where such assumptions were dismantled and reconstructed. Now, when she reflects on the "knowledge" gleaned from training, she remembers the people, her colearners, inside and outside, *by name*. These quickly formed relationships are intertwined in memory with an increasing grasp of some very complex social issues. Figuratively speaking, these relationships became a mnemonic device that has helped her retain, hone, and use the week's understandings. The week's learning was relational—she learned skills and content *through* her relationships with and the perspectives of others, and through her sense of accountability and responsibility to those with whom she was learning. Later that same summer, Allred was invited to become a member of the Inside-Out Research Committee, which works to advance a collective critical and professional consciousness about social justice, crime, education, and incarceration by exploring the impact of the Inside-Out program.

Allred has taught six Inside-Out courses since 2008. A series of investigative conversations initiated by two incarcerated alumni from the spring 2010 course (not the present coauthors) helped to identify the research questions and instruments that went on to inform both a study by Allred et al. (2013)[3] and this one. Discussing what happens to individuals in an Inside-Out course, they talked about an incremental sense of confidence in oneself and in the group's agency, and how this confidence and sense of connection contributed to a notion of transformation. They identified self-efficacy as a construct of interest, and talked about options for measuring it, also identifying the particular academic skills (dialogue, writing, study habits) in which students in Inside-Out courses developed confidence and capacity. The present study, then, emerges out of a history of collaborative exploration in the larger Inside-Out community: formal and informal deliberations with other instructors and researchers, as well as sustained dialogue with alumni of Inside-Out courses.

Student, Community Educator, Researcher

In the fall of 2011, Belche and Robinson read an announcement soliciting interest in taking a college course within the prison. It was advertised as a 15-week sociology course, where men in the facility would study alongside students from a nearby college. Both assumed it was going to be a typical postsecondary prison course in which the instructor lectures. Their interest in studying sociology, mixing with college students, and carrying out a long-felt desire to pursue a college education led each to sign up.

Both experienced a great deal of anxiety during the first combined session (Week 2), albeit for different reasons. Belche remembers feeling relatively at ease about his prospects for academic success in the course. He was, however, jolted out of his comfort zone when inside and outside students were instructed to sit in an alternating pattern. He was keenly aware of negative public perceptions of prisons and the incarcerated, and the proximity to outside students conjured feelings of intimidation and the prospect of judgment. Robinson remembers feeling a lot of anxiety upon sight of the outside students walking into the classroom for the first time, heightened when the class was reminded that a successful course would require that all students participate in dialogue.

Preliminary concerns proved short-lived, soon giving way to very different views of self- and group identity. Sustained conversations revealed that all members had something of value to offer the learning experience. To each, the program showed that through education and engagement with an element of civic mindedness, this type of learning transforms perceptions of self and prospects for social change.

Shortly after the course ended, Allred, Belche, and Robinson met to discuss developing a peer-education program on hepatitis. Over a series of about five working sessions, drawing on the final project of the course, they designed a one-hour seminar that included easy-to-understand information about the causes, symptoms, and treatments of hepatitis and specific ways incarcerated people are at risk for exposure to the virus. To date, Belche and Robinson have facilitated five sessions, each attended by about ten people incarcerated at their prison.

Relationships and Agency in Community-engaged Learning

Scholarship on engaged learning has increasingly shifted toward a concern with the salience of the learning context ("place-based") and the involvement and perspectives of the community. These models highlight the centrality of reciprocity, equity, or mutuality in some aspect of the college campus-community. At the core of this shift is an emerging consensus that relationships are "defining" and "central" to all aspects of service-learning[4] and that their nature shapes "the center of the experience" in fundamental ways.[5] When asked to assess partnerships with colleges, community constituents identify relationships as the most salient aspect of the student-community partner encounter. According to Sandy and Holland (2006), "The relationship itself is foundational...and...all collaborative activities or projects stem from this."[6]

Given the centrality of relationships articulated by community partners and lauded in the scholarship, one would anticipate a concomitant emphasis on empirical inquiry focused on the range or nature of relationships between campus *and* community partners, along with the variables that shape the degrees of mutuality or equity within them. However, there has been surprisingly little empirical inquiry into reciprocity or the effects of campus-community engagements on community participants. A number of studies lament this dearth of information about the experiences and perspectives of community participants.[7]

Although relationships in general have remained at the periphery of our activities and inquiry, there is an increasing appreciation for the multitude of constituents and potential relationships within the overall structural framework of service-learning endeavors. One of the most comprehensive models of these elements was developed by Bringle, Clayton, and Price (2009) called SOFAR, for *S*tudents, *O*rganizations in the Community, *F*aculty, *A*dministrators on the campus, and *R*esidents [or clients] in the community. Bringle et al.'s identification of these five key stakeholders suggests a minimum of ten dyadic relationships that may be assessed (see Clayton et al. [2010] for a discussion of the structural model of community constituents implicated by this definition). Within this nexus, a small subset of these dyadic community constituent relationships have been examined,[8] commonly documenting relationship of students to community organizations, or of students to community organization representatives (e.g., administrators) as a proxy for the residents in the community. In Hutchinson's 2011 study of an adult literacy program, for example, none of the adult learners who work with student tutors were asked directly about their experiences or perceptions. Rather, their perspective was gleaned from official and unofficial agency queries into adult learner progress in terms of language proficiency.

Our inquiry highlights the voices and perspectives of both college students and residents of the community with whom the students engaged on a weekly basis. Further, our personal experiences resonate with scholarship on the centrality of relationships: our own learning experiences seemed so intertwined with student relationships that they became a central part of it, as they have to others who described engagement pedagogy experiences elsewhere.[9]

Connections between Transformation, Closeness, and Efficacy in Service-learning

Given the consensus that relationships in service-learning are the portal through which all other aspects of service-learning flow, we report on two features of the learning experience that were suggested by inside alumni as critical and are described elsewhere as directly affected by relationships: transformative perspectives,[10] and self-efficacy.

A central claim of Inside-Out is its ability to "transform."[11] As Pompa writes, "People really *do* begin to see themselves as potential change agents—as being able to make a difference in the world. For many of the incarcerated students, it provides a radical change from seeing oneself (or being seen) as the problem—to seeing oneself as part of the *solution* to the problem."[12] Relevant scholarship, too, suggests that feelings of transformation and confidence contribute to a preparedness to "lean into the waves"[13] of life's opportunities and challenges.

By all accounts, "transformative learning is a tall order."[14] In an Inside-Out course, transformation emerges from closeness within a relational learning experience, where the focus shifts from potential individual change (e.g., dismantling stereotypes) to a collaboratively forged understanding of larger, more complex community issues (e.g., what are the implications of current inconsistencies between laws and the behavioral sciences as they pertain to crime, punishment, and mental illness?), constructed through respectful and sustained engagements.[15]

As described elsewhere in this volume, each course session involves a multifaceted structure that maximizes opportunities for dialogue among inside and outside students, described by Allred (2009) as a "smorgasbord of interactional templates." Through these opportunities for exchange, student expectations about the objective course outcomes become infused with meaningful relationships fostered through sustained dialogue. Herein lies the seed of transformative learning and deeper understandings of self, community, and others: they originate within "actual relations between people."[16] By contrast, in more transactional relationships, the relationship is perceived as mutually beneficial, but tends to be viewed as more focused on explicit, project-oriented goals, and imbued with a preservation of separate identities among community partners.

Many describe transformational experiences in conjunction with feelings of agency, confidence, or efficacy. In general, self-efficacy is endemic to particular social contexts[17] rather than a mere function of personality characteristics[18] or objective, individual aptitudes.[19] Social-cognitive theory frames self-efficacy as socially constructed and malleable, [20] involving a "triadic, reciprocal, causal relationship among individuals' social environments, behaviors, and cognitions."[21] Equally important, self-efficacy is an important indicator of self-perceived capabilities with implications for whether and how we pursue challenges and opportunities.[22]

More specifically, socially constructed but individually held "subjective convictions that one can successfully carry out given academic tasks at designated levels"[23] have both direct and indirect implications for academic achievement (Bassi, Steca, Fave, and Caprara, 2007; Gore, 2006).

Among college populations, academic self-efficacy has been examined extensively. Most often, assessment tools are lengthy (70–108 items) and focus on multiple domains of college life associated with success (e.g., the Student Readiness Inventory [SRI] [ACT], College Student Inventory [CSI], the College Success Factors Index, Learning and Study Strategies Inventory [LASSI], and Motivated Strategies for Learning Questionnaire [MSLQ]).[24] Here, we have more specific interests. We discuss students' belief in their ability to perform well in an Inside-Out

214 • Allred, Belche, and Robinson

course independent of course content. Specifically, how confident were students with regard to three skill sets: study habits, dialogue with class members, and writing assignments?

Study Hypotheses

Drawing from myriad sources (e.g., colleagues in Inside-Out, student alumni), this study describes students' attitudes about themselves and the course, and whether these change during the semester. Specifically, we compare student responses at two times (Time 1, which occurred during Week 3, and Time 2, which occurred during week 14). There are four main questions the quantitative data allow us to examine. By Time 2, will students experience greater closeness toward each other as learners? If so, why? If not, why not? Will students experience higher levels of academic self-efficacy by Time 2 compared with Time 1? Will outside students report higher levels of academic self-efficacy at Time 1? If so, why? If not, why not? Last, did students perceive the learning experience as relatively transactional at Time 1, and how did this compare with their assessments of the relationship by Time 2?

The Inside-Out pedagogy is implemented so that "everyone is equal—with an equal voice and an equal stake in the learning process."[25] Thus, we also examined the qualitative data for word choices that communicated perceptions of equity as a part of the unfolding relationship. Clayton et al. (2010) offer the distinction of "thin" versus "thick" reciprocity,[26] which we found to be a helpful construct in thinking about measurement possibilities.

Detailed information about the research setting, the host institutions, course protocols, and participant profiles are available in the full essay at www.insideout-center.org.

The Research Setting

Allred was the instructor for the upper level, elective sociology class called *Social Inequality* that is the data source for this project. It focused on the causes and consequences of inequality in the United States and the interface between social inequality, crime, and incarceration. Weekly discussion topics included: How do race, class, and gender fit into theories of crime, patterns of punishment, and social attainment? How is offending related to race, class, and gender? How is incarceration differentially experienced? What is the impact of incarceration on prospects for social mobility?

Classes were held in an all-male, medium security county prison with the capacity to house 448 people. The college is an independent, coeducational, comprehensive liberal arts college in the southeast. The student body includes about 1,930 undergraduates, with nearly 70 percent from the host state. The course initially enrolled 15 inside and 18 outside students. Aligning our research protocol with the Inside-Out philosophy on equitable, respectful, and beneficent relationships, this study opportunity and the mechanisms for opting in or out were responsive to issues of confidentiality and voluntary participation experienced in an Inside-Out course. Our procedures enabled students to take part or decline participation without either the instructor or other students knowing their participation status.

The intentional structuring that was part of this Inside-Out learning experience purposefully harnessed student interests with each other, the reading materials, and the compelling problems, policy options, and change activities that we write about. Through this inquiry, we highlight some outcomes and processes forged through the medium of such relationships.

Analytic Goals and Measures

We incorporate both quantitative and qualitative data in the study. The quantitative measures reveal at two time periods (Week 3 and Week 14), perceptions of closeness in the learning relationship, assessments of the learning encounter as a relatively transactional or transformational experience, and students' levels of academic self-efficacy.

Closeness as Learners

Closeness in learning relationships may be measured with an emphasis on several specific dimensions (e.g., variety of interaction engagements, occurrence of interactions, etc.) or more general aspects of closeness. For several reasons we adopted a measure developed by Mashek, Cannady, and Tangney (2007), which uses a set of two-circle Venn diagrams as a prompt (see figure 22.1). This tool offers a graphic representation of closeness with increasingly overlapping circles. Students were instructed to indicate which of the six Venn diagrams best represented their "thoughts about the current degree of closeness they feel in their relationship as learners with other students." Clayton et al. (2010) describe this evaluative tool as "a good summary of closeness that is short, nonverbal, and user-friendly."[27]

Transformational–transactional

In keeping with the goal of brevity in measurement tools, this study uses Clayton and Scott's (2008, presented and described in Clayton et al., 2010) single-item

CIRCLE THE LETTER (A-F) THAT BEST REPRESENTS HOW YOU SEE THE CURRENT DEGREE OF CLOSENESS IN THIS CLASS.

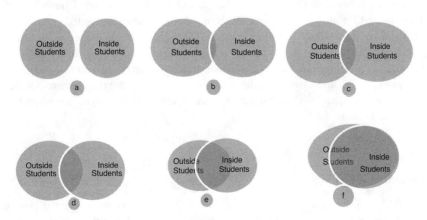

Figure 22.1   Venn diagram of perceived closeness in relationship as learners.

indicator of a transactional–transformational learning experience. Clayton et al. (2010) suggest that the measure used here is a "sufficient proxy"[28] for a more multidimensional phenomenon that they delineate through measurement of nine core aspects of relationships in engaged pedagogies. [29]

See Clayton et al., (2010) for a description of the single-item indicator for assessments of the transformational quality of the course experience and the definitions of the terms "transactional" and "transformational" used here. Each time the survey was administered in this study, students were asked to "think about the nature of the learning partnership" and to "circle the number" indicating their rating of the class experience at that time, where "1" is *completely* trans*actional*, "5" means *somewhat* trans*actional/somewhat* trans*formational*, and "10" is *completely* trans*formational*."

Academic Self-efficacy

For the psychometric of academic self-efficacy, this project uses a strategy best described as a "bottom-up approach."[30] Based on earlier participant-led conversations about the general areas of academic competency that are associated with academic success in an Inside-Out course, we identified three key skill sets: study habits adequate for the volume and level of readings commensurate with a college course, participation in structured and spontaneous opportunities for dialogue with course members, and writing assignments. These skill sets are measured through a listing of ten items that measure three academic competencies (study habits, dialogue with course members, and writing) relevant to an Inside-Out course: studying, asking questions in class, keeping up with the required readings, writing papers, getting papers done on time, managing class preparation, getting the grades I want, talking with the teacher, participating in class discussions, finding time to study. Students rated each item on a 5-point scale, where "1" was "not at all confident" and "5" completely confident for how they felt about the particular academic ability or skill during Week 3 and Week 14 of our class.

Ethical Considerations

This study adheres to the *Guidelines for Ethical Inquiry* (Research Committee of The Inside-Out Prison Exchange Program, 2010). We implemented procedures identical to those described elsewhere.[31] They benefit from deliberations across many contexts (e.g., Research Committee meetings, work sessions in the prison), integrate some important college and community constituent recommendations and perspectives, and involve mechanisms for opting in or out that were responsive to issues of confidentiality and voluntary participation uniquely experienced within an Inside-Out course.

Results

Quantitative Findings

We used one-sided *t*-tests to determine whether the comparisons suggested by our hypotheses were due to chance or statistically significant. We applied an alpha level of .05 for all *t*-tests (see table 22.1).

Table 22.1 Academic self-efficacy mean scores: Global and task specific (B, C, and D)

A) *Global academic self-efficacy mean scores*
   (10 items listed in Appendix A, scores ranging from 10–50, where 50 is high self-efficacy)

	Time 1 (n: SD)*	Time 2 (n: SD)
Student Group		
Inside (I)	a) 35.07 (15: 9.60)	d) 41.91 (11:7.22)
Outside (O)	b) 40.73 (15: 3.65)	e) 43.67 (18: 3.82)
Combined (I & O)	c) 37.90 (30: 7.69)	f) 43.00 (29: 5.31)

** H #1: a vs. d, $t = -2.07$, $p < .05$, b vs. e, $t = -2.56$, $p < .05$, c vs. f, $t = -2.97$, $p < .05$
   H #2: a vs. b, $t = -2.13$ $p < .05$, d vs. e, NS

B) *Academic reading and comprehension self-efficacy mean scores*
   (3 items # 1, #3 , and #10, scores ranging from 3–15, where 15 is high self-efficacy)

	Time 1 (n: SD)*	Time 2 (n: SD)
Student Group		
Inside (I)	a) 11.27 (15: 2.99)	d) 12.45 (11: 2.60)
Outside (O)	b) 11.80 (15: 2.01)	e) 11.90 (18: 1.63)
Combined (I & O)	c) 11.53 (30: 2.52)	f) 12.14 (29: 2.01)

** H #1: a vs. d, NS, b vs. e, NS c vs. f, NS
   H #2: a vs. b, NS, d vs. e, NS

C) *Academic dialogue self-efficacy mean scores*
   (3 items # 2, # 8, and #9, scores ranging from 3–15, where 15 is high self-efficacy)

	Time 1 (n: SD)*	Time 2 (n: SD)
Student Group		
Inside (I)	a) 11.20 (15: 2.51)	d) 13.10 (11: 1.64)
Outside (O)	b) 11.87 (15: 2.17)	e) 13.61 (18: 1.38)
Combined (I & O)	c) 11.53 (30: 2.33)	f) 13.41 (29: 1.48)

** H #1: a vs. d, $t = -2.33$, $p < .05$, b vs. e, $t = -2.69$, $p < .01$ c vs. f, $t = -3.32$, $p < .01$
   H #2: a vs. b, NS, d vs. e, NS

D) *Academic writing self-efficacy mean scores*
   (2 items # 4, #5, scores ranging from 2–10, where 10 is high self-efficacy)

	Time 1 (n: SD)*	Time 2 (n: SD)
Student Group		
Inside (I)	a) 7.13 (15: 2.61)	d) 8.22 (11: 1.64)
Outside (O)	b) 8.87 (15: .83)	e) 9.11 (18: .90)
Combined (I & O)	c) 8.00 (30: 2.10)	f) 8.79 (29: 1.45)

** H #1: a vs. d, NS, b vs. e, NS, c vs. f, NS
   H #2: a vs. b, $t = -2.46$ $p < .05$, d vs. e, NS
* n = number, SD = standard deviation ** Indicates Hypothesis #1 or Hypothesis #2

Academic Self-efficacy
Our first hypothesis was supported: students experienced an increase in their over-all sense of academic self-efficacy. All students and ten items combined, the aver-age self-efficacy score was a 37.90 at Time 1, versus a 43.00 at Time 2, with the difference being statistically significant. As expected, the starting points for inside and outside students were significantly different, even though each subgroup expe-rienced significant increases by Time 2. At Time 1, inside students had a lower average academic self-efficacy rating compared with outside students, and this dif-ference was also statistically significant ($t = -2.13$, $p < .05$).

Within our global measure of academic self-efficacy, recall that we asked about three general academic competencies relevant to this learning context: study habits, dialogue with course members, and writing. Statistically significant findings con-cern transitions in the aspects pertaining to dialogue (enhancements reported by all students) and to writing competencies (expressed at Time 1 by inside students only). Specifically, whether combined or considered separately (inside compared with outside), students experienced statistically significant increases in their sense of confidence concerning class dialogue (i.e., asking questions in class, talking with the teacher, and participating in class discussion).

Nature of the Learning Partnership: Transactional or Transformational
Although initial assessments of a transformational environment seemed high, this may be because Time 1 data were collected *after* the first combined (and often exhilarating) meeting. Regardless, all students expressed a large increase in their assessment of the learning partnership. The responses indicate that the perception of the learning experience went from somewhat transformational to very transfor-mational (see table 22.2).

Degree of Closeness as Learners
Students were provided with a graphic representation of perceived closeness with others as learners through the use of Venn Diagrams with five pairs of increasingly overlapping circles. The pattern revealed an increased sense of closeness that was statistically significant when responses were combined, as well as when assessed separately for inside and outside students. Time 1 means did not differ significantly between inside and outside students. However, at Time 2, outside students had a

Table 22.2   Nature of the learning partnership mean scores

	*Time 1 (n: SD)**	*Time 2 (n: SD)*
Student Group		
Inside (I)	a) 6.00 (15: 1.60)	d) 7.91 (11: 1.87)
Outside (O)	b) 7.07 (15: 1.49)	e) 9.22 (18: 1.12)
Combined (I & O)	c) 6.53 (30: 1.61)	f) 8.72 (29: 1.59)

scores range from 1 (transactional to 10 (transformational)
* H #1: a vs. d, $t = -2.73$, $p < .05$, b vs. e, $t = -4.48$, $p < .01$, c vs. f, $t = -5.27$, $p < .01$
H #2: a vs. b, NS, d vs. e, $t = -1.31$ $p < .05$

Table 22.3 Degree of closeness felt in the relationship as learners with other students (Venn diagram)

	Time 1 (n: SD)*	Time 2 (n: SD)
Student Group		
Inside (I)	a) 3.90 (15:1.53)	d) 4.82 (11: 1.17)
Outside (O)	b) 3.80 (15: 1.27)	e) 5.78 (18: .43)
Combined (I & O)	c) 3.87 (30: 1.38)	f) 5.41 (29: .90)

scores range from 1 (not close at all) to 6 (very close)
* H #1: a vs. d, t = -1.73, p < .05, b vs. e, t = -5.77, p < .01, c vs. f, t = -5.08, p < .01
H #2: a vs. b, NS, d vs. e, t = -.96, p < .05

higher average rating of closeness compared with inside students and the difference was statistically significant (see table 22.3).

The next section offers a presentation and discussion of the themes that were identified in prose responses to the question about closeness in the learning relationship. We offer direct quotes from student participants to emphasize coherence of thematic categories.

Qualitative Themes Concerning Closeness as Learners

Students were invited to provide comments explaining their choice of Venn diagram to represent the degree of closeness they perceived and the average number of words per comment. At both Time 1 and Time 2, fewer inside students offered comments compared with outside students (see tables 22.4 and 22.5).

Increasing consensus exists that the relationships in service-learning facilitate the most meaningful and educative processes and outcomes. Important aspects of such relationships include: "mutually beneficial agenda, understanding the capacity and resources of all partners, participating in project planning, attending to the relationship, shared design and control of project directions, and continual assessment of partnership processes and outcomes."[32] But when learning partners approach engagement experiences with fundamentally different background assumptions, to what extent might this be reflected in their descriptions of early and later encounters with each other? Sandy and Holland (2006) remind us that constituents in the learning relationship often approach the experience with diverse assumptions, concerns, or perceptions. More successful engagements recognize these possibilities, and openly forge ongoing "negotiations to ensure these different needs"[33] are acknowledged. Learners describe the early nature of their relation as transactional, "with distinct objectives," yet when understandings and goals shift to "shared interest," the connections become transformational.

Within this Inside-Out course, such paradigm shifts were first apparent in ways that reflected the notion of a relationship among the entire group as a real or concrete thing. Students were invited to use labels or phrases in their open-ended rating of the closeness in the learning relationship. At Time 1, 15 percent of the students identified the relationship with a positive group label (e.g. friend, group of learners). Only outside

Table 22.4 Inside and Outside students with comments offered to describe rating of closeness as learners. (# with no comments/# of those who participated)

	T1	T2 (% with no comments)
Inside	35.7% (5/14)	57% (8/14)
Outside	26.7% (4/15)	20% (3/15)

Table 22.5 Word counts: Average number of words per comment

	T1	T2
Inside	21.8 (196/9)	21.2 (127/6)
Outside	37.2 (335/9)	21.5 (258/12)

students offered a label to describe their rating of closeness as learners. By Time 2, 44 percent of all students combined name the experience with a positive group label (unity, family, one, friends rather than acquaintances, friends). At this point, a similar fraction of inside (50%) and outside (42%) students named the relationship.

Two other themes emerged: perceived equity and a sense of connection. At Time 1, 25 percent of the students (9% of outside students, 44% of inside students) expressed that perceptions of equity, fairness, or impartiality informed their sense of themselves as colearners. Inside student comments about the salience of perceived equity were consistent (e.g., "I feel like both Inside and Outside students are learning the same material and information together," "both Inside and Outside students are equally focused and participating in class").

By Time 2, 44 percent of all students who offered comments mentioned equity as one of the reasons for their ranking of closeness, saying "we came together as partners in learning," "we all learned so much from each other," and "we have blended into one group of learners." This pattern resonates with the authors' experiences as students also as Belche and Robinson both initially wondered whether they were "real" students in the class and later recognized that both subgroups of students (inside and outside) were genuine course members.

Last, at Time 1, 60 percent of the students expressed a sense of emerging connection to each other as learners. Among inside students, nearly 55 percent indicated the sense that people were "getting closer" or "feeling a bond already" as learners. Among outside students, about 64 percent shared similar sentiments. By Time 2, this pattern remained constant. That is, an overwhelming majority (72%) of all students indicated strong connections to others as learners. Half of the inside students expressed this opinion and about three-fourths of outside students did, as well.

Discussion

Several of these findings are noteworthy. The act of naming the nature of closeness may be viewed as representing perceptions of an authentic bond or connection between the students as learners. While the frequency of phrases that "name" the encounter may also reflect other factors (e.g., gender differences in expressions), the qualitative data suggest some important transitions in the learning toward deeper connections among students.

Recall that at Time 1, none of the inside students used a label or noun to describe the closeness of the relationship, despite the observation that their objective ranking was no different from the average for outside students. This divergence in reification at Time 1 may be connected to the differences in the group's attunement to issues of equity or attitudes toward relationships in general. At Time 1, inside and outside students enter the learning context with different background assumptions about the nature of the learning. On the one hand, some inside students enter the class with a mix of negative concerns that await affirmation: will inside students be guinea pigs in some study designed to benefit the educational experience of outside students? Outside students likely begin the course with impartiality, equity, or similarity of experience as a background assumption, perhaps because it is not a feature of their learning experiences that has been disrupted or they do not occupy a stigmatized role early in this course.

Early differences in perceived equity likely emerge from the experience of incarceration. Belche and Robinson suspect that relationships and bonds between men in prison tend to emerge relatively slowly. Further, the context of prison may render individuals more restrained in their willingness to trust the authenticity of an encounter, in part due to the limited access to information that may corroborate its realism.

Conclusion

The findings shared here are best interpreted in the context of study limitations. First, this study examines a particular pedagogic model, and a particular dyad of colearners (incarcerated and campus-enrolled students). Second, we relied on measures developed by others for two key constructs of interest: academic self-efficacy and closeness in the learning relationship. Given the participants in the vetting process, we have confidence in their face validity for this project. However, future inquiry may consider applying more traditional reliability and validity assessments, and involving a broader group of community constituents in their consideration. Third, this study's sample size was small, working with one class in one site.

That said, the findings would suggest the value of extending such research. Overall, we found that Inside-Out students have a transformative, educative experience during this type of engaged learning. The outcome is part-and-parcel to the context (prison) and the ways in which people are guided on a weekly basis to interact as colearners through dialogue and reflection. Taken together, the course elements enhanced a subset of academic self-efficacy, namely confidence in participating in sustained dialogic interaction. Students developed close bonds as learners, and viewed these bonds as an essential thread in the deeply engaging fabric of their learning endeavor.

Notes

1. Marie Sandy and Barbara A. Holland, "Different Worlds and Common Ground: Community Partner Perspectives on Campus-community Partnerships," *Michigan Journal of Community Service Learning* 13, no. 1 (Fall 2006): 33.

2. Ibid.

3. Sarah Allred, Lana D. Harrison, and Daniel O'Connell, "Self-Efficacy: An Important Part of Prison-based Learning," *Prison Journal* (2013), doi: 10.1177/0032885512472964.

4. Patti H. Clayton, Robert G. Bringle, Bryanne Senor, Jenny Huq, and Mary Morrison. "Differentiating and Assessing Relationships in Service-learning and Civic Engagement: Exploitative, Transactional, or Transformational," *Michigan Journal of Community Service Learning* (Spring 2010): 5.

5. Jamie Beran and Aleeza Lubin, "Shifting Service-learning from Transactional to Relational," *Journal of Jewish Communal Service* 87 (2012): 88.

6. Sandy and Holland, "Different Worlds and Common Ground," 34.

7. See studies by Ellen Skilton-Sylvester and K. Erwin, "Creating Reciprocal learning Relationships across Socially Constructed Boarders," *Michigan Journal of Community Service Learning* (Fall 2000): 73; Laurie Worrall, "Asking the Community: A Case Study of Community Partner Perspectives," *Michigan Journal of Community Service Learning* (Fall 2007): 5; Robert G. Bringle, Patti H. Clayton, and Mary F. Price, "Partnerships in Service-learning and Civic Engagement," *Partnerships: A Journal of Service-learning and Civic Engagement* 1, no. 1 (Summer 2009): 1–20; Clayton et al., "Differentiating and Assessing Relationships," 5.

8. Bringle et al., "Partnerships in Service-learning and Civic Engagement," 1–20.

9. Sylvia Ashton-Warner, *Teacher* (New York: Touchstone, Simon, and Schuster, 1963).

10. Ellen Skilton-Sylvester and K. Erwin, "Creating Reciprocal Learning Relationships across Socially Constructed Boarders," *Michigan Journal of Community Service Learning* (Fall 2000): 72.

11. L. Pompa, "One Brick at a Time: The Power and Possibility of Dialogue across the Prison Wall," *The Prison Journal*, 2013.

12. Ibid.

13. Skilton-Sylvester and Erwin, "Creating Reciprocal Learning Relationships," 69.

14. Beran and Lubin, "Shifting Service Learning," 88.

15. Ibid., 89.

16. Skilton-Sylvester and Erwin, "Creating Reciprocal Learning Relationships," 65; L. S. Vygotsky *Mind in Society: The Development of Higher Psychological Processes* (Harvard University Press, 1978), 57.

17. C. L. Staples, M. L. Schwalbe, and V. Gecas, "Social Class, Occupational Conditions, and Efficacy-based Self-esteem," *Sociological Perspectives* 27, no. 1 (1984): 85–109.

18. J. W. Jackson, "Enhancing Self-efficacy and Learning Performance," *The Journal of Experimental Education* 70, no. 3 (2002): 243–254.

19. V. Gecas, and M. A. Seff, "Social Class, Occupational Conditions, and Self-esteem," *Sociological Perspectives* 32, no. 3 (1989): 353–364. J. T. Mortimer, and J. Lorence, "Occupational Experience and the Self-concept: A Longitudinal Study," *Social Psychology Quarterly* 42 (1979): 307–332. Staples, et al., "Social Class."

20. Staples et al., "Social Class."

21. Allred et al., "Self-Efficacy"; Bandura. *Social Foundations of Thought and Action: A Social-cognitive View* (Englewoods Cliffs, NJ: Prentice Hall, 1986).

22 Staples et al., "Social Class," 90.

23. Bong, Mimi. "Academic Motivation in Self-efficacy, Task Value, Achievement Goal Orientations, and Attributional Beliefs," *The Journal of Educational Research* 97, no. 6 (2004): 288.

24. Carol L. Barry and Sara J. Finney. "A Psychometric Investigation of the college Self-Efficacy Inventory." *Measurement and Evaluation in Counseling and Development* 42, no. 3 (October 2009): 197–222, doi: 10.1177/0748175609344095.

25. Pompa, "One Brick at a Time. "
26. Clayton et al., "Differentiating and Assessing Relationships," 18.
27. Ibid., 15.
28. Ibid.
29. These nine dimensions include the following: outcomes of the service-learning partnership, the extent to which constituents have common goals in service-learning collaboration, the degree to which constituents collaborated on decisions, the balance of constituent contributions of resources, the extent to which conflicts emerged in the service-learning relationship, the role of the partnership in work and identify formation, the balance of power in the relationship, the extent to which constituents perceive significant outcomes, perceptions of change and benefit from the perspective of all constituents.
30. Barry and Finney, "A Psychometric Investigation."
31. Allred et al., "Self-Efficacy."
32. Sandy and Holland, "Different Worlds and Common Ground," 34.
33. Ibid.

References

Allred, Sarah L. "The Inside-Out Prison Exchange Program: The Impact of Structure, Content, and Readings." *Journal of Correctional Education* 60 no. 3 (September 2009): 2.

Allred, Sarah, Lana D. Harrison, and Daniel O'Connell. "Self-Efficacy: An Important Part of Prison-Based Learning." *The Prison Journal* 93 (June 2013): 211–233Andrews, Mark. "Who is being heard? Response-bias in open-ended responses in a large government employee survey." (Paper presentation at AAPOR. The ASA section on Research Methods A, 2005), http://www.amstat.org/sections/srms/proceedings/y2005/Files/JSM2005–000924.pdf.

Ashton-Warner, Sylvia. *Teacher.* New York: Touchstone, Simon, and Schuster, 1963.

Bandura, Albert.. *Social Foundations of Thought and Action: A Social-cognitive View.* Englewoods Cliffs, NJ: Prentice Hall, 1986.

Barry, Carol L. and Sara J. Finney. "A Psychometric Investigation of the College Self-efficacy Inventory." *Measurement and Evaluation in Counseling and Development* 42, no. 3 (October 2009): 197–222, doi: 10.1177/0748175609344095.

Basi, Marta, Patrizia Steca, Antonella Delle Fave, and Gian Vittorio Caprara. "Academic Self-efficacy Beliefs and Quality of Experience in Learning." *Journal of Youth and Adolescence* 36, no. 3, (2007). 301–312.

Behrman, Carolyn. "Food for Thought: Coalition Process and a Community-based Research and Service-learning Project." *Annals of Anthropological Practice* 35 (2011): 79–95.

Beran, Jamie and Aleeza Lubin. "Shifting Service-learning from Transactional to Relational." *Journal of Jewish Communal Service* 87, no. 1/2 (2012): 88–92.

Bong, Mimi. "Academic Motivation in Self-efficacy, Task Value, Achievement Goal Orientations, and Attributional Beliefs." *The Journal of Educational Research* 97 no. 6 (2004): 287–297.

Borden, Amanda Welch. "The Impact of Service-learning on Ethnocentrism in an Intercultural Communication Course." *Journal of Experiential Education* 30, no. 2 (2007): 171–183.

Bringle, Robert G., Patti H. Clayton, and Mary F. Price. "Partnerships in Service-learning and Civic Engagement." *Partnerships: A Journal of Service-Learning and Civic Engagement* 1, no. 1 (Summer 2009): 1–20.

Brown, Phil. "Popular Epidemiology and Toxic Waste Contamination: Lay and Professional Ways of Knowing." *Journal of Health and Social Behavior* 33 (1992): 267–281.

Brown. Phil."Who is the Community? What is the Community?" http://www.brown.edu/research/research-ethics/sites/brown.edu.research.research-ethics/files/uploads/Who%20is%20the%20community%20-%20Phil%20Brown_0.pdf. (2004). Accessed March 3, 2013.

Celio, Christine I., Joseph Durlak, and Allison Dymnicki. "A Meta-analysis of the Impact of Service-learning on Students." *Journal of Experiential Education* 34, no. 2 (2011): 164–181.

Clayton, Patti H., Robert G. Bringle, Bryanne Senor, Jenny Huq, and Mary Morrison. "Differentiating and Assessing Relationships in Service-learning and Civic Engagement: Exploitative, Transactional, or Transformational." *Michigan Journal of Community Service Learning* 16, no. 2 (Spring 2010): 5–22.

Conti, Norm, Linda Morrison, and Katherine Pantaleo. "All the Wiser: Dialogic, Space, Destigmatization, and Teacher-activist Recruitment." *The Prison Journal* 93 (June 2013): 163–188.

Cruz, Nadinne, and Dwight E. Giles, Jr. "Where's the Community in Service-learning Research?" *Michigan Journal of Service Learning* 7, no. 1 (2000): 28–34.

Ferla, Johan, Martin Valcke, and Yonghong Cai. "Academic Self-efficacy and Academic Self-concept: Reconsidering Structural Relationships." *Learning and Individual Differences* 19 (2009): 499–505.

Gecas, Viktor and Seff, MonicaA. "Social Class, Occupational Conditions, and Self-esteem." *Sociological Perspectives* 32, no. 3 (1989): 353–364.

Gore, Jr. Paul A. "Academic Self-efficacy as a Predictor of College Outcomes: Two Incremental Validity Studies." *Journal of Career Assessment* 14, no. 1 (2006): 92–115.

Hutchinson, Mary. "Measuring Engagement Impact on Communities: Challenges and Opportunities." *Journal of Higher Education Outreach and Engagement* 15, no. 3 (2011): 31–44.

Jackson, Jay W. "Enhancing Self-efficacy and Learning Performance," *The Journal of Experimental Education* 70, no. 3 (2002): 243–254.

Mabry, J. Beth. "Pedagogical Variations in Service-learning and Student Outcomes: How Time, Contact, and Reflection Matter." *Michigan Journal of Community Service-Learning* 5, no. 1 (Fall 1998): 32–47.

Mashek, Debra, Lisa W. Cannady, and JuneP. Tangney. "Inclusion of Community Self-scale: A Single Item Pictorial Measure of Community Connectedness." *Journal of Community Psychology* 35, no. 2 (2007): 257–275.

Mortimer, Jeylan T. and Lorence,Jon "Occupational Experience and the Self-concept: A Longitudinal Study." *Social Psychology Quarterly* 42 no. 4 (1979): 307–332.

Niehaus, Kate, Kathleen Moritz Rudasill, and Jill L. Adelson. "Self-Efficacy, Intrinsic Motivation, and Academic Outcomes among Latino Middle School Students Participating in an After-school Program." *Hispanic Journal of Behavioral Sciences* 34, no. 1 (2012): 118–136.

Nelson, Lynn Hankinson. *Who Knows: From Quine to a Feminist Empiricism* Philadelphia: Temple University Press, 1990.

Pettijohn II, Terry F. and Ginny M. Naples. "Reducing Ethnocentrism in U.S. College Students by Completing a Cross-cultural Psychology Course." *The Open Social Science Journal* 2 (2009): 1–6.

Pompa, Lori. "One Brick at a Time: The Power and Possibility of Dialogue across the Prison Wall." *The Prison Journal* 93 (June 2013): 127–134.

———. "Service-learning as a Crucible." *Michigan Journal of Community Service* 9, no. 1 (2002): 67–76.

Pompa, Lori and Melissa Crabbe. *The Inside-Out Prison Exchange Program: Exploring Issues of Crime and Justice Behind the Walls, Instructor's Manual (Revised Edition)*. Philadelphia: Temple University, 2004.

Sandy, Marie and Barbara A. Holland. "Different Worlds and Common Ground: Community Partner Perspectives on Campus-community Partnerships." *Michigan Journal of Community Service Learning* 13, no. 1 (Fall 2006): 30–43.

Simons, Lori and Beverly Cleary. "Student and Community Perceptions of the 'Value-added' for Service-learners." *Journal of Experiential Education* 28, no. 1 (2005): 164–188.

Skilton-Sylvester, Ellen and Eileen K. Erwin. "Creating Reciprocal Learning Relationships across Socially Constructed Boarders." *Michigan Journal of Community Service Learning* 7 (Fall 2000): 65–75.

Staples, Clifford L., Michael L. Schwalbe, and Viktor Gecas. "Social Class, Occupational Conditions, and Efficacy-based Self-esteem." *Sociological Perspectives* 27, no. 1 (1984): 85–109.

Stevens, Tara, Arturo Olivarez Jr., William Y. Lan, and Mary K. Tallent-Runnels. "Role of Mathematics Self-efficacy and Motivation in Mathematics Performance across Ethnicity." *Journal of Educational Research* 97 no. 4 (2004): 208–221.

Vygotsky, Lev S. *Mind in Society: The Development of Higher Psychological Processes*. Boston: Harvard University Press, 1978, 57.

Worrall, Laurie. "Asking the Community: A Case Study of Community Partner Perspectives." *Michigan Journal of Community Service Learning* 14, no. 1 (Fall 2007): 5–17.

CHAPTER 23

Evaluating the Impact of Community-based Learning: Participatory Action Research as a Model for Inside-Out

Angela Bryant and Yasser Payne

Introduction

The last two decades have seen significant growth in US university initiatives to promote civic engagement for undergraduates through service or community-based learning (CBL) experiences,[1] with 60 percent of graduates engaging in at least one course during their academic career (The National Task Force on Civic Learning and Democratic Engagement, 2012). Some describe the current era as representing the fourth wave of a reemphasis on civic engagement in higher education (National Service-learning Clearinghouse, January 2008). A recent report from The National Task Force on Civic Learning and Democratic Engagement designates this era as a "crucible moment," given that the research clearly demonstrates that "students who participate in civic learning opportunities are more likely to: persist in college and complete their degrees; obtain skills prized by employers; and develop habits of social responsibility and civic participation" (2012, v). Bridging theory or textbook material learned in the classroom with the reality of these ideas in practice better prepares undergraduates for the work force and can engage college students in the life of their communities. It is no surprise that there is a concurrent call for universities to continue measuring the impact of such programs on students, community partners, and the university as a whole, and to continue developing innovative methods to evaluate these initiatives.

Studies of CBL primarily test John Dewey's (1938) concept of transformation through experience and David A. Kolb's (1984) stages of experiential learning as the source of quality learning and development. Empirical research has traditionally been gathered by survey questionnaires or assessments of self-reflection and has focused on the impact of CBL on student perceptual shifts and civic engagement. In general, comparative studies demonstrate significant improvement for students involved in CBL courses in areas of course satisfaction, political awareness, social justice attitudes, problem-solving skills, community involvement, empowerment, diversity awareness, leadership, moral development, rejection of individualistic expectations of social problems, and a reduction of ethnocentrist views (Borden, 2007; Hollis, 2002; Lewis, 2004; Markus et al., 1993; Marullo, 1998; Mayhew and Fernandez, 2007; Mobley, 2007; Simons and Cleary, 2005). There is also evidence of an increase in motivation for current or future volunteering (Einfeld and Collins, 2008), shifts in perceptions of race and inequality (Borden, 2007; Hale, 2008; Marullo, 1998; Mayhew and Fernandez, 2007; Mobley, 2007), a deeper under-standing of cultural and social diversity (Einfeld and Collins, 2008; Hughes, Boyd, and Dykstra, 2010) as well as collective responsibility for social problems (Reed et al., 2005; Singer et al., 2002), and an increased ability to apply course material and theory to real-life situations (Blieszner and Artale, 2001; Redhawk-Love, 2008) (for a larger review of the CBL research see Finley, 2012).

In this chapter, we focus on the limitations of existing CBL research and pro-vide a theoretical framework for participatory action research (PAR) as a model for evaluating the impact of CBL. We believe that the most significant limitation of existing CBL research is that it fails to fully incorporate the perspectives of partici-pants outside the university. At the same time, there are historical and persisting concerns regarding research with the "vulnerable" and/or marginalized populations that are generally the focus of CBL courses. We utilize a case study of Inside-Out to provide a blueprint for implementing PAR as a framework for both addressing these ethical concerns and ensuring that the perspectives of *all* CBL participants, and in particular members of marginalized populations, are incorporated into any research conducted.

Limitations of CBL Research

One main limitation of existing research on the impact of CBL is the representa-tiveness of the samples. Most research assesses the impact of CBL on college stu-dent participants over the course of a semester and rarely incorporates assessments from the perspective of the community partner and/or the community participants that the partner organization serves. Other concerns include: inherent bias in self-report surveys, student selection bias (e.g., research shows that students who enroll in CBL are qualitatively different from those who do not, see Vogelgesang and Astin, 2000), lack of generalizability of qualitative studies of reflection papers, and objectivity bias from the faculty standpoint. Most studies utilize either qualitative or quantitative measures, but not both, and do not reveal whether the benefits of CBL differ for short-term versus longer-term experiences. The combination of qualitative and quantitative measures and a comparative sample of students not enrolled in CBL courses may overcome many of these weaknesses currently found in the literature (Simons and Cleary, 2005), yet there is still scant research showing whether and how CBL courses promote students' participation in social change (Mobley, 2007). Published evaluation and research into whether and how student transformation occurs in Inside-Out courses have been similarly limited (but do see Allred, 2009).

Theoretical Framework for Assessing the Impact of Inside-Out: PAR

Inside-Out courses support CBL objectives by providing campus-based students with exposure to the context of prison while convening critical discussions between those outside and inside prison walls. In this weekly dialogue, all voices are equal (including the instructor's), and, especially in Inside-Out courses with a criminal justice theme, participants are encouraged to confront stereotypes and assumptions held about crime, "offenders," and justice. Weekly exposure to the context of prison life, the creation of a safe space to explore critical sociological issues and problems in society, and the individual and group activities, assignments, and projects allow participants to move beyond the class and see themselves as agents of social change (see present volume, chapter 2, for a thorough discussion).

Similar to previous research on the impact of higher education on prisoners (Torre and Fine, 2005), Inside-Out instructors describe perceptual shifts among student participants from seeing themselves as passive objects to seeing themselves as active subjects. They develop a sense of critical, personal agency, and an active, collective responsibility. However, empirically measuring the impact of Inside-Out courses poses significant challenges. During recruitment for the course, we specifically tell inside students that we are not there to study them or presume any differences in expertise. We are simply there to hold a college class, study issues together, and learn from one another in a context in which all voices are equal, including that of the instructor. This information is important to convey, given the history of abuse of prisoners in the name of research. Hence, conducting research specific to measuring the effects of Inside-Out courses challenges instructors' efforts at establishing and building trust with the inside students.

As a methodological framework, PAR extends this pedagogy by organizing Inside-Out students to conduct empirical research. Inside-Out courses culminate with an empirically grounded group project conceived and designed by the class participants. Often, these projects are based on some element(s) of the criminal justice system that the students believe can and should be changed, and the final product is formally presented to representatives of the prison, university, and community at the public closing ceremony. Utilizing a PAR framework for group projects alleviates the legitimate concern about a long and pernicious history of research "on" people in prison. Instead, as an extension of the final projects that are already a hallmark of the Inside-Out curriculum, such projects would enable Inside-Out students, as well as academic, civic, and political leadership more generally, to better understand the needs, concerns, and overall perspectives of individuals remanded to correctional facilities. PAR experiences can benefit all participants involved, providing both inside and outside students the skills and products that support future employment and educational opportunities.

In the PAR model, representatives of the population being studied are part of the research team. The inclusion of members of the population under study as researchers results in fairer and more effective analysis of the data and helps to address some of the legitimate fear and distrust identified as a barrier to doing research about (rather than *with*) "vulnerable" communities (Brown, 2010; Brydon-Miller and Maguire, 2009; Payne, 2006a; Payne and Brown, 2010). PAR members are expected to be involved in every phase of the research project, including shaping and developing the: (1) research question/hypothesis; (2) theoretical framework; (3) methodological design; (4) data collection and analysis; (5) formal publications; (6) formal presentations; and (7) sociopolitical organizing in response to data outcomes. Ideally, all PAR members are fairly or equitably compensated for all time committed to the project, and partner organizations (e.g., academic, political, nonprofit, correctional) provide institutional support, helping to generate commitment on the part of all stakeholders involved with the project.

A primary tenet of PAR is that it seeks to empower those who are often studied from a deficit or pathological framework in the field of criminology (Dupont, 2008). PAR as a method has been increasingly used by educational and public health scholars, who conclude that:

> PAR has become much more widely accepted as an effective teaching, learning, and research practice...that offers principles and frameworks to enable teacher and/or school-based practitioner inquiry to become more participatory, collaborative, and democratizing in ways that meaningfully engage students, families, and other educators in the full range of the action research cycle, from problem identification to making project results and implications public. (Brydon-Miller and Maguire, 2009, 82–83)

There are several key concerns to be addressed when integrating PAR with Inside-Out. It is necessary to assure ensure prison officials that Inside-Out is not a "whistle-blowing" program or an avenue to conduct unauthorized research. As the Inside-Out program (http://www.insideoutcenter.org/clarification.html) explicitly states:

> Inside-Out is not an opportunity for anyone to gain access to prison populations as a pretext for doing research unrelated to Inside-Out. People on the inside have a realistic concern about being treated as "guinea pigs" (a phrase often used by those inside) for research that, too often, is exploitative, harmful, and invalid.

Such perceptions could have a chilling effect, undercutting efforts to provide Inside-Out college courses in prisons across the network. We believe that, when implemented thoughtfully, however, PAR provides a robust avenue for conducting innovative research than can produce necessary change without jeopardizing the integrity of the Inside-Out program or other CBL programs. The key for PAR to realize its potential in CBL work is in the process of developing courses. Faculty must participate in open discussions of such initiatives with community partners (for Inside-Out, prisons) and university officials. This engagement is similar to the preparatory work necessary for offering Inside-Out courses, where the instructor must develop trust and rapport with the organization (prison) officials and with participants. Thus, we suggest that seasoned instructors are best suited for piloting PAR initiatives in their courses. While there are of course official processes that must be accomplished for PAR projects (such as Institutional Review Board IRB processes for both the university and prison site), many more informal conversations should take place with all involved to ensure as much transparency as possible. In our collective experiences, PAR projects can produce many positive results for all involved, but require time and resources at all stages of development and implementation.

Furthermore, we advocate and recommend the specific use of Street PAR as the *particular* PAR methodology to be used by Inside-Out courses and/or correctional facilities, since people of color, including indigenous people, are highly overrepresented in North American prisons. Street PAR is a methodological framework or a phenomenological research orientation that requires a deep appreciation and full respect for men and women of color who hold a street identity. Street PAR calls for a comprehensive analysis of the lived experiences of street-identified Black, Brown, and Red people by way of understanding their identity through an agency-structure theoretical, methodological, and empirical lens.

Street PAR

Sites of resilience (SOR) theory guides street PAR by arguing that a critical mass of Black and Brown people, as a function of *structural violence*—particularly in the forms of blocked economic, educational, and political opportunity—have turned to *the streets* as a way to locate resilience (Payne, 2011; see also chapters 4, 7, and 17 in this volume for individual reflections on this trajectory). Street PAR explicitly organizes Black and Brown persons who are active in the streets, who embrace or have embraced street life and/or crime as a central or core identity, and/or who have at some point been involved with the criminal justice system to empirically document the lived experiences of street-life-oriented people in local street communities, schools and/or correctional facilities (Payne, 2006a, 2008, forthcoming; Payne and Brown, 2010). The assumption is that individuals who are actively or formerly involved with the streets are best poised to critically examine the intimate and structural experiences of a population that have usually been ignored or dismissed, even in the racial and ethnic neighborhoods in which they reside. Community researchers interested in organizing research designs with *the streets* have to more aggressively reframe explanations and methods for studying street-life-oriented behavior, identity, or culture—so that interventions and policies can better reflect and improve their lived experiences. It should be underscored that Street PAR in no way encourages or endorses crime. Rather, by examining the most adaptive features of a street identity, Street PAR provides a deep phenomenological analysis that could greatly inform and improve interventions developed for those who lead a street lifestyle.

Street PAR projects can take many forms, but at the very least, such projects must reflect the following three features: (1) research orientation; (2) intervention for Street PAR members; and (3) a vehicle for action or activism that extends to local community members. Street PAR understands itself as an aggressive intervention designed to transition those in *the streets* out of *the streets* and into much improved structural opportunity, by providing high quality and rigorous economic and educational opportunities that can help to offset the poor academic, employment, and/or criminal backgrounds that many in *the streets* have accrued across time. As method and intervention, Street PAR has proven to develop participants' reading, writing, and analytical skills, as well as generating professional experiences and products (publications, presentations, etc.) viewed favorably by colleges, employers, and society overall. As such, it contributes to the endeavor to learn how to intellectually engage individuals held inside correctional facilities to which educators and community professionals should be persistently committed. Unlike most current correctional practices, and like other higher education in prison initiatives (Batiuk et al., 2005), Street PAR can also dramatically improve reentry and/or reduce recidivism rates among those returning home from incarceration.

Street PAR projects are expected to organize activism in the communities or with the street population they presume to serve. Questions for Inside-Out Street PAR projects include: what does authentic research, intervention, and activism look like inside correctional facilities? And how can this vision be realized within Inside-Out courses and initiatives?

Although small in number, there are in fact some examples of PAR work being designed and generated with and by "street-life"-identified Black and Brown populations (Brown, 2010; LIFERS, 2004; Payne, 2006, 2008; Payne and Brown, 2010). For example, a scholarly and activist-based group of men serving life sentences in Pennsylvania have remained steadfastly determined to offer their recommendations and analysis for responding to street culture (LIFERS, 2004). Some among this group, including Paul Perry (chapter 4) and Tyrone Werts (chapter 17), have also been influential and longtime members of Inside-Out's Graterford Think Tank, the core group that developed The Inside-Out Prison Exchange Program into a continent-wide program. The LIFERS say:

> …it is unrealistic to think that any serious efforts to address the problem of drug addiction could be successful while simultaneously excluding drug users, who consume illegal substances, and drug dealers, who market them, from such efforts. It is logically inconsistent, therefore to expect a reduction in crime simply by galvanizing law enforcement, legislators, and a few select community groups, while excluding those deemed to be criminal elements from the process. (2004, 51)

More recently, the second author here organized a PAR team of four "street-life"-oriented Black men to examine attitudes toward economic and educational opportunity in a community sample of "street-life"-oriented Black men ranging between the ages of 16–65 (Payne, 2008; Payne and Brown, 2010). Data for this project were collected from street communities in Harlem, New York City, and Paterson, NJ, in the form of 371 surveys, 20 individual interviews, and two group interviews. Like Paul Perry, Kyle Daniel-Bey, and Tyrone Werts, whose narratives are included in this volume, the young men (16–19) in the study understood a street identity and related activities as adaptive or sensible within school environments perceived to be hostile. These young men perceived school violence, overcrowded class rooms, or underpreparation as signs of neglect or evidence of a hostile environment—and this neglect, from their perspective, allotted them permission to embrace a street identity as a way to maximize their limited opportunities.

Street PAR Blueprint for Inside-Out Research

As these examples illustrate, Street PAR is not a *single* method (e.g., focus groups, survey) but an approach or framework that can shape multiple kinds of projects that use data to address pressing social concerns and actualize social justice. Across these variations, Street PAR is grounded in nine core dimensions, explicit standards by which to understand and measure the design, application, or implementationof a Street PAR project, and the Street PAR teams are expected to have completed formal research methods training prior to data collection. These nine dimensions (see Brown, 2010; Fine et al., 2004; Payne, 2006b, 2008, forthcoming) are organized into two subareas: (1) project organization (five dimensions include project identity, ethics, resources and incentives, timeline, and methodological design); and (2) community and activism (four dimensions include local history, audience, The People, and the action plan). Of these nine standards, we will here zero in on ethical project organization, project significance to The People, and the development of a meaningful action plan, as we consider an Inside-Out case study. As stated above, all Street PAR projects have a research orientation, function as interventions for participants, and serve as a vehicle for action that extends to benefit the larger community.

Research Orientation

Ethics

Research methods curricula must organize their ethics component as responsible to both traditional and nontraditional discourses on ethics. The team is expected to be taught the formal process of seeking university approval to conduct research. In fact, the team should review the actual institutional review board application that was approved. This will provide an opportunity for the team to be made aware of their own legal and moral rights as they work on the project, as well as of the rights of the respondents. Also, at most academic institutions, Inside-Out students conducting PAR work will be required to provide evidence to the host university that they have completed some type of national research ethics education curriculum, such as the Collaborative Institutional Training Initiative (CITI).

Crucially, nontraditional discussions of ethics should be held as well. Team members should be well informed, by way of the literature and other credible and creative sources (e.g., the Inside-Out Ethical Guidelines for Research), of how marginalized populations have been exploited in past academic research. Also, the team needs to explore together how most research operates from the assumptions and interests of those who conduct the research rather than the value system of those being studied. Considering the power dynamics inherent in research and knowledge production, the team must explicitly determine *who owns the project* (especially the data), and what *ownership* means to various members on the team (e.g., inside students, outside students, faculty members, prison staff and administrators). Also, students should discuss how such projects can benefit the overall careers of both inside and outside students and faculty who are involved, such as entrance into college or graduate school, grant and/or employment opportunities, tenure and promotion, and other forms of recognition at the prison site for inside students that can provide benefits upon release for employment and/or educational endeavors. Finally, Street PAR projects are mandated to engage in activism or change. As a consequence of this charge, it would be unethical not to organize and implement instances of advocacy and/or action throughout the Inside-Out group project.

The first author has offered Inside-Out courses every fall since 2009 at a minimum- and medium-prison for men. It was through different Inside-Out course experiences that the realization of PAR as a methodological framework for this context came to fruition. In one iteration, at the conclusion of an Inside-Out course, four students asked to coauthor an article about the experience. The instructor coordinated monthly meetings at the prison for them to work together on the paper until the men were released, at which time we held the last few meetings on campus. The paper was completely driven by the students in terms of the framing of the topic, literature reviews, analyses, and writing. The article was accepted in October 2012 for publication in an undergraduate journal focused on CBL. At the same time, two inside students sought to write a paper about the role of higher education in their individual process of transformation in prison. Again, the instructor coordinated the meetings, but the men brought the paper to fruition, which is currently in Revise & Resubmit status for the *Journal of Prisoners on Prisons*.

Intervention for Street PAR members

The People

Street PAR projects must find a way to formally assess how the project was received by the larger group under study. For instance, if the project examined access to physical activity, then the team has to poll men or women outside of the sample (or some representative group) on their views of how the Street PAR project impacted change in physical activity. All too often, PAR projects claim to have an impact on the larger communities under study without conducting an impacts assessment. No project should invoke social justice goals until the people presumably being served by the project understand the efforts of the Street PAR study as social justice.

For example, it has been common in the first author's courses for inside students to report that the prison administrators do not effectively communicate the purpose of various assessments administered or explain the benefits of the programs being offered at the institution. Consequently, prisoners report not completing assessments honestly or finding it difficult to make informed decisions about program enrollment. Two Inside-Out cohorts focused their final group projects on providing the correctional system with evidence-based research on how the state can meet the goal of reducing the prison population. One element of the second cohort's report focused on enhancing communication to all prisoners about programs available and ensuring more attention is given to determining what programs actually help people in prison attain knowledge and skills for successful reentry to their communities. At the conclusion of this course, two outside and four inside students decided they wanted to conduct a survey themselves to determine which programs prisoners find beneficial beyond reasons related to judicial release (e.g., being able to demonstrate to the court that they have completed different rehabilitation programs). They conducted the literature reviews and designed a survey of six questions. Two of the inside students administered 74 anonymous surveys to men currently incarcerated at the prison who have completed one or more of the programs. Two additional inside and two outside students analyzed the data and drafted the findings with feedback from all project participants. The project members presented their findings to administrators at the prison, which came at a crucial time of programmatic decision-making, as the prison was transitioning to house a "reintegration dorm."

Street PAR as a Vehicle for Action or Activism That Extends to Local Community Members

Action Plan

Activism or Action can and should be part of PAR projects on the inside, but such projects should be wisely developed. *Authentic instances of social justice or activism* as defined by the local population under study will always be challenging to conduct inside correctional facilities, so activism needs to be conceptualized in ways that benefit the larger institutions without compromising the integrity of the project. Street PAR teams should review formal theories of social justice (Bowman, 1991; Tuck, 2009; Knight, 2003; Payne, 2006, forthcoming) to guide the action plan. Given that the full gravity of an action plan occurs not just at the end but across the duration of a project (Tuck, 2009), Street PAR teams must organize an "action" subteam responsible for developing an action schedule with formal steps to be approved by the larger team and implemented throughout the course of the project.

For example, in the group project focused on recommendations for the implementation of evidence-based reentry programs, one key recommendation was to develop a partnership between the prison and the university to enable college students to cofacilitate some of the needed reintegration dorm programs in order to address the issue of staff shortages and budget cuts at the prison. The prison site was very receptive to the plan and we began this pilot initiative in spring 2013. College students are enrolled in a college course and have been trained by both the prison and faculty member to cofacilitate four different programs for approximately 80 men housed in the reintegration dorm. This can be described as a win–win partnership for all involved: university students are gaining the educational and career benefits of working in a correctional environment, incarcerated men are gaining the educational skills developed through the programs as well as completing hours necessary toward an employability certification offered to assist them in reducing barriers for gainful employment upon release, and the prison is able to implement required reintegration programs without incurring additional costs. The first author plans to submit the required materials to the university to be able to offer this program as a permanent course offering.

This project shares many features with the sustained transformative potential of the Think Tanks and other Inside-Out group projects across the network. For example, Jeri Kirby of West Virginia University facilitates Inside-Out classes at the United States Penitentiary at Hazelton. Her 2010 Inside-Out class developed a 12-month residential reentry program. Prison officials were very receptive, implemented the program, and graduated the first cohort of participants in 2012. Alumni of that 2010 course, inside and out, have gone on to play key roles in running the program itself (see The Inside-Out Center Newsletters, Fall 2011 and Summer 2012). In Ohio, Inside-Out alumni have coordinated an annual alumni dinner, presented at local and national conferences, and been invited as guest lecturers at universities across the state of Ohio to discuss their experiences in prison, Inside-Out, and reentry. Similar to other Inside-Out initiatives geared toward bridging the pathway of prison to college, since 2011, interested inside students can obtain the college credit for the Inside-Out course (funded by nonstate subsidies) and the instructor supports both inside and outside students in their higher education pursuits. The examples of the organic growth of initiatives born out of group projects demonstrate the promise of Street PAR in the Inside-Out context. Specifically, these examples provide some potential answers to the question posed earlier regarding what authentic research, intervention, and activism can look like inside correctional facilities:

1. Members of the team participate in each element of the research project, from design to analysis to presentations to publication (a research orientation).
2. Teams are specifically geared toward changing some aspect of the prison system, as in the example of ensuring that people in prisonhave access to effective programs to assist in reentry (an intervention for Street PAR members).
3. Inside-Out group projects enable students and other stakeholders to better understand the needs, concerns, and overall perspectives of individuals remanded to correctional facilities in order to create effective short- and long-term solutions, with some solutions implemented (a vehicle for action).
4. Inside-Out students have developed research projects and programs, written journal articles, spoken at community-based and college events, and continued higher education pursuits upon release (showing how PAR experiences provide Inside-Out students with valuable social-cultural, educational, and economic capital to be used to obtain better employment and educational opportunity).

Conclusion

In this chapter, we demonstrate the potential of PAR as a framework for CBL courses in order to achieve multiple outcomes. We argue that PAR provides an overarching theory and methods that support a truly reciprocal university–community partnership, benefiting all participants involved, and not solely university students. PAR provides the avenue for all stages of development of the course, from identification of community needs, to involvement in project design, to the utilization of project findings to advocate for and implement change. The PAR framework not only addresses the development and implementation of community-based projects but also overcomes many of the ethical concerns and methodological weaknesses found in community-based research or evaluation of CBL courses.

Inside-Out courses as a specific form of CBL provide a model for what PAR, and specifically Street PAR, can achieve, even in one of the most restrictive community settings, the prison. We also recognize that perhaps the biggest challenge of PAR is the time necessary to develop and implement projects. While we utilize the Inside-Out group project approach as an avenue for PAR, we also see the benefits of conceptualizing CBL projects in general over the course of two semesters rather than one. For example, the first semester course (e.g., a research methods course) could be utilized to train PAR members in five dimensions of project organization (project identity, ethics, resources and incentives, timeline, and methodological design) and the second-semester course could focus on the necessary dimensions of community and advocacy (local history, audience, The People, and the action plan). We also suggest that seasoned CBL faculty engage in the PAR model, given the time and commitment necessary to develop any CBL course—let alone one in which the entire process is guided by multiple voices and requires a strong ongoing relationship with the community partner to navigate potentially difficult conversations and transparency of projects.

In general, Street PAR's building of context through the thoughtful and necessary dimensions of projects is an innovative and effective ethical and methodological framework. By engaging participants as informed researchers and incorporating action or social advocacy as a necessary component for implementing short- and long-term solutions to community-defined social problems, it aligns practice with principle and builds capacity for *all* participants. In sum, the PAR model provides the necessary context for the continued evolution of CBL initiatives in higher education.

Note

1. We use the term community-based learning (CBL) to encompass civic engagement, experiential learning, and service learning concepts, and to highlight the reciprocity this type of transformational learning espouses. While service learning has sometimes emphasized providing "services" to those in need, CBL emphasizes the role of the community members in defining their needs and incorporates social advocacy or action to meet those needs (see Tony Robinson, "Dare the School Build a New Social Order?" *Michigan Journal of Community Service Learning* (2000): 142–157). Community-based research (CBR), like CBL and in contrast to traditional academic research, similarly privileges the powerless with an explicit goal of action to address the community-defined concern (see Kerry J. Strand, "Community-based Research as Pedagogy," *Michigan Journal of Community Service Learning* (2000): 85–96).

References

Allred, Sarah L. "The Inside-Out Prison Exchange Program: The Impact of Structure, Content, and Readings," *The Journal of Correctional Education* 60, no. 3 (2009): 240–258.

Batiuk, Mary Ellen, Karen F. Lahm, Matthew McKeever, Norma Wilcox, and Pamela Wilcox. "Disentangling the Effects of Correctional Education: Are Current Policies Misguided? An Event History Analysis," *Criminal Justice* 5, no. 1 (2005): 55–74.

Blieszner, Rosemary and Lisa M. Artale. "Benefits of Intergenerational Service Learning to Human Services Majors," *Educational Gerontology* 27 (2001): 71–87.

Borden, Amanda Welch. "The Impact of Service-learning on Ethnocentrism in an Intercultural Communication Course," *Journal of Experiential Education* 30, no. 2 (2007): 171–183.

Bowman, Phillip J. "Race, Class, and Ethics in Research: Belmont Principles to Functional Relevance." In *Black Psychology*, 3rd ed. Edited by Reginald L. Jones, 747–768. Berkeley, CA: Cobb & Henry, 1991.

Brown, Tara M. "Arise to the Challenge: Partnering with Urban Youth to Improve Educational Research and Learning," *Perspectives on Urban Education* 7, no. 1 (2010): 4–14.

Brydon-Miller, Mary, and Patricia Maguire. "Participatory Action Research: Contributions to the Development of Practitioner Inquiry in Education," *Educational Action Research* 17, no. 1 (2009): 79–93.

Dewey, John. *Experience and Education.* New York: Macmillan, 1938.

Dupont, Ida. "Beyond Doing No Harm: A Call for Participatory Action Research with Marginalized Populations in Criminological Research," *Critical Criminology* 16 (2008):197–207.

Einfeld, Aaron, and Denise Collins. "The Relationships between Service-learning, Social Justice, Multicultural Competence, and Civic Engagement," *Journal of College Student Development* 49, no. 2 (2008): 95–109.

Fine, Michelle. "Bearing Witness: Methods for Researching Oppression and Resistance—A Textbook for Critical Research," *Social Justice Research* 19, no. 1 (2006): 83–108.

Fine, Michelle, Rosemarie A. Roberts, Maria E. Torre, Janice Bloom, April Burns, Lori Chajet, Monique Guishard, and Yasser A. Payne. *Echoes of Brown: Youth Documenting and Performing the Legacy of Brown V. Board of Education.* New York: Teachers College Press, 2004.

Finley, Ashley. *Making Progress? What We Know about the Achievement of Liberal Education Outcomes.* Washington, DC: Association of American Colleges and Universities, 2012.

Hale, Aileen. "Service Learning with Latino Communities," *Journal of Hispanic Higher Education* 7, no. 1 (2008): 54–69.

Hollis, Shirley. "Capturing the Experience: Transforming Community Service into Service Learning," *Teaching Sociology* 30 (2002): 200–213.

Hughes, Carolyn, Elizabeth Boyd, and Sara J. Dykstra. "Evaluation of a University-based Mentoring Program: Mentors' Perspectives on a Service-learning Experience," *Mentoring & Tutoring: Partnership in Learning* 18, no. 4 (2010): 361–382.

Knight, Michelle. Through urban youth's eyes: Negotiating K-16 policies, practices, and their futures. *Educational Policy,* 17 no. 5 (2003) 531–557.

Kolb, David A. *Experiential Learning: Experience as the Source of Learning and Development.* Englewood Cliffs, NJ: Prentice Hall, 1984.

Lewis, Helen M. "Participatory Research and Education for Social Change." In *Handbook of Action Research: Participative Inquiry and Practice.*Edited by Peter Reason and Hilary Bradbury-Huang, 356–362. London: Sage, 2001.

Lewis, Tammy L. "Service Learning for Social Change? Lessons from a Liberal Arts College," *Teaching Sociology* 32 (2004): 94–108.

LIFERS. "Ending the Culture of Street Crime," *The Prison Journal* 84, no. 4 (2004): 48–68.

Markus, Gregory B., Jeffrey P. F. Howard, and David C. King. "Integrating Community Service and Classroom Instruction Enhances Learning: Results from an Experiment," *Educational Evaluation and Policy Analysis* 15, no. 4 (1993): 410–419.

Marullo, Sam. "Bringing Home Diversity: A Service-learning Approach to Teaching Race and Ethnic Relations," *Teaching Sociology* 26 (1998): 259–275.

Mayhew, Matthew J. and Sonia DeLuca Fernandez. "Pedagogical Practices That Contribute to Social Justice Outcomes," *The Review of Higher Education* 31 (2007): 55–80.

McIntyre, Alice. *Inner-city Kids: Adolescents Confront Life and Violence in an Urban Community.* New York: New York University Press, 2000.

Mobley, Catherine. "Breaking Ground: Engaging Undergraduates in Social Change through Service Learning," *Teaching Sociology* 35, no. 2 (2007): 125–137.

National Service-learning Clearinghouse. "History of Service Learning in Higher Education," January 2008, http://www.servicelearning.org/history-service-learning-higher-education, retrieved January 16, 2013.

Payne, Yasser A. "Participatory Action Research and Social Justice: Keys to Freedom for Street-life-oriented Black Men." In *Free at Last?: Black America in the Twenty-first Century.* Edited by Juan Battle, Michael Bennett, and Anthony Lemelle, Jr., 265–80. New York: Transaction, 2006a.

———. *Participatory Action Research and HIV/Aids in Newburgh, New York State.* Greater Hudson Family Health Center, HIV/AIDS Department, 2006b.

———. "'Street Life' as a Site of Resiliency: How Street-life-oriented Black Men Frame Opportunity in the United States," *Journal of Black Psychology* 34, no. 1 (2008): 3–31.

———. "Site of Resilience: A Reconceptualization of Resiliency and Resilience in Street-life-oriented Black Men," *Journal of Black Psychology* 37, no. 4 (2011): 426–51.

———.*The People's Report: The Link between Structural Violence and Crime in Wilmington, Delaware.* Hope Commission and University of Delaware, Forthcoming.

Payne, Yasser A. and Tara M. Brown. "The Educational Experiences of Street-life-oriented Black Boys: How Black Boys Use Street Life as a Site of Resiliency in High School," *Journal of Contemporary Criminal Justice* 26, no. 3 (2010): 316–338.

Pompa, Lori. "Service Learning as Crucible: Reflections on Immersion, Context, Power, and Transformation," *Michigan Journal of Community Service Learning* (Fall 2002): 6776.

Redhawk-Love, Sharon. "Keeping it Real: Connecting Feminist Criminology and Activism through Service Learning," *Feminist Criminology* 3, no. 4 (2008): 303–318.

Reed, Virginia A., G. Christian Jernstedt, Jill K. Hawley, Emily S. Reber, and Courtney A. DuBois. "Effects of a Small-scale, Very Short-term Service-learning Experience on College Students," *Journal of Adolescence* 28 (2005): 359–368.

Robinson, Tony. "Dare the School Build a New Social Order?" *Michigan Journal of Community Service Learning* 7 (2000): 142–157.

Simons, Lori and Beverly Cleary. "Student and Community Perceptions of the 'Value Added' for Service Learners," *Journal of Experiential Education* 28, no. 2 (2005): 164–188.

Singer, Jefferson A., Laura A. King, Melanie C. Green, and Sarah C. Barr. "Personal Identity and Civic Responsibility: 'Rising to the Occasion' Narratives and Generativity in Community Action Student Interns," *Journal of Social Issues* 58, no. 3 (2002): 535–556.

Strand, Kerry J. "Community-based Research as Pedagogy," *Michigan Journal of Community Service Learning* 7 (2000): 85–96.

The National Inside-Out Center Newsletter.2 (Fall 2011), 3: 8. http://www.insideoutcenter.org/newsletter.html.

The National Inside-Out Center Newsletter. 3 (Summer 2012), 2: 6–7. http://www.insideoutcenter.org/newsletter.html.

The National Task Force on Civic Learning and Democratic Engagement. *A Crucible Moment: College Learning and Democracy's Future.* Washington, DC: Association of American Colleges and Universities, 2012.

Torre, María Elena and Michelle Fine. "Bar None: Extending Affirmative Action to Higher Education in Prison," *Journal of Social Issues* 61, no. 3 (2005): 569–594.

Tuck, Eve. "Suspending Damage: A Letter to Communities," *Harvard Educational Review* 79, no. 3 (2009): 409–428.

Vogelgesang, Lori J. and Alexander W. Astin. "Comparing the Effects of Community Service and Service Learning," *Michigan Journal of Community Service Learning* 7 (2000): 25–34.

PART VI

Leaning into the Future: Helping Change Endure

CHAPTER 24

Inside-Out as Law School Pedagogy*

Giovanna Shay

In the fall of 2010, and again in spring 2012, I taught a course titled Gender & Criminal Law inside the Western Massachusetts Correctional Alcohol Center in Springfield. Participants in the course included roughly equal numbers of law students from my home academic institution, Western New England University School of Law (WNE), and residents of the facility. For 14 weeks, we met on Friday mornings at the institution to discuss issues including domestic violence law reform, the role of family ties in sentencing, and gender issues in prisoner reentry.

I taught my course in a modified form of the Inside-Out format....[1] This chapter reflects on that experience. It makes the case for Inside-Out as a particularly useful form of experiential learning for law students. It also describes some techniques that I learned through teaching an Inside-Out course that can be implemented in a more traditional law school setting. Inside-Out joins with other vehicles designed to promote exchange between law students and incarcerated people...., fulfilling the role the legal academy can play in examining the nation's over-reliance on incarceration.

Why Inside-Out?

After several years of teaching criminal law and related electives in a traditional law school format, I began looking for ways to enrich my curriculum. I came to teaching after practicing as a public defender, and held a clinical teaching fellowship before transitioning to podium teaching. Although I absolutely believed in the value of learning "to think like a lawyer" through case analysis, I also saw that my students' views were heavily shaped by their life experiences and intuition. I thought that they would be better-prepared lawyers if they had more direct exposure to the criminal punishment system.[2]

I was considering the idea of approaching a correctional facility to develop a collaborative project when I met Amherst College Professor Kristin Bumiller (see chapter 19). She told me that a group of professors was already doing what I was considering—through the Inside-Out network. I visited Kristin's Inside-Out class, offered at the county jail in Northampton, Massachusetts, and I enrolled in training.

Soon I found myself at a retreat center outside of Philadelphia in an intense week-long training program that included time in the Philadelphia jails and at Graterford prison. At Graterford, we participated in a two-day mini version of an Inside-Out course, led by a group of experienced "inside" (incarcerated) students, alumni of the program.

It may be easy to guess why Inside-Out is valuable to those in prison. There is an unprecedented number of incarcerated people in the United States—currently 2.3 million.[3] Most of them have received a grossly inadequate education.[4] Despite this tremendous need, incarcerated students are restricted from receiving many important sources of funding for education, such as federal Pell grants.[5]

The racial disparities in incarceration[6] make this educational divide morally intolerable. Commentators describe a racialized "school-to-prison-pipeline," in which substandard free-world education and harsh criminal punishment policies work together to produce synergistic, subordinating effects.[7]

There are also pragmatic reasons why education for people in prison benefits the free world. The vast majority of those incarcerated will be released.[8] Studies suggest that schooling may reduce recidivism.[9] One 1997 study for the US Department of Education reported that participating in some type of schooling while incarcerated reduced the risk that a student would return to prison by 29 percent.[10]

But these are not the reasons that I decided to teach a law course in an Inside-Out format. I did it because I believed that it was invaluable for the law students. My hope is that the law students will draw on this experience in their legal careers. Today's law students someday will be in a position to make many decisions—as prosecutors, defense attorneys, judges, legislators, and state attorneys general. Their choices can greatly impact the administration of our criminal stigma systems. I wanted future lawyers to view people in the criminal punishment system as human beings, and to understand all of the costs of incarceration.[11]

It took some time to find the right facility. In Western Massachusetts, Inside-Out is so popular among undergraduate professors that it is difficult to find a space in which to teach. Institutions have limited facilities in which classes can meet, and at some correctional institutions, there is considerable turnover, or only a small number of individuals with educational qualifications sufficient to take advantage of the opportunity. I approached a few institutions before being referred to a secure, residential facility with a welcoming staff.... Most residents leave four days per week for work release, so we met on Friday mornings, when residents are typically in programming.

Although Inside-Out.... (described in detail elsewhere in this volume) aspires to improve the educational attainment of those who are imprisoned, and many Inside-Out courses offer college credit to inside students through cooperating institutions, traditional correctional education is not its main focus. By contrast, Inside-Out is designed as a "transformative" educational experience.[12] It is described as an "embodied experience," meaning that the learning that occurs is not solely cerebral.[13]

Outside students gain personal experience of the criminal punishment system by placing themselves in new and sometimes uncomfortable settings. Outside students actually experience some corrections routines; they meet officers andinmates; they take classes within rooms at the correctional facility; they talk with people in prison about the experience of incarceration. The goal is for inside and outside students to reexamine their preexisting notions about crime and punishment through conversation with one another.[14] Pompa's goal in creating the program was to spur students to question—to ask who is incarcerated, how the system operates, and what students might do to change it.[15]

Inside-Out is not about advocacy to change conditions in correctional facilities, or about political activism. In my previous work, I had functioned as an attorney, and, later, as a teacher for future advocates. However, I was willing to forego my accustomed lawyer role in order to create this educational experience for law students. And although I see the importance of political engagement to reduce the nation's reliance on incarceration, I am willing to invest in dialogue and experiential learning to promote change in the long term.

In my course, I expressly addressed the potentially exploitative aspects of the program. One concern that can surface is what tangible benefit inside students gain if they are not receiving course credit. The converse question is why the inside students should receive a free course, when outside students pay tuition. My response to both these questions is that the program has intrinsic intellectual and experiential value for both groups of participants. Students have to judge for themselves whether it is worth it.

Another controversial aspect of Inside-Out is the facility tour. The typical curriculum provides for a tour of the institution for outside students during the course. Some view this as intrusive and voyeuristic, while others argue that it is an integral part of the experience for the outside students. The first semester that I offered the course, our outside group made the decision not to tour the facility, a choice that I maintained the second semester that I taught. Instead, we invited the inside students, accompanied by our facility liaison, to visit WNE for our penultimate class. Our academic dean greeted our guests; we held class in our moot courtroom; and the law students hosted a potluck for our inside colleagues. The campus meeting was so successful that we repeated it when I offered the course a second time. This facet of our semester is one advantage of teaching in a permeable, low-security facility.

Teaching Law in an Inside-Out Format

Inside-Out courses are typically undergraduate classes. They cover a wide range of subject areas (although many do address some aspect of criminal punishment).[16] My course was different because it was a class in the law. Not surprisingly, there were many challenges to teaching a law school course, including traditional law students, in a correctional facility. How much reading should I assign? What should I select as an entry point for discussion? How much background should I provide to the legal doctrines discussed in the cases?

I chose to adapt my Gender & Criminal Law course to an Inside-Out format. In the traditional law school classroom, the first half of the course is devoted to two feminist law reform efforts—rape law and domestic violence—and critiques of those movements, from the right and the left. The second half of the traditional seminar is devoted to issues of gender in sentencing and corrections.

For the Inside-Out version, I modified my materials in a number of ways. I eliminated the rape law reform movement unit, because I did not want to begin with a topic that is so fraught in an environment that is inherently sensitive, and in which we were building trust. Since we met once per week in a longer class (to reduce travel time and time lost to security checks), I consolidated units. I reduced the amount of reading somewhat, but not significantly. For each unit, I continued to assign a couple of cases, as well as some very short (and I hoped provocative) excerpts from law review articles. As in my traditional course, I required response papers. The first time I taught Inside-Out, I required these papers of a couple of discussion leaders each week. I found the reflection papers to be so helpful in promoting engagement that the second time around, I asked all students to write a reflection paper every week. As I do in some first-year courses, I distributed reflection questions designed to direct the students to the most important concepts in the reading.

The second time I taught Inside-Out, I hired one of the law students who had completed the course the previous year as my Research and Teaching Assistant. He visited the facility a couple of times per week outside of regular class hours, to support inside students with their writing.

I did some additional framing for the Inside-Out version of the course. The model Inside-Out curriculum suggests that the inside and outside groups meet separately the first week, to receive an orientation to the rules. The second class is the first meeting of the two groups, which includes some structured group activities designed to promote interaction. The third class meeting is again separate, with an opportunity to debrief and address any issues. This format obviously takes a significant amount of class time. One potential solution is to require Inside-Out law school participants to attend a couple of class meetings before the semester begins (as do many law school clinics), or in addition to regularly scheduled class meetings. The second semester that I taught, I adopted this approach, doing some of the debriefing in additional sessions outside of regularly scheduled class time.

Inside-Out courses typically are organized in an interactive discussion format.[17] I adapted some of these techniques for the legal curriculum. I should caveat this passage by noting that I was reluctant at first because some of these methods may seem hokey, particularly to hard-nosed law teachers. However, I can attest that they proved effective. By relieving students of the responsibility of mingling and making conversation, these formats reduced awkwardness and provided participants with a sense of security. For example, I invited my students to sit in a circle, alternating inside and outside participants—an Inside-Out technique designed to promote a nonhierarchical atmosphere and interaction between inside and outside students.[18]

At the beginning of the semester, as is typical in Inside-Out courses, participants developed their own guidelines for discussion.[19] Believe it or not, this collaborative process really did help students to maintain a collegial tone; manage conflict when it arose; and keep their comments to a reasonable length.

I also broke students into small groups to discuss specific questions and report to the larger group. For example, I might put up a quote from an opinion or from an author and ask the groups to discuss. I might ask them to parse the reasoning of an opinion in their small groups, and to explain it to one another. Or I might ask them to talk about whether they agreed with the majority or dissent in a case. I would frequently circulate to pass out readings for the following week and keep tabs on whether the groups were on track. As in a traditional classroom, I found this to be a good device for generating discussion rather than asking for volunteers in a large group in which students might feel uncomfortable. However, more than in the regular law school classroom, the small group exchanges provided an opportunity for students to engage in real dialogue about criminal justice issues.

Another technique used in Inside-Out training is to pose the same check-in question to each participant in turn at the opening of the session I adapted this to the law course by asking a question related to the week's readings. I would ask which case or article excerpt participants most wanted to discuss—or which most angered or surprised them. On a number of occasions, this check-in prompted me to alter the order of my lesson plan, to take advantage of the momentum of the students' interest. For example, in the domestic violence unit in the traditional classroom, I typically begin with an excerpt from a law review article describing how domestic violence was treated in the courts in the nineteenth century.[20] During my Inside-Out semester, however, the students overwhelmingly wanted to begin by discussing the *City of Torrington case*,[21] a milestone in the domestic violence movement, which occurred in nearby Torrington, Connecticut.

Although some Inside-Out colleagues initially questioned whether a law school class would work in an Inside-Out format, in many ways, legal courses may be a particularly effective vehicle for Inside-Out. Commentators have argued that legal education is well-suited to a carceral setting because law courses can be participatory; they help people in prisonto develop their analytical capacities; and they can change students' views of the law's relationship to society.[22] After visiting my class, Kristin Bumiller noted the advantages of the case method. Cases are stories—they are accessible; often compelling; and, in Kristin's words, cases are "bounded," meaning that they provide students with a shared text and finite number of facts and concepts to discuss. Many of the issues in the cases are timely and relevant to both groups of students.

There were a couple of tactics that I used to make the case method more manageable for inside students. I provided a short sketch of legal doctrine as background, to a greater extent than I would in a typical upper-division law school course. I also found it useful, at least in the beginning, to call on inside students to state the facts of the case, and then to ask a law student to take the first shot at answering questions regarding legal analysis. This leveled the playing field, to an extent. Because many of our inside students read very carefully (the law students were amazed), they often had extremely detailed knowledge of the facts. A law student could then take the lead in helping us through the legal reasoning. After unpacking the legal analysis, I could ask some opinion or policy questions that would open up dialogue for all participants. That final step—the exchange of participants' views on policy choices—is the greatest comparative strength of the Inside-Out model.

Benefits of Inside-Out for Law Students

There were numerous benefits to teaching in an Inside-Out format. Inside-Out is described by its founder as an "embodied" experience, and that is certainly the case. The reality of going through security and of meeting inside the facility makes an impression on law students that simply cannot be duplicated by a speaker's description, a reading, or even a film.[23]

As might be expected, inside students' contributions to the discussions enriched the course. Typically, my traditional Gender & Criminal Law seminar includes some spirited exchanges. But as in many law school courses, students tend to fall into roles for the semester—the progressive, the social conservative, the libertarian. In the Inside-Out classroom, inside students sometimes voiced counter-intuitive views, which would undermine stereotypes. Our discussion of cases about substance-abusing pregnant women, for example, was much more nuanced because of the presence of inside students.

Inside students sometimes also spoke about their own experiences in a way that helped us all to understand the human cost of criminal punishment policies. For example, in the traditional seminar, I assign excerpts from readings about the role of family ties in sentencing. Not surprisingly, the Inside-Out classroom discussion was much more hard-hitting than the typical abstract seminar exchange. Discussions of policing, police interrogation tactics, and parole supervision were also much richer.

Through our class discussions, the law students realized how their life experiences (and the limits of those experiences) could affect their lawyering. In a class on mothers accused of killing children, I assigned an article by Michelle Oberman that described possible circumstances that may have produced the fatal injury of a child.[24] Our discussion helped the outside students to realize that, as lawyers, they might miss key facts about a case if they rely on assumptions about clients' or victims' lives, rather than asking questions or seeking to educate themselves.

The most notable benefit of the course was one that I had not fully anticipated. It was the behavior of the law students. I have never seen law students speak or think as carefully about issues of criminal law, sentencing, and corrections policy as in an Inside-Out course. In a traditional law school classroom, in which we place a premium on the development of rhetorical skills, it is all too easy to fall into knee-jerk positions (whether law-and-order or bleeding heart liberal). In the presence of the inside students, however, the law students were thoughtful and deliberate in their comments. I did not perceive that they edited themselves unduly, or avoided controversial positions. However, unlike my experience in some traditional settings, the law students refrained from making provocative remarks for the shock value alone; they listened and responded to one another rather than getting into back-and-forth exchanges to show off or score points; and they avoided glib generalizations.

Applying Inside-Out in a Traditional Law School Format

My Inside-Out experience added some new dimensions to my regular law teaching. After Inside-Out, I incorporated more participatory, interactive techniques into my traditional classroom teaching. For example where I previously would arrive to class prepared to do a brief review and then launch into my lesson plan, I increasingly posed a question to the class about the prior lesson or the day's reading, Inside-Out style. Once I started doing this, it struck me as strange that I formerly had jumped into the day's subject matter without first taking the temperature of the class. I also found that, in contrast to the traditional Socratic Method in which one student is asked to perform while the others are permitted to tune out, asking the same question of each student, both kept the pressure on by requiring a response from everyone, and took the pressure off by ensuring that no one person was singled out for interrogation.

Of course, the success of this check-in approach depends in large part on the value of the entry-point question that is posed. A concrete question about the facts will not provide much grist for discussion, and a question that is too general (e.g., "Any reactions to the readings?") will not provoke very interesting responses. I found the most effective queries to be open-ended questions that provided some focus (questions that are "ajar"). For example, I would ask what people were most excited to discuss, or whether they agreed with a particular judge's or author's view.

Another benefit of the course was indirect and not only unique to Inside-Out, but also worth noting. Because no electronic devices are permitted in the correctional facility, law students were not able to bring in their laptops and phones. As a result, the conversation was much more engaged. We were all in a room together— talking with one another. The novel nature of the exchange only heightened the intensity of the dialogue. Indeed, my Inside-Out experience was so powerful that it has prompted me to consider banning laptops in my traditional law school classes, a position that other law teachers have championed.[25]

With the support of my law school and our collaborating facility, I plan to teach a course in an Inside-Out format again in the future. I hope that other law professors will join me considering this model, as well as other methods for engaging incarceration in our law teaching.

Notes

* This chapter is an edited version of an article by the same name that first appeared in the *Journal of Legal Education* 62, no. 2 (November 2012): 207–217.

1. Villanova University School of Law has subsequently offered an Inside-Out course, and at the time of the writing of this article, law professors at schools including Yale and Notre Dame also had completed Inside-Out training.

2. I will follow the example of Teri Miller, Dean Spade, and others by using the term "criminal punishment system" rather than "criminal justice system." See, for example, Teresa A. Miller, "Lessons Learned, Lessons Lost: Immigration Enforcement's Failed Experiment with Penal Severity," *Fordham Urban. Law. Journal* 38 (2010): 217; Dean Spade, "Keynote Address: Trans Law Reform Strategies: Co-optation, and the Potential for Transformative Change," *Women's Rights Law Reporter* 30 (2009): 288.

3. Incarceration, The Sentencing Project, *available at* http://www.sentencingproject.org/template/page.cfm?id=107.

4. US Department of Education Office of Education & Research, "Literacy behind Prison Walls: Profiles of the National Adult Literacy Survey at xviii" (October 1994) (finding

that seven of ten inmates perform at the lowest two levels of literacy, as measured on a five-level instrument).

5. Daniel Karpowitz and Max Kenner, "Education as Crime Prevention: The Case for Reinstating Pell GrantEligibility for the Incarcerated," Annandale-on-Hudson NY: A Bard Prison Initiative Report, 2003,7, Available at https://www. stcloud-state.edu/continuingstudies/distance/documents/EducationasCrimePrevention TheCaseForReinstatingthePellGrantforOffendersKarpowitzandKenner.pdf.   They writethat the number of postsecondary education programs for the incarcerated in New York State fell from 70 to four after the abolition of Pell grants to the incarcerated in 1994; Laura E. Gorgol and Brian A. Sponsler, "Unlocking Potential: Results of a National Survey of Post-secondary Education in State Prisons," (May 2011): 2, 6–8, 18, An issue brief from Institute of Higher Education (IHEP). Available at http://www. ihep.org/Publications/publications-detail.cfm?id=143 (noting that the number of post-secondary correctional education programs had rebounded to pre-1994 levels by 2005, and that some federal sources of funding had been made available to youth offenders, but still concluding that "incarcerated persons are ineligible for nearly all federal and state need-based financial aid programs").

6. "Racial Disparity, the Sentencing Project," http://www.sentencingproject.org/template/page.cfm?id=122 (reporting that African-American and Latinos comprise 60% of those in US prisons).

7. See Katayoon Majd, "Students of the Mass Incarceration Nation," *Howard Law Journal* 54 (2011): 343, 346–347 (arguing that "the education and justice systems...have developed a 'symbiotic relationship,' effectively working together to lock out large numbers of youth of color from societal opportunity and advantage") (internal citations omitted). See, for example, NAACP, "Misplaced Priorities: Over-incarcerate, Under-educate (April 2011) (drawing a direct connection between increased state spending on prisons and reduced resources for schools for poor children of color).

8. Gorgol and Sponsler, "Unlocking Potential," *supra* note 6, at 16 (estimating that 95% of those in prison will return to the free world); Justin Brooks, "Addressing Recidivism: Legal Education in Correctional Settings," *Rutgers Law. Review* 44 (1992): 699, 702–705.

9. Karpowitz and Kenner, *supra* note 6, at 4–6; *see* Gregory A. Knott, "Cost and Punishment: Reassessing Incarceration Costs and the Value of College-in-prison Programs," *North Illinois University Law Review* 32 (2012): 267, 268 (arguing that "college-in-prison programs are an effective response to prison population growth and costs explosions."); Michelle Fine, Maria Elena Torre, Kathy Boudin, Iris Bowen, Judith Clark, Donna Hylton, Migdalia Martinez, "Missy," Rosemarie A. Roberts, Pamela Smart, Debora Upegui, "Changing Minds: The Impact of College in a Maximum Security Prison" (September 2001) (reporting that "women who attended college while in prison [at Bedford Hills] were significantly less likely to be reincarcerated (7.7 percent) than those who did not attend college while in prison (29.9 percent)"); Correctional Education Association, Education Reduces Crime: Three-State Recidivism Study (2003) (demonstrating statistically significant lower rates of recidivism for participants in corrections education in Ohio and Minnesota); Sylvia G. McCollum, "Prison College Programs," *The Prison Journal* 73 (1994): 51, 58–59 (listing studies that suggest a lower recidivism rate for thosewho have completed educational programs while incarcerated).

10. Karpowitz and Kenner, *supra* note 6, 4 n.7 (quoting Steurer, Smith, and Tracy, *The Three State Recidivism Study*, US Department of Education (1997)).

11. See James Forman, Jr., "Why Care About Mass Incarceration?" *Michigan Law Review* 108 (2010): 993, 1007 (arguing that "America's prison policies hurt us all" because prisons have too little education and too much "violence and unnecessary degradation").

12. See, for example, Lori Pompa, "Breaking Down the Walls: Inside-Out Learning and the Pedagogy of Transformation," in *Challenging the Prison-industrial Complex*, edited by Stephen John Hartnett (Champaign, IL: University of Illinois Press, 2011), 253–272.

13. Philosophy, College of Liberal Arts Temple University (2010), *available at* http://www. insideoutcenter.org/philosophy.html.

14. Ibid.

15. Pompa, "Breaking Down the Walls," *supra* note 13, 67.

16. Ibid., 259 (describing "dozens" of courses in "many and varied disciplines"); see Simone Weil Davis, Inside-Out: The Reaches and Limits of a Prison Program, in *Razor Wire Women,* edited by Jodie Michelle Lawston and Ashley E. Lucas (Albany NY: SUNY Press, 2011), 203 (describing a writing course in an all-women's facility, involving "outside" students from a women's liberal arts college, that focused on therapeutic writing).

17. See, for example, Sarah Allred, "The Inside-Out Prison Exchange Program: The Impact of Structure, Content, and Readings," *Journal of Correctional Education* 60 (2009): 240 (concluding based on student reflection papers and feedback that the structure of the course promoted student learning).

18. Pompa, "Breaking Down the Walls," *supra* note 13, 72.

19. Ibid.

20. See, for example, Reva Siegel, "The Rule of Love: Wife Beating as Prerogative and Privacy," *Yale Law Journal* 105 (1996): 2117.

21. "Thurman v. City of Torrington," 595 F. Supp. 1521 (D. Conn. 1984).

22. Brooks, "Addressing Recidivism" *supra* note 9, 719, 721, 727.

23. Nicholas de B. Katzenbach, "Reflections on 60 Years of Outside Scrutiny of Prisons and Prison Policy in the United States," *Pace Law Review* 30 (Fall 2010): 1446, 1451 (suggesting that judges and law students should visit prisons).

24. Michelle Oberman, "Judging Vanessa: Norm Setting and Deviance in the Law of Motherhood," *William & Mary Journal of Women and the Law* 15 (2009): 337.

25. See, for example, David Cole, "Laptops vs. Learning," *Washington Post*, April 7, 2007, available at http://www.washingtonpost.com/wp-dyn/content/article/2007/04/ 06/AR2007040601544.html.

CHAPTER 25

Teaching the Instructors

Matt Soares

I see now how appropriate it is that Inside-Out opens its first class with a circle. Just as our lives begin in a perfect little circle, a single cell that holds within it infinite potential, that first wagon wheel exercise ignites a spark of intellectual life that enlivens every successful Inside-Out class. This spark of intellectual life, sustained in dialogue circles across the Inside-Out network, is tough to describe, but it definitely exists, and not by chance, but by design. Through Inside-Out we trust in the process that kindles that intellectual spark over and over again, knowing it will propagate and grow, venturing out into the world spreading among fertile minds.

A single question can be finite, but the quest for knowledge is infinite. To master a working knowledge of a subject, is just the beginning of knowing; it becomes entirely different when you find yourself faced with the challenge of teaching your chosen subject to someone else. And this challenge will grow exponentially when sharing it with 30 individuals. The spark I felt as a student has been magnified over and over again in my evolution from student to facilitator to trainer of other facilitators and back again as I have helped to train new Inside-Out instructors.

Based on my experiences as an instructor trainer, I feel that two major factors are key to cultivating and sustaining that spark. The first is setting a solid foundation and taking enough time to establish a safe environment in which dialogue can flourish. This process cannot be rushed. And the second is carefully considering the students in the class, their challenges, and their interests. It is critical to set the tempo from the start to engage and unify 30 students on a common intellectual journey.

Another important point that we try to stress to the trainees is to focus on the facilitation practices, not a set curriculum. After establishing a safe learning environment, to me, the second step is a mix of the dialogic approach and what Paulo Friere and others define as the banking system (Friere 1970). The teacher must create a balance between setting a base of common knowledge to be learned by the students, and then creating activities and open dialogue through which to explore and engage the topic.

In many ways, I'm still trying to understand the amount of self-control and work it takes to stay neutral in the teaching process. There is a fine line between providing answers and guiding your students to find their own answers. A successful Inside-Out facilitator finds creative ways to engage students to search for these answers, instead of merely requiring them to repeat known material.

During our first training this was a struggle for me, as well as several of my peers. The task of creating an activity during the Inside-Out training is so much easier when you are on the outside looking in. As we reflected, we found many metaphors for this process.

Perhaps a curriculum is like developing a recipe for baking a cake from scratch—even with some steps to follow, the teacher has to know how to prepare the ingredients, how to add individual touches, how to avoid burning the cake.

Or perhaps leading a class is more like being a parent. In our think tank, the Theory Group, we jokingly refer to our group as a family, in our case, one with a strong matriarch. As Mario Carines recounts in chapter 10, we have had our sibling rivalries, but with creative guidance from our professors, we as a group have matured and learned to work together successfully over time. Or perhaps it is like teaching a child to ride a bike. The teacher must figure out when to remove the training wheels and eventually when to let go of the bike altogether. Theory Group members all feel a strong desire to succeed and further our educational pursuit, not because our professors tell us to, but because of the respect we now have for ourselves as well as our professors.

The new instructors we were to assist in our first Training Institute were very accomplished and established people. As we learned in the initial brainstorming session we organized, they included a psychologist, several tenured professors, and a sociologist who specializes in restorative justice. To say that we were intimidated at first would be an understatement. So it was very interesting and surprising for us as trainers to see and hear many of the same questions, confusions, and struggles surface that we had experienced only a month earlier, during our "Train the Trainers" session, when we had been assigned the same task our trainees were now facing: to create and demonstrate an experiential learning activity. We quickly identified with their struggle, which allowed us to engage the group constructively. After all, not much builds a team's unity like overcoming a shared obstacle. Interestingly, as we were trying to create a safe learning environment for the trainees we were again trusting the process and also creating a safe learning environment for ourselves as trainers.

Then came the second, more frustrating and daunting struggle. How were we to subtly guide these professionals in their fields without directing and limiting them? Their task was to develop an out-of-the box way to engage their students in learning a new subject. Ironically, it is hard to take a hands-off approach to teaching a hands-on experience. And it was tough for us to even attempt to undo years of established teaching methods in an hour or so of brainstorming. We ended up just putting the dots out there and letting them figure out how to connect them in their own way. We had a real sense of pride as the next generation took up the reins.

The goal for the next day was for them to develop the activity. We thought we had alerted the trainees to some common activity-ruining missteps: flipping back and forth between lecture, small groups and large groups, or trying to cram two hours of information into a 30-minute exercise. They left that day with what appeared to be confidence in their product. Doubt, however, must have crept in during their downtime that night. The years of established teaching methods they were familiar with won them over, or perhaps they didn't like being outside of their comfort zone.

When they came back the following day they had revised their entire activity, and it was a shadow of its former self. It lacked that "oomph" and its deep-rooted message just got lost in the translation. Lo and behold, despite repeated advice against it they combined several of the typical styles we had warned them against. Their new activity was a lecture followed by a large group discussion, then a small group discussion, and a return to a large group discussion, with two hours of information and unsuccessful dialogue crammed into 30 minutes, which seems like a long time, until you try to convey a message and get 35–40 people to actively participate.

The end result may have been a little flat, but this process was itself by no means a failure. You can learn just as much, if not more, from a failure with which you struggled than from simple success on your first attempt. After all, for most of us the true learning is not upon reaching the destination but through the journey that gets us there.

The trainees were frustrated that they couldn't convey the message that they intended with the format they chose. Together, they realized that they had not trusted in the process. They were embarrassed, and a couple of them actually apologized to us for not listening to our advice.

*   *   *

Reflecting back on my own journey as this first Training Institute hosted by the Michican Theory Group drew to a close, I remembered its beginning. I remember sitting there on the first day like a deer caught in the headlights staring and being stared at by a college professor, whose opening statement more or less amounted to "I can't believe I'm in prison." My own opening statements were roughly "What? You teach where? I can't believe I'm talking to a professor from Notre Dame!" No offense to our treasured professors from University of Michigan, Dearborn, but I have always dreamed of attending Notre Dame. I was awe-struck.

There was something very reassuring, though, in the fact that this training was starting in the very same manner as my original Inside-Out class had started, with the wagon-wheel activity. I could almost hear Lori Pompa repeating, "Trust in the process." So I trusted in the process and once again watched the ice breaker work its magic, as the body language and facial expressions of all those involved in the activity changed and relaxed, as that intellectual spark ignited and gained energy. Participating the first time was extraordinary. To be given the privilege to experience it for a second and a third time was absolutely amazing, like witnessing the spark of new life being created again and again.

Most of the rest of the training was a blur of questions, activities, and stimulating conversations shared over a meal. Friendly and productive, it was a very satisfying culmination of months, in fact years, of preparation unfolding over the course of a very intellectually exhausting week.

Very few people are given the opportunity to use their personal experience as a teaching tool. One of the highest forms of respect that I can offer to Lori Pompa, the Graterford Think Tank, and all of those involved in Inside-Out across the country (and, more recently, the world), is to pass on this opportunity. There is something very satisfying about initiating a peer, a future brother or sister of mine, part of a group of future Inside-Out facilitators. All our hard work as trainers was brought to fruition when the trainees came to see us as experts in *our* field of study.

For those of you considering participating in an Inside-Out Training Institute, here is some advice:

1. Trust in the process.
2. Less is more.
3. Relax and enjoy the experience.
4. A simple activity can be an important tool, allowing people to discover for themselves an understanding of a complex problem.
5. It's worth repeating: Trust in the process to be able to relax and enjoy the experience, and you will sustain the spark.

References

Freire, Paulo. *Pedagogy of the Oppressed* (New York: Continuum, 2007), Chapter Two.

CHAPTER 26

Beyond "Replication": Inside-Out in Canada

Simone Weil Davis

S everal years into what is still a new initiative, I reflect briefly in this chapter on Inside-Out Canada, the first national iteration of Inside-Out in a country other than the United States.[1] Any US-originated program may confront questions as it moves toward international expansion—questions about national differences and how to see and act past the blind spots of internalized US hegemony. Educators who work in study abroad or in globally focused intercultural dialogue are deeply engaged with these questions, of course, and some propose answers.[2] But many programs that start with a one-country focus, like Inside-Out, grow toward an international presence and understand the process only as they go. Perhaps Inside-Out Canada's experiences can suggest some things about how program replication is best conceived and framed more generally.

Today, enthusiasm seems particularly high for national replications and roll-outs. This demand for proven approaches to pressing social problems may be due in part to funding patterns in a lean economy. In prison education alone, Inside-Out and the Bard Prison Initiative have received major grants for national replication, and an array of community-oriented educational initiatives have scaled up as national programs, from 826 Valencia to KIPP and Teach for America. Is "replication" the most useful concept for this kind of growth? Perhaps there are better conceptions for the expansion of a program model, more in keeping with the value of mutual exchange that undergirds the best community-based learning (CBL). Dissemination? Collaboration? Evolution?

To share a good idea and the training that enables it seems like...a good idea. But people like to own what they do. Imbedded in distinct contexts, we all bring a lifetime of our own resources, connections, analyses, and habits to whatever we pick up, and we all must respond to different regional, cultural, and perspectival urgencies, constraints, and possibilities. These concerns are relevant for all kinds of programs that try to scale up and duplicate—even from one school to two, or one city to two. Working locally always involves understanding a particular microculture, building alliances, extending roots of commitment, and learning from those "who live there." In a query that also drives Melissa Crabbe's chapter (chapter 3), here I ask how a program model can adhere to the principles and practices that define it, while extending a truly open invitation to the people who will be building it locally. These questions are thrown into more urgent relief when we consider the launch of a national program outside the borders of the originating country.

In 2009, I returned to Toronto (where I had lived as a child) after decades in the States. Upon first return, still starry-eyed, I found myself feeling that even with a federal administration that leans neoconservative, overall, Canadian society seemed to be less harshly bound by neoliberal assumptions, and more civil than its twenty-first-century American counterpart. The people I was meeting struck me as unbowed by dog-eat-dog fatalism, resourceful in coping with inequities. And despite political, social, and economic problems old and new, the notion of a common good, a collectively shared public interest that deserved to be considered and upheld, seemed to have more currency across the body politic than in the States. As the Harper administration put forth a raft of new sentencing and crime bills that would mean more people in prison for longer spans even as access to higher education for people in Canadian prisons constricted, I was struck by the need for a program that would work in the way that Inside-Out does. Despite federally appointed watchdogs like Howard Sapers, the federally mandated but independent work of the Canadian Association of Elizabeth Fry Societies, and other vital community voices, Canadians overall did not seem fully aware of the big changes afoot in the criminal justice system, which were disproportionately impacting people of color, Indigenous peoples, and the economically disenfranchised. In informal conversations, at conferences and in structured information sessions across several provinces, I tested the waters to see if there was interest,[3] and I learned about many rich engagements with criminal justice issues and with CBL within and beyond the academy. Illustrative examples include Nadia Duguay's project idAction in Montreal, which offers critical thinking workshops to criminalized young adults; and the remarkable access program, Beginning University Successfully, through the University of Winnipeg's Urban and Inner-City Studies program, which maintains its site in the heart of the North End community.[4] Living in a region that helped found the restorative justice movement, I asked people at Aboriginal Legal Services of Toronto, Inc., Peacebuilders International, and Kitchener's Community Justice Initiatives about their work. That first summer back in Toronto, I joined a local commemoration of Prisoner Justice Day and saw a grassroots-generated memorial event hosted by one of the most heterogeneous and effective community cohorts imaginable. (Held across Canada each year, Prisoner Justice Day started in prison in the mid 1970s and remembers those who have died behind bars.)

As a result of these initial conversations, in Fall 2011, Inside-Out saw its first Canadian courses run. In Vancouver, British Columbia, Jane Miller-Ashton, and Hollis Johnson of Kwantlen Polytechnic University offered a criminology course at Matsqui Penitentiary.[5] Meanwhile, in Kitchener, Ontario, Shoshana Pollack at Wilfrid Laurier University's Faculty of Social Work gave the first Inside-Out course at Grand Valley Institution for Women and initiated a robust, ongoing program there that has since become the institutional home for Inside-Out Canada[6] (see also chapters 6 and 14). Strengthened immeasurably by the think tank at Grand Valley (the Walls to Bridges Collective, whose mission statement is in this book's Appendix), Inside-Out Canada hosted its first Instructor Training Institute in July 2013, and the 18 faculty members and community educators who attended brought the number of trained Inside-Out instructors in Canada up to 34, across five provinces. The think tank members coaching participants were the first to do so in a Canadian prison, the first in a prison for women, and the first to foreground a feminist framework.

*　　*　　*

Apparent through this process are some very important distinctions between the United States and Canadian contexts for this work—political, societal, and cultural influences that impact how people do collaborative work in Canada, what is possible here, what is needed here, and what is appropriate here. Two distinctions from the U.S. context must centrally shape prison education here: a profound difference in the scale of incarceration, and the blistering and tragic scale of criminalization and overincarceration of Indigenous people in Canada.

First, and very significantly, there is no mass incarceration in Canada—yet. (The Omnibus Crime Bill C-10 (2012) bundles mandatory minimums, Truth in Sentencing, and much more. Along with new policies and practices around policing and parole, a new surge in incarceration rates looms, particularly among Indigenous and immigrant populations.)[7] Though Canada's incarceration rate is by no means a source of pride, it remains the case that the US rate is around *five times* that of Canada's (Walmsley, 2011). Meanwhile, despite our huge landmass, the country's total population is around one-tenth that of the United States. In 2012, California (with roughly the same population as Canada) had 130,000 people in prison (and 8,900 others imprisoned out of state) while all of Canada held around 38,000 people in custody on any given day (StatsCan, 2012).

What do these differences in scale and rate mean for Inside-Out? Though there is much for an American to learn about the lived consequences of a less vast system, I will just explore one, here. With far fewer really long sentences, and many inside students getting out more rapidly, the need for programs that prepare for and address reentry, that offer continuity of academic support and courses in outside as well as inside venues, may be even more pressing than in the States. And because a higher percentage of the inside students in a prison classroom have release dates close at hand, there is more of an active and immediate call for working alumni communities that can stay cogent and shift gears when people get out. Also, community corrections has a larger proportional footprint, so there is demand from correctional administrators for Inside-Out-style courses with classes to be held 50 percent in halfway houses and 50 percent on campus. In sum, shorter sentences shift the work's context, which leads to adaptation.

Unsurprisingly, innovations in community engagement and venues beyond the correctional are key to Inside-Out's beginnings in Canada.[8] One new project, inspired in part by and in solidarity with Inside-Out Canada, was collectively con-ceived by faculty from the University of Saskatchewan and community educators. This educational partnership between university students, mature students from Oskayak High School, which practices Indigenous pedagogy, and "non-traditional" learners from STR8UP, a local initiative for youth and adults who have exited gangs, will offer participants the opportunity to explore and further the decoloniz-ing potential of education. The long-term plan is to offer cross-listed courses in Law, English, and Native Studies in a community rather than correctional setting. They began with a series of working dinners, where future students from all three com-munities met to brainstorm together about desired course curricula.

Working in a country that incarcerates fewer of its citizens, the American prison educator gets to ask herself or himself a useful if unsettling question: if a program has been conceived and developed inside the cauldron of hyper-incarceration and inhumanly long sentences, are its own vision and practice distorted by the excep-tional conditions it attempts to ameliorate? It is good—crucial—to be jarred loose from the presumption that "inside" students will continue to remain inside for many years. In that moment of adjustment, I become more receptive to new ideas and less confined, myself, by the impacts of mass incarceration. With the help of new colleagues, new students, and new alumni, I am "moving beyond the walls that separate us," as the Inside-Out mission requires.

* * *

Second, Canada's racial politics are distinct from those in the United States, and this has a crucial bearing on the face and practice of criminal justice and correc-tions here. Racism and its bitter consequences are here in full force, but they have been hammered out on a different historical forge. African Canadians and other visible minorities are overrepresented in prison, and there is at present a complex interplay between shifting federal practices about immigration and the processes of criminalization.

And there is unbelievably stark overrepresentation of Indigenous people in Canada's prisons and jails. Especially dramatic in correctional facilities in the prairie provinces (where 90 to 98 percent of the people in a prison or jail may be Aboriginal),[9] overall Indigenous people make up between three and four percent of the population here, but 23 percent of those in Canada's federal prisons and a staggering 33 percent of the women in the federal correctional system (Canadian Press, 2012).[10]

As M. Kay Harris argues in chapter 5, to do Inside-Out responsibly in the US context, one *must* be able to understand the historical flow that links slavery to convict leasing, to Jim Crow laws, to ghettoization, to prejudicial and disempow-ering foster care and welfare systems, to hyper-incarceration. Meanwhile, to do Inside-Out in Canada, one *must* understand the historical flow between colonial-ism, forced removals, land loss, cultural genocide, broken treaties, the Indian Act, the cataclysmic ruptures and violence of residential schools, child welfare practices like the infamous Sixties Scoop that took children from reserve communities, urban dislocation, and the hyper-incarceration of Indigenous peoples (Rudin, 2007). The contexts created by these historical flows are not just ideas—they are the lived web of meaning and experience that directly affect how everyone involved, especially Indigenous people and black people, experience North American criminal justice systems. Crucial too are the informal or unsanctioned learning and healing practices that happen and have happened among African American and Indigenous people throughout North American prison history, along with the game-changing prisoner-run campaigns for educational and culturally appropriate programming inside, from the demand for educational access at Attica to the hunger strikers who called for spiritual services at Kent Institution in Agassiz, British Columbia.[11]

So, to work with Indigenous people in and/or out of prison, a contemporary CBL educator, regardless of racial identity, would do well to think of forming an alliance built on collaboration and shared listening, rather than expecting a previously formulated program to be accepted and instituted as-is. For an American working in Canada, double that. Slowly built and carefully sustained relationships based on earned respect and mutual learning will be immeasurably stronger with an awareness of what you cannot quickly "pick up" about Indigenous ways of knowing, and a willingness to learn.

An example might be the exchange that can happen around the resonances and differences between Indigenous approaches to circle work and the way it shows up in the Inside-Out practice.[12] Both sorts of circles are far more than a grouping of chairs—the Introduction to this volume as well as chapters 2 and 26 discuss this point vis à vis Inside-Out. As with restorative justice circle work, Inside-Out sometimes uses a talking piece, which ensures that everyone has the opportunity to speak without interruption and which emerges out of Indigenous practice. But there are key differences as well, and in the wake of a history of cultural appropriation, those differences matter.[13] Though I can responsibly do no more than point toward the large history of native circle work ("Don't talk about us without us"), it certainly manifests a material worldview that is at great variance to settler society's. A non-indigenuous perspective on working in a circle would rarely consider, for instance, the significance in that circle of the four directions. And course readings and instruction would more likely follow the linear logic of text than the circular structure of the medicine wheel, itself a circle divided into four quadrants.[14]

* * *

There are distinct but related reasons to go slow when bringing a program model to a new context: one wants to build intentional relationships, and one chooses to build collaborative ties rather than to seek recruits. Interestingly, as Melissa Crabbe similarly learned in Oregon: relationship-building, especially when it is multidimensional and two-way, is more effective than formal recruitment. Of course, organic growth is to some extent inevitable, and as we can see in this book, it offers profound and very welcome lessons of its own. But the willy-nilly growth that programs often experience, what we call "organic," can sometimes unintentionally favor the status quo, simply because power relations can be invisible due to their familiarity.[15] Here's one relevant example. Imagine, say, that a Caucasian, tenure-stream faculty member spreads the word about a program in a way that seems straightforward and realizable to that person (e.g., information sessions at universities, using the personal network, the collegial network and the mode of expression that come ready to hand). He or she opens the doors to whomever seems intrigued, registers interest, and happens to have the training fee handy. Seems reasonable enough; but in the process, that well-meaning individual may have just accidentally favored as collaborators white people who share a professional network and a certain way of talking about things, who have expendable wealth or institutional privilege, people who are less financially strapped than (community) college instructors and sessionals and adjuncts, and less overextended than many faculty of color, who often shoulder significant institutional responsibilities. Forging more heterogeneous partnerships from the ground up is absolutely essential to the vitality and social significance of CBL work...and it may take a lot more slow relationship-building, a profound commitment to organizational practices that foster equity, and a very conscious addressing of hurdles caused by cultural difference and/or power and privilege inequities. These connection and communication hurdles can emerge out of cultural differences (language, communication styles, social circles, etc.) and the impacts of racism (from poverty and access issues to mutual suspicion, often quite unintended). So, for a program initiator to spread the word and throw the door open to whomever responds may in practice be anything but an "open-door" policy. To address this justice work intentionally and to be open to evolution beyond our own blind spots, educational administrators and CBL directors must take the time required to *use,* on the organizational level, the sorts of skills and values we champion—critical reflection and mutual engagement.

* * *

Rich opportunities for mutual learning open up through the dissemination of a model across many distinct contexts, and especially across national borders. To relish those differences as the occasion for shared learning and discovery, and to incorporate the wisdom of local allies as integral to the program, however, replication needs to be consciously reconceived. If we clutch too tightly to the original model as it spreads, we may unintentionally reduce the goal of replication into mere duplication, dulling our senses to the expertise and engagements of people on the ground. If, however, program components remain somewhat flexible, local players can truly reshape the model so it makes sense in their context.

At the same time, there are important reasons to avoid an "anything goes" approach to variations on the Inside-Out theme. The model needs to stay coherent enough that its ethical and philosophical underpinnings stay solid, especially those that highlight constructive dialogue; experiential learning; teaching as facilitation rather than dominance; a shared concern for safety, mutual respect and well-being; nonexploitation; and a conscious commitment to learning in a just and trusting community. This is work that can be done badly, so concerns about maintaining standards are legitimate. The most lasting and profound solutions lie, I would suggest, in a deep and patient embrace of mutual exchange on the programmatic level as well as in the work itself.

Both to preserve what's finest and most urgent about the original model and to allow for meaningful exchange, respectful collaboration, and a proliferation of helpful learning communities, Inside-Out Canada seems to offer this lesson above all: there are benefits to slow, purposeful growth. Sustained and patient interrogation of our own blind spots; attentive receptivity to new collaborators and new contexts; deep respect for the purpose, practice, and process of dialogue: all these allow us to grow beyond the confines of replication toward an evolutionary process.

A model that evolves and disseminates, with easy "ownership" by the local players who pick it up, allows the variations to have value both locally and for the whole network. In the evolutionary process in the natural world, variations strengthen a living species both locally (because adaptations to lived context are key to survival) and globally (because genetic diversity contributes to overall species hardiness). As with species evolution, local variations of an educational program prove crucial for the whole endeavor, which benefits as an entirety when new questions are posed and new, strong practices are discovered. Ideally, network-wide solidarity and communication across difference confer the benefits of a genuine and free exchange of ideas and outcomes, so that wheels need not be reinvented, and so that local discoveries can inform all the rest of us. And we can and should understand this practice of mutual exchange itself as part of the social transformation we espouse: we are doing things differently when we climb from our silos and share broadly the lessons learned in our work.

Notes

1. Warm thanks to Peter Armstrong, Gale Cyr, Chandler Davis, Phil Goodman, Larry Morrissette, Shoshana Pollack, Barbara Roswell, Priscilla Settee, and the Walls to Bridges Collective.
2. See, for instance, the mission, vision, and value statements for the global ethical service and learning program Amizade: http://amizade.org/about/mission-vision-and-values/.
3. For example, in 2010 Lori Pompa and I offered information sessions at the University of Toronto, McGill University, Carleton University, Queens University, and Wilfrid Laurier University. In 2011, I presented at the annual CACSL conference and Shoshana Pollack and I presented at McMaster University at the annual meeting of the Canadian Association of Elizabeth Fry Societies.
4. Exeko, Inclusion through Innovation in Culture and Education, http://www.exeko.org. Beginning University Successfully (BUS): seehttps://www.uwinnipeg.ca/index/faculty-of-arts-bus. Re BUS and other Winnipeg initiatives, see Larry Silver, ed. *Moving Forward, Giving Back: Transformative Aboriginal Adult Education.* Winnipeg: Fernwood, 2013. Further examples include Canadian Alliance of Community Service Learning: http://www.communityservicelearning.ca/en/; Core Neighborhood Youth Coop, http://www.cnyc.ca/index.htm; or the Front Step Research Cooperative: http://frontstep.ca.
5. On the Coast, CBC. Radio Broadcast: "Kwantlen University Prison Outreach" (January 26, 2012). http://www.cbc.ca/onthecoast/episodes/2012/01/26/kwantlen-prison-outreach/.
6. This was made possible through the commitment of the Faculty of Social Work and Wilfrid Laurier administration and the generous backing of The Lyle S. Hallman Family Foundation.

264 • Simone Weil Davis

7. For legislative history, see Justin Piché's blog, "Tracking the Politics of Criminalization and Punishment in Canada." http://tpcp-canada.blogspot.ca.

8. Pennsylvania's Drexel University is one US site also working on Inside-Out collaborations with *noncorrectional* community partners (though the "community"-based students often have experience with being criminalized).

9. See Jody Porter, "Kenora jail holds 'shocking' number of Aboriginal women" (October 30, 2012). CBC News. http://www.cbc.ca/news/canada/thunder-bay/story/2012/10/30/tby-kenora-jail-aboriginal-women-stats.html.

10. Howard Sapers, Final Report October 2012. *Spirit Matters: Aboriginal People and the Corrections and Conditional Release Act.* http://www.oci-bec.gc.ca/rpt/oth-aut/oth-aut20121022-eng.aspx#TOC17 For a province-by-province breakdown, see "Chart 7 Aboriginal Adult Admissions to Custody, by Province and Territory, 2010/2011," *Statistics Canada.* http://www.statcan.gc.ca/pub/85–002-x/2012001/article/11715/c-g/desc/desc07-eng.html.

11. On education at Attica, see Marie Gottschalk, *The Prison and the Gallows: The Politics of Mass Incarceration in America.* (London: Cambridge University Press, 2006), 180. On the spiritual fast at Kent Institution, see James Burgess Waldram, *The Way of the Pipe: Aboriginal Spirituality and Symbolic Healing in Canadian Prisons.* (Toronto: University of Toronto Press, 1997), 5–20.

12. See former outside student Sharla Johnson: "Importance of the Circle," *Inside-Out Newsletter,* 8 (Winter 2013). http://www.insideoutcenter.org/PDF_newsletters/Winter2013_Newsletter_color.pdf.

13. See, for instance, the 1993 "Declaration of War against Exploiters of Lakota Spirituality," http://www.thepeoplespaths.net/articles/ladecwar.htm.

14. See Four Directions Teaching at http://www.fourdirectionsteachings.com/Teacher_Resource_Kit.html and see *Indigenous Knowledges in Global Contexts: Multiple Readings of Our Worlds*, George J. Sefa Dei, Dorothy Goldin Rosenberg, and Budd L. Hall, eds (Toronto: University of Toronto Press, 2002).

15. Re equity-driven organizational decisions that can avoid accidental replication of an inequitable status quo, see, for instance, Ilana Shapiro, *Training for Racial Equity and Inclusion: A Guide to Selected Programs.* (Washington, DC: The Aspen Institute, 2002). http://www.aspeninstitute.org/sites/default/files/content/docs/rcc/training.pdf.

References

826 Valencia. http://www.826valencia.org. Site last accessed June 2, 2013.

"Aboriginal Women Imprisoned in Soaring Numbers: New Report Describes Growing 'Crisis' for Aboriginal Women." Ottawa: The Canadian Press, 2012. September 27, 2012. CBCNews. http://www.cbc.ca/news/canada/story/2012/09/27/aboriginal-women-prison-report.html

Bard Prison Initiative. http://www.bpi.bard.edu. Site last accessed June 2, 2013.

Dauvergne, Mia. "Adult Correctional Statistics in Canada, 2010/2011." *Statistics Canada,* 2012. http://www.statcan.gc.ca/pub/85–002-x/2012001/article/11715-eng.htm.

Knowledge is Power Program (KIPP). http://www.kipp.org. Site last accessed June 2, 2013.

Medina, Jenifer. "California Sheds Prisoners but Grapples with Courts," *New York Times,* 21 January, 2013. A18. http://www.nytimes.com/2013/01/22/us/22prisons.html.

Rudin, Jonathan. "Aboriginal Peoples and the Criminal Justice System," 2007 Report for the Government of Ontario's Ipperwash Inquiry. http://www.archives.gov.on.ca/en/e_records/ ipperwash/policy_part/research/pdf/Rudin.pdf.

Teach for America. http://www.teachforamerica.org. Site last accessed June 2, 2013.

Walmsley, Roy. *World Prison Population List.* 9th ed. International Center for Prison Studies: Sussex, UK, 2011. http://www.idcr.org.uk/wp-content/uploads/2010/09/WPPL-9-22.pdf.

Wesley, Amanda. "Marginalized: The Aboriginal Women's Experience in Federal Corrections." Ottawa: The Wesley Group, 2012. http://www.publicsafety.gc.ca/res/cor/apc/_fl/apc-33-eng.pdf.

PART VII

Closing Circle

CHAPTER 27

Preconceived Notions

Nyki Kish

Preconceived notions. We are all guilty of harboring them. Notions of what we think things are supposed to be. Things like prison, and education. Of what and who the student is, and what and who the convict is.

These notions have many aliases. They can be called assumptions. Generalizations. Stereotypes. Archetypes. Call them what we may, they are dangerous, for they draw the deep lines, framing the societal and cultural confines that keep us all apart. That keep us all oppressed.

Today, those lines are blurred. Today there is no distinction between student and convict and education and prison . . . . because today, right here, we are all students. Learning. Evolving. Erasing. Celebrating.

We are tearing free from our preconceived notions. Breaking down the walls. Building bridges, building communities. Linking education to rehabilitation. And growing internally all the while.

This is the lesson I have taken from the Inside-Out program. And what a great program it is. When I first applied, I suspected something very special was beginning here—but I had no idea. How could anyone understand what a profound experience this is? This class has a lot to offer. The voices of the class have a lot to offer.

Each person has given me inspiration. Given me the confidence to speak up. The whole class—from its structure, to every person in it—has given me hope. From learning the content, to listening to all your stories and ideas, fears, and dreams, I have realized that I am not as alone as I thought I was. That you are all strong and brave people, and that this world isn't an easy place for any of us.

I have realized something else too. We have got to hold onto programs like this. We have got to embrace them, as we most certainly have here. For this class has let us be strong and brave together. It has become a text we can reference as we follow our individual endeavors. A tool that we can use together to mend what is broken. And a beginning from which something awesome is blossoming.

Standing here today, I understand more than oppression, marginalization. and diversity; I understand liberation too. Because today, I am free. Not in body, but in mind and heart. And that's because of this class, because of all of you. Thank you.

CHAPTER 28

Barriers Comin' Down: An Inside-Out Rap

Damien Arnaout and Shawn Brown

This Rap was first performed at the Kwantlen-Matsqui Inside-Out Closing Ceremony, Vancouver, British Columbia, December 2011.

Beat: Track 15 off of *Paper Trail*, T.I.[1]

Hook

Round and round here we go
The cycle we let it spin
The longer we let it roll
When will it ever end
The inside are lookin out
The outside are comin in
Barriers comin down
And this is where it begins.

Verse 1 (Shawn)

From the inside out to the outside in, see this is how I spit it comin out of the pen
I was trying to feed my fam, not tryin to live in sin
The judge didn't give a damn; my time, did it with a grin
Five years I've been sitting in, lifers call that a fin
Eight years gotta serve a bid n girl she just had a kid
My father he wasn't there – now look at how I begin
One of my biggest fears, now I'm starting to look like him
I admit there were some days, when life lookin kind of grim
If only for just my son, I keep pushin, I gotta win

Decided to make a change, started it from within
so the day that I touch the street, I'm a better not bitter man
Hoping my son he grows to be comfortable in his skin
and prayin my nephew learn from the places that I have been
Teach them so that they know to pass it down to they kin
Make them put it out to the world and hope that it sets a trend.

Hook

Verse 2 (Damien)

From inside to da outz, and da outside comin in,
A handful of students, and some g'z up in da pen
Come to keep it real, no one needin to pretend,
Breakin down barriers, strangers become friends—
Stories that we've shared, the way we get it in,
No judgements in da circle, whether good or bout da sin,
We lost each other's labels, just some cats who study crime,
If given another chance, I'd do it all again—
I've broadened my horizons, I look through different lens,
We represent humanity, da women and the men,
Same wants and needs, it's amazing when you blends
Cats of all backgrounds, givin time and space to spend—
Getting to know each other, new ways to make amends,
Time just flyin by, when we wished it would suspend,
Prof Jane and Hollis, you two I do commend,
We are the pioneers, too soon it had to end!

Hook

Verse 3 (Shawn)

Now as I'm lookin out my window, sitting watching the rain
I start to think about my life, all the joys and the pains
situations of the world could drive a person insane
so I just focus on the positives and try to maintain
There's no gains without pains I guess so no regret
The slip ups that I made helped me correct my step
so now I step correct sit back and reflect:
a journey of a thousand miles begins wit just one step
I've come a long way, still got a long way to go
but ima reach my destination that's a fact that I know
I got love for all my haters cause they forced me to grow
I learned from every situation, ain't the same as before

If you plant a seed then who knows it might grow.
The inside are lookin out
The outside are comin in
Barriers comin down
And this is where it begins!

Note

1. T.I., *Paper Trail.* Atlantic Records/Grand Hustle Records (2008).

CHAPTER 29

The Essence of Inside-Out

Lori Pompa

"All changed, changed utterly:
A terrible beauty is born."

W. B. Yeats[1]

I have loved these words for decades. They bespeak the mystery and majesty of the human heart. And they convey, with quiet power, the experience of being turned inside-out. It is a quiet thing, something that happens in the deep places within, sometimes when we least expect. And it is a thing of power, a tectonic shift that realigns what we thought we knew—about ourselves, about one another, about the world, sometimes about life itself.

What is this thing called "Inside-Out?" On one level, it is a class—though not an ordinary one. In this class, roles are intermingled: everyone is the teacher, everyone is the learner. The process of investigation and discovery is a communal enterprise. We explore together, we grapple together, we create new knowledge together—and we challenge one another to go deeper, always deeper.

But there is more. In a most unlikely setting, Inside-Out provides a space of liberation, a place in which each person is recognized and celebrated for the unique contribution that he or she brings to the whole. In the face of the many forms of imprisonment that we bear in our lives—some internal, some external—this experience offers an intimation of freedom. In this shared space, we can be who we are, say what we know, and call forth the best in one another.

And in our wider social reality, Inside-Out is about walls—some of our own making, some made by others. Some walls are made of bricks—but all are held in place by the mortar of fear and ignorance. We fear what we don't know—in others, in the world, even in ourselves. We build walls, thinking we can keep ourselves safe from whatever we imagine is threatening us. It is a dangerous delusion.

Inside-Out moves through the walls—it is an exchange, an engagement—between and among people who live on both sides of the prison wall. It is through this exchange, realized through the crucible of dialogue, that the walls around us and within us begin to crumble. We are then brought closer to our truest nature. In the words of Robert Frost, "Something there is that doesn't love a wall, that wants it down!"[2] The hope is that, in time, through this exchange, these walls will become increasingly permeable and, eventually, extinct—one idea, one person, one brick at a time.

Notes

1. W. B. Yeats, *Easter, 1916.* Lines 15–16. The Poetry Foundation. http://www.poetry-foundation.org/poem/172061
2. Robert Frost, "Mending Wall" (1914), in *The Norton Anthology of American Literature, Seventh Edition.* Volume D, Nina Baym, ed. (New York: Norton, 2007), 1390.

APPENDIX 1

What They Say

I learned a lot from the course about myself. For example: my ability to socialize with people of different ethnic groups, creeds, nationalities, and social status. Like this light being turned on in a vacuum of pitch-blackness, the Inside-Out program has given me hope and filled me with optimism about the future. (Inside Student)

Inside-Out is a platform. One of many stepping-stones I'm utilizing to make myself a better person. I'm finding that I can do the work of college level courses and even do well. This is an empowering feeling and I'm grateful to all those who've made this opportunity possible. (Inside Student)

It put me in touch with my humanity in a normal way. It goes back to pre-jail, like my mother and my family and the church… being sensitive, caring, thoughtful. It was ok to be nice to other people and guys, and it didn't make you a punk. (Inside Student)

I started seeing things I could do. In the eight years I've been incarcerated, I've never felt so strong about wanting to make a change. (Inside Student)

The impact of crime and prison on poverty-stricken families… I didn't realize it was that great. (Inside Student)

The most important aspect of the course was the humanizing effect. Each and every Friday, I was made to feel almost fully human. (Inside Student)

History

The Inside-Out Prison Exchange Program is based on the simple hypothesis that incarcerated men and women and college students might mutually benefit from studying crime, justice, and related social issues together as peers within a prison context. Founded in 1997 by Lori Pompa, who teaches in Temple University's Criminal Justice Department, the original idea for Inside-Out came from a man serving a life sentence in Pennsylvania named Paul. Since the first Inside-Out class in Philadelphia, more than 260 instructors from 37 states and abroad have been trained in the Inside-Out methodology, and classes have been offered in 25 states, involving at least 9,000 inside and outside students. Classes have been held inside correctional facilities across the country, with courses in a wide range of disciplines: African-American Studies, Anthropology, Criminal Justice, Economics, English, Gender Studies, History, Humanities, Public Health, Philosophy, Political Science, Psychology, Theater, and more.

CONTACT US

Please feel free to email, write, or call THE INSIDE-OUT CENTER with your questions or comments. Inside and outside students who have taken and completed an Inside-Out course are invited to send articles, essays, reflection papers, or any writings about their Inside-Out experience to The Inside-Out Center to be considered for inclusion in the Inside-Out Newsletter, other Inside-Out publication projects, or posted on the Inside-Out website. Finally, the Inside-Out Alumni Blog is an exciting and dynamic space for students participating in the Inside-Out community; past students administer it, and the content is 100 percent alumni-generated.

Please check it out here:
http://insideoutalumni.blogspot.com/

THE INSIDE-OUT CENTER
Suite 331, MB 66–10
1810 LiacourasWalk
Philadelphia, PA 19122
Phone: 215–204–5163 | Fax: 215–204–3872
http://www.insideoutcenter.org

THE INSIDE-OUT COURSE

Inside-Out creates a dynamic partnership between institutions of higher learning and correctional systems in order to transform the way we understand and approach crime, justice, freedom, inequality, and other issues of social concern. Inside-Out is a unique educational experience that provides students with a challenging learning environment through action-oriented dialogue. The core of the Inside-Out program is a semester-long course that meets weekly and includes an equal number of "outside" (i.e., university-based) and "inside" (i.e., incarcerated) students attending class together inside a jail or prison.

The course allows the university students to reconceptualize what they have learned in the classroom, gaining insights that will help them to pursue the work of creating a more just and equitable society. At the same time, it challenges men and women on the inside to place their life experiences in a larger social context and rekindles their intellectual self-confidence and interest in further education. Equally important, Inside-Out encourages inside and outside students alike to recognize their capacity as agents of change—in their lives as well as in the broader community.

THE INSIDE-OUT APPROACH TO LEARNING

PEDAGOGY

In the traditional "banking" method of education, a term coined by renowned educator Paulo Freire, students are mere receptacles of knowledge. Teachers, through lectures and textbook reading assignments, fill students' minds with tons of information, as if people were nothing more than bank deposit boxes. Inside-Out employs a pedagogical model in which knowledge is not only acquired from textbook material, but also generated from the learners themselves through a sharing of perspectives, beliefs, and personal experiences. Crucial to the Inside-Out pedagogy is the powerful exchange that occurs between "inside" and "outside" students. It is the reciprocity and authenticity of this exchange that makes Inside-Out unique.

To the new inside-Out student:

Welcome
from the
Graterford Inside-Out
ThinkTank

The Inside-Out Prison Exchange Program®
Promoting Transformative Education
and Social Change

METHODOLOGY

Creating a safe space that can engender a transformative learning experience is accomplished through the incorporation of a five-component methodology: (1) *Dialogue*, (2) *Group Process*, (3) *Facilitation*, (4) *Shared Learning, and* (5) *Perceived Others*.

Dialogue: The first and most important component of the Inside-Out methodology is *dialogue*. Inside-Out employs dialogue in two ways: *Personal and Collective. Collective. Personal Dialogue* takes the form of individual sharing of subjective thoughts, ideas, beliefs, and experiences in reference to a topic or issue under discussion. *Collective Dialogue* refers to the incorporation of both individual subjective input and information derived from other, presumably objective, source materials (i.e, textbooks) into group discussions that address a variety of social issues. This mixing and meshing of personal and collective dialogue often produces new insights into complex personal and social issues, empowering students with a deeper understanding of self and a variety of macrolevel social issues.

Group Process: *Group Process* is the galvanizing element of Inside-Out. The process includes a series of exercises and activities strategically designed to induce an amalgamation of two diverse groups—people who are incarcerated and college students—into a single cohesive entity. This is accomplished through large and small group interaction. In a Criminal Justice course, for example, throughout the semester, inside and outside students complete readings from a variety of Criminal Justice texts, as well as writing assignments. These activities foster a challenging and transformative learning experience involving critical thinking, collaborative problem-solving, and civic engagement. In the final few weeks of most Inside-Out courses, students work together on a class project.

Facilitation: Students are generally receivers of information dispensed by the teacher, information they are expected to regurgitate during tests. In Inside-Out classes, the instructor takes on the role of *facilitator*, bringing forth knowledge, insight, and the ability to make connections that are within students with the use of various facilitation tools and techniques. Students become the source of knowledge generated from their individual and collective group experience.

Shared Learning: The fourth and most crucial component, *Shared Learning,* is the crux of the Inside-Out teaching model. Inside-Out classes are not characterized by competition and debate, but instead have an atmosphere of mutuality. Students listen, respond, interact, and engage in new ways. Inside and outside participants alike have equal rights as participants and speakers. Incarcerated students and campus students learn from each other and the classroom becomes a crucible for learning where viewpoints can be heard across what would normally be gaps of social separation. This atmosphere of Shared Leaning is made possible in large part by the use of *Community Dialogue Circles* that facilitate *"Conversational Learning." Community Dialogue Circles* create a space of equality by eliminating barriers of separation that tables and rows of chairs create.They help create a sense of shared power where people feel a sense of being in a discussion with equals, as opposed to being talked at or down to by someone in authority.

Perceived Others: The fifth and final component of the Inside-Out model involves identifying and addressing instances *of Perceived Others.* Inside-Out defines "other-ing" as comments, gestures, remarks, or conversation that use stereotypes to single out individuals or groups as different in ways that effectively exclude the voice of a person or group. Inside-Out endeavors to make students aware of the concept of "other-ing"and explicitly requests that program participants refrain from using labels that would normally function as tools of dehumanization. Inside-Out embraces a philosophy that recognizes and names ways of "other-ing" that allows students to move beyond normalized mental blocks, creating the possibility of learning in fuller and deeper ways.

APPENDIX 2

Sample Student-Created Guidelines for Discussion

Inside-Out at Grand Valley Institution for Women, Fall 2011

These guidelines were developed by students in the Fall 2011 Inside-Out course "Diversity, Marginalization, Oppression," Wilfrid Laurier University Faculty of Social Work, conducted at Grand Valley Institution for Women, Kitchener, Ontario. The instructor was Shoshana Pollack.

1. Respect.
2. What we say here should stay here.
3. Free of judgment.
4. No cross talk (one person speaks at a time).
5. Try not to take things personally.
6. Request clarification if needed
   i. *Red flag*—speak up if something does not feel right
   ii. *Park it*—Write down an issue on the board if you wish to revisit and discuss, if you do not feel comfortable talking about it in the moment or if it is "too big" to talk about right away.
7. No rolling eyes, remember positive body language.
8. Come ready to be "present" and participate.
9. Indicate if you relate to someone's thoughts with a sign
   i. Nonverbal way of communicating, encouraging, validating what the speaker is saying.
10. Talk freely, share, try not to hold back.
11. Be open minded.
12. Consider what people are saying, no assumptions.
13. Be aware that we are coming from different contexts.
14. A bit of debate is good.
15. Silence can be ok.

16. Everyone's opinion counts; we may all have different views on a topic.
17. Voice where you are at, let the class know about factors that are influencing your participation and behavior.
18. Outside students: remember you are safe!
19. Be kind and gentle even when disagreeing or debating.
20. Be yourself.
21. Bring "stuff" back to class.
22. Have fun and laugh.
23. Agree to disagree with ideas.

Radio Control: Sample Student-Created Arts-Based Workshop

Lyrics on Lockdown Students

Objectives

Examine radio as an artistic outlet to communicate, converse, provoke thought in others, and to convey ideas, concerns, questions, thoughts, viewpoints, and self-expression. These may be in forms including, but not limited to, spoken word, lyricism, and poetry. Students create a piece of spoken word that conveys the truth of life in prison that is uncensored. Students feel as though they can freely express their feelings about family, life in prison, what life is going to be like when they are released. Students develop an artistic outlet for their emotions that can be applied even after theworkshop is over.

Materials

Pens, paper, CD player to play the public service announcement and Hip-Hop songs.

Ice Breaker

No specific icebreaker used in this workshop; choose one from "ice breaker" list.

Workshop Core

Public Service Announcement

Read to the students (or play audio) a few real Public Service Announcements, all with themes that relate to the prison crisis, youth violence, etc. Alternate each with a stanza of a Hip-Hop song that reflects the same message. Explore the connection between creative work and possible service it could do for the community. (10 min.)

Response Questions

Students will respond to each question on paper. (3 min each)

1. What would you want to tell your mother about your experiences here?
2. What would you tell your younger sibling, cousin, niece/nephew (someone who looks up to you)?
3. What would you want to tell your local politician?
4. What would you want to tell your role model?
5. What would you want to tell your old teacher, or a teacher in your life?
6. What would you want to tell your best friend?
7. What would you want to tell your worst enemy?
8. Choose one more person whom you haven't been able to speak to honestly about your recent experiences, and write down what you would want to tell them? (24 min)

Group Activity

Break into groups of three to four to share and discuss responses. Group members combine their answers, thoughts, and any questions or other sentiments this discussion brings up to create a public service announcement that can be modeled after the public service announcement shared at the beginning of the workshop. Announcement may be in the form of spoken word, lyricism, and/or poetry and should last at least one minute. Each member should have a speaking role in radio announcement. Groups can mimic announcement format heard in class or design original format. (15 min)

Wrap up

Each group shares the radio announcement they created.

Discussion

Can radio/poetry/music change the way people think? What truths do you know that you think others should know? What issues do you want the public to hear you out on?

Inside-Out in Alternative Community Settings: Drexel University Courses from across the Curriculum

"Once Upon a Lifetime (so far)"—Memoir Writing

Except within their immediate families, young adults and senior citizens rarely go out of their way to make conversation, to exchange ideas, or even to sit next to one another in a room. The two generations that divide these groups form a gulf, leaving wonderful stories untold. This course will bring together Drexel students and resident senior citizens at the nearby Mantua Apartments for conversation, writing, and exchange. All students will read creative nonfiction, keep a weekly journal, engage in writing as a process and as a way to facilitate vital conversation, and write several short pieces of memoir, including an exchange of stories they will write about one another. Throughout the course, Mantua Apartments residents will write memoirs alongside the Drexel students. The course will culminate with an anthology of writing created in the course.

Talking the Walk

This course examines types of civic dialogue in an immersive learning environment. Students from Drexel will join with students from the LIFT community to create presentations around issues of social justice that are important to them and practice publically delivering those messages in front of a live audience. Types of speaking will include mock election speeches, public debates, and town hall, neighborhood, or city council meetings. Students will also learn how to identify the various methods speakers use to influence audiences. The final project will include creating and ideally implementing a campaign around a current issue. The class will meet at LIFT in Philadelphia, a nonprofit organization dedicated to combating poverty with resource centers that draw clients from a wide variety of Philadelphia neighborhoods.

Healthy Green Spaces: Urban Farming and Community Organizing

This course will explore community organizing as it relates to urban farming and community gardens. Students will learn how to effectively communicate with neighbors and local governments to create healthy green space and will spend time at The Walnut Hill Community Farm. Students will learn alongside residents of West Philadelphia who are building healthy green spaces from empty lots.

Being Human: Internal Workshop for the Graterford Think Tank

Erin Howley and Kempis (Ghani) Songster

Introduction: Why Are We Interested in this Topic?

GHANI—James Boggs readings—being more fully human vs. human rights

ERIN—Group work and question: What does it mean to be responsible in relationship to others?

This may seem like an abstract topic. There could be many different ways of having a conversation on what it means to be human; we hope to keep exploring this question in subsequent workshops and other venues.

Opening Exercise and Discussion

6:40—7:00: Hand out the following quotes and GHANI reads the quotes aloud with the group:

> "A human being is part of the whole called by us 'universe', a part limited in time and space. He experiences himself, his thoughts and feelings as something separated from the rest—a kind of optical delusion of his consciousness. This delusion is a kind of prison for us, restricting us to our personal desires and to affection for a few persons nearest to us.
>
> Our task must be to free ourselves from this prison by widening our circle of compassion to embrace all living creatures and the whole nature in its beauty."
>
> —Albert Einstein

> "I am a human being. Nothing human can be alien to me."
> —Maya Angelou (quoting Terntius Afer [185–159 BCE])

What do these quotes mean to you? What do they reflect or say about what it is to be human? (Ghani)

Individual and Group Reflection

7:00–7:15: Please take some time to write about *what is involved in the quest to be fully human*, from your position, circumstance, environment, or status. For example, you might choose to focus on this question from the perspective of being a man or a woman, poor, gay, Black or White, incarcerated or living in a big city, the oldest child or youngest child in your family, etc. Please choose a frame or a combination of frames that feel particularly relevant to you, and write about what stands out to you in your journey to become fully human. (Erin)

7:15–7:40: Let's discuss what came about in your writings. This discussion is not about reading word for word what you wrote on your piece of paper, but about the insights and thoughts that arose for you. (Erin)

(Possible comment or observation: There is no single way to approach the quest of becoming fully human. We all stand in different places; we all approach this from different angles. But though we are all very different, does it mean that we are separate from each other in this journey? Is there any way to be unified in this quest to become fully human, given our differences in circumstance and status, as well as our different ways of perceiving?)

Individual and Community: Group Conversation

7:40–8:10: Read James Boggs quote and group conversation. (Ghani)

"...in order to be human, we need to feel that we can walk the streets without fearing each other, that we don't need to spend millions of dollars each year on police dogs and security locks and electronic gadgets to protect our homes and our personal possessions, and that our security doesn't come from policemen or from police dogs but from the value and concern each of us has for the others because we value and cherish human beings more than we cherish material things and individual success. In order to be human, we need to feel that we belong to a community where people of different ages and interests have grown to depend upon one another because over the years our personal lives and the life of the community have become interdependent. We need to feel that we can look to our neighbors for help in keeping the streets clean, in raising our children, in looking out for each other. In order to be human, we need to feel that the work we do is useful and that we are doing it not just for pay or profit, but because it is socially necessary. That is, we are making things that people really need. In order to be human, we need to feel that we are in control of our lives. We need to believe that our decisions and actions make a difference in how we and our co-citizens live, in making our community one that we can be proud of, and in how our country is run."

—James Boggs, from "Toward a New Concept of Citizenship" November 9, 1976

What fundamental shifts in our personal and societal values must take place to enable our full human development, for us to be more fully human individuals and a fully human society? What would it take to live by these values? (Ghani and Erin)

Closing

Summary of the conversation and final reflections in circle. (Ghani and Erin)

APPENDIX 6

Walls to Bridges Vision and Mission

Walls to Bridges Collective (W2BC)

Who We Are

The Walls to Bridges Collective was created by the first Inside-Out Prison Exchange class at Grand Valley Institution for Women in November 2011. All members are alumni or instructors of Inside-Out courses. Walls to Bridges Collective members meet bi-weekly and engage in a variety of different activities, discussions, advocacy and educational experiences in a supportive, anti-oppressive, and nurturing environment. We aim to be active in both the prison and the outside community and encourage dialogue for meaningful transformation.

Our Mission

Through collaboration with people living inside and outside prison walls, we will strive to connect and build bridges by educating, informing, and advocating about social justice and education for criminalized women and trans people.

Our Vision

We envision change by embracing diversity, achieving equality, and rethinking incarceration to create a socially just world.

- *Moving Beyond The Walls That Separate Us* -

Walls to Bridges Collective (W2BC)

Bi-weekly Circle Process

Our collective gathers in a circle format and models the Inside-Out framework. We commence our gathering with an opening activity and/or check in where members are encouraged to voice how they are coming to the circle and if there are factors influencing participation. We select a minutes-taker and two facilitators for the evening, cocreate the meeting's agenda, and then proceed from there.

Principles of Engagement

- We are guided by the principles of the circle and have agreed to engage them through the following actions:
- Commitment to steering committee project timeline
- Respect confidentiality (what we say in the circle, stays in the circle).
- Come ready to be present and engaged
- Be open minded, free of judgment and assumption
- Be ourselves and value different opinions, views, and ways of knowing
- Silence is okay
- Be kind and gentle, even when disagreeing
- Don't personalize
- If something has been unresolved, bring it to the group
- Request clarification when needed
- Speak from our whole selves
- Have fun, laugh, and celebrate.

 *- Moving Beyond The Walls That Separate Us*

Confined Minds Think Tank Conference Program

The Inside-Out Theory Group

CONFINED MINDS

INCARCERATION - EDUCATION - TRANSFORMATION

RYAN CORRECTIONAL FACILITY
APRIL 23, 2010

Special Thanks

Warden Raymond Booker Deputy Warden Scott Nobles
ADW Rita Crittenden
Program Director, Steve Horton
Culinary Arts Director, Duraman Daramy
Prisoner Benevolent Fund at Ryan Correctional Facility

VERY Special Thanks

Patricia Caruso
Director of Michigan Department of Corrections
Michael Switalski
State Senator

Inside-Out Theory Group at
Ryan Correctional Facility

When Director Patricia Caruso declared Michigan an "Inside Out Prison Exchange class friendly state/" the opportunity opened to begin a unique approach to education, Ryan Correctional was the first facility to take on the challenge.

The Inside-Out Prison Exchange is a national program with a classroom curriculum that goes beyond text books. The class helps to break down barriers and erase the stigmas and stereotypes "outside students" might have about imprisoned people. It gives "inside" and "outside" students a chance to broaden our perceptions and hear issues from diverse points of view. It also produces some discussions that give us all something to think about. It provides the "inside students" with a chance to open a dialogue with people we may never have had the opportunity to communicate with. Through this shared learning, we have built social capital together.

The Theory Group is an extension of the class. The "inside students" wanted to continue stretching their intellectual horizons. In the Theory Group, we continue to read books, write papers, and discuss our views and analyses in a dialectical setting.

We also discussed how we wanted others to share our experiences. We decided, in a consensus manner, to plan a day-long conference on education in prison that would: (1) provide opportunities to explore innovative ways to encourage higher education in prison, without additional expense to taxpayers; and (2) to help expand the reach of Inside-Out in the state. Respecting the integrity and the rules of the institutions involved (Ryan and UM Dearborn), agreement was forged to plan this day of activities and explorations.

Inside-Out Prison Exchange has changed the lives of all the students (and their instructors) who have participated. Higher education is the catalyst that brought us together. We want to share this amazing experience with our incarcerated peers. Research indicates that most people in prison who obtain even partial higher education experiences have an increased chance of success on the outside.

We welcome you to this day. We hope that you leave committed to bringing higher education back into the prison system. Peace. Shalom. Namaste.

Jemal (Inside Student)

Program

Confined Minds: Incarceration—Education—Transformation
Ryan Correctional Facility
April 23, 2010

8:15–9:15 a.m.
Refreshments

9:15–10:15 a.m.
Opening Remarks
Welcome
Keynote Speaker
Patricia Caruso
Director, Michigan Department of Corrections

10:15–10:30 a.m.
Break

10:30 a.m.–Noon
Panel 1 Room 130
"Does higher education [in-prison] affect the revolving door?"
Rev. Christian C. Adams (Hartford Memorial Baptist Church)
John Adams (Director, Bureau of Juvenile Justice)
Mark Fancher (Staff Attorney, ACLU)
Darren X (Inside Student)
Facilitated by **Andrea Isom** Fox 2 news Detroit

Panel 2 Chapel
"Can higher education benefit the institution?"
Kathleen Schaefer (President at Professional Probation-Parole
Consulting, Inc.)
Warden Millicent Warren (Warden, Huron Valley Correctional)
Dr. Connie Banks (Principal at Ryan Correctional Facility)
Kyle (Inside Student) Facilitated by **Jeff Gerritt** (Detroit Free Press)

Noon–1:30 p.m.
Lunch Introduced by **Darnell** (Inside Student)

Speaker, Toni Bunton

Student—Master of Arts in Liberal Studies
University of Michigan, Dearborn
Inmate for 17 years

Speaker, Dr. Ahmad Rahman

Associate Professor of History
University of Michigan, Dearborn
Inmate for 22 years

1:30 p.m.–3:00 p.m.
Panel 3 Room 130
"Do outside communities benefit from education inside?"
Raphael Johnson (Author and National Motivational Speaker),
William Tregea (Professor of Sociology, Social Work, and Criminal
Justice, Adrian College)
Vincent Tilford (Executive Director at Habitat for Humanity
Detroit)
Matt (Inside Student)
Facilitated by **Dave Leval** (TV 20 News Reporter)

Panel 4 Chapel
"What is inside out and why is it good for you?"
Lori Pompa (Director, The Inside-Out Prison Exchange Program)
Sue Hyatt (Regional Director, Inside-Out)
Lynn (Inside Student) **Susan Schmidt** (Outside Student)

3:00–3:45 p.m.
Keynote Speaker
Honorable John Conyers
Representative
US House of Representatives

3:45—4:00 p.m.
Concluding Remarks

IN OUR OWN WORDS

What does education mean to me?

Deciding to run towards education rather than away from it was the turning point in my life. I decided to stop doubting and second guessing myself and, when I did that, I realized that I was in my own way. I've found a new vision of myself through education. It has helped me cleanse my mind of all things that hinder my ability to grow intellectually. My classes have made it possible for me to trust myself instead of always trusting the methods of others. Through education, I now believe more in myself. If it wasn't for education, Inside-Out would have never crossed my path, and without this union, my new found perception of history, literature and how the world works would not exist. Thanks to both education and Inside/Out for making it possible for me to renew my life, in a place where I was, I felt like I was a failure.

(Rock)

This seemingly simple question is surprisingly difficult to answer. This class had as much meaning to me as the importance of water for my body. Without this water in my body, it would dry up and die. The same is true for this class when I think about all of the things that I have received from my participation. The learning experience changed all my views and understandings about social structure. Inside-Out allowed me to look at myself and my life "outside the box." I learned how to live in the shoes of the victim's family, and that has allowed me to have a new relationship with them. That is the most important thing that this class has helped me develop. What I learned in Inside-Out allowed the rehabilitation process to unfold for me and the healing process to continue for them. This class also helped to develop a personal balance in my life that I never had. It helped me believe in myself to where I can hold my head up high and not be insecure with people who have more education. I now think that I can do anything if I put my mind to it. Honestly, naming what this class means to me minimizes its significance, because this class cannot be understood in words. The experience is life altering.

(Freeman)

The first thing Inside-Out has done for me is that it has enhanced my desire to pursue higher education while I am incarcerated and to further it when I return to my community. The dedication of the U of M Dearborn Faculty and the creativity and intellectual discourse that the Inside and Outside students engaged in during class showed me that when people come together for the common good, anything is possible. I now have faith in a brighter future. I witnessed young and old leaders from different ethnic, cultural, political and religious persuasions rise above their ideological differences to produce a true dialogical exchange of ideas. All ideas were valued.

Moreover, for the inside students and alums from the first three classes, the Inside-Out Program extended into the Theory Group (that planned today's conference). Participation in this extension of IO has given me an outlet to express myself in an environment devoted to serious educational and intellectual development and promotion.

(Darren-X)

Education has saved my life. When I think about where I was mentally compared to what I have become today, it's literally like looking at night and day. Education has allowed me to step outside of the box I was voluntarily living in for much of my life. The box I'm talking about is called ignorance. Ignorance is closed minded, hateful, and downright harmful to the world as a whole. Through education, I was able to step into the light of knowledge, which illuminated my previous, erroneous ways of thinking, and put me on a path of continued self-improvement. Every day I try to better myself, by learning a new word or by helping someone find their own way out of ignorance, I do something educationally positive.

The Inside-Out Prison Exchange Program has been a major influence in making me a more compassionate and more thoughtful man. The program opened my eyes to a multitude of issues I need to address personally and with the people around me. This includes concepts like gender privilege and other habitus mindsets which cause injustices to continue between people of different genders, races, sexual orientations and social classes. The Inside/Out class is a catalyst that made it possible for me to become a productive member of society and of the world at large, through educating myself and others around me.

(Darnell)

To me the true meaning of existence is measured within the sum of collective life works, habitual thoughts, and behaviors. For most of my life I engaged in a social behavior that I understand was appropriate to my upbringing; it was commonly practiced within my household and within the community where I lived. To be exposed to drugs and violence. To watch my neighborhood deteriorate because of a lack of resources or human desire for something better. The social structure, or subculture, of the community influenced my mental development. I viewed my reality as normal. Inside-Out has given me the proper tools to engage society with a better developed understanding of social ills and cultural diversities. It has done more than just allow me to continue my education, I truly have undergone a remarkable catharsis since entering the program. But more than anything, it has given me the impetus to discover more about myself, as I continue to grow within the dynamic structure of Inside-Out.

(Lynn)

While sitting alongside campus students, discussing issues of social inequality, the Inside-Out program sparked in me a new understanding about the importance of higher education. Having a better comprehension of justice as well as the underlying causes of crime, race divisions, gender discrimination, etc. is changing my world perspective. Higher education is also improving the way in which I identify and harmonize with other human beings. The divisive lines that I used to see are disappearing, and my focus is on the human potential of those in need. I feel fortunate for the opportunity that Inside Out gave me and feel great whenever I'm able to motivate someone in a positive way. Thus, the professional skills that a higher education can give me to assist others in need is the most important aspect to me.

(Mario)

Only by searching and mining are gold and diamonds discovered. We can all find truth if we dig deep into our souls. We are the makers of our own character and the molders of our lives, as well as the builders of our destinies. It is through patience, practice and seizing opportunities that we can advance our educations.

(Little)

Education is and has been a fundamental element for the complete actualization of the person I was meant to be. The opportunity to educate myself mandated that I refine myself continuosly, bringing about the unveiling of my fundamental being. Education opened vistas for self-understanding, while allowing me to unendingly refine my thoughts, ideas and perceptions. It is impossible to know everything. But by this process of constant challenge, I continue to expand my knowledge base. Through this process, I have experienced the joy of learning for learning's sake as I forge ahead in greater understanding of this life I am living.

The Inside-Out Prison Exchange Program offered me the one of the best opportunities to experience this educational motivation. It has been a unique experience, in a setting like no other, and ripe with possibility and mind-expanding concepts. Yet still being, oddly enough, therapeutic in it's inconclusive and provoking format. Ideas I've long held crumble before the reality of people who refuse to be pigeonholed in any way. Exposure to their trials and challenges sensitized me to those needs we all share, rather than the ones I thought were exclusively mine. Sharing these experiences impressed upon me greater humanity than what I was ever used to contemplating. For this and so much more, I will be forever grateful to Inside-Out and will remain involved as the program will have me.

(Kyle)

The Theory Group is not just a place where students, inside and outside, gather to discuss social concerns, but it is a place where critical thinking takes place with the emendations of the group needed by two professors, exercising careful judgment of the subject matter.
(Kenneth)

Education is a tool for mental and moral development. As an educated man, I can help my family and benefit the community as well.
Education is more than basic knowledge, it is a survival tool that I use in day-to-day living. It has allowed me the opportunity to reach outside my box and achieve things that at one time, I thought were impossible.
The Inside-Out prison exchange program allowed me to open up my mind and push into a field that I never knew anything about—sociology. This class offered me one of the best opportunities to experience the wisdom and knowledge of others through books, articles, and dialogue. For this and many more reasons, I will forever be grateful for this Inside-Out class and our two professors.
(Donald)

Higher education helps quench my thirst for utilitarian learning. It invigorates and gives me self confidence. I feel a sense of accomplishment with the more purposeful knowledge I obtain. I understand that the more I learn, the more I am capable of achieving. Having a higher level of education expands my options for being productive for myself and in society!
Inside-Out has broadened my outlook on life, by helping me heed life from various perspectives. It has opened my eyes to the bigger picture of life and how we all affect each others lives, by the perceptions we have of others, am now more conscience of the decisions I make because of the lessons learned in Inside-Out, and not just from the text books!
(Jemal)

Inside-Out has changed my life for the better. This class has taught me that I can achieve any goal I set forth with hard work and dedication. I have received a higher level of education inside than I could have outside. It has given me a great boost in my self-confidence. This class has opened my mind to the way social systems work, and it has changed some of the views and perceptions that I had about college and society. Due to this program, I have become more equipped to deal with situations by utilizing the critical thinking methods that I learned.
I now look at things from more than one point of view. I can take another person's reasoning into consideration before acting or speaking about my own.

I am elated that I have had the privilege and opportunity to participate in this educational opportunity. My hope would be that more institutions would implement this program in their facilities for everyone's benefit.

(Frank)

The Inside-Out program is an amazing educational experience that was created so that students, both inside and outside, could share knowledge and life experiences. Before attending the course my belief in myself and my ability to participate in a program that varied on different educational levels was nonexistent. I felt I didn't have the prerequisite level of understanding and knowledge.

I was wrong. Participating in the different assignments and discussing the ideas, I came to recognize that my aptitude was not the issue. I had given up on myself and settled for not wanting more out of life. This program showed me that I could do better and that I deserved better by giving me confidence in myself. The teachings that came along with the course forced me to strive towards something beyond the confines of my present life circumstances.

My ability to understand amd analyze different texts are on a completely different level than before. Even though some may say I've always held these qualities, I give the credit to this program because without this experience I do not believe these qualities would have ever manifested themselves.

I believe Charles F. Haanel described it best, "We must be before we can do, and we only can do to the extent which we are, and what we are depends upon what we think." This course encourages the insight needed to not only become a better person but also a better thinker. I must be before I can do. I now believe I can be and do whatever I put my mind to.

(Maurice)

Education encompasses a variety of meanings for me, and it's undisputable that a world class education allows an individual to develop (what could be) boundless potential. But above all, education is a key that allows me to unlock the shackles that have contained and confined me since even before my conception. It is the key that breaks through the shackles of ignorance, the shackles of poverty, the shackles of drugs, the shackles of recidivism, the shackles of misunderstanding, the shackles of racism, the shackles of classism, the shackles of sexism, and the shackles of incarceration. So what does education mean to me? Education means my continuous freedom, a freedom of the mind, because when we as a people know better, we do better!

(Tiny)

To me, education is the key that unlocks the door to the dark room and opens the closet of chance, opportunity and resolution. Education lightens a life weighed down by the lack of knowledge, insecurity and obscurity.

Education gives me the opportunity and the capability to associate with others who make positive, stable, and progressive decisions that help keep communities and neighborhoods intact.

Education grows and spreads, connects and sustains a place in life not only myself but for those I love and care about. For it is via education that I can further assist others and not feel like an outsider.

(Dee Bee)

Higher education makes me feel proud because I am the first one in my family to take a college course. Having the chance to recognize my potential is allowing me to push the limits of my education as far as I can.

I feel more confident and secure in myself knowing that I have surpassed the expectations of my high school teachers. I obtained my GED in 1999, took a Horticulture course in 2000, graduated from the Inside-Out Program in 2007, completed a Family Violence course in 2009, and currently I am part of the Theory Group for the Inside-Out Program.

(Cowboy)

The Inside/Out program has transformed me by giving me confidence in myself in the classroom. I feel that I have advanced to the point that I can excel in my studies and achieve the goal of obtaining my degree in Behavioral Sciences. Education is a tool to assist me in overcoming the obstacles that are placed in front of me. It prepared me for the challenges that I may encounter upon leaving prison.

My objective is to be a productive member of society. Education has me focused on the things that matter in my life, and I am now more analytical in my thinking. I am focused on the positive things that I have the ability to integrate and implement in my daily life. I let go of what I can't change.

(A'Don)

"If you give a man a fish he eats for a day, but if you teach a man to fish, he eats for a lifetime." I've heard this old adage time and time again over the course of my life. It wasn't until recently that I truly understood it. Today as in the past, I have found that I need to nourish myself physically, spiritually, and mentally.

Education is a major puzzle piece in the attempted completion of my human equation. The equation for me is a striving for perfection in all that I do. I see the importance of education now.

I've spent the past several years during my incarceration working on improving myself physically and spiritually, but I always felt incomplete. I've now found and only begun to explore, this new missing piece. Educational aspirations are now part of my new internal quest for self empowerment, improvement, and the endless quest for completion of the human equation.

We may never be truly complete, but the importance is in the journey. The Inside-Out program has opened my eyes and mind to educational pursuits that I never would have acknowledged, much less considered in the past. For that, I will forever be grateful.
(Matt)

PRINTED BY PRINT XPRESS 313–846.1644
CONFINED MINDS
INCARCERATION—EDUCATION—TRANSFORMATION
CONFINED MINDS
INCARCERATION—EDUCATION—TRANSFORMATION
RYAN CORRECTIONAL FACILITY APRIL 23, 2010

Contributors' Biographies

Editors

Simone Weil Davis is the coordinator of Inside-Out Canada, home-based at Wilfrid Laurier University. Davis supports teaching and learning practices that move us past an unjust status quo and toward each other. With a Ph.D. in English and specialties in American Studies and Gender Studies, she has been teaching since 1991 and has been involved with Inside-Out since 2005. Simone lives in Toronto.

Barbara Sherr Roswell teaches writing at Goucher College and is founding director of the Goucher Prison Education Partnership, a program that offers a liberal arts education to men and women incarcerated in Maryland and stimulates meaningful dialogue about justice, incarceration, and educational access. She has been teaching Inside-Out courses since 2006. Founding editor of *Reflections: A Journal of Public Rhetoric and Service Learning,* she is co-author of *Reading, Writing and Gender* (Eye on Education, 2002) and *Writing and Civic Engagement* (Bedford, 2010).

Contributors

Sarah L. Allred is Associate Professor in the Department of Sociology and Anthropology at Berry College, Mt. Berry, Georgia. Her research and teaching focus on the social construction of mental illness, health and health-care issues, social inequality, and research methodology. Her recent works appear in the *Journal of Correctional Education, Disability & Society, Ecopsychology, The Prison Journal,* and the *International Journal of Environmental Health Research.*

Damien Arnaout is a rapper, writer, and artist, living in British Columbia. He writes that he was "privileged enough to be a part of the Inside-Out program, which has helped nurture the change in me that I never thought possible." He treasures the friendships, bonds, and memories and recommends to others this "life-changing and horizon-broadening experience."

Shahad Atiya participated in an Inside-Out sociology class as an undergraduate University of Michigan-Dearborn and was then invited to join the Theory Group.

An active member of the group for over three years, Shahad has had members of her family invited for workshops, which was a life-changing experience for them. She began law school in the fall of 2013.

Nathan Belche is an alumnus of the Inside-Out Prison exchange Program. He participated as an Inside student in the spring of 2012. Following this course, he helped design a health education program on hepatitis prevention, symptoms, and treatment at the facility where he is incarcerated. Along with two other men incarcerated at his facility, he continues to serve as a teacher in this peer-led program.

Charles Boyd, an active member of the Graterford Think Tank since 2003, has served as coach in 23 Inside-Out's Instructor Trainings to date. At Graterford, he is a peer facilitator and internal coordinator for both the Restorative Justice and Alternatives to Violence Projects; Chairman of the Lifers, Inc., Public Relations Committee; and a volunteer for the Hospice Care Program. Author of several published articles, Charles loves reading, writing, dancing, traveling, meeting new people, and nature.

Shawn Brown
Aka Skary Brown
Inside out student
Father brother son

Angela Bryant is Assistant Professor of Sociology at The Ohio State University, Newark. Her research focuses on theoretical and substantive questions concerning the organizational contexts of juvenile/criminal courts, racial/ethnic, gender, and class disparities in case processing decisions, and the implementation and consequences of formal/informal crime control policies for offenders. She has taught Inside-Out courses every fall since 2009, serves as the Inside-Out instructor co-coordinator for the state of Ohio, and is a member of the International Inside-Out Prison Exchange Program Steering Committee.

Kristin Bumiller is the author of *In an Abusive State* (Duke University Press, 2008) and *The Civil Rights Society* (Johns Hopkins University Press, 1988). Her journal publications span a broad range of interests from anti-discrimination policy, feminist theory, gender and punishment to disability rights. She has served on the Board of Trustees for the Law & Society Association and is currently on the National Steering Committee for the Inside-Out Program.

Gitte Wernaa Butin is Assistant Professor of Multidisciplinary Studies at Cambridge College in Boston. Her commitment is to teach for transformation and self-discovery. Her interdisciplinary research engages the fields of philosophy, religious studies, and modern/contemporary literature and focuses on narrative identity and its advantages and disadvantages. She has published in *Kierkegaardiana*, *Kerygma*.

Mario Carines was raised in Guatemala, and illegally immigrated to the United States where he eventually married. After many hardships he had enrolled in college just a few months prior to the tragedy that landed him in a Michigan prison with a life sentence. A member of the Theory Group, he helps to design and facilitate workshops, conferences, and trainings promoting justice and access to education.

Melissa Crabbe, MPP, is Inside-Out's Associate Director. In 1992, she met Calvin, a man then on California's death row and now serving a life sentence. That meeting started her on the path that led her to UC Berkeley's Graduate School of Public Policy, the Pennsylvania Prison Society, and Inside-Out. Crabbe's work focuses on developing training curricula, program planning and development, and training facilitation.

Kyle Daniel-Bey is a member of the Michigan Theory Group and in that capacity coaches at Inside-Out Instructor Training Institutes and helps to design and facilitate public education forums, workshops, and conferences on restorative justice and educational justice. A juvenile lifer incarcerated since 1995, Kyle is dedicated to bringing about personal and social transformation through education.

Kayla Follett recently completed the Master of Social Work Program at Wilfrid Laurier University in Kitchener, Ontario. She attended the first Inside-Out course in Canada and continues to be involved with the Think Tank, the Walls to Bridges Collective. Kayla recently returned to St. John's, Newfoundland, where she is originally from, to be with her family and friends and to work as an Education Coordinator for a Sexual Assault Crisis Center.

Phil Goodman is Assistant Professor of Sociology at the University of Toronto, Mississauga. His research interests include punishment, incarceration, and race and ethnicity. Inside-Out courses (including a fall 2012 course at Grand Valley Institution for Women, and a fall 2013 course at Vanier Centre for Women) are among his favorite to teach.

Keisha L. Green earned her PhD in Educational Studies at Emory University. Formerly a Presidential Postdoctoral Fellow at Rutgers University's Graduate School of Education, Keisha joined the School of Education faculty at the University of Massachusetts in Fall 2013. Her most recent study focused on the intersection of youth radio, literacy, and civic engagement. Keisha's publications include a forthcoming chapter in the edited volume *Humanizing Research: Decolonizing Qualitative Inquiry With Youth and Communities*.

Gillian Harkins is Associate Professor of English at the University of Washington in Seattle, where she works with University Beyond Bars (UBB), Freedom Education Project Puget Sound (FEPPS), and the Black Prisoners Caucus (BPC) TEACH to create higher education programs for people incarcerated in the Puget Sound area.

M. Kay Harris is Associate Professor Emeritus of Criminal Justice at Temple University. She serves on the National Inside-Out Steering Committee and has taught seven Inside-Out classes. She volunteers with the Think Tank and with the LIFERS Incorporated Public Safety Initiative at the state prison at Graterford and facilitates "Living with Life" workshops for students at the state prison at Chester, PA. She has published on sentencing, reducing prison and jail populations, and restorative and transformative justice.

Erin Howley is an educator and community artist with a passion for using arts and dialogue in intergroup settings to access new avenues for learning and growth. Erin worked for five years as Program Coordinator with The Inside-Out Prison Exchange Program, assisting with the infrastructure and development of the international program. She graduated in 2008 from Temple University with a degree in Adult Education and Organizational Development.

Nyki Kish is a musician, artist, and community activist. She is imprisoned with a life sentence, but continues her involvement in arts and advocacy projects, including Books to Bars, the books to prisoners' organization she founded. She has been involved with Inside-Out since its first Canadian course was offered in 2011. A founding member of the Walls2Bridges Collective, Nyki believes intensely in the program and in making education accessible to all human beings.

Amelia Larson completed her Master of Social Work degree in June of 2013. She currently works as a family interventionist with an agency in Calgary, Alberta, that operates from an experiential learning framework. She continues to advocate for experiential learning opportunities for populations in vulnerable situations. On the weekends, Amelia can be found in the Rocky Mountains, hiking, camping, or snowboarding.

Jim Nolan is Associate Professor of Sociology and Anthropology at West Virginia University, where he was named the 2010 CASE Professor of the Year. Coauthor of *The Violence of Hate* and *The Essential Hate Crime Reader*, his research primarily focuses on democratic forms of policing neighborhoods. Trained in 2006, he has led an Inside-Out course at Pruntytown Correctional Center almost every semester since.

Yasser A. Payne is an associate professor in the Department of Black American Studies at the University of Delaware. Using Participatory Action Research, he explores notions of resiliency *with* the streets of Black America: projects include *The Streets of Harlem: How Black Men in the Streets Adapt to Structural Violence* (forthcoming collaboratively created video). Publications include *Echoes of Brown: Youth Documenting and Performing the Legacy of Brown V Board of Education* (NY: Teachers College Press, 2004).

Paul Perry has been involved with Inside-Out since its inception. A founding member of the Graterford Think Tank and the LIFERS Public Safety Initiative, he has served as Internal Director of Graterford's Prison Literacy Project, a member of the Graterford Hospice team, and as developer and facilitator of numerous educational programs. An award-winning author and musician, Paul plays the guitar, saxophone, and keyboards. He earned his BS degree in 1992.

Shoshana Pollack is a professor in the Faculty of Social Work at Wilfrid Laurier University. Since 1991, she has been working with and beside incarcerated women as a therapist, researcher, scholar, and educator. She currently coordinates the Inside-Out program at WLU and Grand Valley Institution for Women (a federal facility in Kitchener, Ontario), and facilitates a think tank called the Walls to Bridges Collective.

Lori Pompa is Founder and Director of The Inside-Out Center at Temple University, International Headquarters of The Inside-Out Prison Exchange Program and has been on the Criminal Justice faculty at Temple University since 1993. As a 2003 Soros Justice Senior Fellow, she collaborated with others on both sides of the prison wall to develop Inside-Out into an international model of transformative pedagogy. Pompa has taken more than 12,000 students into correctional facilities through a variety of courses and exchanges and often speaks about Inside-Out's contributions, most notably at the Clinton School of Public Service and at the Fetzer Institute's Global Gathering on Love and Forgiveness in Assisi, Italy.

Todd Robinson is an alumnus of the Inside-Out Prison Exchange Program. He participated as an Inside student in the spring of 2012. Following this course, he helped design a health education program on hepatitis prevention, symptoms, and treatment at the facility where he is incarcerated. Along with two other men incarcerated at his facility, he continues to serve as a teacher in this peer-led program.

Jessie Rodger is a Masters of Social Work candidate at Wilfrid Laurier University in Kitchener-Waterloo, Ontario. Jessie was part of the first Inside-Out class in Canada at Grand Valley Institute for Women. She continues to support criminalized people through her work as a board member with St. Leonard's Community Services in London.

Steven Shankman is Distinguished Professor of English and Classics at the University of Oregon, and UNESCO Chair in Transcultural Studies, Interreligious Dialogue, and Peace. He is the author of the book *Other Others: Levinas, Literature, Transcultural Studies* (SUNY Press, 2010).

Giovanna Shay is Professor of Law at Western New England University School of Law. Previously, Giovanna was a Clinical Teaching Fellow at Yale Law School, a Staff Attorney at the Public Defender Service for DC, and a Soros Justice Fellow at the ACLU National Prison Project. Giovanna participated in Inside-Out training in 2009, the first law professor to do so. She has facilitated two Inside-Out courses at the Western Massachusetts Correctional Alcohol Center.

Matt Soares, a member of the Michigan Theory Group, coaches instructors at Inside-Out Training Institutes and helps to lead workshops and conferences that bring incarcerated and nonincarcerated people together for educational programs. Incarcerated since 2006 on a 7–15 year sentence, Matt is a husband and father of three beautiful girls.

Daniel Stageman, the Director of Research Operations in the Office for the Advancement of Research, John Jay College of Criminal Justice, is a PhD Candidate in Criminal Justice at the CUNY Graduate Center. He has worked as an educator serving middle- and high-school students as well as prisoners and ex-prisoners of all ages. He strives to incorporate what he learned about racial and social justice as a practitioner into his research, which currently focuses on the influence of political/economic context and profit motive on federal-local immigration enforcement partnerships.

Ella Turenne is currently Assistant Dean for Community Engagement at Occidental College and a long-time cofacilitator of Inside-Out's Instructor Training Institutes. Ella is an artist, activist, and educator.

Tony Vick, born in 1962 into a two-parent, lower-middle-class home in Clarksville, Tennessee, attended the University of Tennessee, Knoxville, and Austin Peay State University. Convicted in 1996 of two murders, Vick is serving two life sentences at Riverbend Maximum Security Prison. He works to bring educational opportunities into prison, develops Inside-Out programming, and serves as editor of the prison newspaper, *Maximum Times*.

Tyrone Werts, a founding member of Inside-Out's original Think Tank, coordinates public relations for the Inside-Out Center in Philadelphia. Out of prison after 36 years through a governor's commutation in 2011, Werts was formerly president of the Lifers Association inside SCI-Graterford. Werts was recently named a Soros Justice Fellow for his Public Safety Initiative, which calls on the many resources of formerly imprisoned Philadelphians in a coordinated effort to end the culture of street crime.

Lucas B. Wilson attended the Inside-Out training institute in 2005 and has been an active member of the Inside-Out National Steering Committee. He teaches Economics and Africana Studies at Mount Holyoke College in South Hadley, Massachusetts.

Index

Printed and bound in the United States of America